FLORIDA STATE
UNIVERSITY LIBRARIES

MAY 1 1995

TALLAHASSEE, FLORIDA

Organization Charts

Organization Charts

Structures of more than 200 businesses and non-profit organizations

Edited by Judith M. Nixon

With a Foreword by John G. Maurer

HD
58.65
O74
1992

Editor: Judith M. Nixon

Author of Foreword: John G. Maurer

Coordinating Editor: Kathleen Droste
Senior Editor: Linda Metzger

Production Manager: Mary Beth Trimper
Production Assistant: Mary Winterhalter

Art Director: Arthur Chartow
Graphic Design Supervisor: Cynthia Baldwin
Graphic Designer: Kathleen A. Hourdakis

While every effort has been made to ensure the reliability of the information presented in this publication, Gale Research Inc. does not guarantee the accuracy of the data contained herein. Gale accepts no payment for listing; and inclusion in the publication of any organization, agency, institution, publication, service, or individual does not imply endorsement of the editors or publisher. Errors brought to the attention of the publisher and verified to the satisfaction of the publisher will be corrected in future editions.

This publication is a creative work copyrighted by Gale Research Inc. and fully protected by all applicable copyright laws, as well as by misappropriation, trade secret, unfair competition, and other applicable laws. The authors and editors of this work have added value to the underlying factual material herein through one or more of the following: unique and original selection, coordination, expression, arrangement, and classification of the information.

Gale Research Inc. will vigorously defend all of its rights in this publication.

Copyright © 1992 by Gale Research Inc.
835 Penobscot Building
Detroit, MI 48226

All rights reserved including the right of reproduction in whole or in part in any form.

™ This book is printed on acid-free paper that meets the minimum requirements of American National Standard for Information Sciences—Permanence Paper for Printed Library Materials, ANSI Z39.48-1984.

ISBN 0-8103-8497-3

Printed in the United States of America

Published simultaneously in the United Kingdom
by Gale Research International Limited
(An affiliated company of Gale Research Inc.)

Contents

Preface

Organization Charts collects more than two hundred graphic representations of actual corporate structures of operating companies in one convenient source. Organizations of many types, sizes, and from a variety of industries have been included: large and small, public and private, profit and nonprofit, international and local.

Students, job seekers, researchers, and business people will use this collection to compare the structures of several companies and within and across industries, identify key positions and areas within an organization, analyze span of control in various corporations, and study how competitive organizations organize their activities.

Compilation Methods

Acquiring the organizational charts of companies is an often suprisingly difficult process. Many companies do not publish their charts or distribute them to outsiders, because they consider their organizational structures to be proprietary information that they are hesitant to share.

To find the charts in this book, the editor culled business journals, Purdue University's large collection of Annual Reports to Shareholders, searched the major databases, and sent direct requests to Fortune 500 corporations. All companies for whom charts were found in published sources were additionally contacted for updates.

Presentation of Charts

To allow easy comparison between the charts, they were redrawn using computer software designed for this purpose. Each chart contains a citation identifying the company whose structure is represented, the organization's national origin if other than the United States, and the source and date of the chart. In addition, the editorial staff has often added brief annotations to aid the reader in understanding what is represented on the chart. (The annotation might note, for example, that the chart focuses on the Marketing Division of an organization.)

Because *Organization Charts* is not intended as a source book for names of current position holders, and because names of position holders change frequently in today's fast-paced business world, only position titles have been listed. For some organizations, not all of the information provided could be included because of the extent of detail represented; in these instances, the editorial staff reproduced the charts exactly as given up to a certain line of authority. Except for these changes, the collected charts reproduce as closely as possible the graphic representations as received directly from the companies, noted in their Annual Reports, or reported in business publications.

Helpful Features

In addition to the classic position charts included in *Organization Charts,* other features illuminate the data.

Inclusion of subsidiary charts. In doing her research the editor found a number of charts identifying subsidiary relationships within parent organizations. These are interfiled with the classic position charts to aid the user studying relationships among companies.

Informative foreword. An essay by John G. Maurer, professor of business at Wayne State University, discusses the history of organization charts, analyzes various types of structures employed by organizations to accomplish their goals, and notes differences and similarities in the charts included in this work.

Detailed index. A detailed cumulative index includes all company names, including parent organizations and subsidiaries, provides subject access to the companies listed in terms of specific areas of an industry or product lines, and lists major divisions within organizations.

Comments Are Welcome

The editor welcomes any comments regarding this publication. Please address correspondence to: Editor, *Organization Charts*, Gale Research Inc., 835 Penobscot Bldg., Detroit, Michigan 48226-4094; or call toll-free 1-800-347-4253.

Judith M. Nixon
Purdue University Libraries
West Lafayette, Indiana

Foreword

Organization charts depict in a two-dimensional manner how individual positions (jobs) are specialized and coordinated. The horizontal dimension depicts "who does what," that is, the nature and degree of specialization. The vertical dimension depicts how specialized positions are coordinated by means of authority relationships. Organization charts represent a depiction of the essence of organization structure, namely, the specialization of jobs and the coordination of these specialized jobs.

History

David C. McCallum constructed the first U.S. organization chart in 1854 when he was appointed General Superintendent of the New York and Erie Railroad. McCallum's chart resembled a tree with roots (Board of Directors and President), branches (the five operating divisions and two departments), and leaves (e.g., ticket agents, foremen). By 1910, organization charts had been widely implemented by U.S. businesses, with DuPont and General Motors as prominent adopters (Chandler, pp. 156-157).

Caplow notes that while organization charts are relatively new, the concept they operationalize is very old. He traces the concept back to the Ts'in and Han dynasties in China, the Roman republic, the Prussian civil service, and the Venetian constitution (Caplow, pp. 50-55). Shafritz and Ott (pp. 10-23) provide an interesting chronology of organization theory from 1491 B.C. to 1990. In 1491 B.C., Jethro advises Moses to delegate authority along hierarchical lines (Exodus xviii: 14-22). In 500 B.C., Sun Tzu's *The Art of War* points out the importance of hierarchical organization. In 1377 A.D., the Muslim scholar Ibn Khaldun in *The Muqaddimah: An Introduction to History* introduces concepts of formal and informal organization.

The Horizontal Dimension

Specialization (also often referred to as division of labor or functionalization) is the process whereby the overall task of the organization is divided into smaller activities or components. Each square or rectangle on the organization chart represents a position to which has been assigned a different and smaller part of the organization's overall mission. The organization chart of the Webb Companies of Webb/America (p. 209) shows that the overall task of this organization has been initially divided into forty-three different positions (rectangles).

One way to understand specialization is to examine the chart of an organization as it grows from a one-person to a larger more complex organization (Scott and Mitchell, p.38). [See exhibit 1]

In Stage 1 of Exhibit 1, the President performs all of the organization's tasks, including engineering, production, and marketing activities. In Stage 2, as the sales and net income of the organization grow, the President begins to divide up the work. He/she specializes the production activity and places a Vice President in charge of it. In Stage 3, futher division of labor occurs. Stage 4 depicts further specialization with the creation of a third vice-presidential position. Notice how specialization results in the addition of organization levels. As we will see in the vertical dimension section to follow, the President's job changes from primarily "doing" (Stage 1) to primarily "managing" (Stage 4), which includes the task of coordinating the jobs of the three Vice Presidents (Stage 4). Job specialization, the horizontal dimension of organization design, also involves the grouping or departmentalization of positions. Positions can be grouped on a functional, self-contained unit, hybrid, or matrix basis.

FUNCTIONAL

This method of departmentalization groups similar positions which are needed to produce and sell a product or service. For example, in a manufacturing firm the functions of Research and Development, Engineering, Manufacturing, and Marketing would each be placed in four separate departments, each department headed by a manager (perhaps a Vice President in a larger firm) who reports to the President. All of the positions associated with the manufacturing process would be placed under the control of the Manufacturing Manager. Stage 4 of exhibit 1 depicts a functional structure.

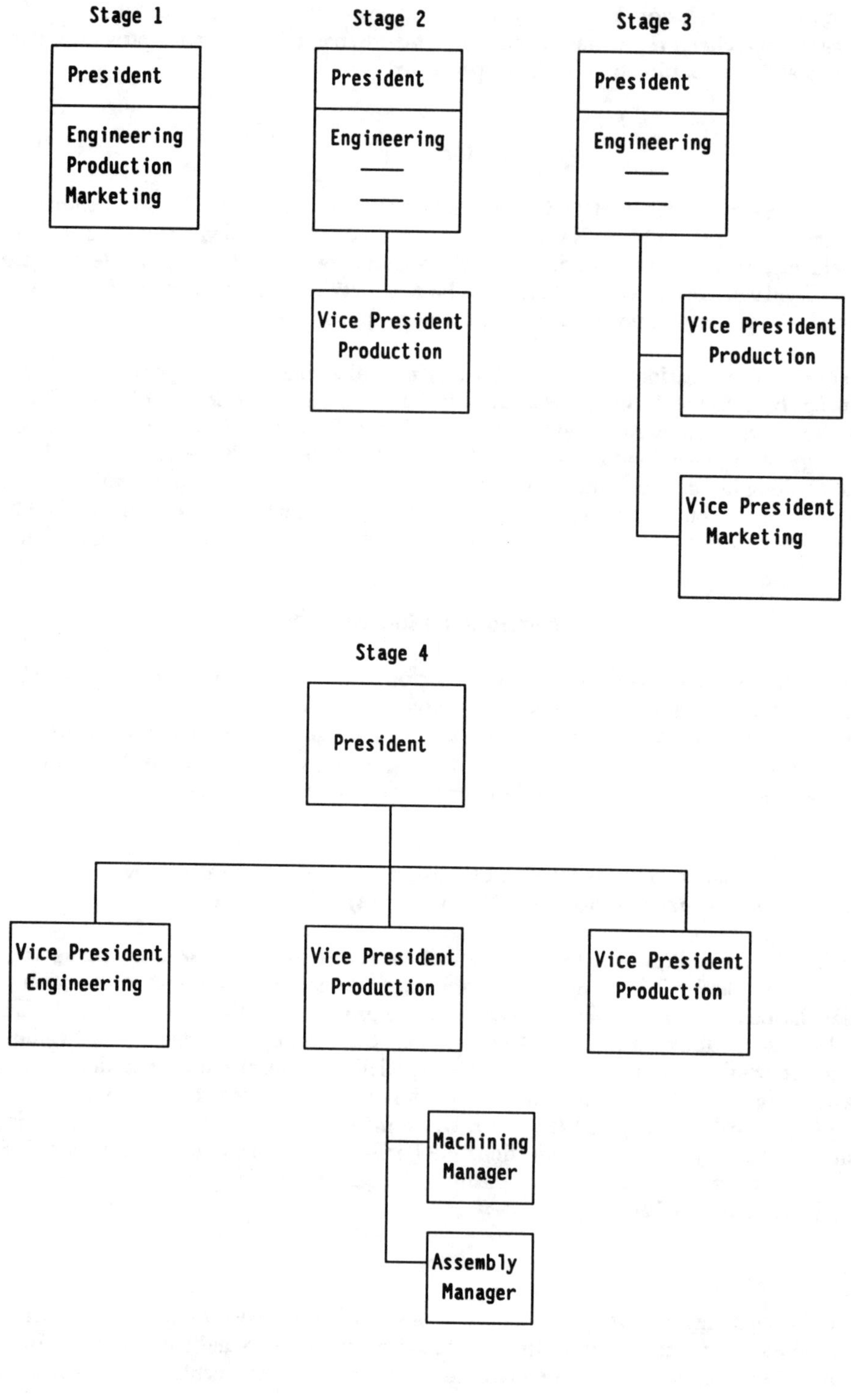

Exhibit 1

Functional structures are typically used for smaller organizations employing a simpler technology and operating in a more stable and simple environment (Daft, p.192). Their major advantage is the efficiency and economies of scale which result from the grouping of specialists within each function. These specialists can attain in-depth skill development (Duncan, p.65). Their major disadvantage is the difficulty of achieving cross-department communication, cooperation, and coordination. There is a decided tendency for specialists within a functional department to focus on the pursuit of departmental goals rather than to cooperate with other functional departments in the pursuit of organizational goals (Robey, p.188). These coordination difficulties may increase the organization's response time to environmental threats and opportunities, since coordination problems must first rise to a higher level in the organization where a position occupant has authority over two or more functional departments experiencing coordination problems. This takes time. But even when the problem finds this "cross-over" point, the coordinating position occupant may be too distant from the problem to be of much help (Mintzberg, pp. 125-126).

SELF-CONTAINED UNIT

As an organization becomes larger (more employees or participants) and more complex in terms of the number and/or types of products produced and markets served, there is a tendency for the organization to change from a functional structure to a self-contained unit structure. This type of departmentalization groups, under a single manager, positions whose occupants are performing dissimilar functions, but who are focusing on: 1) a specific product or group of products; 2) a specific customer or customer/client group; or, 3) a particular geographic area (Baird, p. 202). Nerco, Inc. (p. 147) depicts a self-contained unit structure organized by product: coal, minerals, and oil & gas. Structuring an organization by the use of self-contained units can be thought of as the disassembly of a large organization with a functional structure into a number of smaller companies (e.g., products or product divisions), each of which incorporates its own set of functional activities like manufacturing, marketing, etc.

Organization by self-contained units is typically used by larger organizations which are employing a more complex technology and operating in a more unstable and complex environment (Daft, pp. 194-197). Its major advantages are better coordination between and among functions within the self-contained unit and more intense focus on the product or service (i.e., a customer/client orientation) rather than a primary focus on the processes involved in creating the product or service (Duncan, pp. 65-68). This improved coordination and product/market focus is associated with faster response time to environmental threats and opportunities. The major disadvantages of a self-contained unit structure are the reduction of the benefits in specialization provided by the functional structure, and the difficulties in achieving coordination across the self-contained units (Daft, pp.196-197).

HYBRID

A hybrid organization structure incorporates organization by self-contained units but also contains "functional departments centralized and located at corporate headquarters" (Aldag and Stearns, p. 302). Nalco Chemical Company (p. 132) uses this type of structure. Note on this chart that there is organization by self-contained unit incorporating both geographic (International Operations) and product/service (Water and Waste Treatment Division, Petroleum Chemicals Division, and Process Chemical Division) and organization by function at the corporate level (three Senior Vice Presidents: R & D, Engineering, Corporate Sales, and three Vice Presidents: Marketing and Quality Management, Manufacturing and Logistics, and Environmental Health and Safety).

A hybrid organization structure is typically employed by a large organization facing an uncertain external environment. A major strength of this structural type is that it retains the focus and coordination benefits of the self-contained unit structure and adds to this the benefits of specialization for certain functional areas, e.g., Research and Development, at the top of the organization. A major weakness is that the probability of conflict increases between managers in charge of self-contained units and those functional managers at the top of the organization (corporate level) whose role it is to advise and provide services to self-contained unit managers and their subordinates.

MATRIX

This type of departmentalization represents the simultaneous use or blending of both a functional structure and a self-contained unit structure. One feature of this structure is that some individuals may report to more than one supervisor. In exhibit 2, individuals in cell 1, who are working on a certain project or product, will have a functional supervisor (engineering) and a self-contained unit supervisor (Product A Manager). Functional supervisors "are responsible for developing and deploying, in the form of skilled personnel, a technical resource. Project managers are responsible for project completion" (Bedeian, p. 209). The intent of this complicated structure is to achieve a balance of anthority between product and functional managers, rather than permit either group dominance over the other. If the functional manager dominated, the product may be technologically superior, but may not meet the client's needs (delivery date, price, product features). If the product manager dominates, the customer's needs may be met, but the product may be technologically inferior, e.g., lower quality. The matrix is designed to force colloboration between product and functional managers. Note that the Product A manager must work with three different functional managers, and that each functional manager must work with three different product managers.

Three conditions cause an organization to consider using a matrix structure (Davis and Lawrence, pp.11-24):

Function / Product	FUNCTIONAL MANAGERS		
	Engineering Manager	Manufacturing Manager	Marketing Manager
Product A Manager	1	2	3
Product B Manager	4	5	6
Product C Manager	7	8	9

Adopted from Gibson *et al.*, p. 451

Exhibit 2

1. Strong outside pressure exists for a dual focus on technology (functional groupings) and product (self-contained units). For example, to be effective in the aerospace industry, a firm must "focus intensive attention both on complex technical issues and on the unique project requirements of the customer."

2. Pressures exist for high information- processing capacity. The matrix structure is designed to cope with information overload caused by rapidly changing and relatively unpredictable environmental demands. Reasonable responses to these complex demands requires the interaction of a large number of different individuals.

3. Pressures exist for shared resources. The need for economies of scale in functional areas causes the firm to wish to retain the functional structure, while it adds a product structure. Functional specialists can be shared across self-contained units.

The major disadvantages of the matrix structure "lie in the confusion it creates, its propensity to foster power struggles, and the stress it places on individuals" (Robbins. p.337). Confusion results from the dual command structure, while power struggles occur as functional and product managers wrestle for dominance.

The Vertical Dimension

The solid vertical lines which connect the squares or rectangles on an organization chart depict authority relationships. The occupant of the higher position has the authority to direct and control the activities of the occupant of the lower position, without obtaining prior approval from his/her superior. A major role of the vertical lines of authority on the organization chart is to depict the way in which specialized positions are coordinated. The Baltimore Gas and Electric Company/ Corporate & Utility Organization (p. 22) shows that the Fossil Energy Vice President has the authority to direct and coordinate the positions of Fossil Operations Manager, Fossil Engineering Manager, and General Maintenance Manager. Authority flows in an unbroken line (the chain of command) from the President at the top of the organization to the first-line supervisor at the bottom of the organization. This chain of command also depicts the formal conduit through which formal information and communication flows. As a first approximation, directives flow from the top to the bottom of the organization; information about results flows from the bottom to the top.

Four major decisions must be made regarding authority:

1. Management must insure that the occupants of positions who are being held accountable for the performance of certain duties have sufficient authority to accomplish them.

2. Because there is a limit on the number of positions which one manager can supervise, management must decide the number of positions which should report to a single managerial position. This is referred to as the span of control or span of management. The Ford Motor Company organization chart (pp. 75-77) shows that the span of control of the Executive Vice President for North American Automotive operations is seven. One of these seven positions, the Vice President for Sales Operations, also has seven positions reporting to him. A low average span of management will cause more levels of management to exist in the hierarchy. As the number of employees increase in the organization, the choice between increasing levels of management or increasing spans of management must be made (Child, p. 60).

3. Counting from the top of the organization to the bottom, how many levels of management will exist? The Ford Motor Company chart (pp. 75-77) shows six levels of management from the Chairman of the Board and Chief Executive Officer to the Chief Design Executive of North American Design. Downsizing the organization through the removal of middle management positions will result in less specialization (the managers who remain will have additional and different activities to perform) and their spans of control will increase (Gibson *et al.*, p.445).

4. How shall authority be distributed? Decentralization of authority refers to the systematic delegation of more authority to managers at lower levels in the organization. A self-contained unit structure provides the opportunity to delegate authority by granting product division managers considerable authority over their "smaller businesses" and holding them accountable for "bottom-line" results.

Line-Staff Structure and Conflict

Line authority refers to that authority which exists along the chain of command and which is dedicated to the achievement of the organization's primary objective. Staff positions provide information, advice, and services to line positions, and, in some cases, engage in control activities, e.g., monitoring a line manager's compliance with the company's personnel policies and procedures. There are two types of staff: personal and specialized. Personal staff exists to support a single line manager. Examples of titles of personal staff are Executive Assistant, Assistant to, and Administrative Assistant. Specialized staff supports all positions (both line and staff) which require its assistance (Gerloff, p.253). In the May Institute organization chart (p. 121), the Administrative Assistant is an example of personal staff serving only the Executive Director. The Pizza Hut--Operations Division organization chart (p. 153) provides an example of specialized staff. The Human Resources position provides services to Market managers, Area Managers, and Unit Managers. Managers of Specialized Staff units have line authority over their subordinates within the unit. For example, the Vice President of Human Resources has the right to direct the activities of, e.g., the Employment Manager, the Industrial Relations Manager, etc.

Varying degrees of line-staff conflict may occur depending on whether the staff specialist has: 1) advisory responsibility (staff advises when requested; line managers may accept or reject advice); 2) compulsory staff advice (line manager must obtain staff advice, but need not accept it); 3) concurring staff authority (the line manager and the staff specialist must agree on the decision; or 4) functional authority (prior to making a decision in the staff specialist's area of expertise, the line manager must seek out and accept the advice of the staff specialist (Gerloff, p.253). In types 3 and 4, the line manager may receive "advice" from the staff specialist that not only may conflict with her/his personal judgement, but may also conflict with the directives of his/her immediate line superior and/or with the "advice" of other staff specialists. Attempts to minimize line-staff ambiguity and conflict take the form of using dotted lines on the organization chart to denote staff relationships, labeling staff positions on the chart (White, p.37), and explicating the nature of the relationship in policy manuals which may accompany the chart (Famularo, p. 331, p.351). The Baxter Healthcare organization chart (pp. 27-28) shows the use of labels.

International Organization Structure

Designing the international organization structure adds the problemmatic issues of geography and cultural differences to the horizontal and vertical dimensions of organization structure described above. Phatak (pp. 135-161) proposes that there are five stages in the evolution of the organization structure of international business firms.

Stage 1. Creation of an Export Department. If the company's product line is narrow, the Export department manager typically reports to the marketing manager. If the product line is broad, she/he reports to the president.

Stage 2. The establishment of foreign subsidiaries. Manufacturing plants or service operations are located within the foreign country. Each foreign subsidiary manager reports to the president.

Stage 3. The formation of an International Division Staff. The International Division is headed by a senior executive who reports to the President. This position typically appears on the organization chart on the same horizontal plane on which domestic product division senior executives appear. The subsidiary managers report to the International Division's senior executive.

Stage 4. Departmentalization of the International Division. The International Division is departmentalized by product or geographic area. Product or geographic area managers report to the head of the International Division. Subsidiary managers report to either the product managers or the geographic area managers. The Nalco Chemical Company Chart (p. 132) shows three geographic area vice presidents (Europe, Pacific, and Latin America) reporting to the Executive Vice President for International Operations.

Stage 5. The Global Structure. The emergence of a global structure parallels the change from viewing international operations as an appendage of the company to a view of the company as an integrated world-wide competitor. There are four possible global structures:

1. the global product division structure: each of the previous <u>domestic</u> product division managers is given <u>world-wide</u> authority for his/her specific product group. Each product manager has line authority over all functional activities (e.g., finance, marketing) concerning her/his product division regardless of the country in which they are occuring (Daft, pp. 233-234).

2. the global geographic division structure: the global market is divided into geographic regions

or countries. The regional or country manager is granted authority over all functional activities for all products within his/her geographic area.

3. the global functional division structure: each functional vice president, e.g., vice president of manufacturing, is given authority for her/his specialty across all domestic and foreign operations. As Phatak notes (p. 152), this structure is not commonly used by international firms because of coordination difficulties between and among functions in a given geographic area.

4. The global matrix structure: this structure operationalizes two organization design variables simultaneously, namely, product and area. It is adopted in order to solve problems that are caused by the unidimensional structures described immediately above. For example, in the global product division structure, two or more product managers will be operating independently of each other in the same country. While the global geographic division structure coordinates products within countries, it doesn't promote coordination of product line activities across countries. In order to reduce the disadvantages of these two types, the global matrix structure is used. As Exhibit 3 shows, it blends location with product. This blending causes a dual authority structure to exist, e.g., the foreign subsidiary manager receives directives from two uperiors: the Product 1 Manager and the Country A Manager.

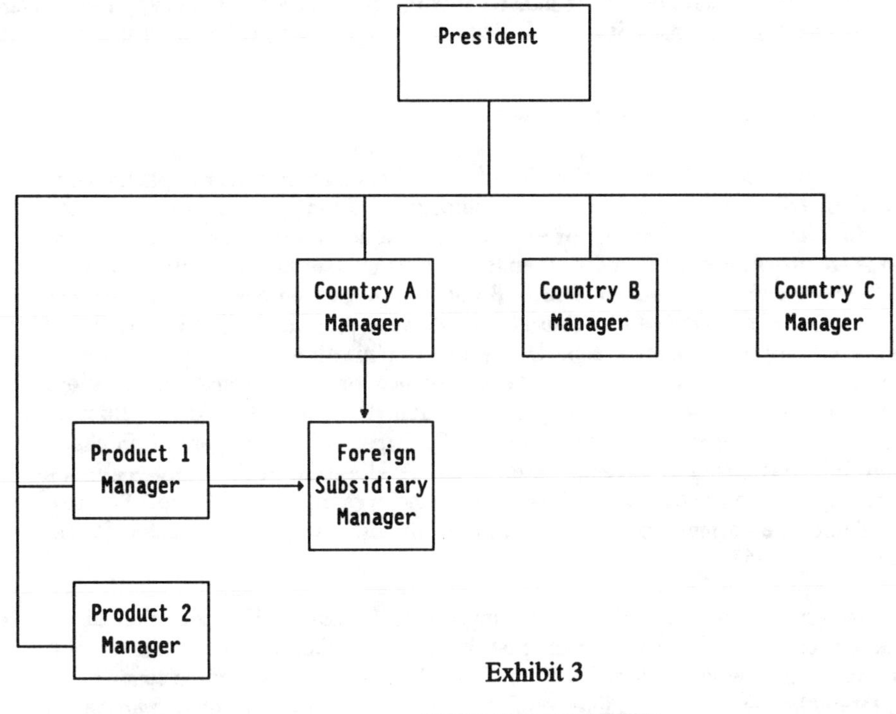

Exhibit 3

Strengths of Organization Charts

Since organizations are created to achieve objectives, it is important to identify which positions in an organization are responsible for which activities, as well as to clarify relationships among positions: who has authority over whom, and who has the authority to coordinate which activities. Organization charts perform these functions. The major strengths of organization charts are:

1. They explain how the work of a position, department, or division connects with the work of other organizational subunits (Gibson *et al.*, p. 436), i.e., how the parts fit into the "big picture." The organization chart can be used to orient new employees or current employees in a reorganization, as well as explain the organization to outsiders (Albanese, p.281).

2. They explain where a position occupant goes to solve a problem (Bedeian, p. 258).

3. They depict the number of management levels, the spans of control, and the bases for departmentalization.

4. Engaging in the process of constructing the organization chart may be more valuable than the ultimate product. The process of drawing the organization chart may cause managers to both perceive and carefully resolve latent division of labor and coordination problems, as well as spot "potential sources of conflict or areas where unnecessary duplication exists." (Stoner and Freeman, p. 266).

Weaknesses of Organization Charts

Very rational managerial actions often result in unintended consequences. The design and use of an organization chart is no exception. Robert Townsend, the former president of Avis Rent-A-Car and the author of *Up the Organization* and *Further Up the Organization*, believes that organization charts are demoralizing to the organization because they tend to imply that higher positions are more important than lower positions in achieving the organization's mission. Lincoln Electric Company has never published a formal organization chart, nor are organization charts commonly found in Japanese companies (Gray and Smeltzer, p.344). Some executives argue that organization charts tend to reduce teamwork, give individuals "occupying a rectangle" too strong a feeling of ownership, and make it more difficult to change the organization's structure (Koontz *et al.*, p.259).

Among the major weaknesses of organization charts are:

1. They do not depict the informal organization. The formal organization is the pre-planned one which prescribes tasks and relationships of authority. Dalton (p. 18) refers to the organization chart as an optimistic chart of expectations about relationships. The informal organization is an emergent phenomenon. It arises "spontaneously as people associate with one another" (Davis and Newstrom, p. 308). Because organization designers are neither clairvoyant nor omniscient, they cannot construct in advance an organization structure that can anticipant all future contingencies, especially for an organization coping with an instable and unpredictable external environment. The emergence of an informal organization, consisting of vertical, horizontal, and diagonal interactions outside the formal lines of anthority, is essential to the effective functioning of the organization. Organization charts do not capture informal power arrangements, e.g., the development of dominant coalitions of top-level managers who coalesce to set the agenda of the organization (Hall, pp.117-118). Nor so they depict the formulation and operation of middle-level management informal cliques (Dalton, pp. 52-65).

2. They do not reflect the operation of officially-prescribed horizontal linkages like: direct contact between managers across departmental boundaries; liaison roles; task forces; committees; and, full-time integrators (Daft, pp.183-185). While a task force tends to be a temporary lateral linkage, "the standing committee is a more permanent interdepartmental grouping, one that meets regularly to discuss issues of common interest (Mintzberg, p. 164). Organization charts may identify the members of standing committees by placing asterisks in various rectangles, with the title of the committee footnoted on the bottom of the page on which the chart appears. Effective horizontal linkages are vital for an organization that is characterized by a high degree of job specialization.

3. They may cause the reader to make faulty inferences about the amount of formal authority or the amount of influence a given position occupant possesses. In the former case, one may incorrectly infer the amount of formal authority a position occupant possesses by the distance of his/her "rectangle" from the President's (Gray and Smeltzer, p.345). In the latter case, the rectangles of two position occupants may be the same distance from the President's (i.e., they may lie on the same horizontal plane) and they may, in fact, enjoy roughly equivalent amounts of formal authority, but one position occupant may be

considerably more influential than the other. This may occur because she/he possesses greater power. This power may result from better conceptual, administrative, or social skills (including charisma).

4. They may cause managers to adopt an overly narrow view of the required duties and interactions of their positions. Managers may be reluctant to engage in creative or proactive activities and interactions which are not sanctioned by the formal chain of command (Gibson *et al.*, p.437).

5. Organization charts may supply competitors with strategic information in that they provide some indication about the relative status of the various functional areas and the coordination and emphasis that are deemed strategically important. For example, if the sales department is headed by a senior vice-president who reports directly to the president, it is an indication that sales is more influential than manufacturing if manufacturing is headed by a director who reports to the senior vice-president for administration (Porter, p.52 and p.55).

6. Many organization charts become outdated while they are being reproduced and distributed. This is especially true for organizations adapting to high rates of technological and environmental change.

The Pyramid and Other Shapes

Organization charts tend to be depicted as pyramidical in shape with authority delegated from the top position down the hierarchy to the first-line supervisor. If organizations were perfectly pyramidical, the drawing of a horizontal line across the organization chart at any level would result in a larger number of positions below the line than above the line. Few organizations are perfectly pyramidical. For example, some are diamond-shaped, with more of the positions concentrated at the middle levels (Caplow, pp. 58-59).

Some organizations choose to depict the organizational pyramid sideways on the page. See the Toshiba chart on p. 193. There appear to be three reasons for this. First, this represents an attempt to reduce symbolically the emphasis on top-down authority relationships depicted in the traditional chart. Second, the rank or status differences between and among positions are more obscured. Third, if the use of rectangles is eliminated in favor a title line only, a more complete picture of a complex organization can be captured on a single page. Some organizations invert the pyramid to emphasize the primary importance of the workers' contributions to the success of the organization. Placing managers below the workers on the chart is designed to signal the manager's primary role of support for those who are performing the work of the organization. Some inverted-pyramid charts place the customer at the very top in order to symbolically underscore the importance of an organization-wide marketing orientation. A few organizations reject the pyramidical shape in favor of a circular or concentric chart. See the Chemed chart, p. 45, for example. As with the "sideways pyramid," this chart seeks to obscure rank or status differences and to deemphasize top-down authority relationships. In addition, it appears designed to evoke a systems view of the organization, i.e., that an effective organization relies heavily on horizontal relationships between and among positions, in addition to the vertical authority relationships depicted on the more traditional pyramidical organization chart. In some charts the perimeter positions are connected in order to emphasize these horizontal linkages.

Conclusion

Because there is no one best way to design on organization structure, there can be no one best organization chart. Contemporary managers take a contingency approach to the design of organization structures. This means that their objective is to design an organization structure that is congruent with the organization's size, technology, environment, goals, strategy, and culture (Daft, pp. 178-212). There are numerous organizational life cycle models which analyze the types of structural changes that must occur over time as changes occur in the six dimensions listed above (Scott, pp. 177-178). Finally, because organization charts provide only a skeletal depiction of an organization's structure, they should be used in conjunction with written job descriptions and formal policy statements. These tools can identify potential structural problems as well as provide guidelines for their solution, e.g., line-staff relationships (Famularo, pp. 187-194 and pp. 315-361).

References

Albanese, Robert. *Management* (Cincinnati, Ohio: South-Western, 1988).

Aldag, Ramon J., and Stearns, Timothy M. *Management* (Cincinnati, Ohio: South-Western, 1987).

Baird, Lloyd S., Post, James E., and Mahon, John F. *Management: Functions and Responsibilities* (New York: Harper & Row, 1990).

Bedeian, Arthur G. *Management* (New York: The Dryden Press, 1989).

Caplow, Theodore. *Principles of Organization* (New York: Harcourt, Brace & World, 1964).

Chandler, Jr., Alfred D. "Origins of the Organization Chart" *Harvard Business Review,* 66, March-April, 1988, pp. 156-157.

Child, John. *Organization: A Guide to Problems and Practice* (London: Harper & Row, 1984).

Daft, Richard L. *Organization Theory and Design* (St. Paul, MN: West Publishing, 1992).

Dalton, Melville. *Men Who Manage* (New York: Wiley, 1959).

Davis, Keith, and Newstrom, J. *Human Behavior at Work* (New York: McGraw-Hill, 1985).

Davis, Stanley M., and Lawrence, Paul R. *Matrix* (Reading, Mass.: Addison-Wesley Publishing, 1977).

Duncan, Robert. "What is the Right Organization Structure?" *Organization Dynamics,* Winter, 1979, pp. 59-80.

Famularo, Joseph J. *Organization Planning Manual* (New York: Amacom, 1979)

Gerloff, Edwin A. *Organization Theory and Design* (New York: McGraw-Hill, 1985).

Gibson, James L., Ivancevich, John M., and Donnelly, Jr., James H. *Organizations* (Homewood, IL: Irwin, 1991).

Gray, Edmund R., and Smeltzer, Larry R. *Management: The Competitive Edge* (New York: MacMillan, 1989).

Hall, Richard H. *Organizations* (Englewood Cliffs, N.J.: Prentice-Hall, 1987).

Koontz, Harold, O'Donnell, Cyril, and Weihrich, Heinz. *Essentials of Management* (New York: McGraw-Hill, 1986).

Mintzberg, Henry. *The Structuring of Organizations* (Englewood Cliffs, N.J.: Prentice-Hall, 1979).

Phatak, Arvind V. *International Dimensions of Management* (Boston: PWS-Kent, 1992).

Porter, Michael E. *Competitive Strategy* (New York: The Free Press, 1980).

Robey, Daniel. *Designing Organizations* (Homewood, IL: Irwin, 1991)

Robbins, Stephen P. *Organization Theory* (Englewood Cliffs, N.J.: Prentice Hall, 1990).

Scott, W. Richard. *Organizations* (Englewood Cliffs, N.J.: Prentice. Hall, 1992).

Scott, William G., and Mitchell, Terence R. *Organization Theory* (Homewood, IL: Irwin-Dorsey, 1972).

Shafritz, Jay M. and Ott, J. Steven. *Classics of Organization Theory* (Pacific Grove, CA: Brooks/Cole, 1992).

Stoner, James A.F., and Freeman, R. Edward. *Management* (Englewood Cliffs, N.J.: Prentice-Hall, 1989).

White, K.K. *Understanding the Company Organization Chart* (New York: American Management Association, 1963).

Professor John G. Maurer
School of Business Administration
Wayne State University
Detroit, Michigan

3M

Source: Company update, 1991

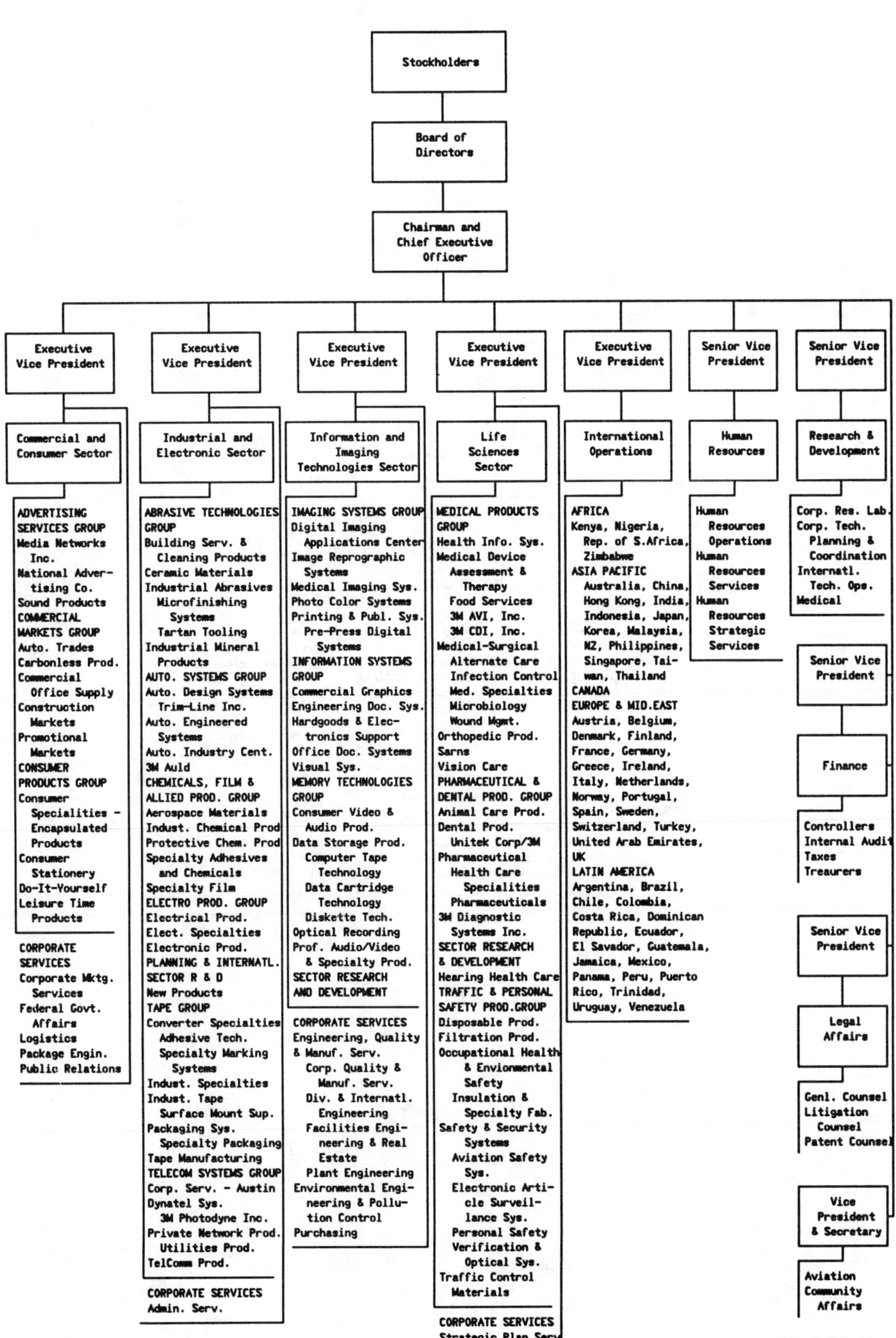

ACUREX CORP.

Source: Company update, 1991

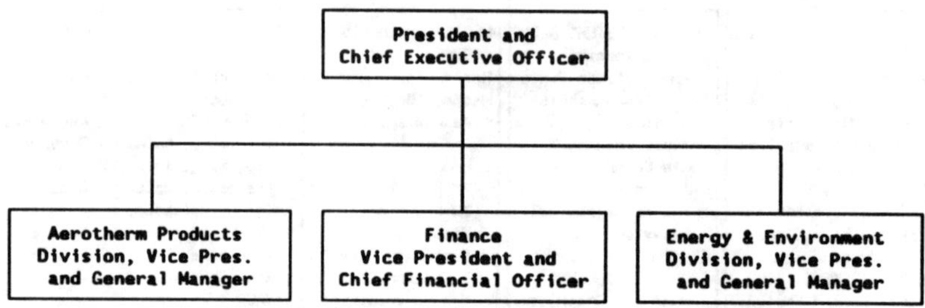

After Acurex reorganized, its operational divisions became responsible for handling their own contracts, finance/accounting, procurement, and human resources.

THE AEROSPACE CORP.

Source: Company update, 1991

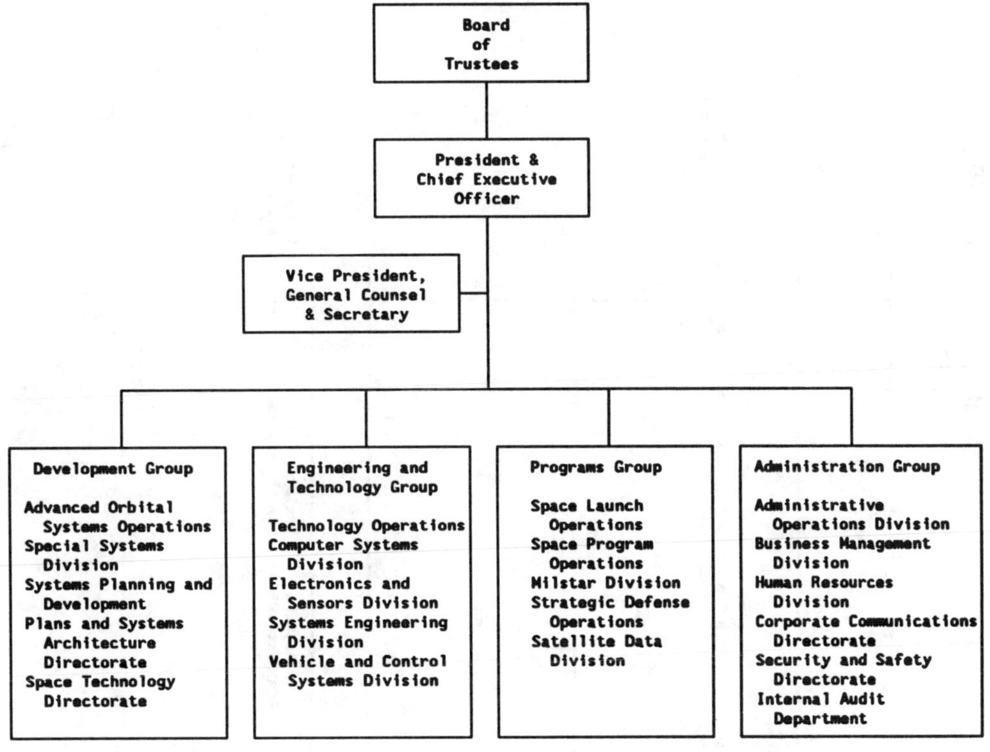
Board
of
Trustees
President &
Chief Executive
Officer
Vice President,
General Counsel
& Secretary
Development Group
Advanced Orbital
Systems Operations
Special Systems
Division
Systems Planning and
Development
Plans and Systems
Architecture
Directorate
Space Technology
Directorate
Engineering and
Technology Group
Technology Operations
Computer Systems
Division
Electronics and
Sensors Division
Systems Engineering
Division
Vehicle and Control
Systems Division
Programs Group
Space Launch
Operations
Space Program
Operations
Milstar Division
Strategic Defense
Operations
Satellite Data
Division
Administration Group
Administrative
Operations Division
Business Management
Division
Human Resources
Division
Corporate Communications
Directorate
Security and Safety
Directorate
Internal Audit
Department

AETNA
HUMAN RESOURCES DEPT.

Source: Company update, 1991

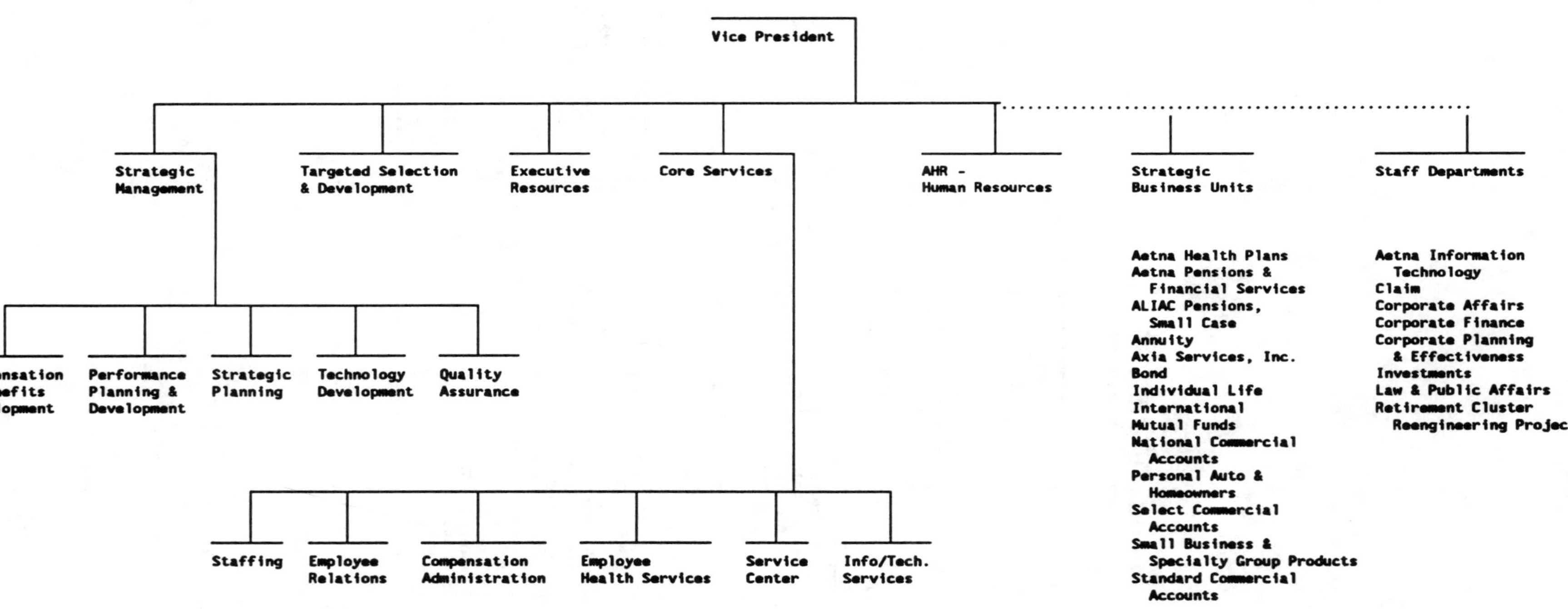

Strategic Business Unit (SBU)/Staff area HR heads report directly to SBU/staff heads while maintaining a dotted-line reporting relationship to Vice-President, Aetna Human Resources.

AGRGXCO (AGRICULTURAL EXPORT CORPORATION OF ISRAEL)

Source: RESEARCH IN MARKETING
4: 253 (December 31, 1988)

AGREXCO's board of directors delegates its authority to three management committees: finance, marketing, and packing and transport. Members of the management committees are members of the board of directors, but not employees of AGREXCO. All major decisions are taken in these committees.

* all products excluding flowers

AIRBUS INDUSTRIE (France)

Source: Company update, 1991

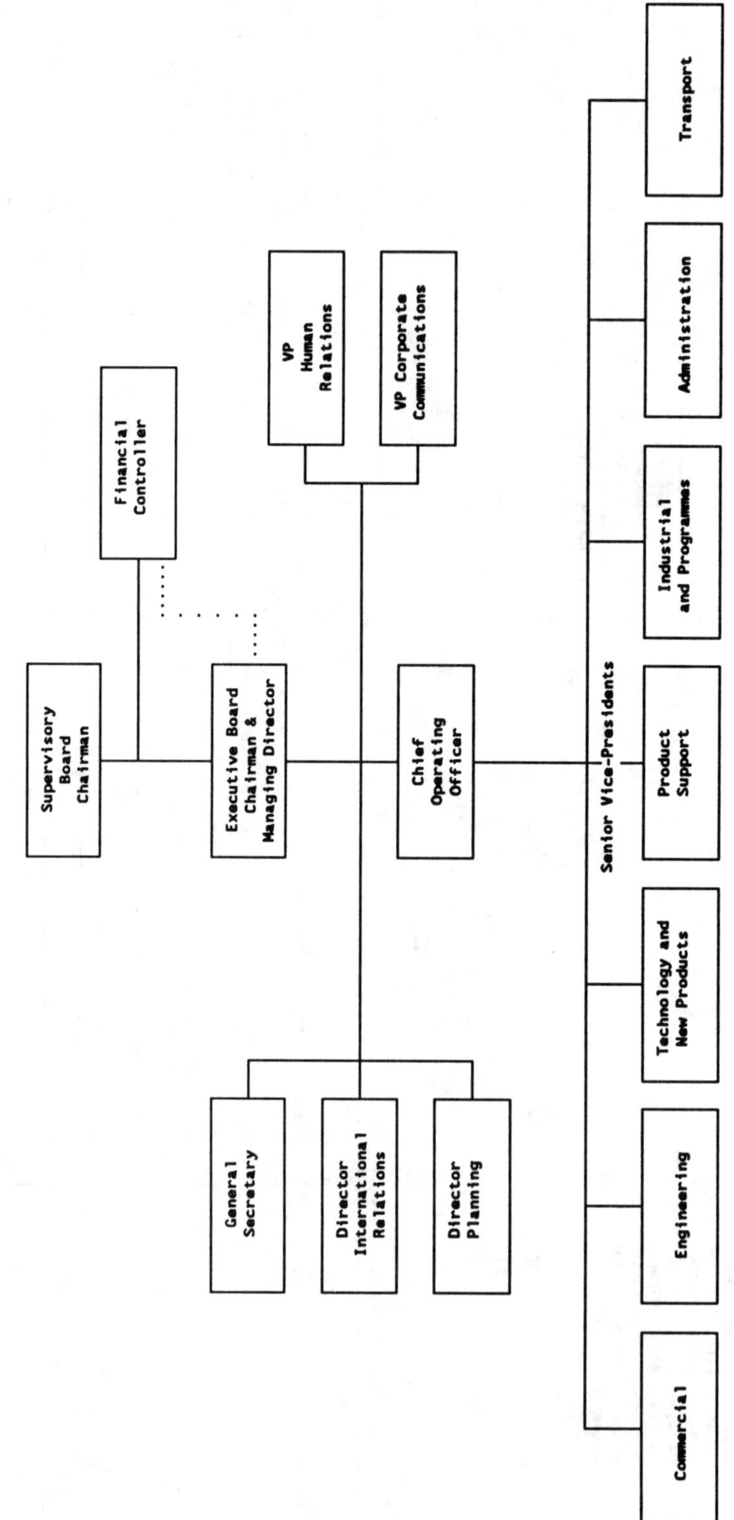

ALLIED-SIGNAL AEROSPACE CO.

Source: AVIONICS REPORT
2: 5 (September 8, 1989)

President

Engine Group President
Garrett Engine Div. President
Garrett Gen'l. Aviation Serv. Div. President
Garrett Aux. Power Div. President
Garrett Airline Serv. Div. President
Garrett GmbH President

Services Group President
Airsupply Division President
Endevco Division President
Bendix Oceanics, Inc. President
Bendix Wheels & Brakes Div. President
Bendix Field Engineering Corp. President
Bendix Kansas City Division President
Garrett Processing Div. President
Bendix Engine Controls Div. President

AIResearch Group President
AIResearch Los Angeles Div. President
Allied-Signal Aerospace Canada President & CEO
Garrett Canada President
Bendix Avelex, Inc. President
Garrett Fluid Systems Div. President
AIResearch Tucson Div. President
Electrodynamics Division President

Avionics Group President
Bendix/King Air Transport Avionics Div. President
Bendix Communications Div. President
Bendix Flight Systems Div. President
Bendix/King Gen'l. Aviation Avionics Div. President
Bendix Electric Power Div. President
Bendix Guidance Systems Div. President
Bendix Test Systems Div. President

Marketing & Customer Support Sr. Vice Pres.
Human Resources Vice President
Planning Vice President
Finance Vice President
General Counsel Vice President
Operations Vice President
Engineering & Technology Vice President
Public Affairs Director

ALTANA INDUSTRIE-AKTIEN UND ANLAGEN AG (Germany)

Source: Annual report, 1990

Altana, Bad Homburg v.d. Hohe

- **Pharmaceuticals**
  - Byk Gulden Lomberg Chem. Fabrik GmbH Konstanz
    - Chemische Fabrik Promonta GmbH Hamburg
    - Roland Arzneimittel GmbH Hamburg
    - E. Tosse & Co. mbH Hamburg
    - Sterimed Gesellschaft fur med. Bedarf mbH Saarbrucken
    - Byk-Sangtec Diagnostica GmbH & Co. KG Dietzenbach
    - Byk Oranienburg Arzneimittel GmbH Oranienburg
    - Cambridge-Life Sciences PLC Ely
    - Byk Nederland B.V. Zwanenburg
    - Byk Belga S.A. Brussel
    - Laboratoires Byk France S.A. Le Mee-sur-Seine
    - Byk Osterreich Gesellschaft mbH Wien
    - Byk AG Kreuzlingen
    - Byk Gulden Italia S.p.A. Cormano
    - Byk Gulden S.A. de C.V. Naucualpan de Juarez
    - Byk Quimica e Farmaceutica LTDA. Sao Paulo
    - Byk-Liprandi S.A.C.I. Buenos Aires
    - Byk Gulden S.A. (Pty.) Ltd. Randburg
    - Nippon Byk Gulden Company Ltd. Osaka
- **Chemicals**
  - BYK-Chemie GmbH Wesel
    - Rhenania Chem. Ges. mbH Grevenbroich
    - Dr. Wiedeking GmbH Kempen
    - BYK-Gardner GmbH Geretsried
    - BYK-Gardner Inc. Silver Spring
    - BYK-Chemie France SARL Le Blanc Mesnil
    - BYK-Chemie Japan KK Osaka
- **Dietetics**
  - Milupa AG Friedrichsdorf
    - Milupa B.V. Amersfoort
    - N.V. Milupa S.A. Sint-Stevens-Woluwe
    - Milupa Limited Hillingdon
    - Milupa A/S Espergaerde
    - Milupa S.A. Paris
    - Milupa S.A. Colmar
    - Milupa S.p.A. Varese
    - Milupa S.A. Domdidier
    - Milupa Ges. mbH Puch
    - Milupa Hellas E.P.E. Athens
    - Milupa S.A. Madrid
    - Milupa Portuguese Limitada Benavente
    - Kasdorf S.A. Buenos Aires
    - Consolidated Foods (Private) Ltd. Karachi
- **Computer software**
  - Deutsch-Atlantische Telegraphen-Aktiengesellschaft Koln

Altana Inc. Melville, N.Y. — incorporating pharmaceuticals, chemicals, dietetics div.

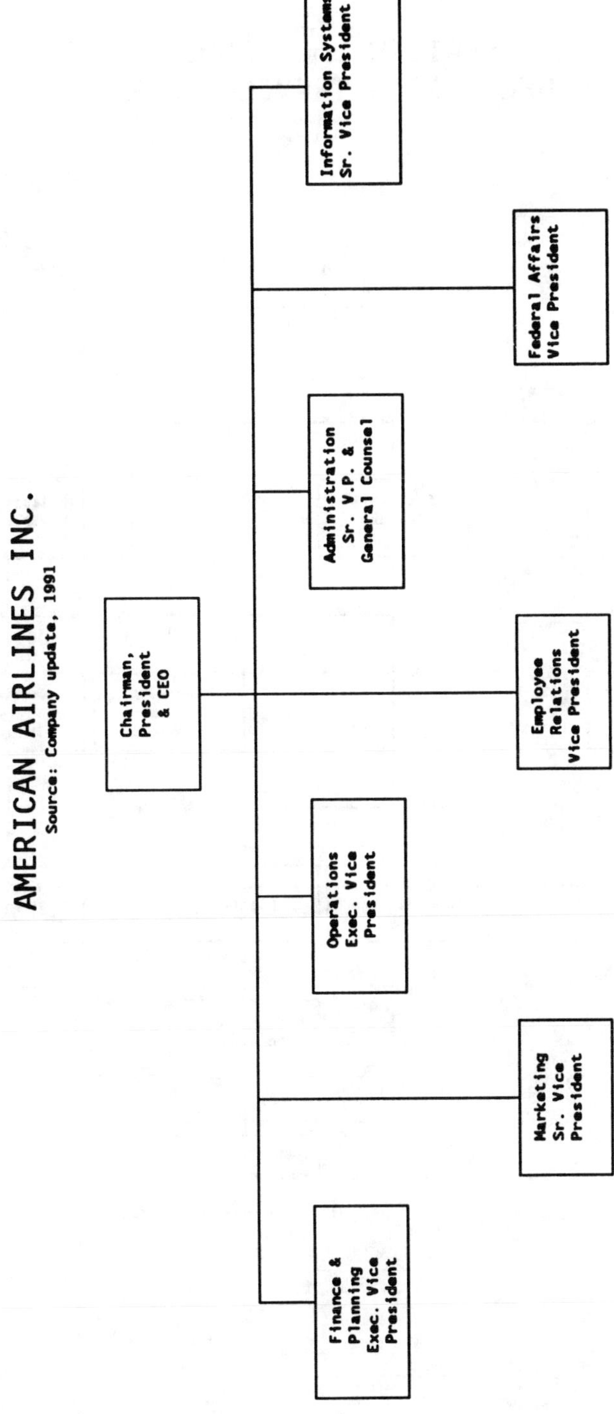

AMERICAN AIRLINES INC.
Source: Company update, 1991
Chairman, President & CEO
Finance & Planning Exec. Vice President
Marketing Sr. Vice President
Operations Exec. Vice President
Employee Relations Vice President
Administration Sr. V.P. & General Counsel
Federal Affairs Vice President
Information Systems Sr. Vice President

AMERICAN BAR ASSOCIATION
MEETINGS & TRAVEL DEPARTMENT

Source: MEETING NEWS
15: 22+ (February 1991)

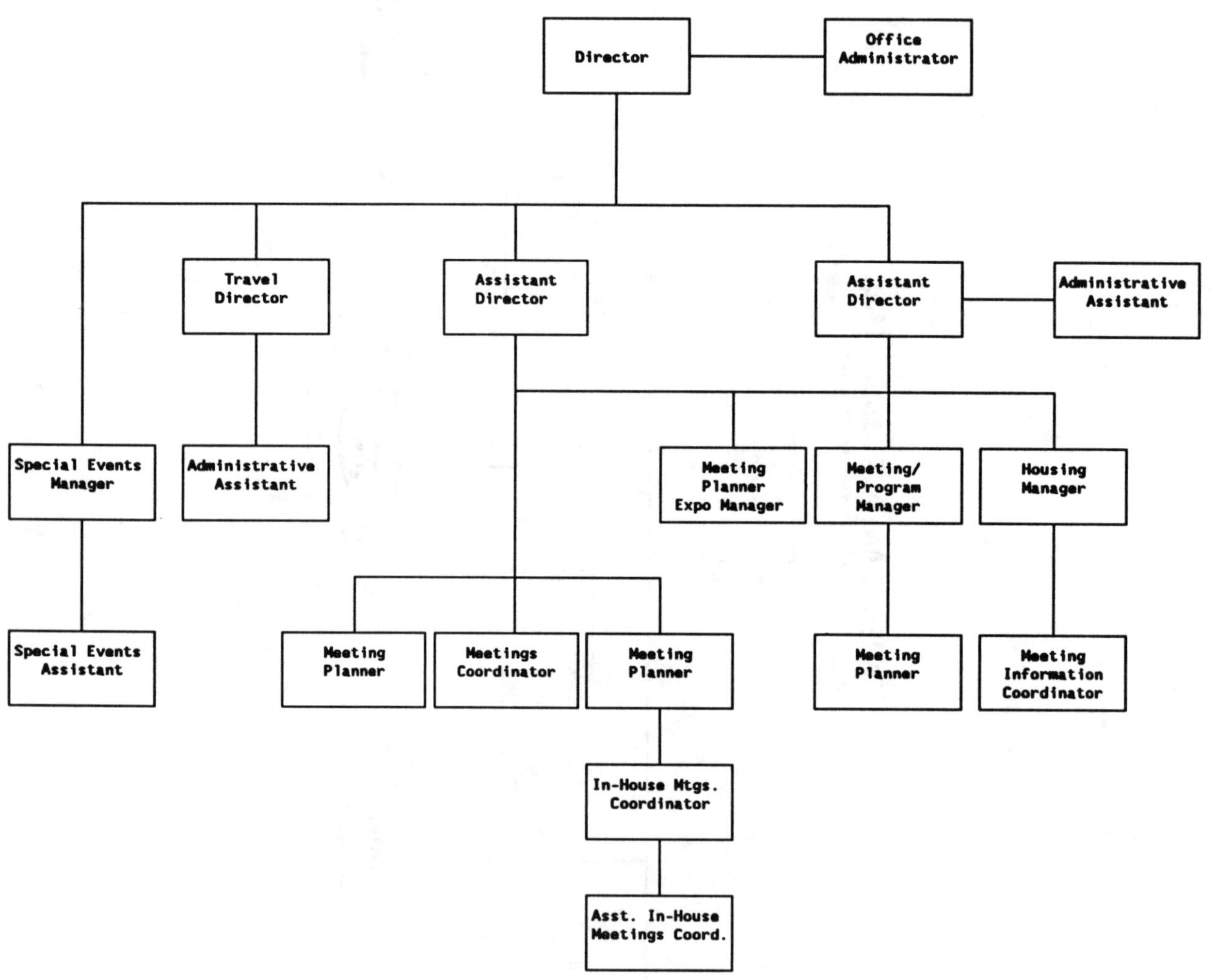

AMERICAN FOUNDRYMEN'S SOCIETY TECHNICAL COUNCIL

Source: MODERN CASTING
80: 38+ (October, 1990)

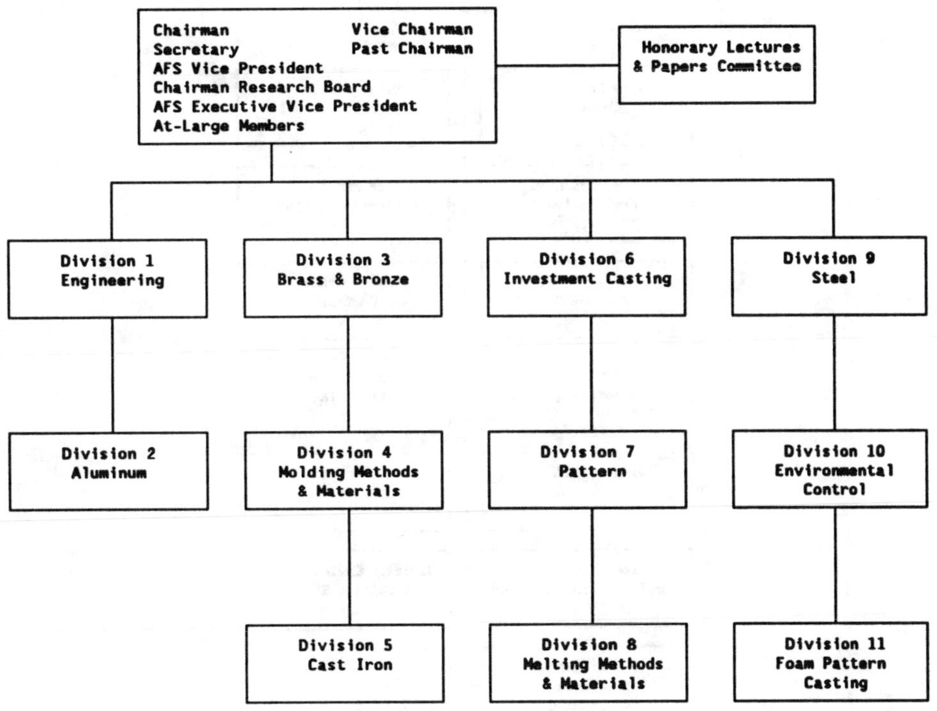

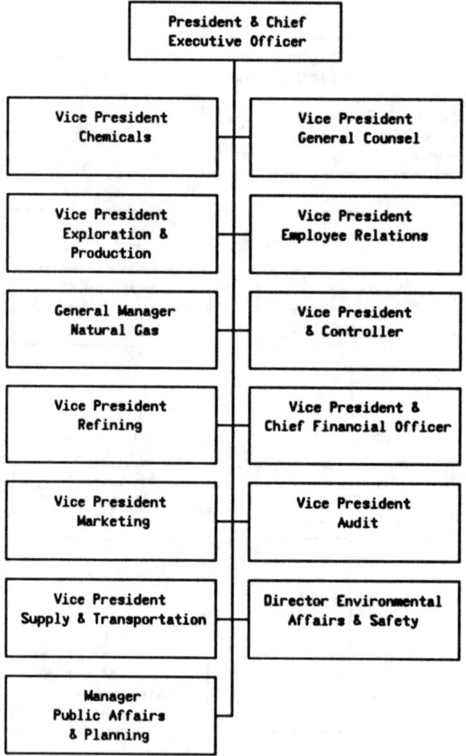
AMERICAN PETROFINA, INC.
Source: Company update, 1991
President & Chief Executive Officer
Vice President Chemicals
Vice President General Counsel
Vice President Exploration & Production
Vice President Employee Relations
General Manager Natural Gas
Vice President & Controller
Vice President Refining
Vice President & Chief Financial Officer
Vice President Marketing
Vice President Audit
Vice President Supply & Transportation
Director Environmental Affairs & Safety
Manager Public Affairs & Planning

AOKI CORP. (Japan)

Source: Annual report, 1988

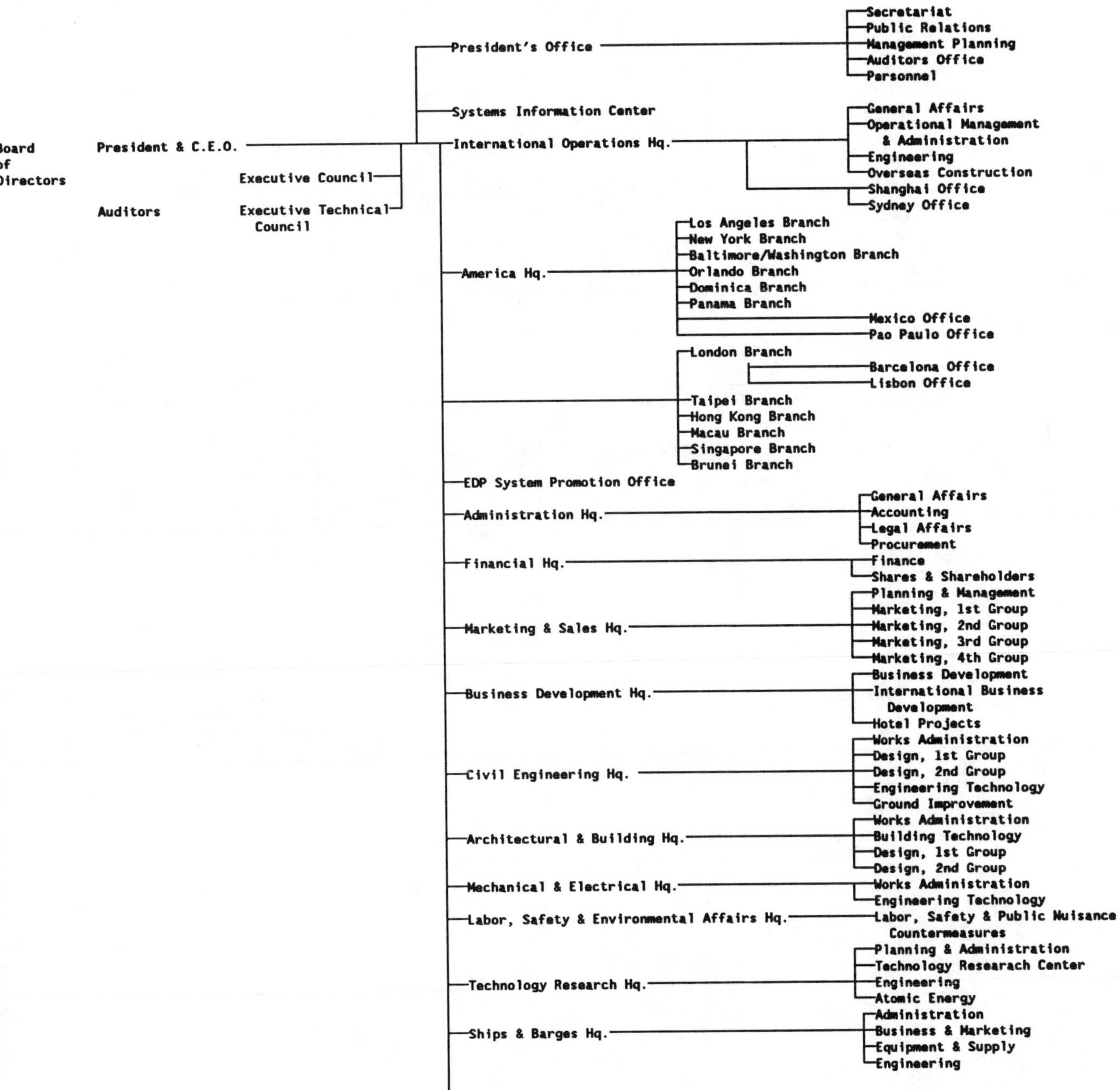
Board of Directors
President & C.E.O.
Auditors
Executive Council
Executive Technical Council
President's Office
Secretariat
Public Relations
Management Planning
Auditors Office
Personnel
Systems Information Center
International Operations Hq.
General Affairs
Operational Management & Administration
Engineering
Overseas Construction
Shanghai Office
Sydney Office
America Hq.
Los Angeles Branch
New York Branch
Baltimore/Washington Branch
Orlando Branch
Dominica Branch
Panama Branch
Mexico Office
Pao Paulo Office
London Branch
Barcelona Office
Lisbon Office
Taipei Branch
Hong Kong Branch
Macau Branch
Singapore Branch
Brunei Branch
EDP System Promotion Office
Administration Hq.
General Affairs
Accounting
Legal Affairs
Procurement
Financial Hq.
Finance
Shares & Shareholders
Marketing & Sales Hq.
Planning & Management
Marketing, 1st Group
Marketing, 2nd Group
Marketing, 3rd Group
Marketing, 4th Group
Business Development Hq.
Business Development
International Business Development
Hotel Projects
Civil Engineering Hq.
Works Administration
Design, 1st Group
Design, 2nd Group
Engineering Technology
Ground Improvement
Architectural & Building Hq.
Works Administration
Building Technology
Design, 1st Group
Design, 2nd Group
Mechanical & Electrical Hq.
Works Administration
Engineering Technology
Labor, Safety & Environmental Affairs Hq.
Labor, Safety & Public Nuisance Countermeasures
Technology Research Hq.
Planning & Administration
Technology Research Center
Engineering
Atomic Energy
Ships & Barges Hq.
Administration
Business & Marketing
Equipment & Supply
Engineering
Other 11 Domestic Branches

APOGEE ENTERPRISES, INC.

Source: Annual report, 1991

Commercial Construction	Installation and Distribution	Glass Fabrication	Window Fabrication
Harmon Contract Harmon Contract U.K. Ltd. Harmon Contract Asia Ltd.	Harmon Glass Harmon Glass Network Glass Depot Midas Muffler	Viracon Viracon West Viracon/Curvlite Viratec Tru Vue Viratec Thin Films Marcon Coatings Marcon West	Wausau Metals Milco Anogee Linetec Wausau Specialty Products Nanik The Shuttery Window Works

Apogee's four divisions operate as free-standing companies, with their own resources, operating units and performance records.--1991 Annual report.

ARCO (ATLANTIC RICHFIELD CO.)

Source: Company update, 1991

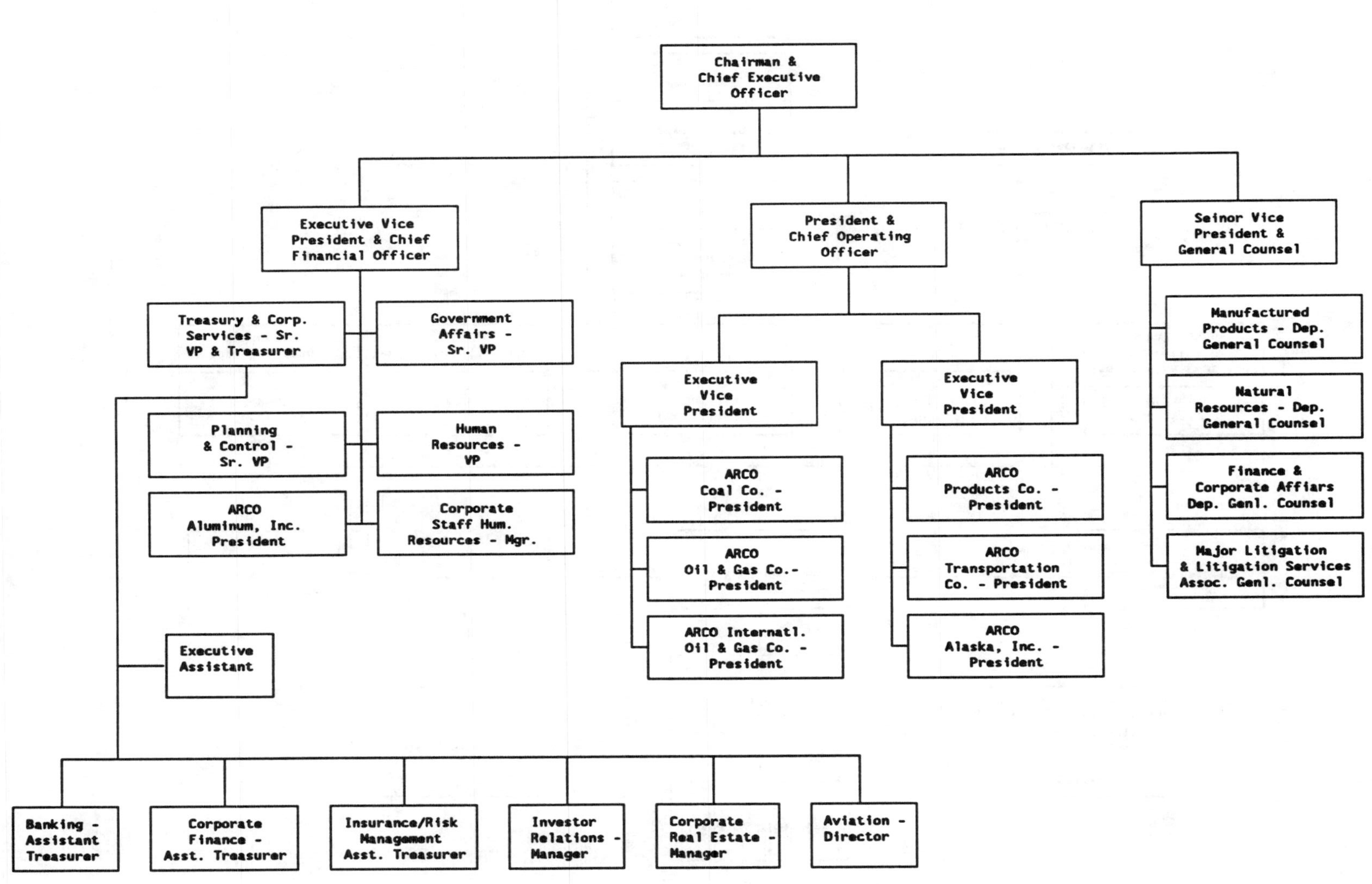

ARMSTRONG WORLD INDUSTRIES, INC.

Source: Company update, 1991

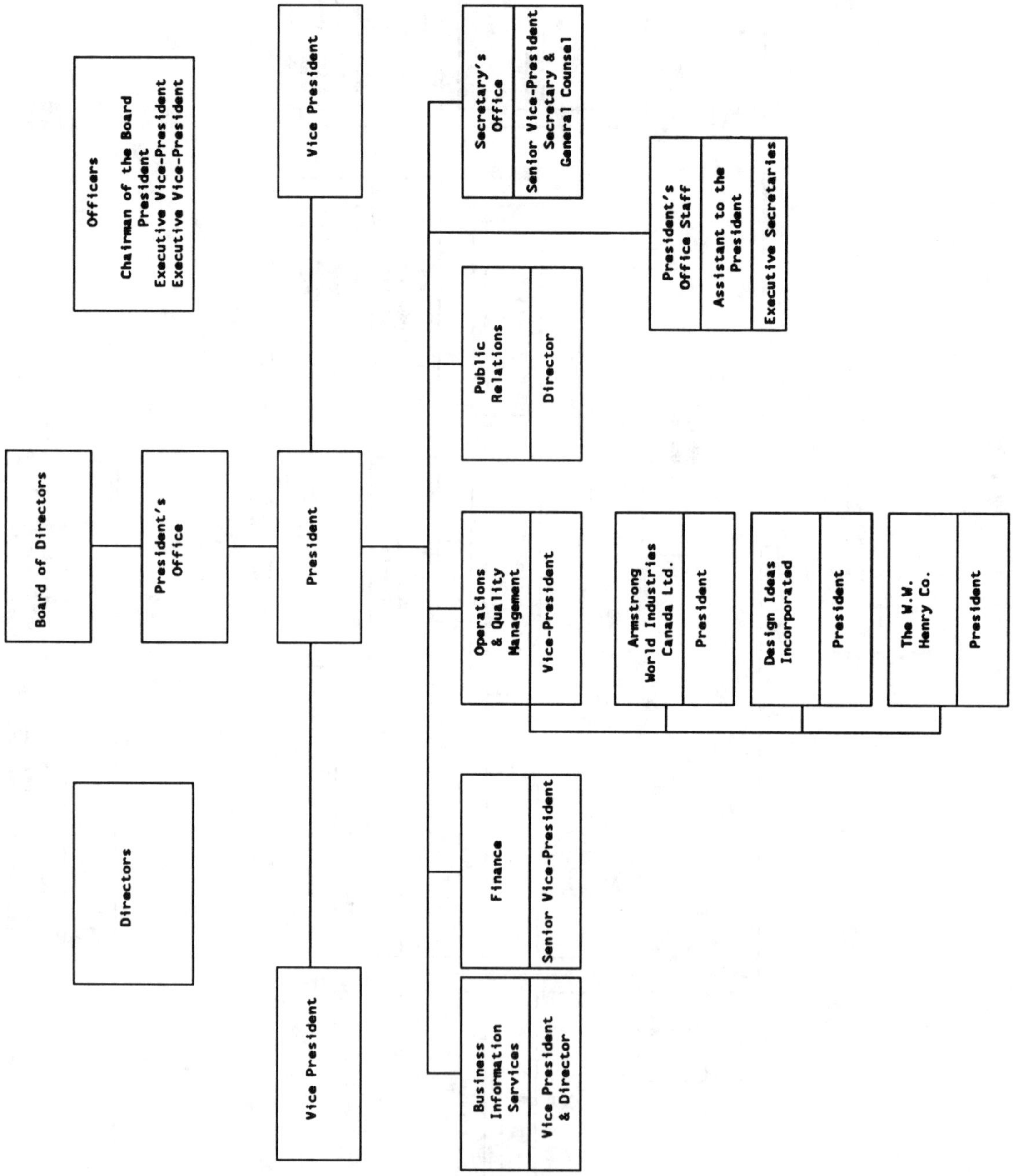

Board of Directors
President's Office
Directors
Officers
Chairman of the Board
President
Executive Vice-President
Executive Vice-President
Vice President
President
Vice President
Business Information Services
Vice President & Director
Finance
Senior Vice-President
Operations & Quality Management
Vice-President
Armstrong World Industries Canada Ltd.
President
Design Ideas Incorporated
President
The W.W. Henry Co.
President
Public Relations
Director
President's Office Staff
Assistant to the President
Executive Secretaries
Secretary's Office
Senior Vice-President Secretary & General Counsel

Continued on next page

ARMSTRONG WORLD INDUSTRIES, INC.
Continued from previous page

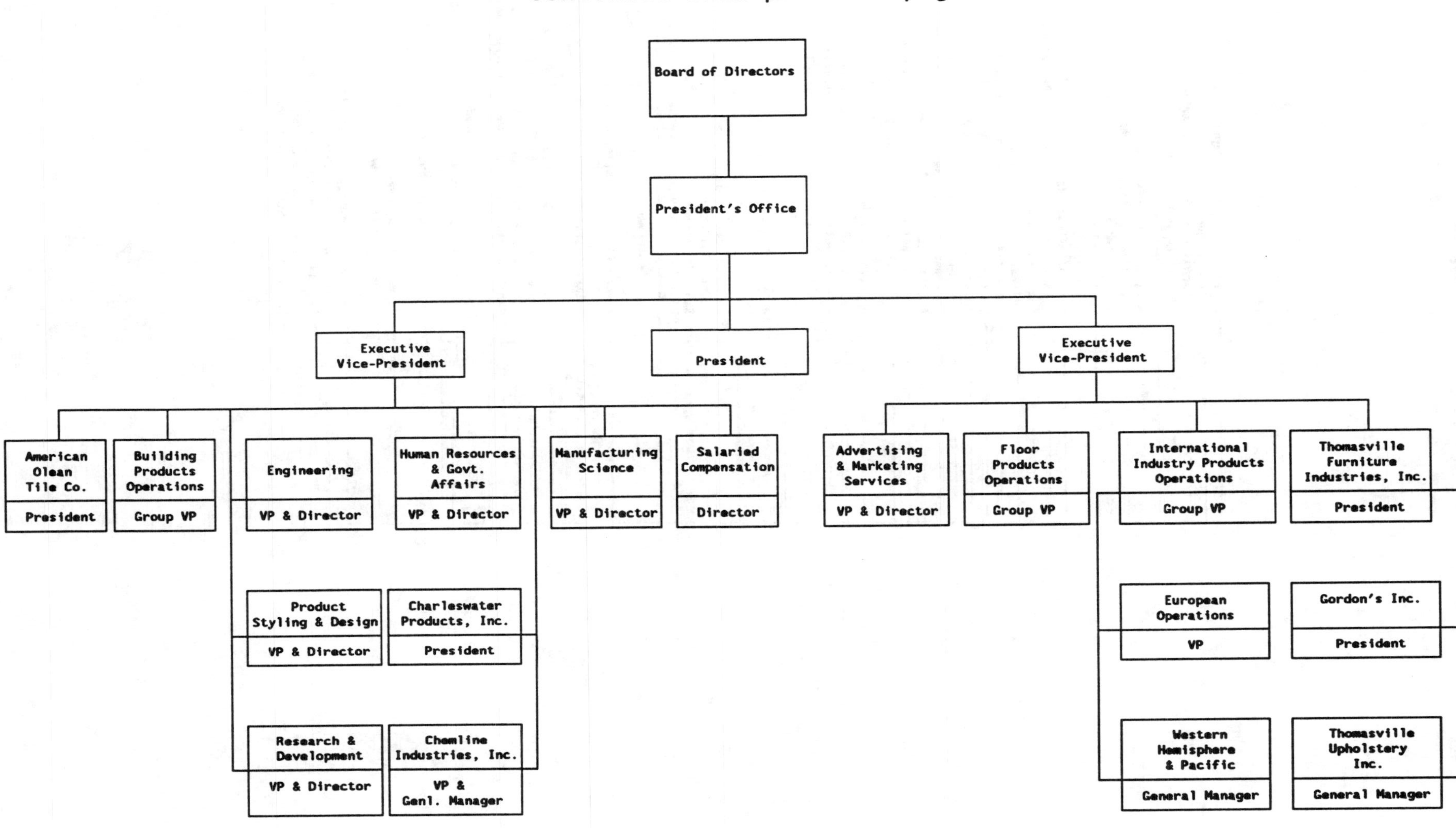

ASAHI BREWERY LTD. (Japan)

Source: Company update, 1991

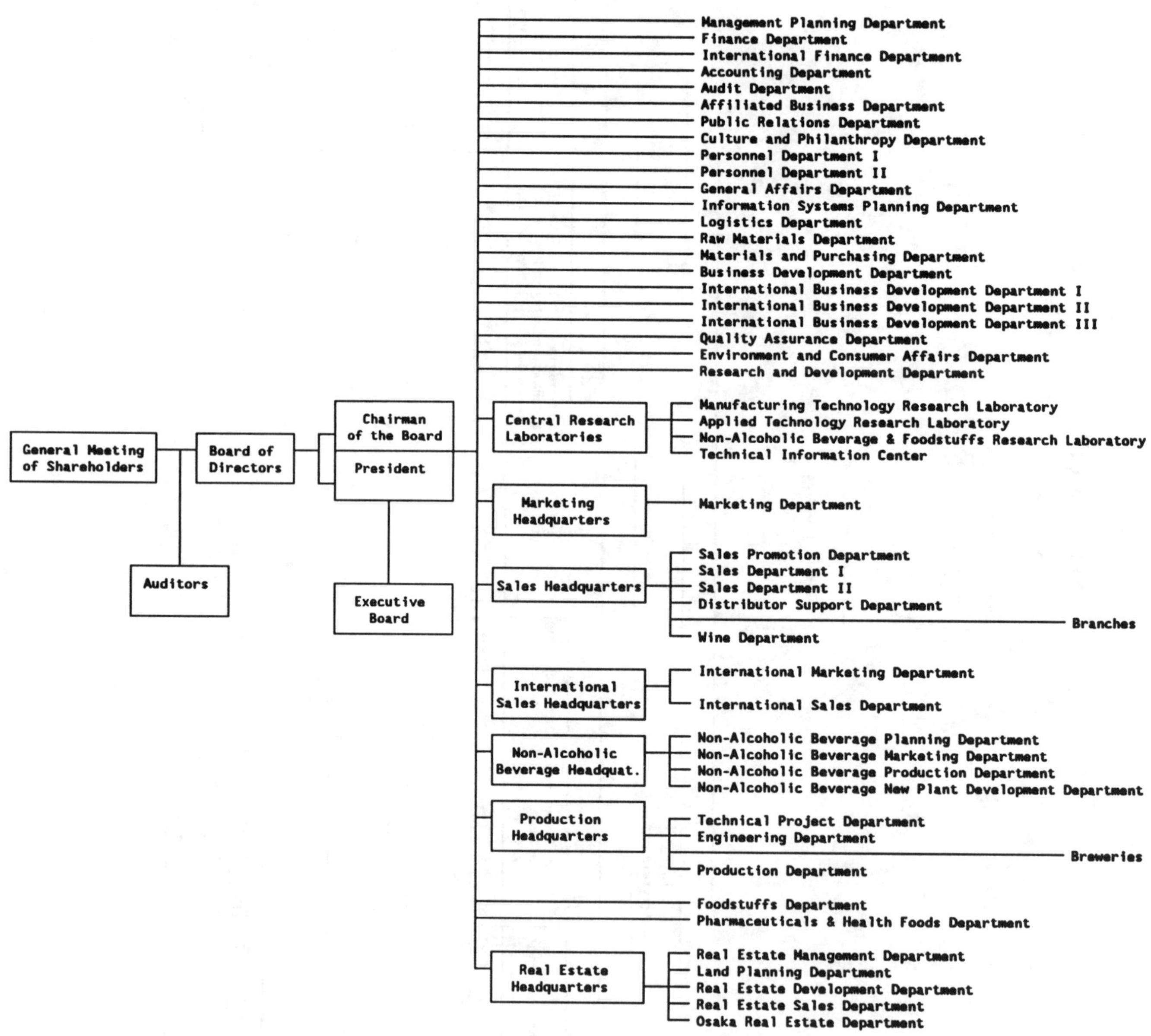

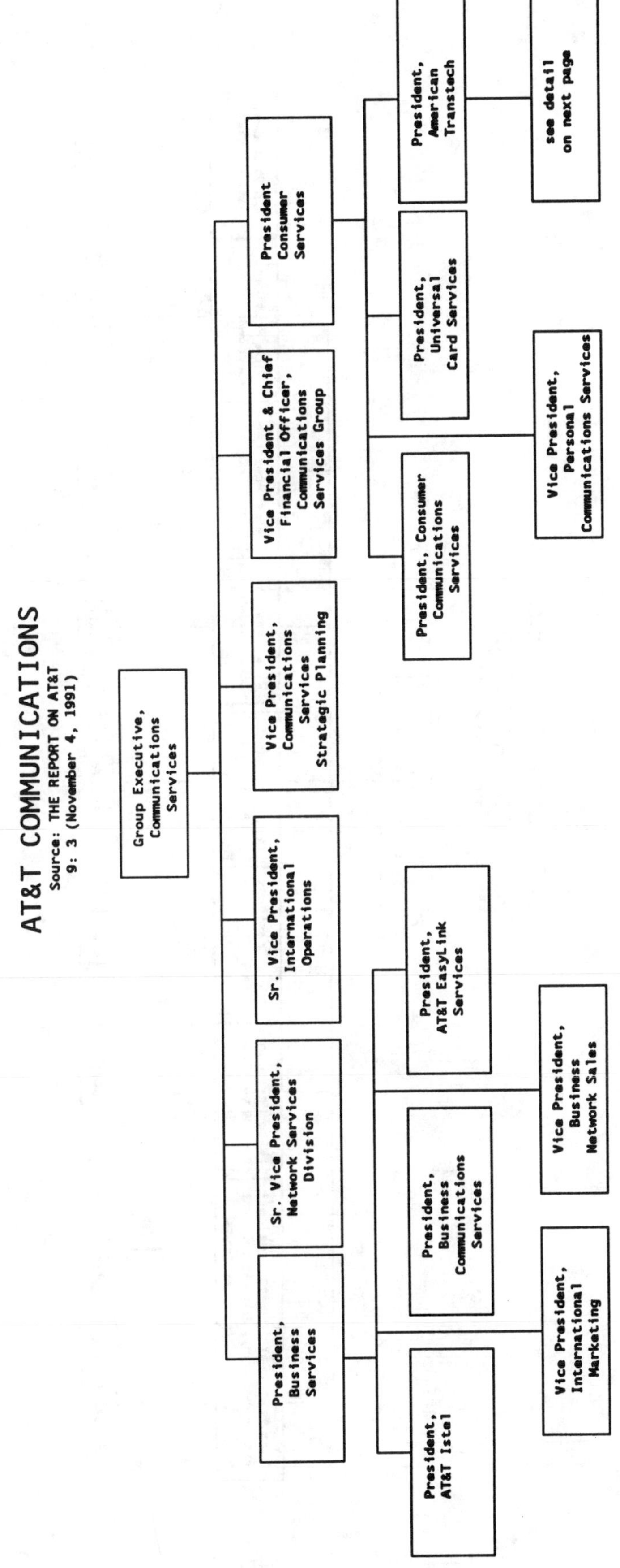
AT&T COMMUNICATIONS
Source: THE REPORT ON AT&T
9: 3 (November 4, 1991)
Group Executive, Communications Services
President, Business Services
Sr. Vice President, Network Services Division
Sr. Vice President International Operations
Vice President, Communications Services Strategic Planning
Vice President & Chief Financial Officer, Communications Services Group
President Consumer Services
President, AT&T Istel
Vice President, International Marketing
President, Business Communications Services
Vice President, Business Network Sales
President, AT&T EasyLink Services
President, Consumer Communications Services
Vice President, Personal Communications Services
President, Universal Card Services
President, American Transtech
see detail on next page

AT&T COMMUNICATIONS
AMERICAN TRANSTECH

Source: Company update, 1991

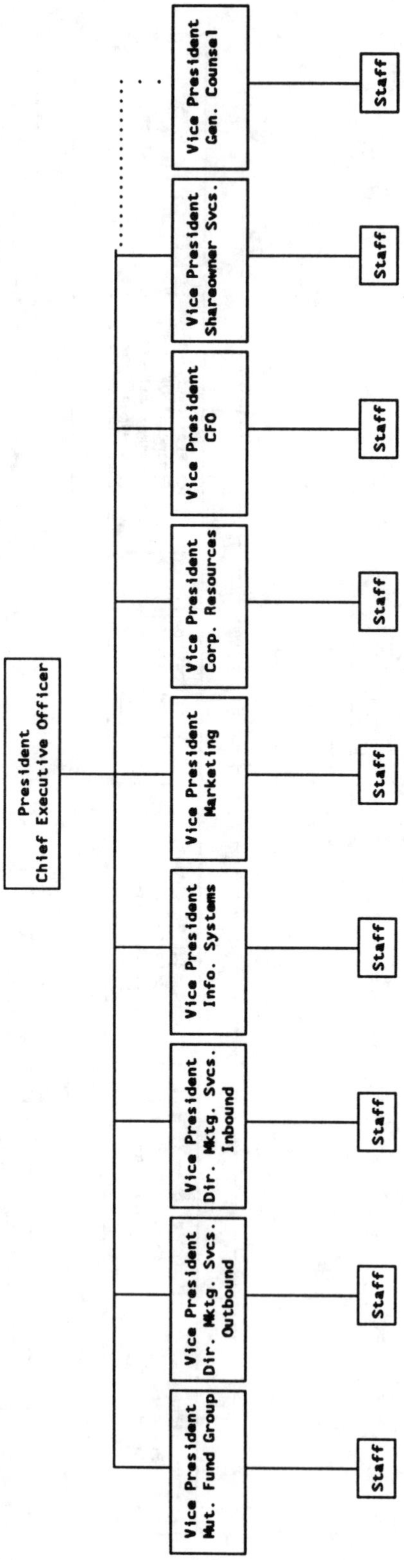

President
Chief Executive Officer

Vice President
Mut. Fund Group

Staff

Vice President
Dir. Mktg. Svcs.
Outbound

Staff

Vice President
Dir. Mktg. Svcs.
Inbound

Staff

Vice President
Info. Systems

Staff

Vice President
Marketing

Staff

Vice President
Corp. Resources

Staff

Vice President
CFO

Staff

Vice President
Shareowner Svcs.

Staff

Vice President
Gen. Counsel

Staff

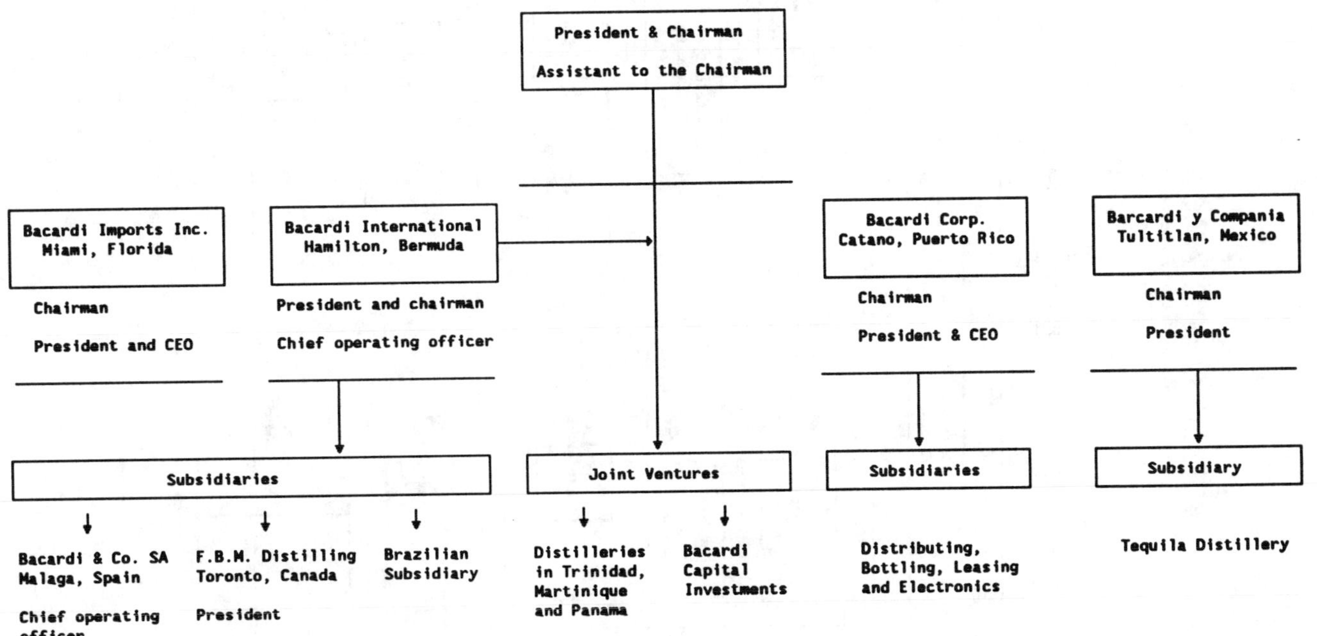
BACARDI & CO. LTD. (Bahamas)
Source: WASHINGTON POST
110: H1+ (May 10, 1987)
President & Chairman
Assistant to the Chairman
Bacardi Imports Inc.
Miami, Florida
Chairman
President and CEO
Bacardi International
Hamilton, Bermuda
President and chairman
Chief operating officer
Bacardi Corp.
Catano, Puerto Rico
Chairman
President & CEO
Barcardi y Compania
Tultitlan, Mexico
Chairman
President
Subsidiaries
Joint Ventures
Subsidiaries
Subsidiary
Bacardi & Co. SA
Malaga, Spain
Chief operating officer
F.B.M. Distilling
Toronto, Canada
President
Brazilian Subsidiary
Distilleries in Trinidad, Martinique and Panama
Bacardi Capital Investments
Distributing, Bottling, Leasing and Electronics
Tequila Distillery
This chart demonstrates the networking of independent companies.

BALTIMORE GAS AND ELECTRIC COMPANY/CORPORATE & UTILITY ORGANIZATION

Source: Company update, 1991

- Chairman of the Board and Chief Executive Officer
  - Vice Chairman of the Board
    - Nuclear Energy Vice President
      - Calvert Cliffs Nuclear Power Plant-Manager
      - Nuclear Engineering Manager
      - Nuclear Qlty. Assurance Manager
      - Nuclear Safety & Planning Manager
      - Nuclear Support Services Manager
      - Nuclear Outage & Proj. Mgmt. Manager
  - Corporate Finance VP & Treasurer
  - Auditing Manager
  - Legal General Counsel
  - Corporate Affairs Vice President
  - Utility Operations President
    - Fossil Energy Vice President
      - Fossil Operations Manager
      - Fossil Engineering Manager
      - Generation Maintenance Manager
    - Electric Interconnection & Transmission VP
      - Electric System Engineering Manager
      - Electric System Operation Manager
      - Electric Test Manager
      - Electric Construction Manager
      - Telecommunications Manager
    - Marketing Vice President
      - Merchandise Manager
      - Marketing & Energy Serv. Manager
      - Gas & Appliance Serv Manager
      - Economic Research Manager
    - Customer Service & Accounting Vice President
      - Accounting Manager
      - Customer Accounts Manager
      - Customer Relations Manager
    - General Services Vice President
      - Information Systems Manager
      - Purchasing & Mats. Mgmt. Manager
      - Faculties Management Manager
      - Transportation Manager
    - Distribution Vice President
      - Northern Distribution Manager
      - Central Distribution Manager
      - Southern Distribution Manager
      - Distribution Engineering Manager
      - Gas Supply Manager
  - Management Services Vice President
    - Employee Services Manager
    - Staff Services Manager
    - Safety & Med. Services Manager

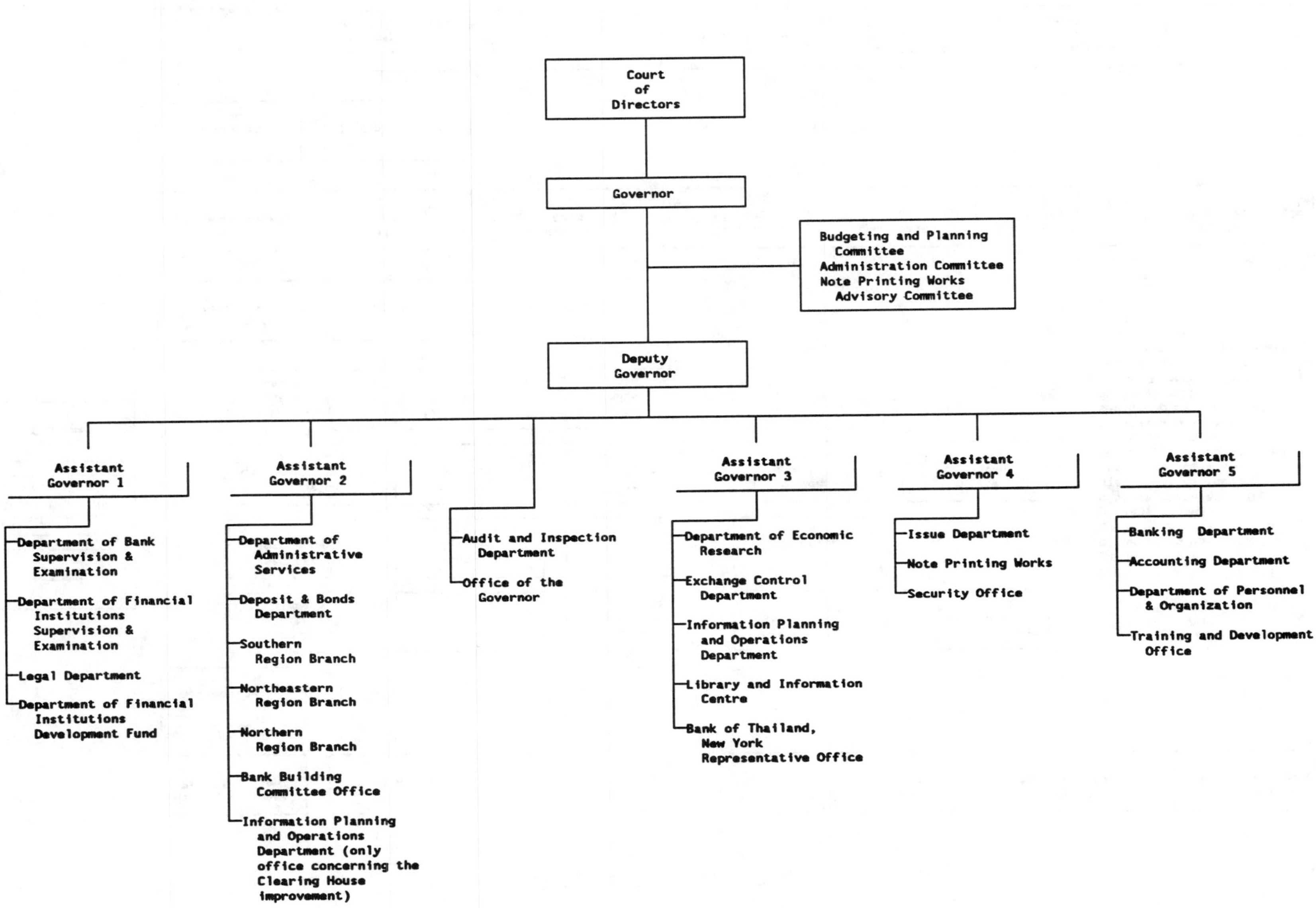
BANK OF THAILAND
Source: Annual report, 1989
Court of Directors
Governor
Budgeting and Planning Committee
Administration Committee
Note Printing Works Advisory Committee
Deputy Governor
Assistant Governor 1
Department of Bank Supervision & Examination
Department of Financial Institutions Supervision & Examination
Legal Department
Department of Financial Institutions Development Fund
Assistant Governor 2
Department of Administrative Services
Deposit & Bonds Department
Southern Region Branch
Northeastern Region Branch
Northern Region Branch
Bank Building Committee Office
Information Planning and Operations Department (only office concerning the Clearing House improvement)
Audit and Inspection Department
Office of the Governor
Assistant Governor 3
Department of Economic Research
Exchange Control Department
Information Planning and Operations Department
Library and Information Centre
Bank of Thailand, New York Representative Office
Assistant Governor 4
Issue Department
Note Printing Works
Security Office
Assistant Governor 5
Banking Department
Accounting Department
Department of Personnel & Organization
Training and Development Office

BARLOW RAND LTD. (South Africa)

Source: Company update, 1991

Chairman

Vice-Chairman & Chief Executive

Deputy Chairman

- Mining & Mineral Beneficiation
  - Rand Mines
  - Rand Mines Coal & Base Minerals
  - Rand Mines Gold & Platinum
  - Rand Mines Properties
  - Pretoria Portland Cement
  - Middleburg Steel & Alloys
- Industry
  - Electronics & Electrical Engineering
    - Reunert
    - Reunert Technology Systems
    - GEC Alsthom South Africa
    - Circuit Breaker Industries
  - Information Technology
    - Technology Systems International
    - ISM
    - RCP Group
  - Earthmoving Equipment, Motor & Appliances
    - Barlows Equipment Co.
    - Barlow Motor Investments
    - Barlow Consumer Electric Products
    - Barlow Handling
  - Building Materials, Steel & Paint
    - Federated-Blaikie
    - Robor Industrial Holdings
    - Plascon
- Packaging & Textiles
  - Nampak
  - Romatex
- Food & Pharmaceuticals
  - Tiger Foods
  - Imperial Cold Storage
  - Oceana Fishing
  - C.G. Smith Sugar
  - Adcock Ingram
  - Logos Pharmaceuticals
- International
  - J. Bibby & Sons
- Group Services & Property
  - Property, Finance & Administration
    - Finance
    - Administration
    - Barlow Rand Properties
    - Barlow Rand Computer Services
    - Rand Registers
  - Human Resources & Public Affairs
    - Human Resources
    - Public Affairs
    - Social Investment

Barlow Rand Ltd. is the parent company of a diversified business group with interests in mining, mineral beneficiation, manufacturing, distribution, food, pharmaceuticals and property. These interests are concentrated mainly in Southern Africa, but the group also has international operations in the United Kingdom, Europe, the United States and the Far East.--1990 Annual report

BASS PLC (United Kingdom)

Annual report, 1990

Chairman & Chief Executive

Corporate

Function	
Group Financial Controller Director of Information Technology Group Insurance Manager Director of Tax and Treasury	Financial Director
Director of Human Resources Director of Pensions	Director
Director of Property	Director
Director of Administration Group Legal Advisor	Company Secretary
Director of Corporate Affairs	

Operational

Function	Company	
Managing Director Human Resources Director Finance and Corporate Planning Director Legal, Estates and Purchasing Director Operations Director Marketing Director Sales Director Technical Director	Britvic Soft Drinks	Chairman
Managing Director Managing Director Managing Director	Augustus Barnett Delta Biotechnology Chateau Lascombes	
Managing Director	Bass Developments	Chairman
Managing Director	Hedges & Butler	

Continued on next page

BASS PLC (United Kingdom)

Continued from previous page

Chairman & Chief Executive

	Operational	
	Division/Company	Function
Chief Executive	Bass Brewers	Commerical Managing Director Managing Director Bass UK Managing Director Bass Brewing Distribution Director Finance Director Personnel Director
Chairman	Bass Export	Managing Director
Chief Executive	Bass Inns & Taverns	Inns & Taverns South, Operations Director Inns & Taverns North, Operations Director Marketing Director Property Director Finance Director Personnel Director
Chairman	Toby Restaurants	Managing Director
Chief Executive	Bass Leisure	Commercial Director Finance Director Human Resources Director Barcrest Managing Director BLMS Managing Director Coral Racing Managing Director Coral Social Clubs Managing Director
Chairman & Chief Executive Officer . . . . Vice Chairman	Holiday Inn Worldwide	Senior Vice President Company Managed Hotels US President Franchise Hotel Div. Senior Vice President/Managing Director Europe, Middle East, Africa Senior Vice President Finance Senior Vice President Corporate Development Senior Vice President Human Resources Senior Vice President General Counsel Senior Vice President Worldwide Marketing Senior Vice President Design & Purchasing

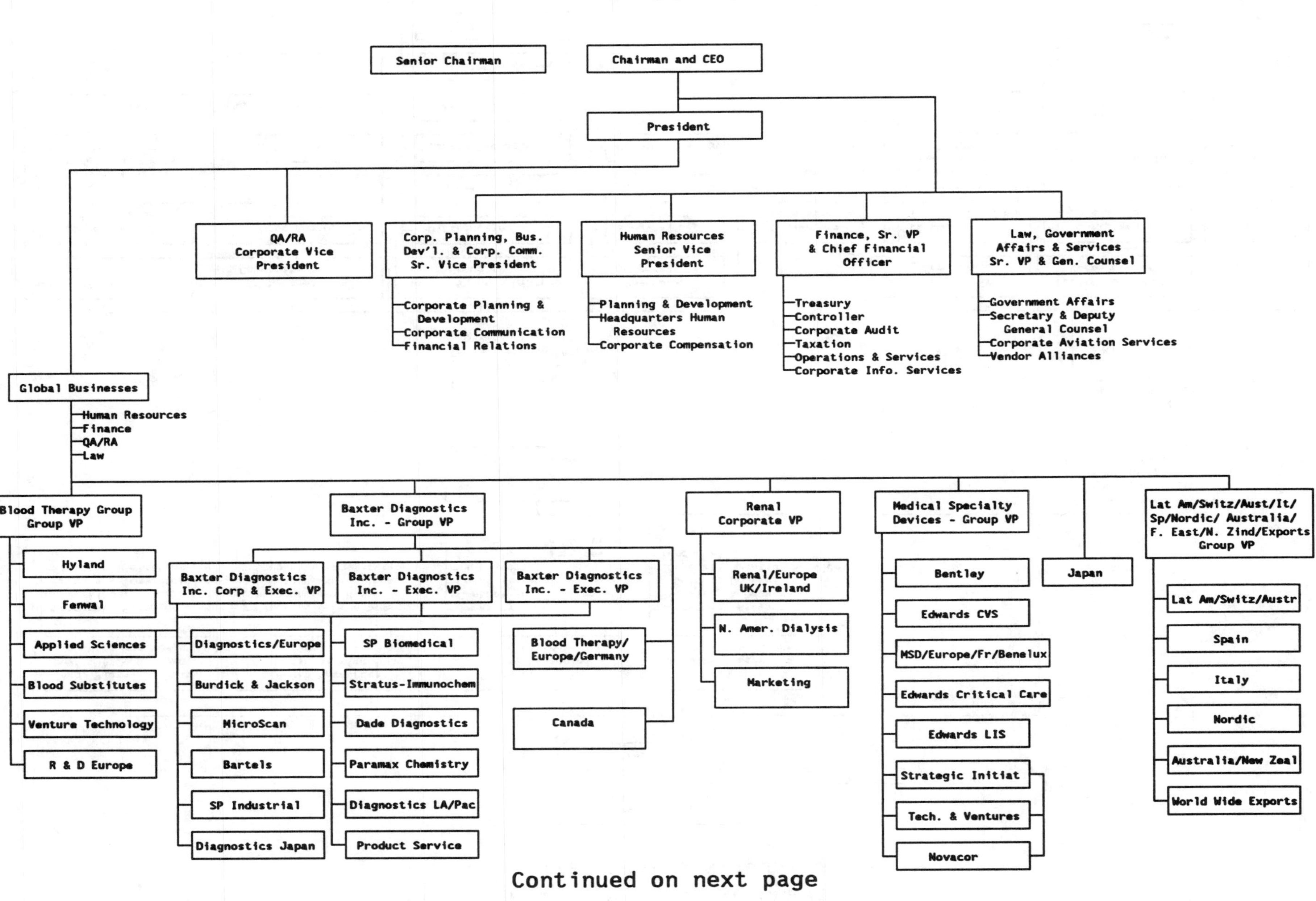

Continued on next page

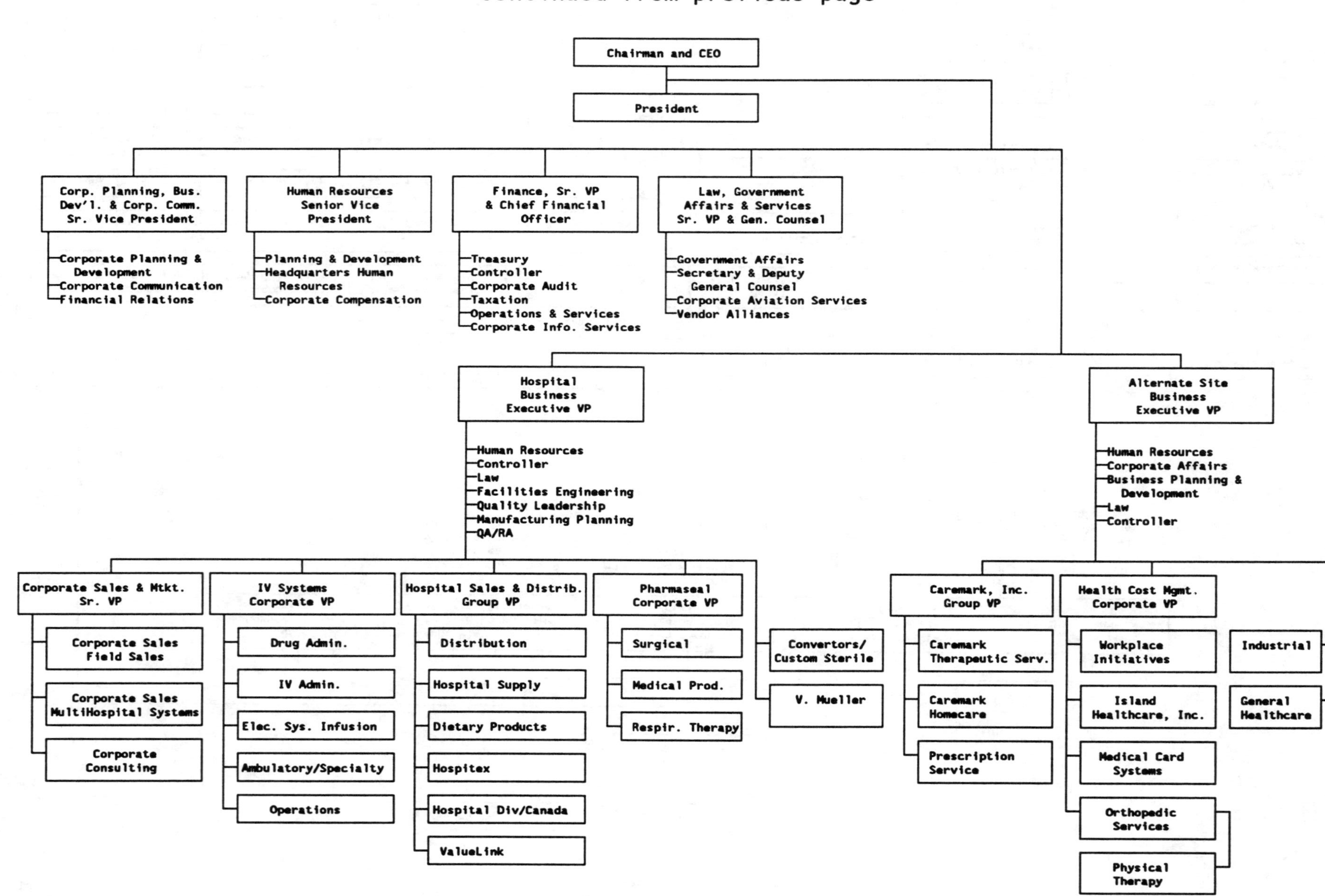

BAXTER HEALTHCARE CORP.
Continued from previous page
Chairman and CEO
President
Corp. Planning, Bus. Dev'l. & Corp. Comm. Sr. Vice President
Corporate Planning & Development
Corporate Communication
Financial Relations
Human Resources Senior Vice President
Planning & Development
Headquarters Human Resources
Corporate Compensation
Finance, Sr. VP & Chief Financial Officer
Treasury
Controller
Corporate Audit
Taxation
Operations & Services
Corporate Info. Services
Law, Government Affairs & Services Sr. VP & Gen. Counsel
Government Affairs
Secretary & Deputy General Counsel
Corporate Aviation Services
Vendor Alliances
Hospital Business Executive VP
Human Resources
Controller
Law
Facilities Engineering
Quality Leadership
Manufacturing Planning
QA/RA
Alternate Site Business Executive VP
Human Resources
Corporate Affairs
Business Planning & Development
Law
Controller
Corporate Sales & Mtkt. Sr. VP
Corporate Sales Field Sales
Corporate Sales MultiHospital Systems
Corporate Consulting
IV Systems Corporate VP
Drug Admin.
IV Admin.
Elec. Sys. Infusion
Ambulatory/Specialty
Operations
Hospital Sales & Distrib. Group VP
Distribution
Hospital Supply
Dietary Products
Hospitex
Hospital Div/Canada
ValueLink
Pharmaseal Corporate VP
Surgical
Medical Prod.
Respir. Therapy
Convertors/ Custom Sterile
V. Mueller
Caremark, Inc. Group VP
Caremark Therapeutic Serv.
Caremark Homecare
Prescription Service
Health Cost Mgmt. Corporate VP
Workplace Initiatives
Island Healthcare, Inc.
Medical Card Systems
Orthopedic Services
Physical Therapy
Industrial
General Healthcare

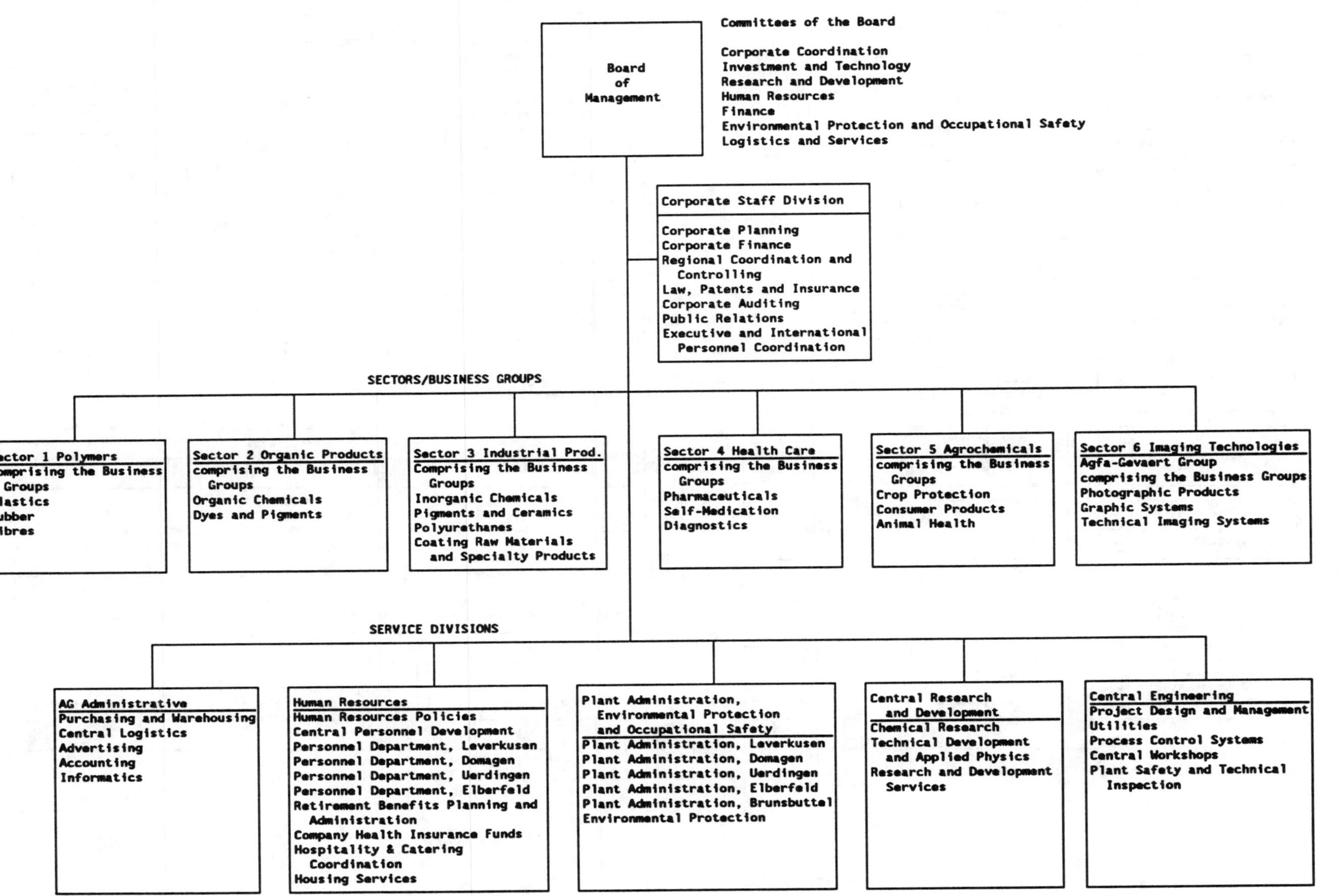
BAYER AG (Germany)
CORPORATE STRUCTURE
Source: Company update, 1991
Board of Management
Committees of the Board
Corporate Coordination
Investment and Technology
Research and Development
Human Resources
Finance
Environmental Protection and Occupational Safety
Logistics and Services
Corporate Staff Division
Corporate Planning
Corporate Finance
Regional Coordination and Controlling
Law, Patents and Insurance
Corporate Auditing
Public Relations
Executive and International Personnel Coordination
SECTORS/BUSINESS GROUPS
Sector 1 Polymers
comprising the Business Groups
Plastics
Rubber
Fibres
Sector 2 Organic Products
comprising the Business Groups
Organic Chemicals
Dyes and Pigments
Sector 3 Industrial Prod.
Comprising the Business Groups
Inorganic Chemicals
Pigments and Ceramics
Polyurethanes
Coating Raw Materials and Specialty Products
Sector 4 Health Care
comprising the Business Groups
Pharmaceuticals
Self-Medication
Diagnostics
Sector 5 Agrochemicals
comprising the Business Groups
Crop Protection
Consumer Products
Animal Health
Sector 6 Imaging Technologies
Agfa-Gevaert Group
comprising the Business Groups
Photographic Products
Graphic Systems
Technical Imaging Systems
SERVICE DIVISIONS
AG Administrative
Purchasing and Warehousing
Central Logistics
Advertising
Accounting
Informatics
Human Resources
Human Resources Policies
Central Personnel Development
Personnel Department, Leverkusen
Personnel Department, Dormagen
Personnel Department, Uerdingen
Personnel Department, Elberfeld
Retirement Benefits Planning and Administration
Company Health Insurance Funds
Hospitality & Catering Coordination
Housing Services
Plant Administration, Environmental Protection and Occupational Safety
Plant Administration, Leverkusen
Plant Administration, Dormagen
Plant Administration, Uerdingen
Plant Administration, Elberfeld
Plant Administration, Brunsbuttel
Environmental Protection
Central Research and Development
Chemical Research
Technical Development and Applied Physics
Research and Development Services
Central Engineering
Project Design and Management
Utilities
Process Control Systems
Central Workshops
Plant Safety and Technical Inspection

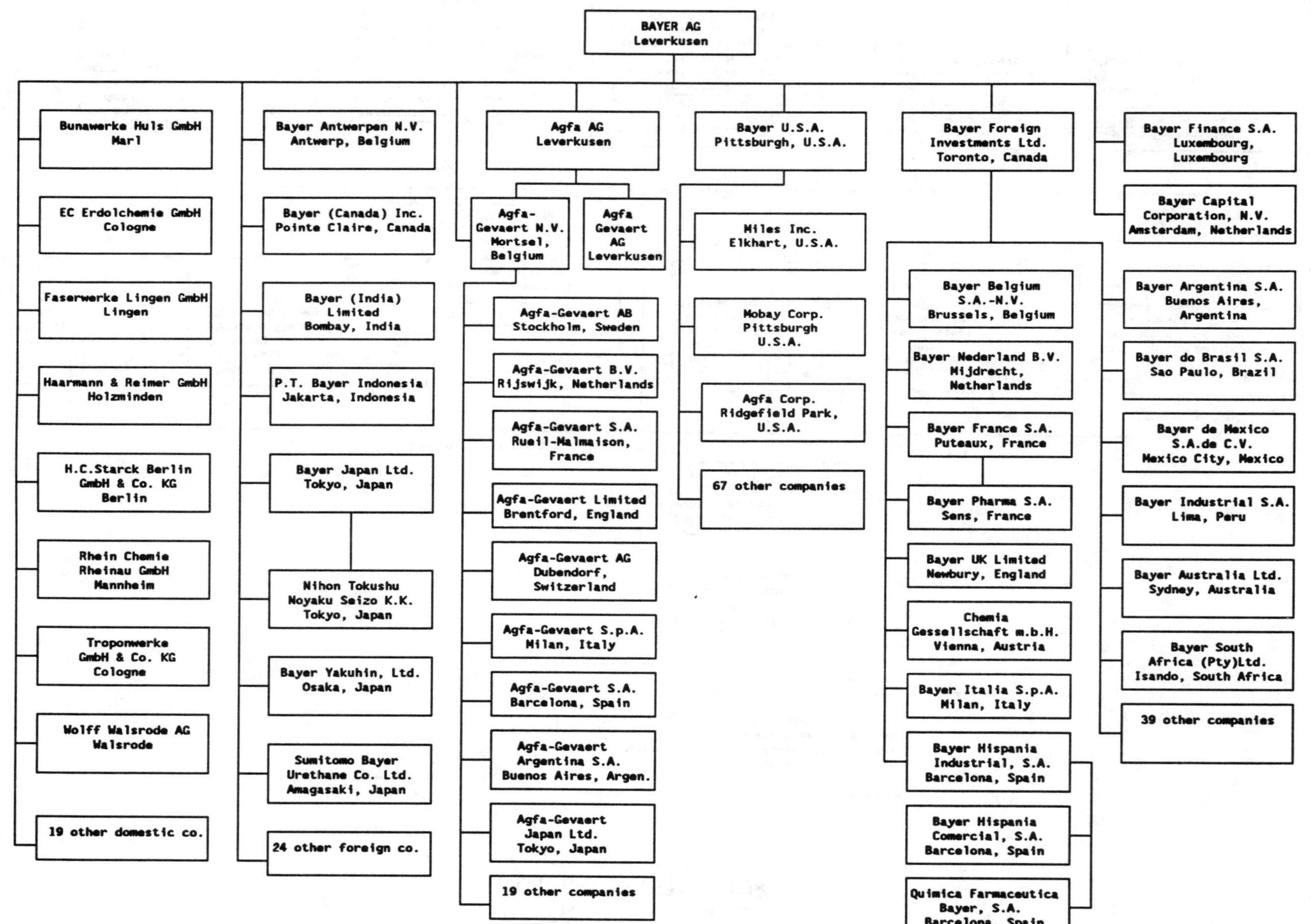
BAYER AG (Germany)
MAJOR AFFILIATED COMPANIES
Source: Company update, 1991
BAYER AG Leverkusen
Bunawerke Huls GmbH Marl
EC Erdolchemie GmbH Cologne
Faserwerke Lingen GmbH Lingen
Haarmann & Reimer GmbH Holzminden
H.C.Starck Berlin GmbH & Co. KG Berlin
Rhein Chemie Rheinau GmbH Mannheim
Troponwerke GmbH & Co. KG Cologne
Wolff Walsrode AG Walsrode
19 other domestic co.
Bayer Antwerpen N.V. Antwerp, Belgium
Bayer (Canada) Inc. Pointe Claire, Canada
Bayer (India) Limited Bombay, India
P.T. Bayer Indonesia Jakarta, Indonesia
Bayer Japan Ltd. Tokyo, Japan
Nihon Tokushu Noyaku Seizo K.K. Tokyo, Japan
Bayer Yakuhin, Ltd. Osaka, Japan
Sumitomo Bayer Urethane Co. Ltd. Amagasaki, Japan
24 other foreign co.
Agfa AG Leverkusen
Agfa-Gevaert N.V. Mortsel, Belgium
Agfa Gevaert AG Leverkusen
Agfa-Gevaert AB Stockholm, Sweden
Agfa-Gevaert B.V. Rijswijk, Netherlands
Agfa-Gevaert S.A. Rueil-Malmaison, France
Agfa-Gevaert Limited Brentford, England
Agfa-Gevaert AG Dubendorf, Switzerland
Agfa-Gevaert S.p.A. Milan, Italy
Agfa-Gevaert S.A. Barcelona, Spain
Agfa-Gevaert Argentina S.A. Buenos Aires, Argen.
Agfa-Gevaert Japan Ltd. Tokyo, Japan
19 other companies
Bayer U.S.A. Pittsburgh, U.S.A.
Miles Inc. Elkhart, U.S.A.
Mobay Corp. Pittsburgh U.S.A.
Agfa Corp. Ridgefield Park, U.S.A.
67 other companies
Bayer Foreign Investments Ltd. Toronto, Canada
Bayer Belgium S.A.-N.V. Brussels, Belgium
Bayer Nederland B.V. Mijdrecht, Netherlands
Bayer France S.A. Puteaux, France
Bayer Pharma S.A. Sens, France
Bayer UK Limited Newbury, England
Chemia Gesellschaft m.b.H. Vienna, Austria
Bayer Italia S.p.A. Milan, Italy
Bayer Hispania Industrial, S.A. Barcelona, Spain
Bayer Hispania Comercial, S.A. Barcelona, Spain
Quimica Farmaceutica Bayer, S.A. Barcelona, Spain
Bayer Finance S.A. Luxembourg, Luxembourg
Bayer Capital Corporation, N.V. Amsterdam, Netherlands
Bayer Argentina S.A. Buenos Aires, Argentina
Bayer do Brasil S.A. Sao Paulo, Brazil
Bayer de Mexico S.A.de C.V. Mexico City, Mexico
Bayer Industrial S.A. Lima, Peru
Bayer Australia Ltd. Sydney, Australia
Bayer South Africa (Pty)Ltd. Isando, South Africa
39 other companies

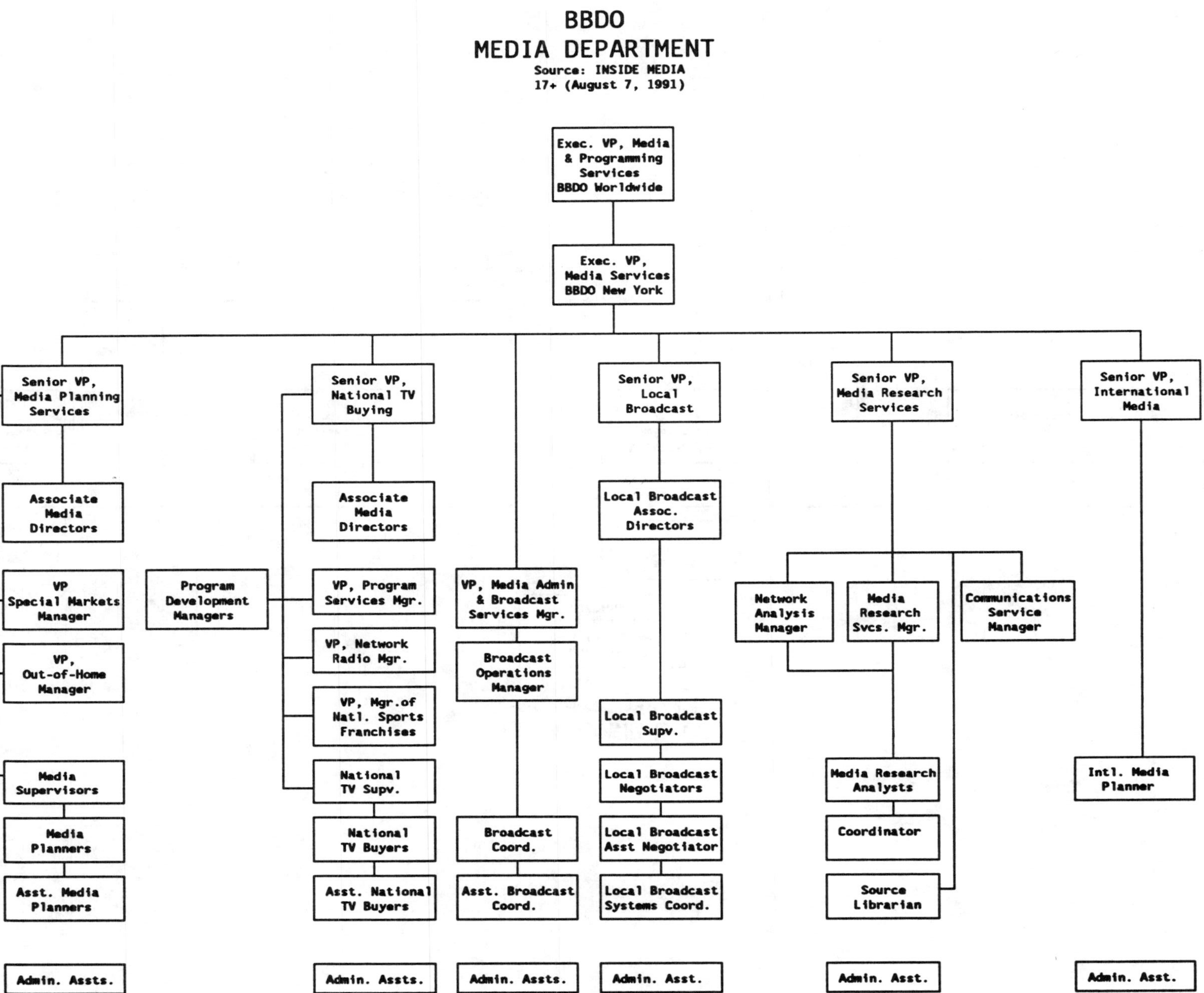
BBDO
MEDIA DEPARTMENT
Source: INSIDE MEDIA
17+ (August 7, 1991)
Exec. VP, Media & Programming Services BBDO Worldwide
Exec. VP, Media Services BBDO New York
Senior VP, Media Planning Services
Associate Media Directors
VP Special Markets Manager
VP, Out-of-Home Manager
Media Supervisors
Media Planners
Asst. Media Planners
Admin. Assts.
Program Development Managers
Senior VP, National TV Buying
Associate Media Directors
VP, Program Services Mgr.
VP, Network Radio Mgr.
VP, Mgr.of Natl. Sports Franchises
National TV Supv.
National TV Buyers
Asst. National TV Buyers
Admin. Assts.
VP, Media Admin & Broadcast Services Mgr.
Broadcast Operations Manager
Broadcast Coord.
Asst. Broadcast Coord.
Admin. Assts.
Senior VP, Local Broadcast
Local Broadcast Assoc. Directors
Local Broadcast Supv.
Local Broadcast Negotiators
Local Broadcast Asst Negotiator
Local Broadcast Systems Coord.
Admin. Asst.
Senior VP, Media Research Services
Network Analysis Manager
Media Research Svcs. Mgr.
Communications Service Manager
Media Research Analysts
Coordinator
Source Librarian
Admin. Asst.
Senior VP, International Media
Intl. Media Planner
Admin. Asst.

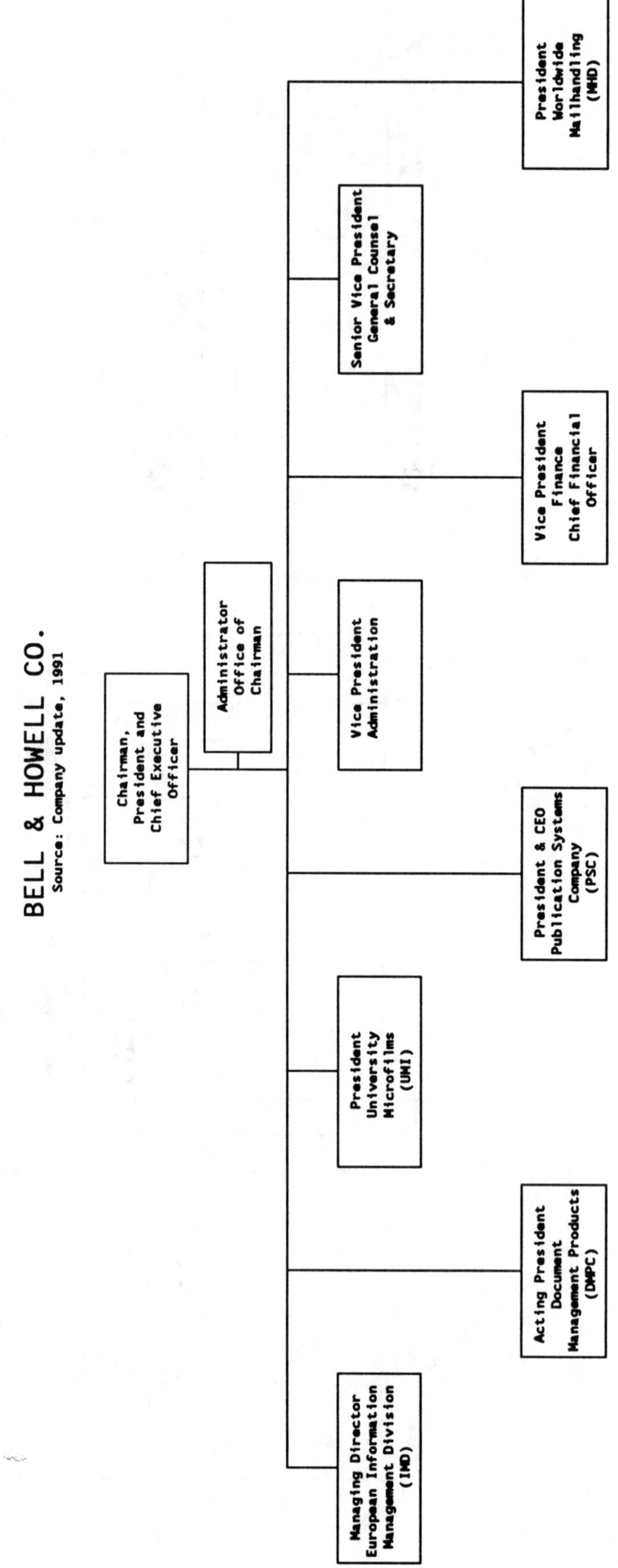
BELL & HOWELL CO.
Source: Company update, 1991
Chairman, President and Chief Executive Officer
Administrator Office of Chairman
Vice President Administration
Senior Vice President General Counsel & Secretary
Vice President Finance Chief Financial Officer
President Worldwide Mailhandling (MHD)
President & CEO Publication Systems Company (PSC)
President University Microfilms (UMI)
Acting President Document Management Products (DMPC)
Managing Director European Information Management Division (IMD)

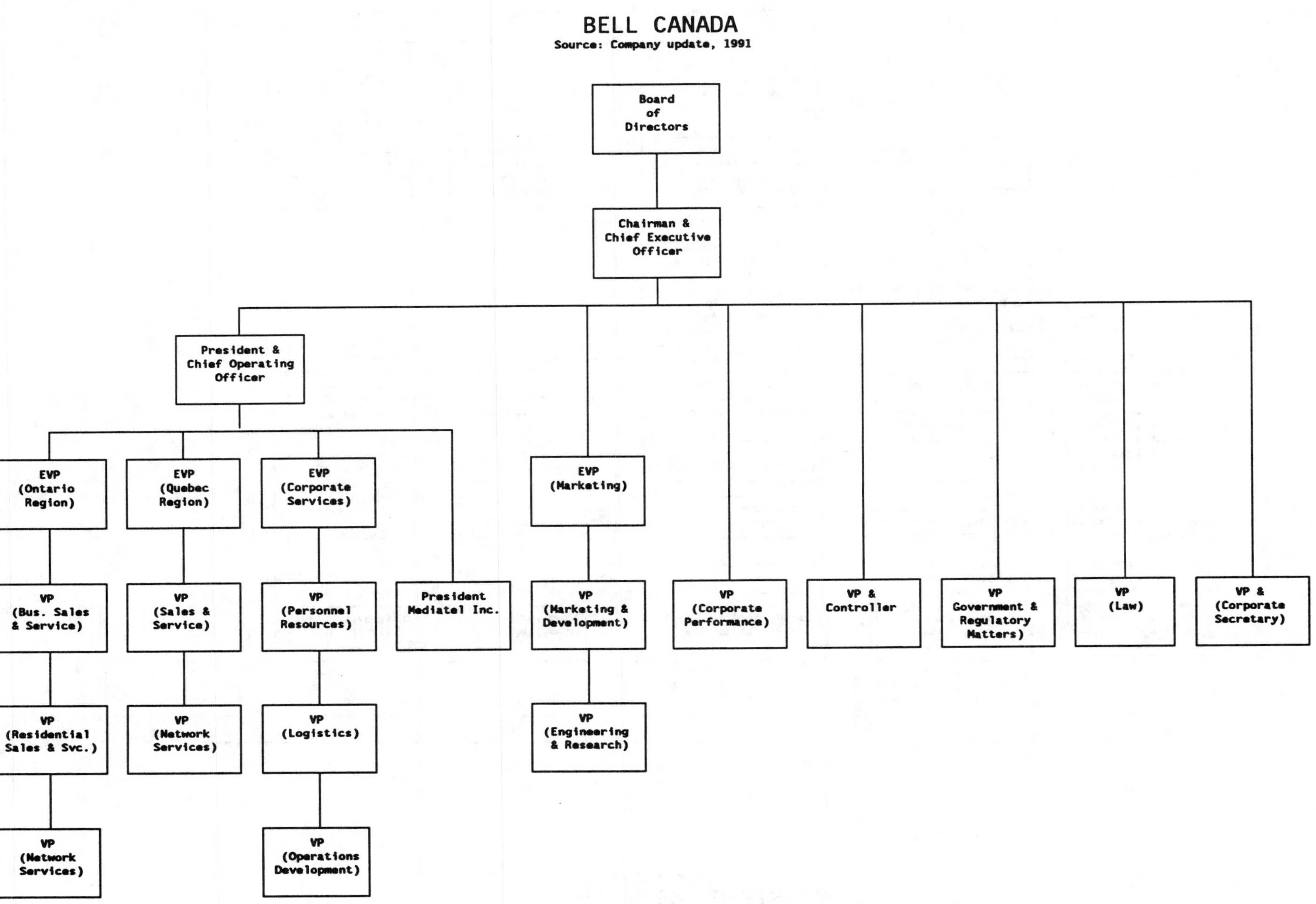
BELL CANADA
Source: Company update, 1991
Board of Directors
Chairman & Chief Executive Officer
President & Chief Operating Officer
EVP (Ontario Region)
VP (Bus. Sales & Service)
VP (Residential Sales & Svc.)
VP (Network Services)
EVP (Quebec Region)
VP (Sales & Service)
VP (Network Services)
EVP (Corporate Services)
VP (Personnel Resources)
VP (Logistics)
VP (Operations Development)
President Mediatel Inc.
EVP (Marketing)
VP (Marketing & Development)
VP (Engineering & Research)
VP (Corporate Performance)
VP & Controller
VP Government & Regulatory Matters)
VP (Law)
VP & (Corporate Secretary)

BELLSOUTH CORP.
BELLSOUTH ENTERPRISES

Source: Company update, 1991

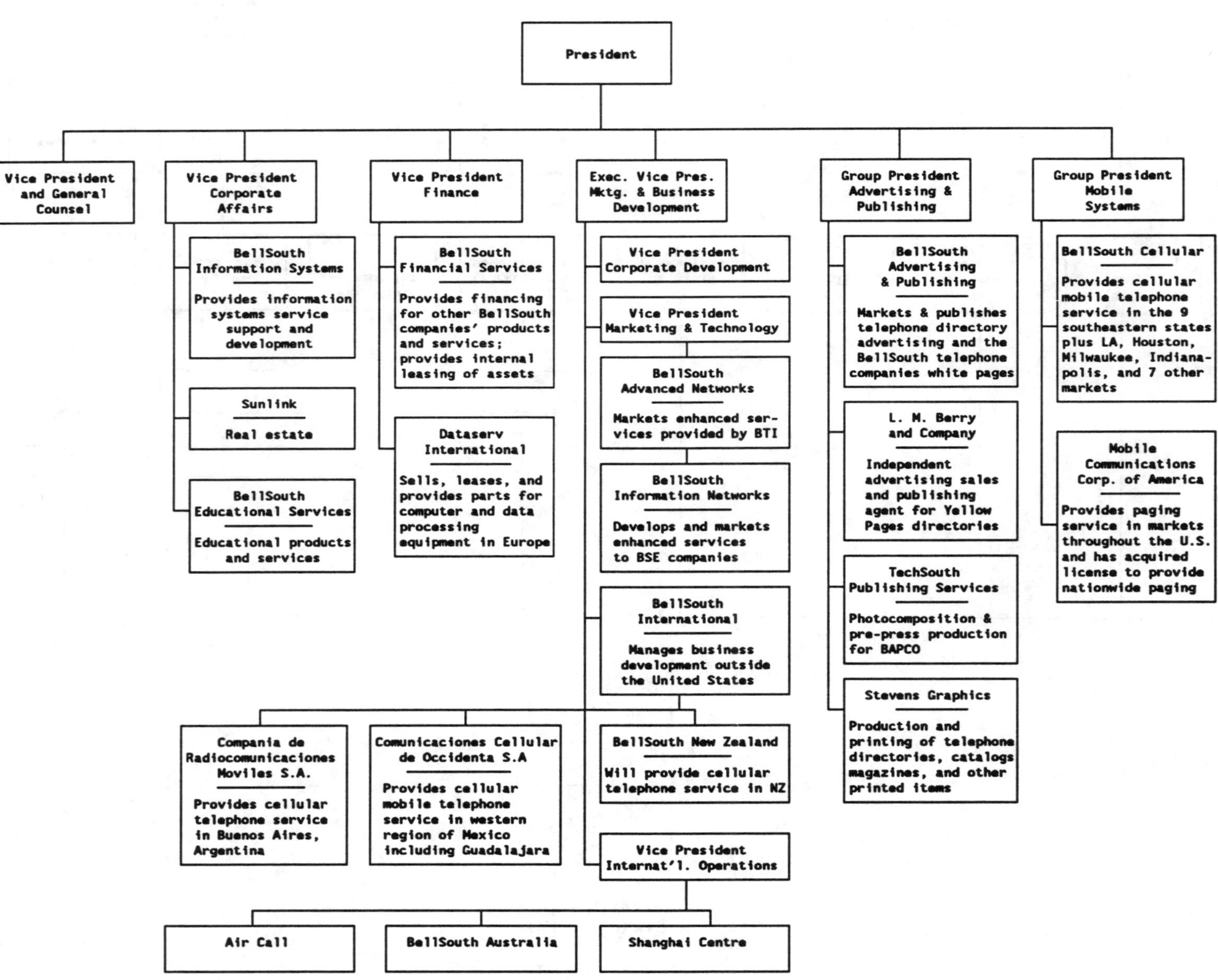

BELLSOUTH CORP.
BELLSOUTH TELECOMMUNICATION
Source: Company update, 1991

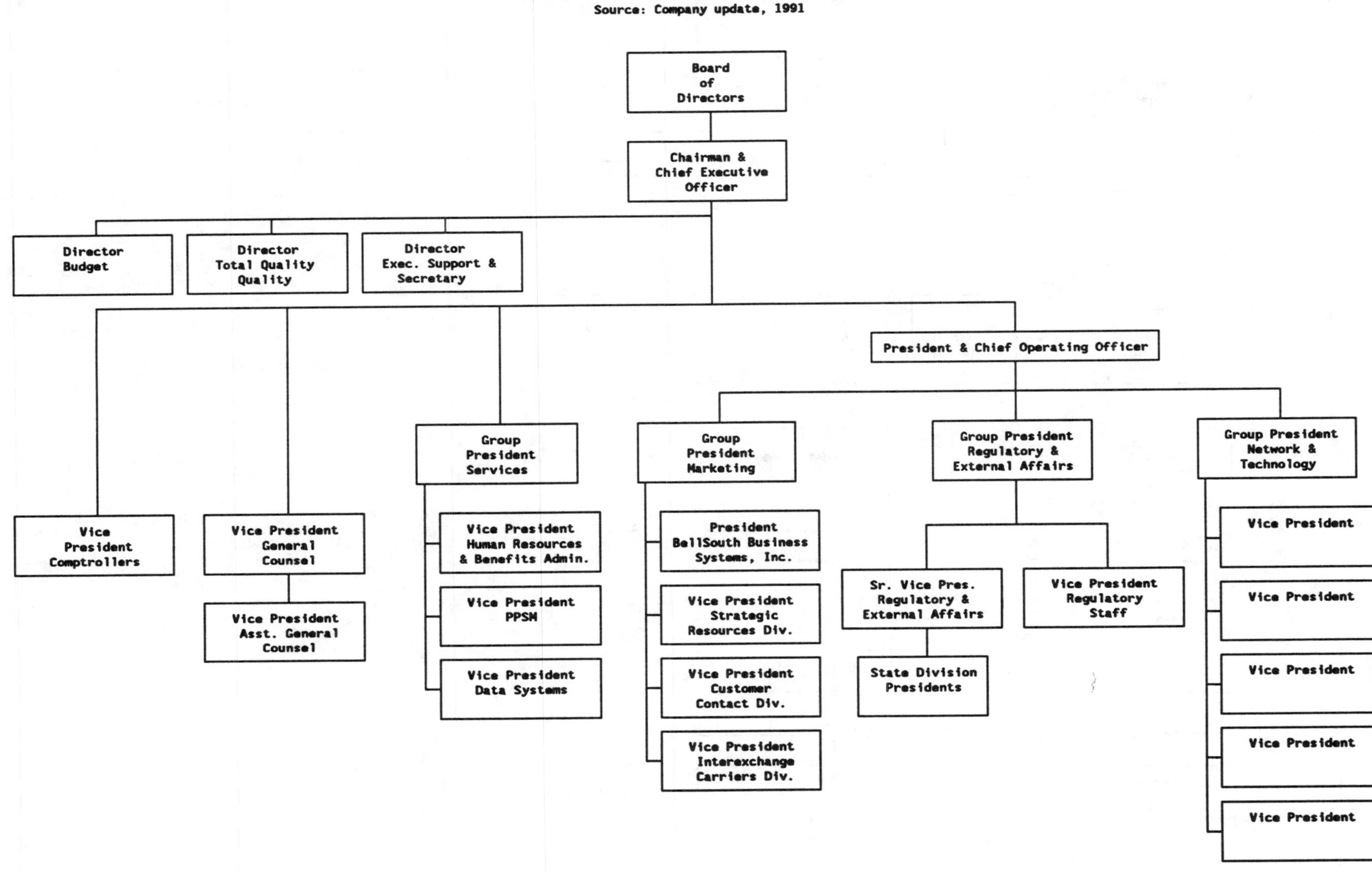

BEROL NOBEL (Sweden)

Source: Company update, 1991

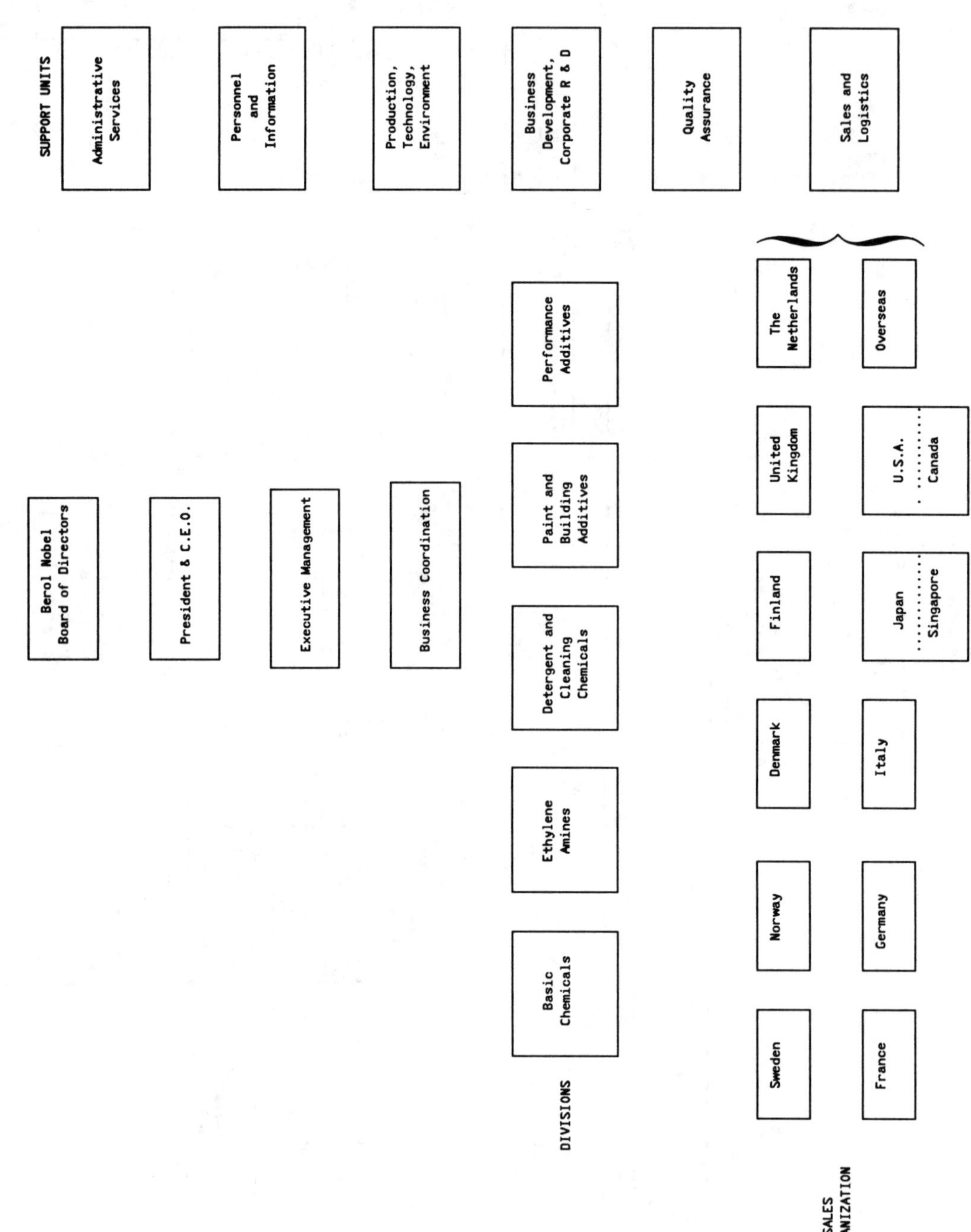
Berol Nobel Board of Directors
President & C.E.O.
Executive Management
Business Coordination
SUPPORT UNITS
Administrative Services
Personnel and Information
Production, Technology, Environment
Business Development, Corporate R & D
Quality Assurance
Sales and Logistics
DIVISIONS
Basic Chemicals
Ethylene Amines
Detergent and Cleaning Chemicals
Paint and Building Additives
Performance Additives
SALES ORGANIZATION
Sweden
Norway
Denmark
Finland
United Kingdom
The Netherlands
France
Germany
Italy
Japan
Singapore
U.S.A.
Canada
Overseas

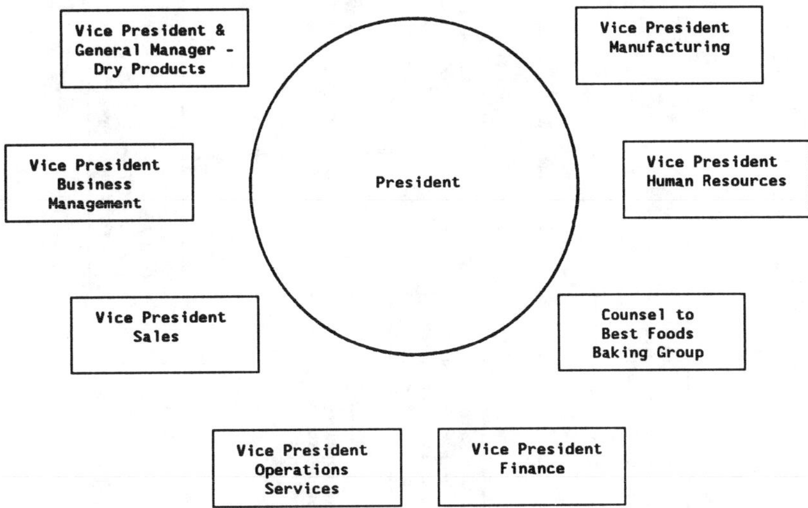

Best Foods' hybrid organizational structure has helped the company combine the benefits of centralization while maintaining responsiveness through decentralized functional lines of authority.

BETHLEHEM STEEL CORP.

Source: Company update, 1991

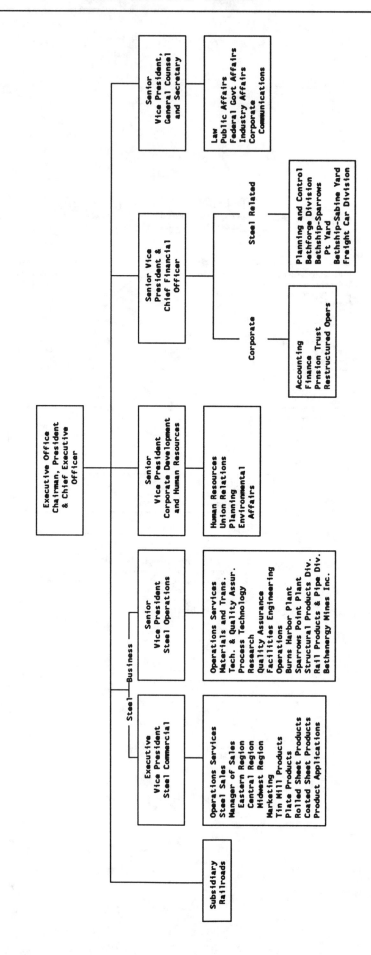

Executive Office
Chairman, President
& Chief Executive
Officer

Subsidiary
Railroads

Steel Business

Executive
Vice President
Steel Commercial

- Operations Services
- Steel Sales
- Manager of Sales
  - Eastern Region
  - Central Region
  - Midwest Region
- Marketing
- Tin Mill Products
- Plate Products
- Rolled Sheet Products
- Coated Sheet Products
- Product Applications

Senior
Vice President
Steel Operations

- Operations Services
- Materials and Trans.
- Tech. & Quality Assur.
- Process Technology
- Research
- Quality Assurance
- Facilities Engineering
- Operations
- Burns Harbor Plant
- Sparrows Point Plant
- Structural Products Div.
- Rail Products & Pipe Div.
- Bethenergy Mines Inc.

Senior
Vice President
Corporate Development
and Human Resources

- Human Resources
- Union Relations
- Planning
- Environmental Affairs

Senior Vice
President &
Chief Financial
Officer

Corporate

- Accounting
- Finance
- Prnsion Trust
- Restructured Opers

Steel Related

- Planning and Control
- Bethforge Division
- Bethship-Sparrows Pt Yard
- Bethship-Sabine Yard
- Freight Car Division

Senior
Vice President,
General Counsel
and Secretary

- Law
- Public Affairs
- Federal Govt Affairs
- Industry Affairs
- Corporate Communications

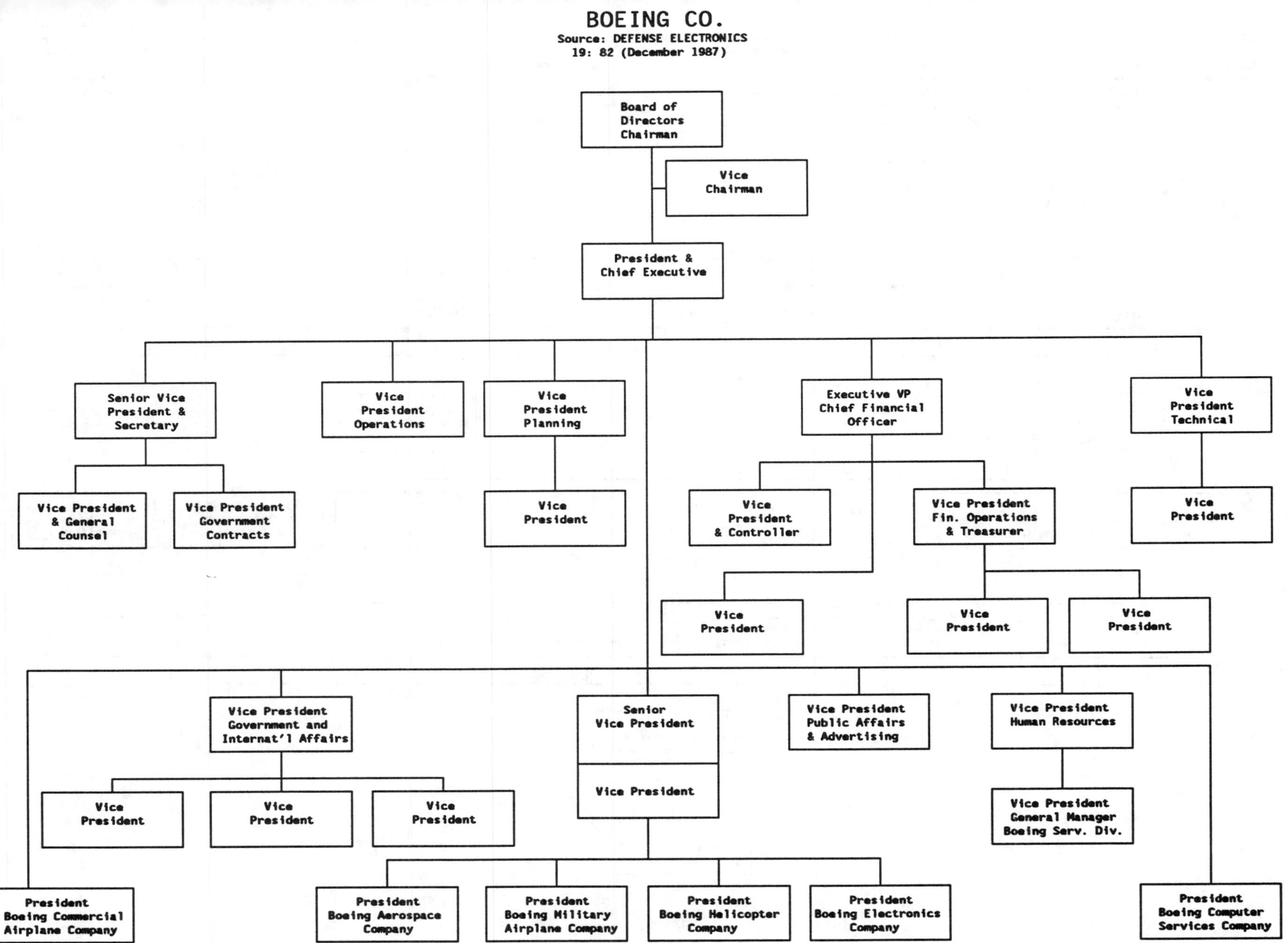
BOEING CO.
Source: DEFENSE ELECTRONICS
19: 82 (December 1987)
Board of Directors Chairman
Vice Chairman
President & Chief Executive
Senior Vice President & Secretary
Vice President Operations
Vice President Planning
Executive VP Chief Financial Officer
Vice President Technical
Vice President & General Counsel
Vice President Government Contracts
Vice President
Vice President & Controller
Vice President Fin. Operations & Treasurer
Vice President
Vice President
Vice President
Vice President
Vice President Government and Internat'l Affairs
Senior Vice President
Vice President
Vice President Public Affairs & Advertising
Vice President Human Resources
Vice President
Vice President
Vice President
Vice President General Manager Boeing Serv. Div.
President Boeing Commercial Airplane Company
President Boeing Aerospace Company
President Boeing Military Airplane Company
President Boeing Helicopter Company
President Boeing Electronics Company
President Boeing Computer Services Company

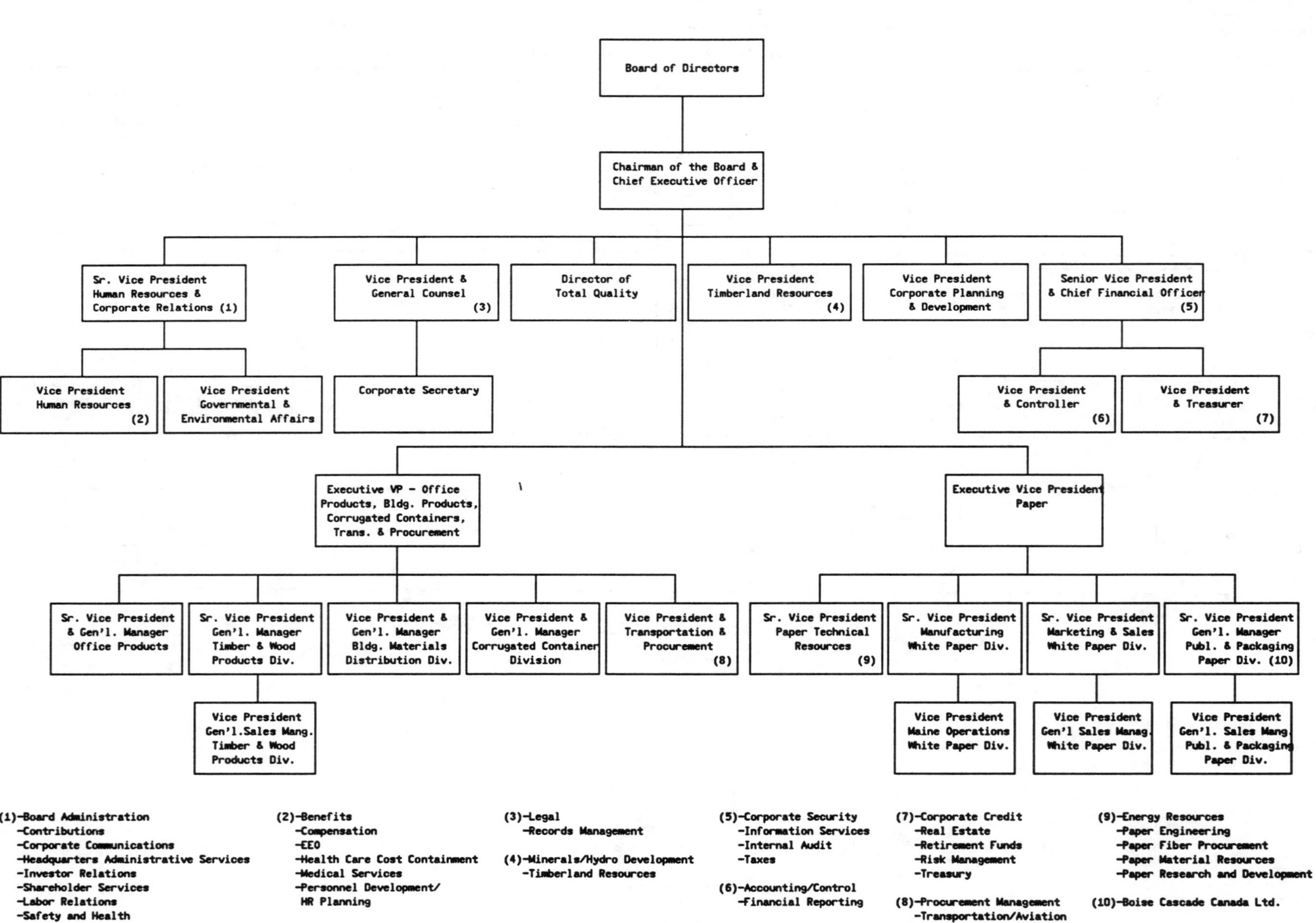
BOISE CASCADE CORP.
Source: Company update, 1991
Board of Directors
Chairman of the Board & Chief Executive Officer
Sr. Vice President Human Resources & Corporate Relations (1)
Vice President Human Resources (2)
Vice President Governmental & Environmental Affairs
Vice President & General Counsel (3)
Corporate Secretary
Director of Total Quality
Vice President Timberland Resources (4)
Vice President Corporate Planning & Development
Senior Vice President & Chief Financial Officer (5)
Vice President & Controller (6)
Vice President & Treasurer (7)
Executive VP - Office Products, Bldg. Products, Corrugated Containers, Trans. & Procurement
Sr. Vice President & Gen'l. Manager Office Products
Sr. Vice President Gen'l. Manager Timber & Wood Products Div.
Vice President Gen'l.Sales Mang. Timber & Wood Products Div.
Vice President & Gen'l. Manager Bldg. Materials Distribution Div.
Vice President & Gen'l. Manager Corrugated Container Division
Vice President & Transportation & Procurement (8)
Executive Vice President Paper
Sr. Vice President Paper Technical Resources (9)
Sr. Vice President Manufacturing White Paper Div.
Vice President Maine Operations White Paper Div.
Sr. Vice President Marketing & Sales White Paper Div.
Vice President Gen'l Sales Manag. White Paper Div.
Sr. Vice President Gen'l. Manager Publ. & Packaging Paper Div. (10)
Vice President Gen'l. Sales Mang. Publ. & Packaging Paper Div.
(1)-Board Administration
-Contributions
-Corporate Communications
-Headquarters Administrative Services
-Investor Relations
-Shareholder Services
-Labor Relations
-Safety and Health
(2)-Benefits
-Compensation
-EEO
-Health Care Cost Containment
-Medical Services
-Personnel Development/
HR Planning
(3)-Legal
-Records Management
(4)-Minerals/Hydro Development
-Timberland Resources
(5)-Corporate Security
-Information Services
-Internal Audit
-Taxes
(6)-Accounting/Control
-Financial Reporting
(7)-Corporate Credit
-Real Estate
-Retirement Funds
-Risk Management
-Treasury
(8)-Procurement Management
-Transportation/Aviation
(9)-Energy Resources
-Paper Engineering
-Paper Fiber Procurement
-Paper Material Resources
-Paper Research and Development
(10)-Boise Cascade Canada Ltd.

BSN GROUPE (France)

Source: Company update, 1991

Dairy Products

Europe
- Gervais Danone
- Laiterie De Ville-comital
- Gervais Danone Austria
- Gervais Danone Belgique
- Gervais Danone AG
- Galbani
- Gervais Danone Italiana
- Gervais Danone Nederland
- Danone SA

International
- LPC Industrias Alimenticias
- Guangzhou Danone Yogurt Co.
- Ajinomoto Danone
- Danone De Mexico
- The Dannon Co.

Grocery Products Pasta & Prepared Dishes

Grocery Products
- Amora
- Diepal
- Generale-Traiteur
- Materne Fruibourg
- Nutri-pharm-elgi
- Segma Liebig-Maille
- Stoeffler
- Liebig Benelux
- Star SpA
- Starlux
- HP Foods
- Lea & Perrins

Pasta and Prepared Dishes
- Panzani SA
- Birkel
- Sonnen-Bassermann
- Agnesi
- Panzani Ponte Liebig
- La Familia

Biscuits
- L'Alsacienne
- Belin
- Heudebert
- Lu
- Vandamme Pie Qui Chante
- General Biscuits Osterreich
- General Biscuits Belgie
- General Biscuits GmbH
- Saiwa
- General Biscuits Nederland
- General Biscuits Espana
- Jacob's Bakery
- Britannia Brands HK Ltd.
- Britannia Industries Ltd.
- Britannia Brands Malaysia
- Britannia Brands New Zealand
- Peerless Foods Pte Ltd.

Beer
- Kanterbrau SA
- Kronenbourg
- Alken Maes
- Henninger Hellas
- Peroni
- Mahou

Mineral Water
- Evian
- Seat
- Boario
- Sangemini Ferrarelle
- Font Vella
- Evian Waters of France

Containers
- Seprosy
- Verreries de Masnieres
- Verreries Souchon Neuvesel
- VMC
- Vereenigde Glasfa-brieken
- Giralt Laporta
- Vidrieria Vilella

BT NORTH AMERICA INC.

Source: Company update, 1991

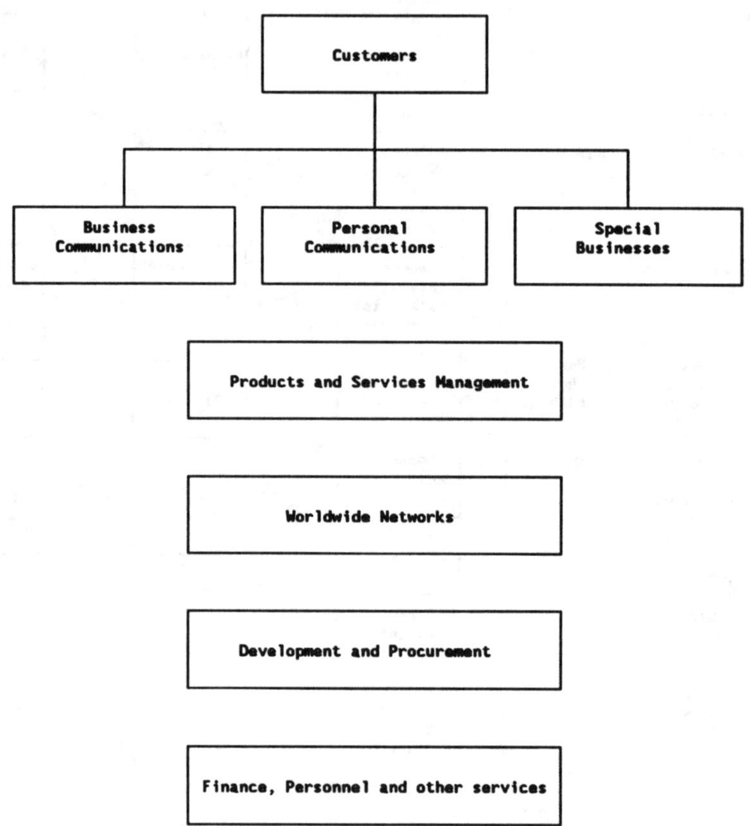

BT's values (from 1991 annual report):

* We put our customers first
* We are professional
* We respect each other
* We work as one team
* We are committed to continuous improvement

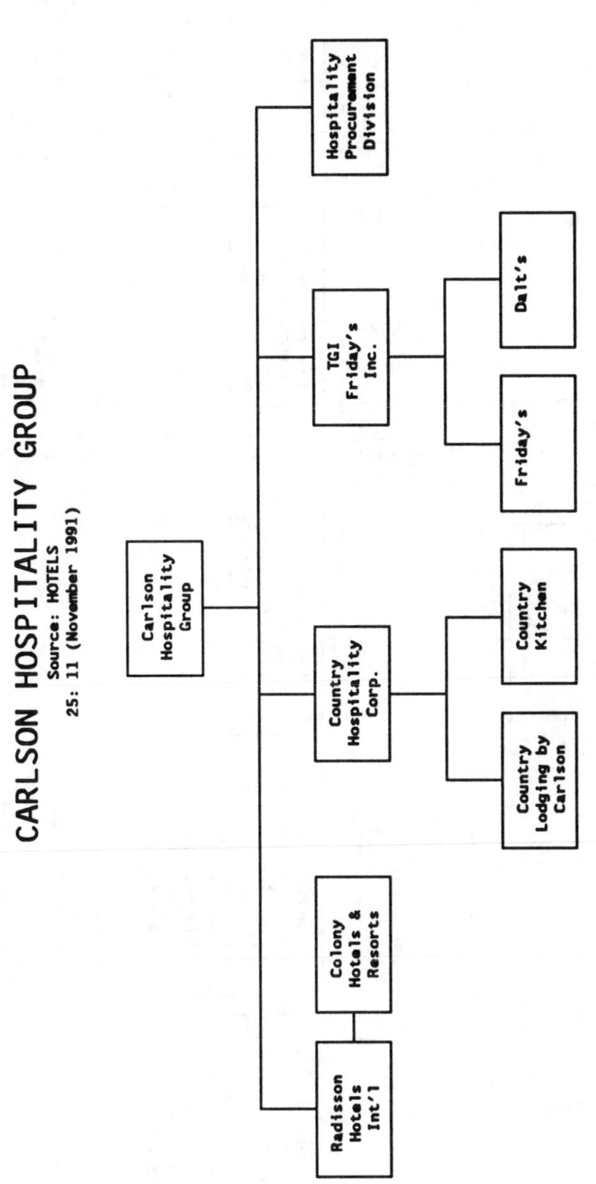

Carlson Hospitality Group's five hotel and restaurant chains are all expanding worldwide. The Procurement Division purchases fixtures, furnishings, & equipment for the group.

CATERPILLAR INC.

Source: Company update, 1991

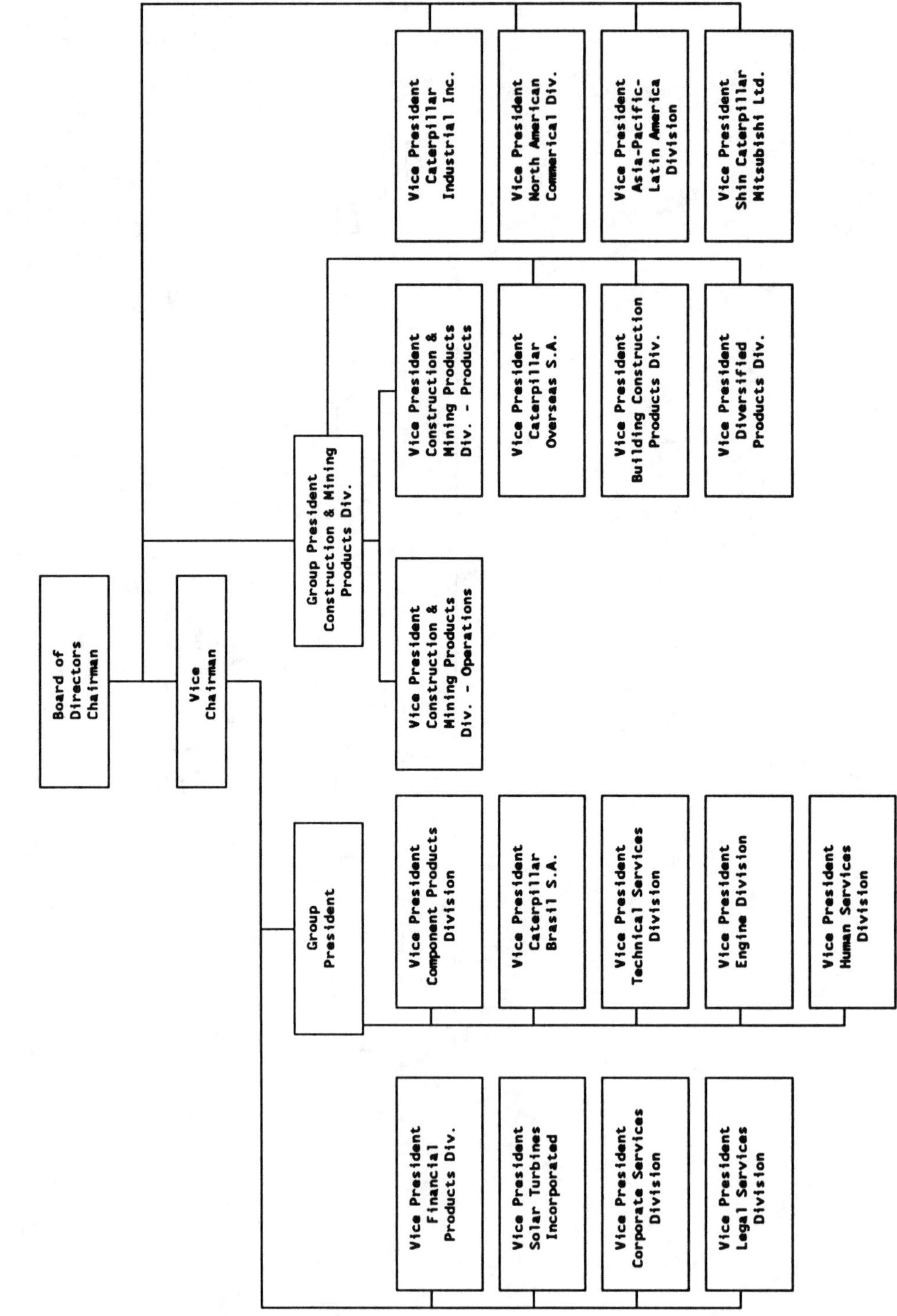

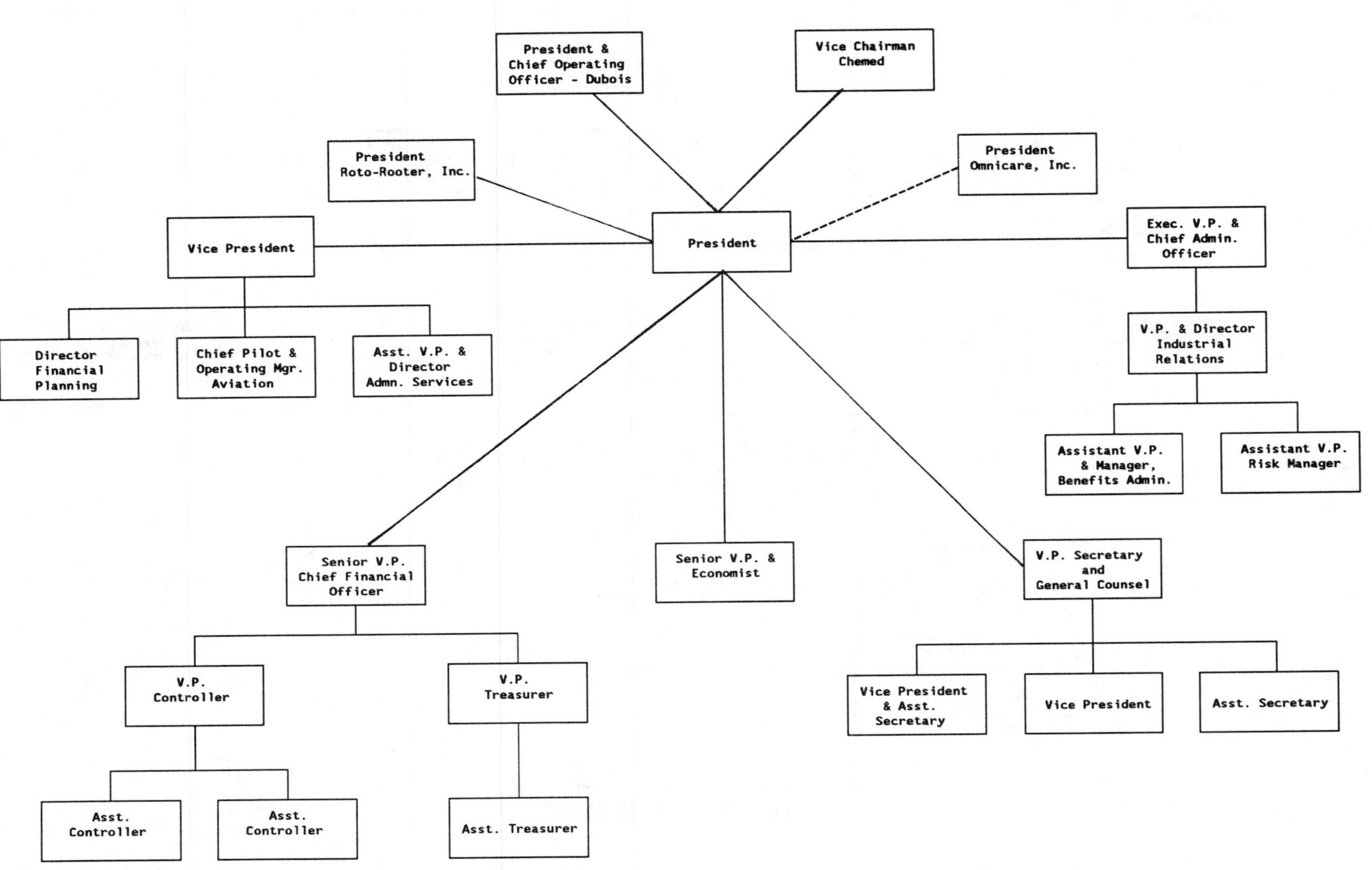
CHEMED CORP.
Source: Company update, 1991
President & Chief Operating Officer - Dubois
Vice Chairman Chemed
President Roto-Rooter, Inc.
President Omnicare, Inc.
Vice President
President
Exec. V.P. & Chief Admin. Officer
Director Financial Planning
Chief Pilot & Operating Mgr. Aviation
Asst. V.P. & Director Admn. Services
V.P. & Director Industrial Relations
Assistant V.P. & Manager, Benefits Admin.
Assistant V.P. Risk Manager
Senior V.P. Chief Financial Officer
Senior V.P. & Economist
V.P. Secretary and General Counsel
V.P. Controller
V.P. Treasurer
Vice President & Asst. Secretary
Vice President
Asst. Secretary
Asst. Controller
Asst. Controller
Asst. Treasurer

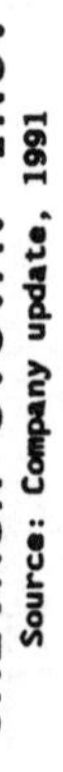

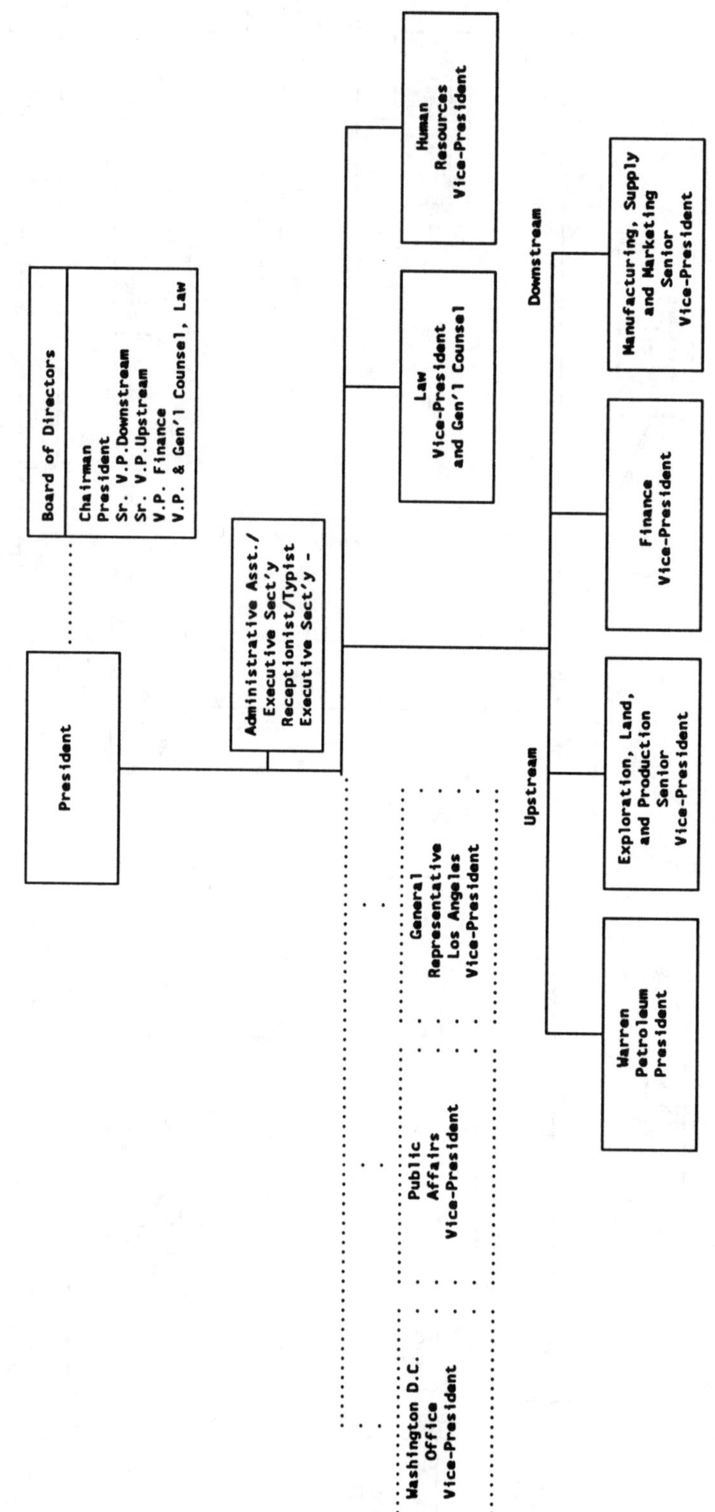

Chevron U.S.A. Inc. is the United States oil & gas subsidiary of the Chevron Corp.

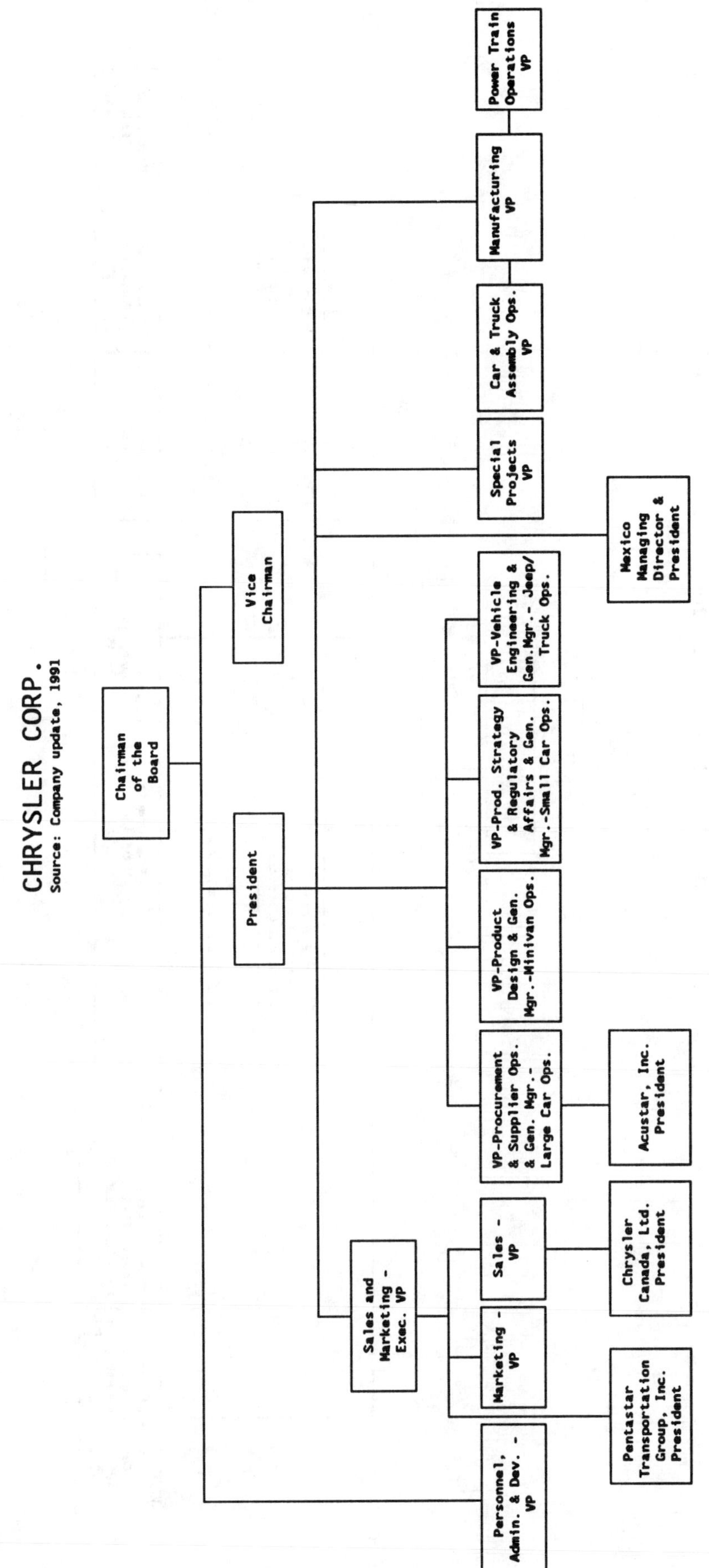

Continued on next page

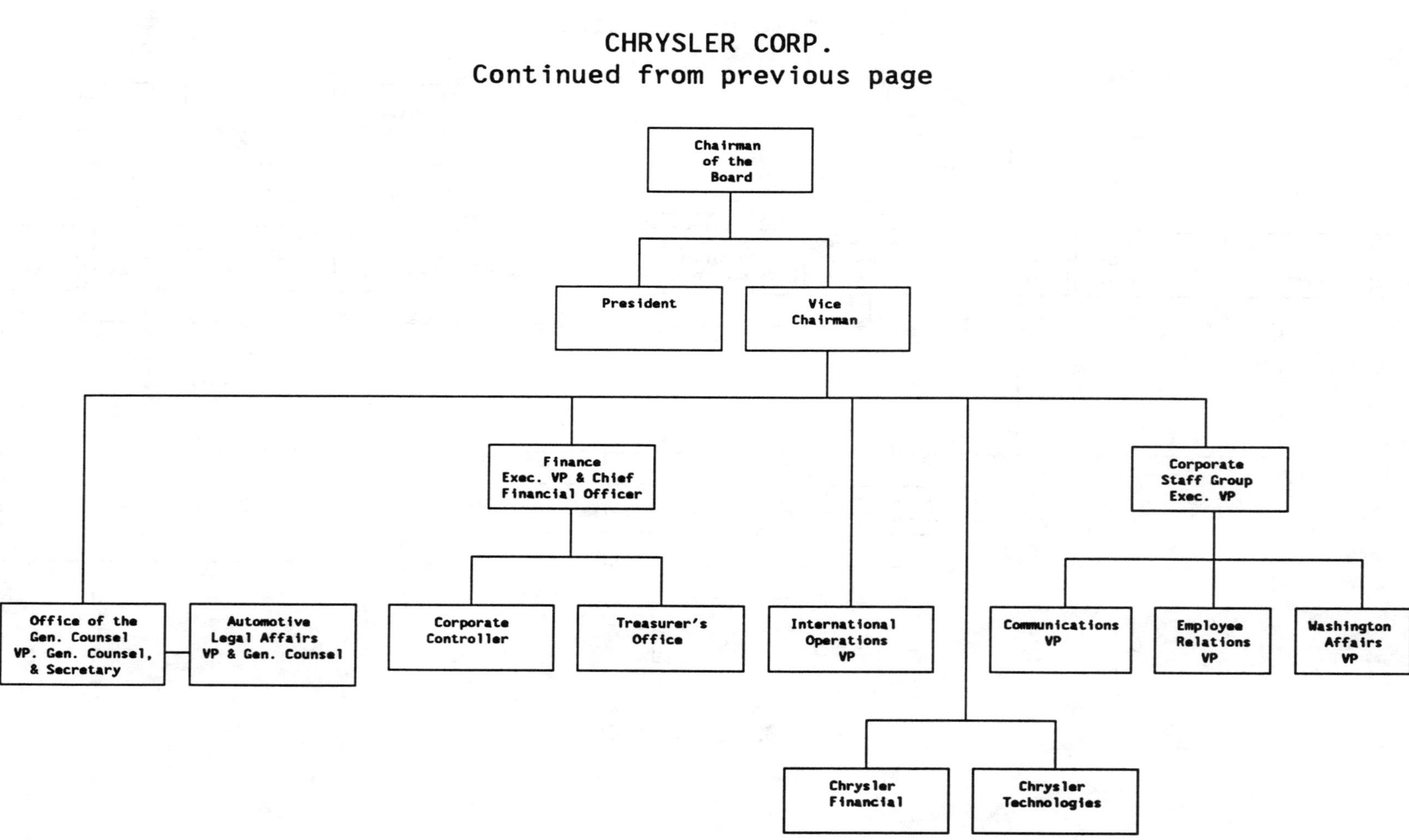
CHRYSLER CORP.
Continued from previous page
Chairman of the Board
President
Vice Chairman
Office of the Gen. Counsel VP. Gen. Counsel, & Secretary
Automotive Legal Affairs VP & Gen. Counsel
Finance Exec. VP & Chief Financial Officer
Corporate Controller
Treasurer's Office
International Operations VP
Chrysler Financial
Chrysler Technologies
Corporate Staff Group Exec. VP
Communications VP
Employee Relations VP
Washington Affairs VP

CHRYSLER CORP.
ACUSTAR INC.
PROCUREMENT AND SUPPLY (Huntsville, AL)

Source: Company update, 1991

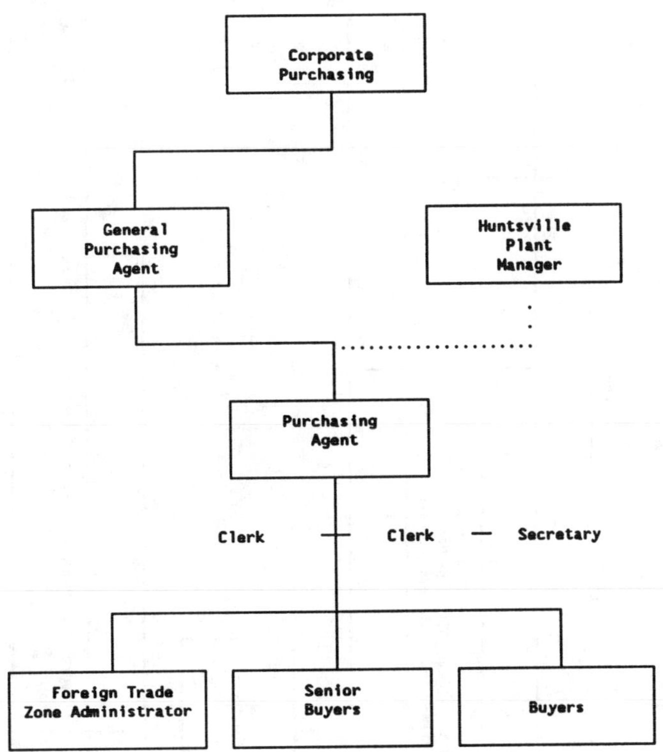

This chart displays the Procurement and Supply Operations at Chrysler Corp.'s Acustar plant in Huntsville, AL.

CHRYLSER CORP.
CHRYSLER CANADA LTD.
SALES

Source: Company update, 1991

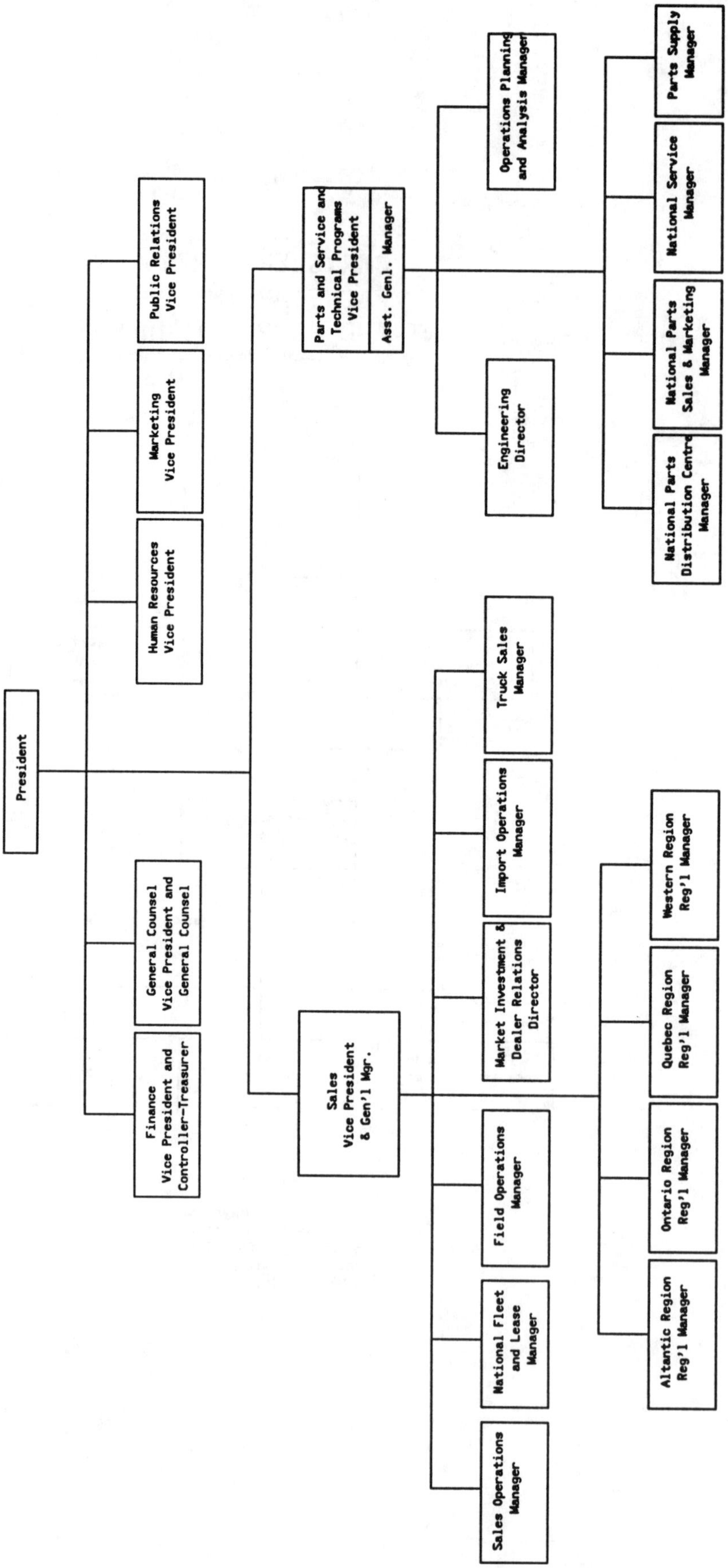

President

Finance
Vice President and
Controller-Treasurer

General Counsel
Vice President and
General Counsel

Human Resources
Vice President

Marketing
Vice President

Public Relations
Vice President

Sales
Vice President
& Gen'l Mgr.

Sales Operations
Manager

National Fleet
and Lease
Manager

Field Operations
Manager

Market Investment &
Dealer Relations
Director

Import Operations
Manager

Truck Sales
Manager

Altantic Region
Reg'l Manager

Ontario Region
Reg'l Manager

Quebec Region
Reg'l Manager

Western Region
Reg'l Manager

Parts and Service and
Technical Programs
Vice President

Asst. Genl. Manager

Engineering
Director

Operations Planning
and Analysis Manager

National Parts
Distribution Centre
Manager

National Parts
Sales & Marketing
Manager

National Service
Manager

Parts Supply
Manager

CILCORP INC.

Source: Company update, 1991

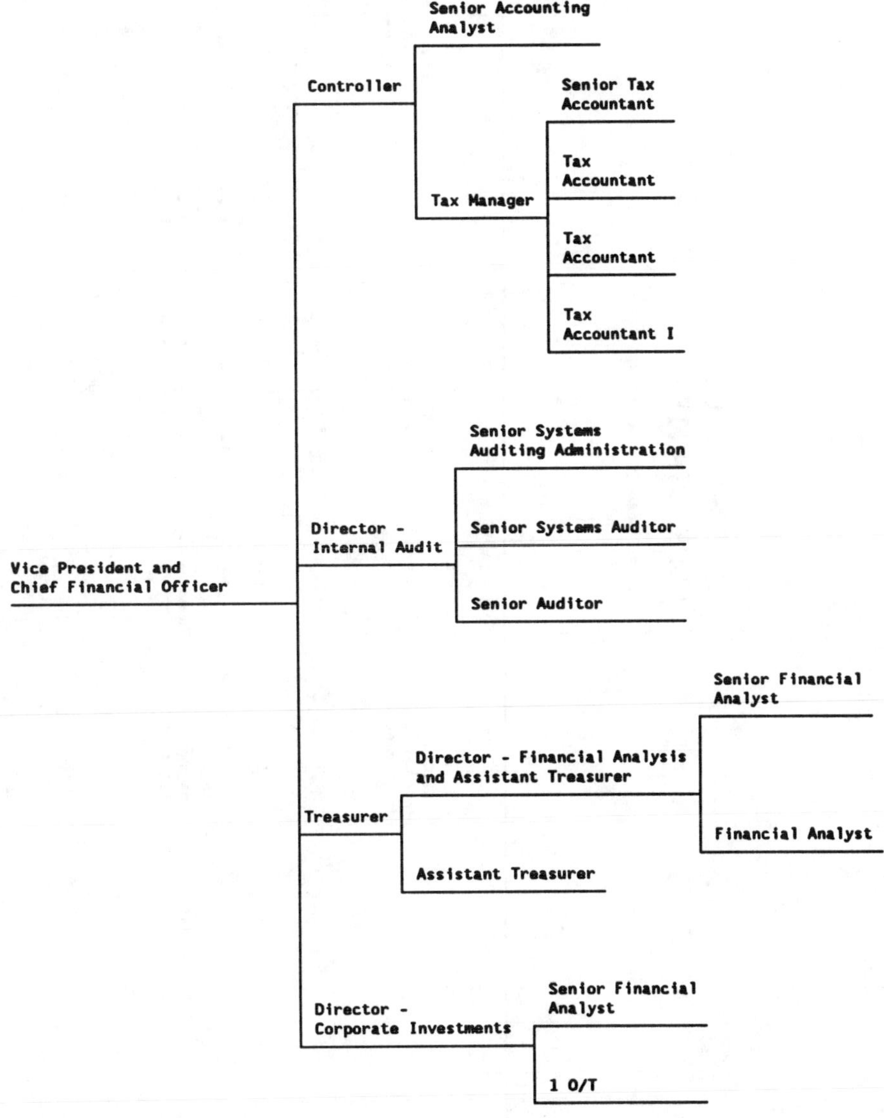

This is an organizational chart of Cilcorp Inc. as it relates to the Cilcorp Vice President and Chief Financial Officer and those management employees who report to him.

CILCORP INC. SUBSIDIARIES

Source: Company update, 1991

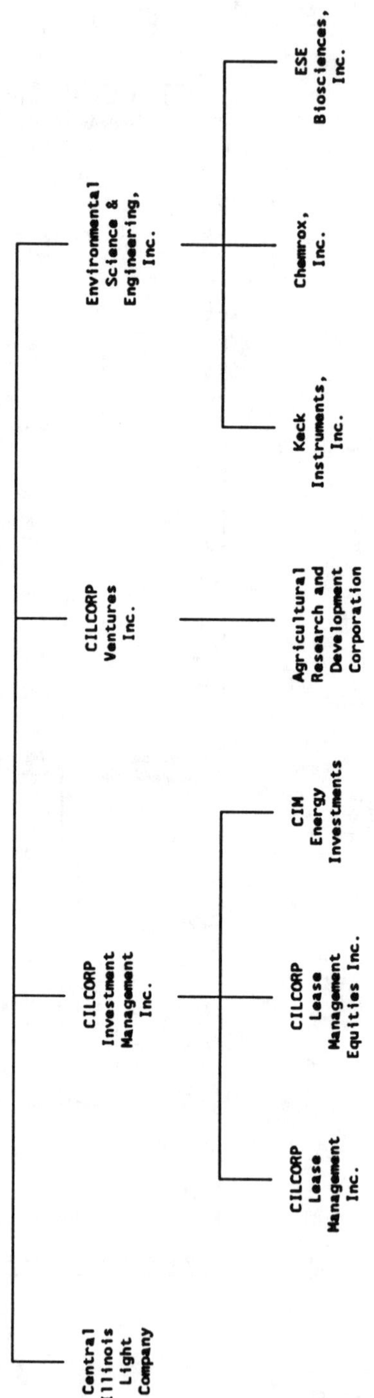

CLARK EQUIPMENT CO.

Source: Company update, 1991

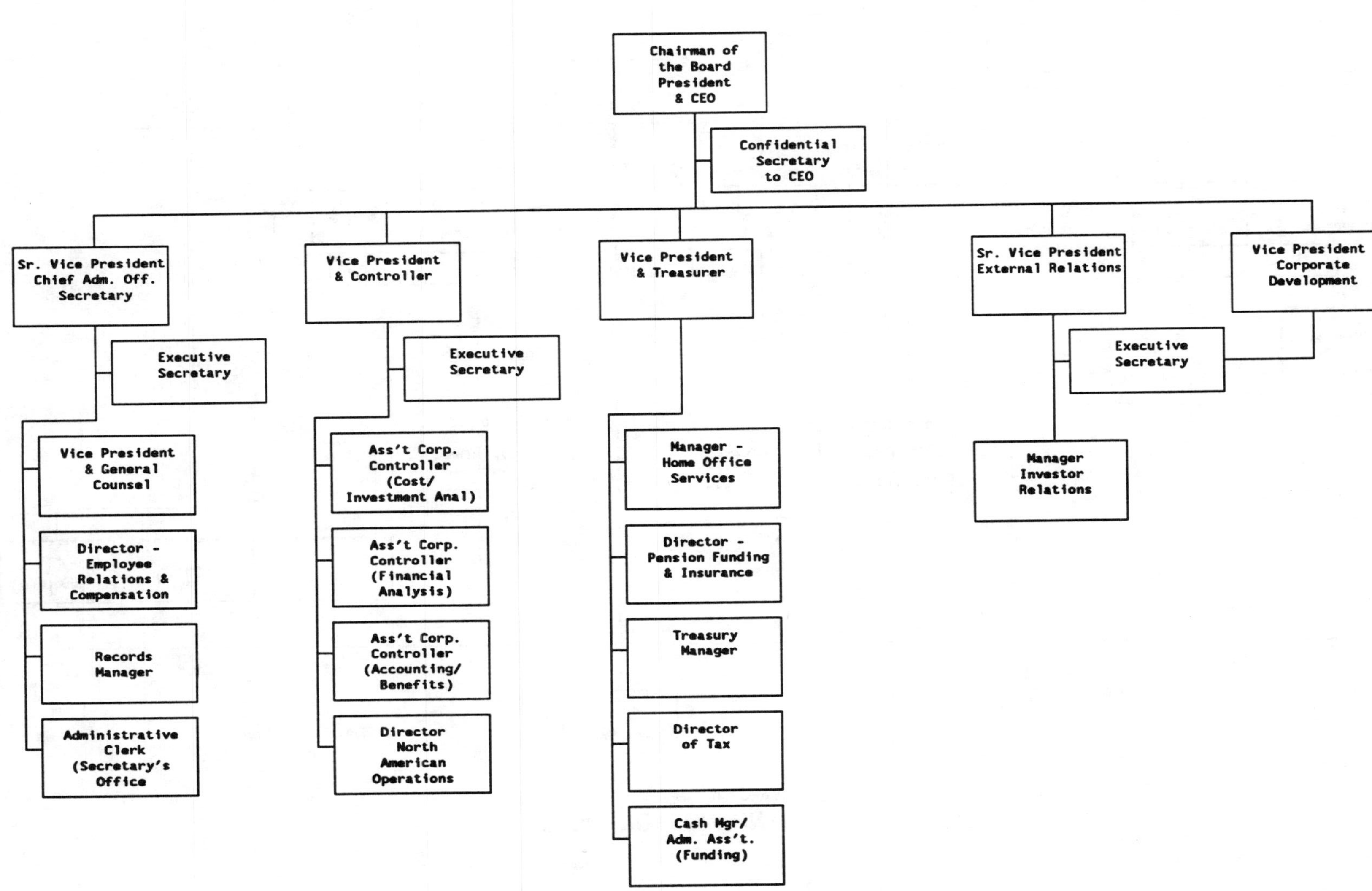

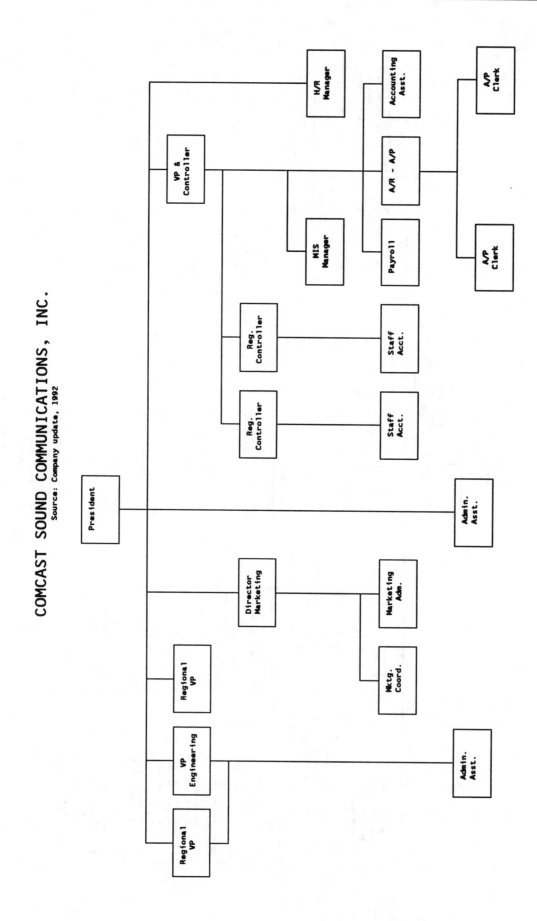

COMCAST SOUND COMMUNICATIONS, INC.

Source: Company update, 1992

President

Regional VP

VP Engineering

Regional VP

Director Marketing

VP & Controller

H/R Manager

Reg. Controller

Reg. Controller

MIS Manager

Mktg. Coord.

Marketing Adm.

Staff Acct.

Staff Acct.

Payroll

A/R - A/P

Accounting Asst.

Admin. Asst.

Admin. Asst.

A/P Clerk

A/P Clerk

COMPAGNIA FINANZIARIA DE BENEDETTI SPA (Italy)

Source: FORBES
139: 36+ (March 23, 1987)

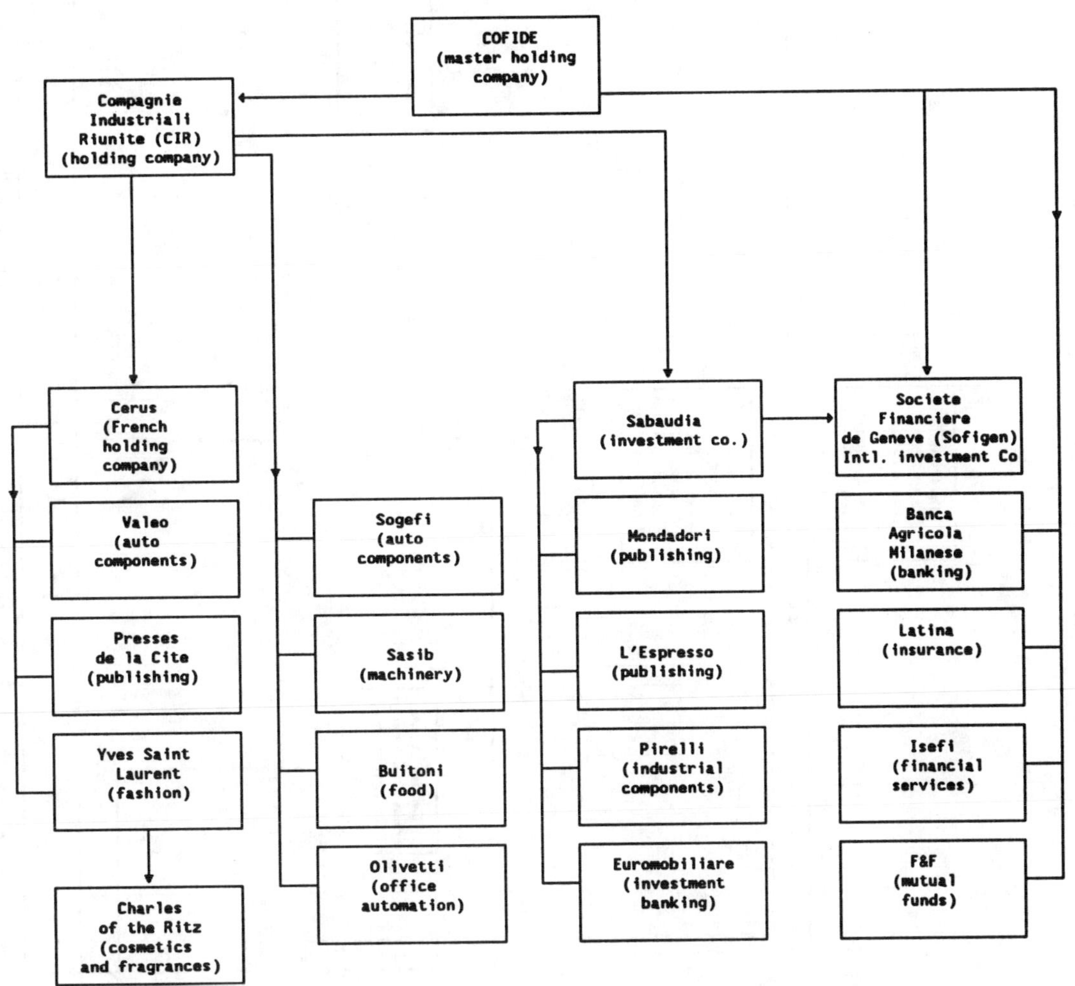

The chart above shows most, but not all, of Cofide's holdings.

CONSUMERS POWER CO. (Jackson, Michigan)

Source: Company update, 1991

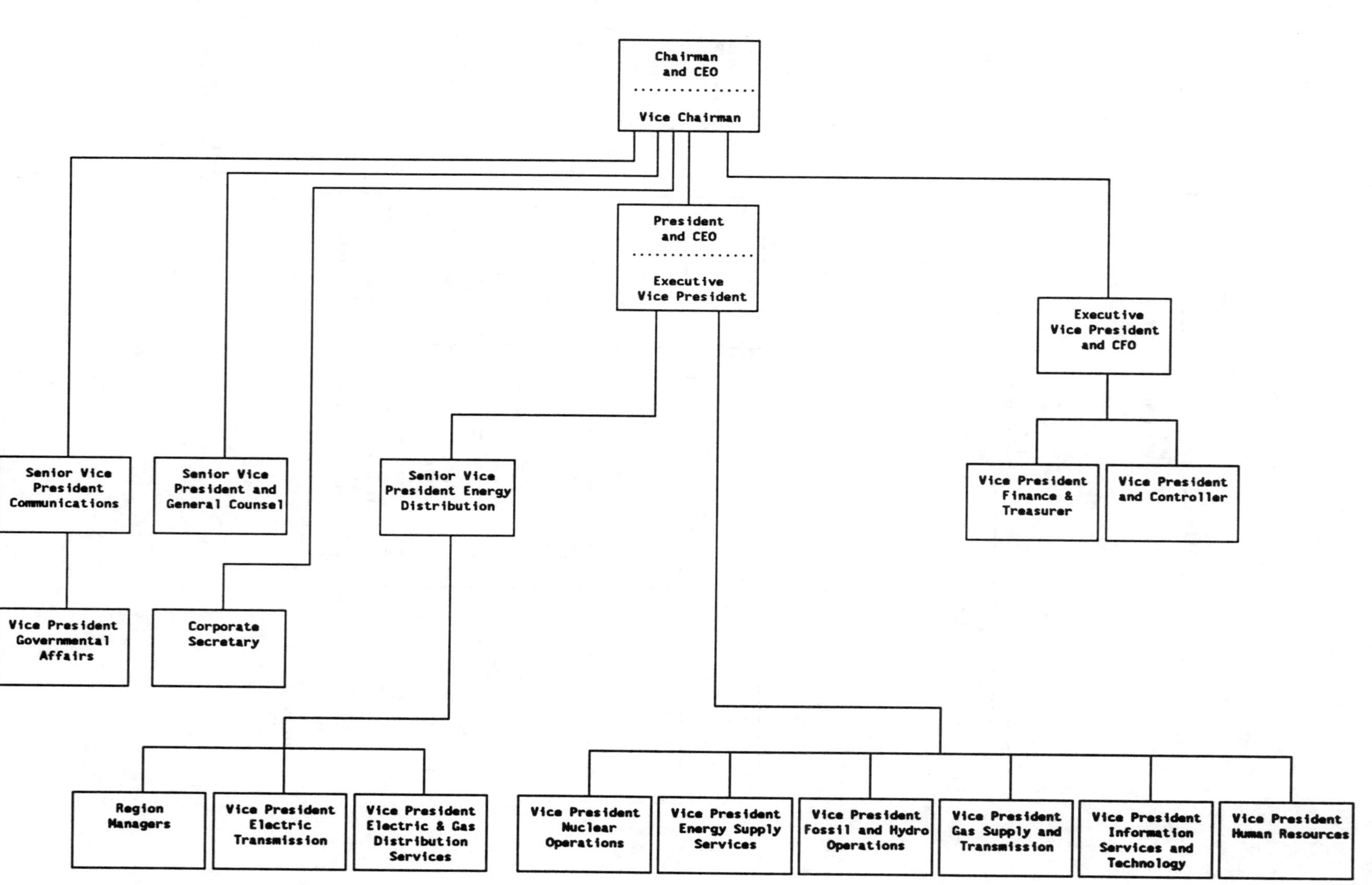

COOPER TIRE & RUBBER CO.

Source: Company update, 1991

- Chairman of the Board Chief Executive Officer
  - President Chief Operating Officer
    - Division President (Tires)
      - Vice President Administration
      - Vice Presidnet Information Systems
      - Vice President Marketing
      - Vice President Operations Mfg. & Tech.
      - Director International
      - Director Planning
      - Director Distribution
    - Division President (Eng. Prod.)
      - Vice President Controller
      - Vice President Sales
      - Vice President Purchasing
      - Manager Information Systems
      - Vice President Manufacturing
      - Vice President Engineering
  - Vice President Purchasing
  - Vice President Chief Financial Officer
    - Controller
    - Treasurer
    - Employee Relations
  - Vice President General Counsel
    - Legal

CRAY RESEARCH, INC.

Source: Company update, 1991

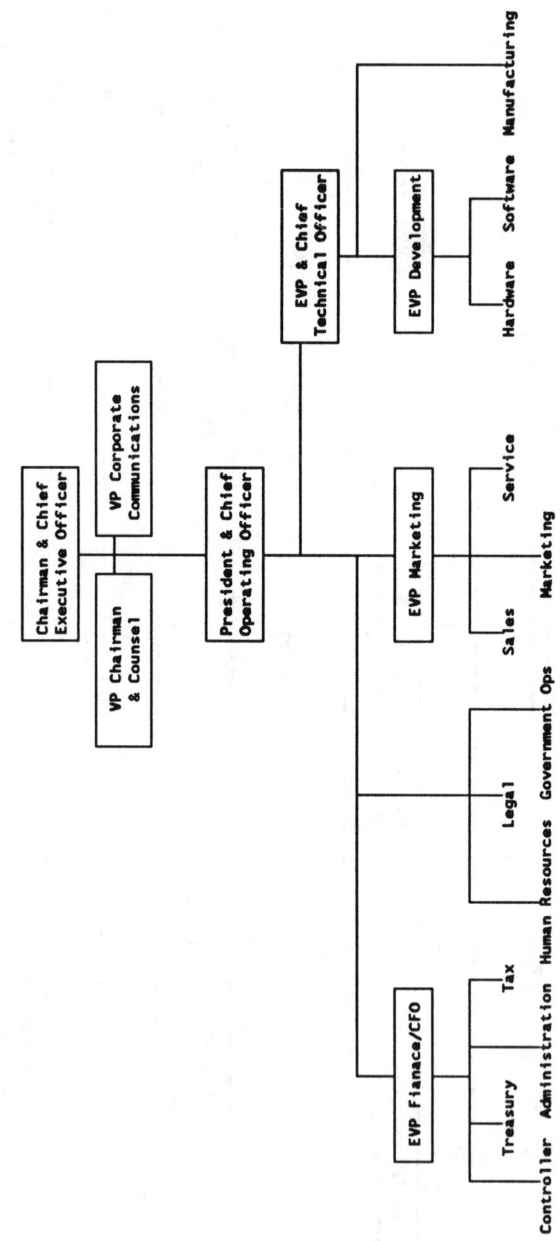

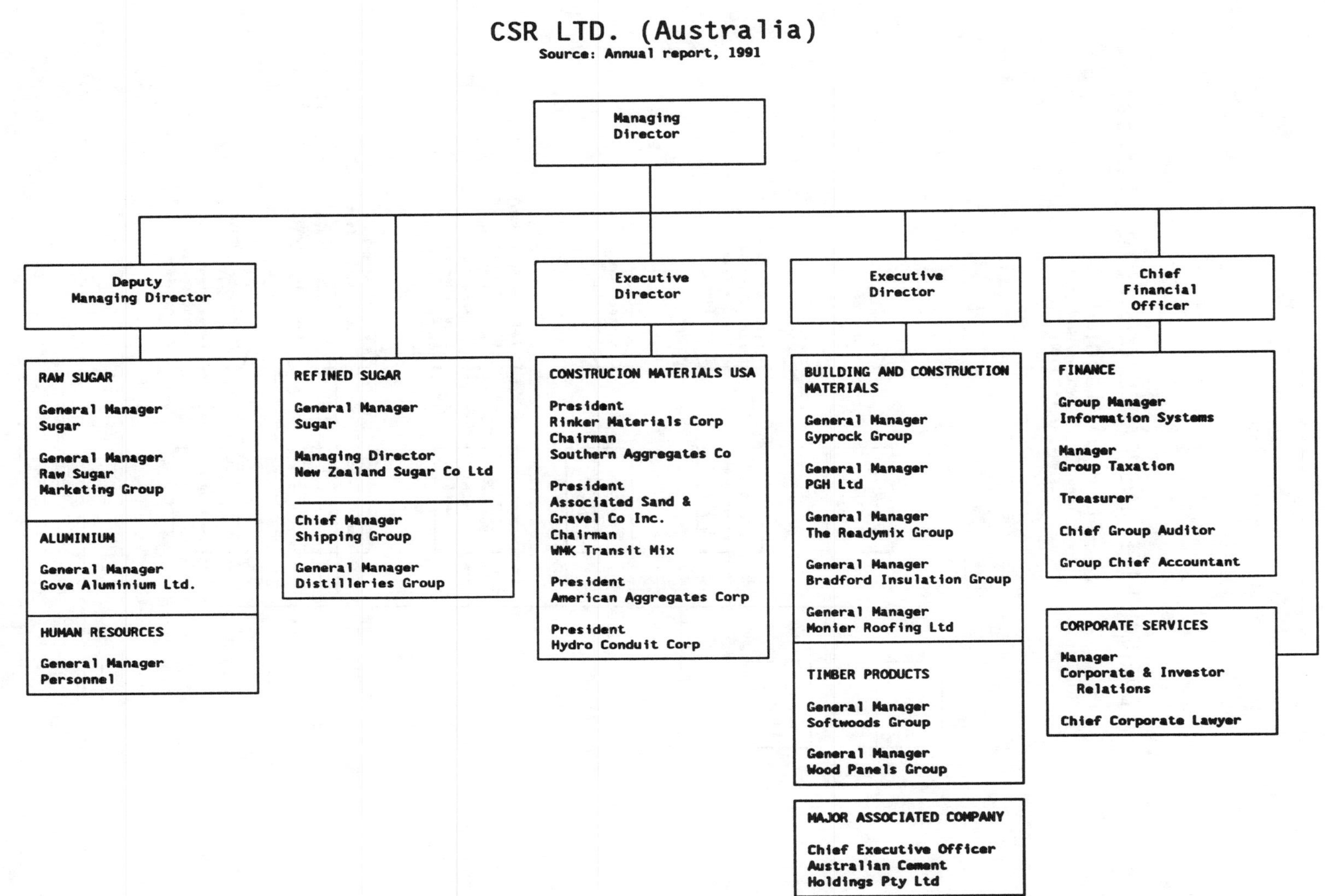
CSR LTD. (Australia)
Source: Annual report, 1991
Managing Director
Deputy Managing Director
Executive Director
Executive Director
Chief Financial Officer
RAW SUGAR
General Manager Sugar
General Manager Raw Sugar Marketing Group
ALUMINIUM
General Manager Gove Aluminium Ltd.
HUMAN RESOURCES
General Manager Personnel
REFINED SUGAR
General Manager Sugar
Managing Director New Zealand Sugar Co Ltd
Chief Manager Shipping Group
General Manager Distilleries Group
CONSTRUCION MATERIALS USA
President Rinker Materials Corp
Chairman Southern Aggregates Co
President Associated Sand & Gravel Co Inc.
Chairman WMK Transit Mix
President American Aggregates Corp
President Hydro Conduit Corp
BUILDING AND CONSTRUCTION MATERIALS
General Manager Gyprock Group
General Manager PGH Ltd
General Manager The Readymix Group
General Manager Bradford Insulation Group
General Manager Monier Roofing Ltd
TIMBER PRODUCTS
General Manager Softwoods Group
General Manager Wood Panels Group
MAJOR ASSOCIATED COMPANY
Chief Executive Officer Australian Cement Holdings Pty Ltd
FINANCE
Group Manager Information Systems
Manager Group Taxation
Treasurer
Chief Group Auditor
Group Chief Accountant
CORPORATE SERVICES
Manager Corporate & Investor Relations
Chief Corporate Lawyer

DAEHAN LIFE INSURANCE CO., LTD. (Korea)
EDP Division

Source: LONGE RANGE PLANNING
23: 69+, (April 1990)

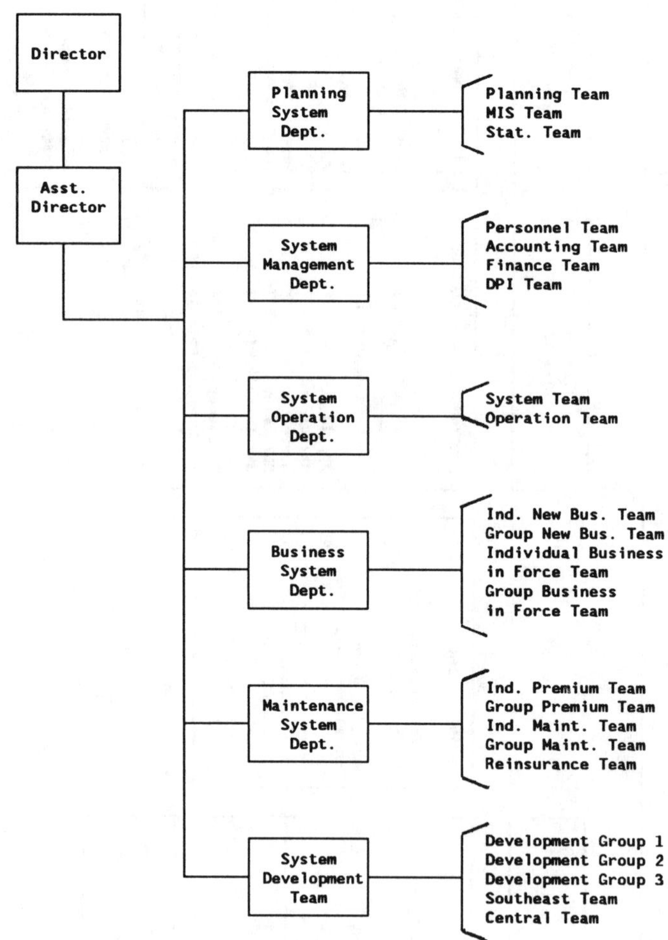

DAIMLER-BENZ AG (Germany)

Source: LONG RANGE PLANNING 24, No. 1: 26+ (1991)

Daimler-Benz AG

CEO | Finance | R&D | Personnel | CEO MB | Dep. CEO MB | CEO AEG | CEO DASA | CEO DEBIS

Mercedes-Benz AG (MB)

CEO | Dep. CEO | Personnel | CEO Cars | CEO Trucks

- Cars
- Trucks

AEG AG

CEO | Finance | Personnel | CEOs Business Units

- Electrotechnical Goods and Components
- Consumer Goods
- Office and Communication Technology
- Automation Technology
- Transportation Systems
- Microelectronics

Deutsche Aerospace AG (DASA)

CEO | Finance | Personnel | CEOs Business Units

- AEG-AS
- Domier
- MTU
- MBB

Daimler-Benz InterServices AG (DEBIS)

CEO | Personnel | CEOs Business Units

- Information Systems,
- Financial Services and Insurance,
- Retail Businesses and Marketing Services,
- ...

The new organizational structure of Daimler-Benz demonstrates the concept that the top managers of important divisions also constitute the top management of the group along with the managers who are responsible for functional areas within the group.

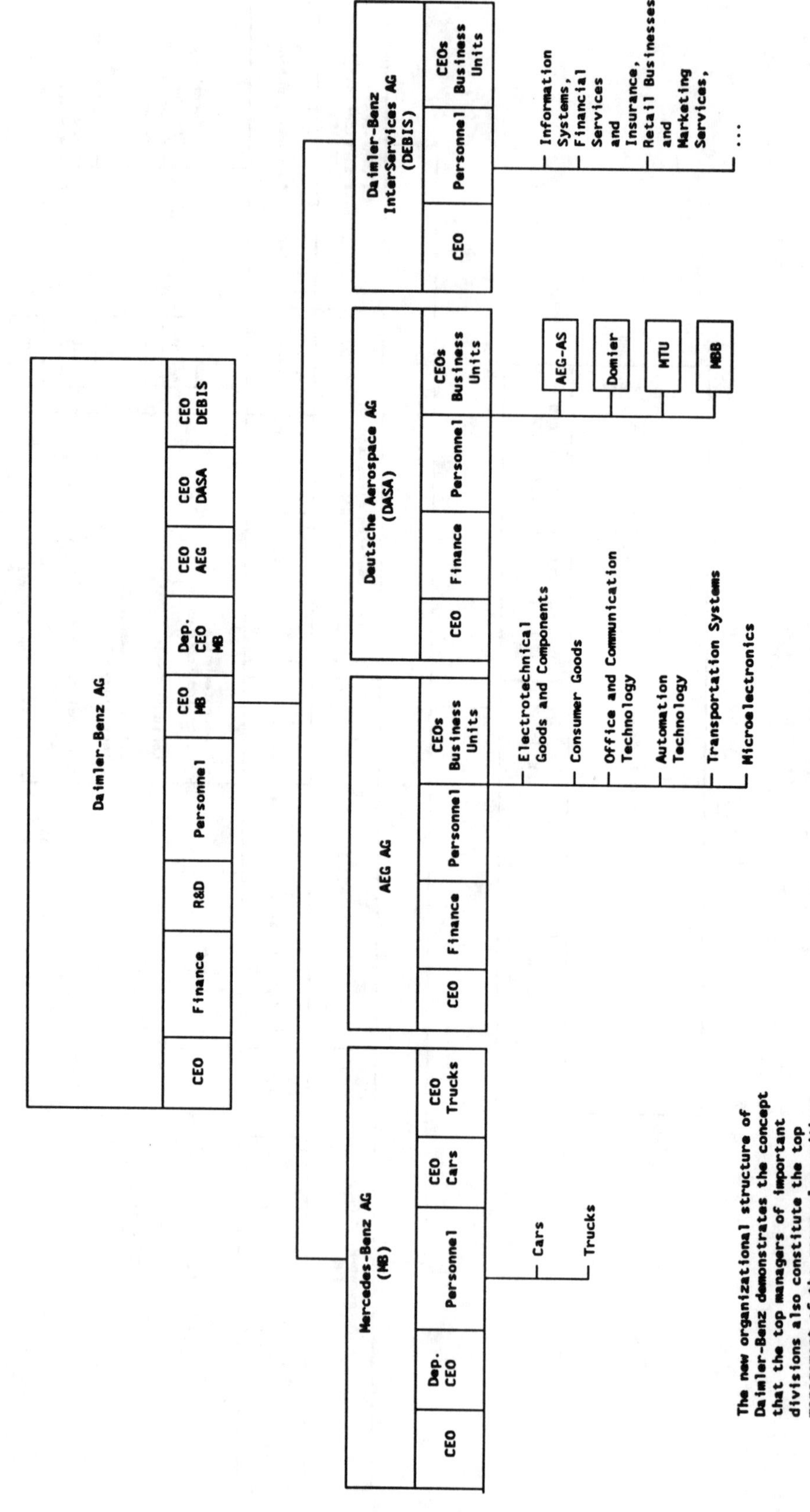
DAIMLER-BENZ AG (Germany)
Source: LONG RANGE PLANNING 24, No. 1: 26+ (1991)
Daimler-Benz AG
CEO
Finance
R&D
Personnel
CEO MB
Dep. CEO MB
CEO AEG
CEO DASA
CEO DEBIS
Mercedes-Benz AG (MB)
CEO
Dep. CEO
Personnel
CEO Cars
CEO Trucks
Cars
Trucks
AEG AG
CEO
Finance
Personnel
CEOs Business Units
Electrotechnical Goods and Components
Consumer Goods
Office and Communication Technology
Automation Technology
Transportation Systems
Microelectronics
Deutsche Aerospace AG (DASA)
CEO
Finance
Personnel
CEOs Business Units
AEG-AS
Dornier
MTU
MBB
Daimler-Benz InterServices AG (DEBIS)
CEO
Personnel
CEOs Business Units
Information Systems,
Financial Services and Insurance,
Retail Businesses and Marketing Services,
...
The new organizational structure of Daimler-Benz demonstrates the concept that the top managers of important divisions also constitute the top management of the group along with the managers who are responsible for functional areas within the group.

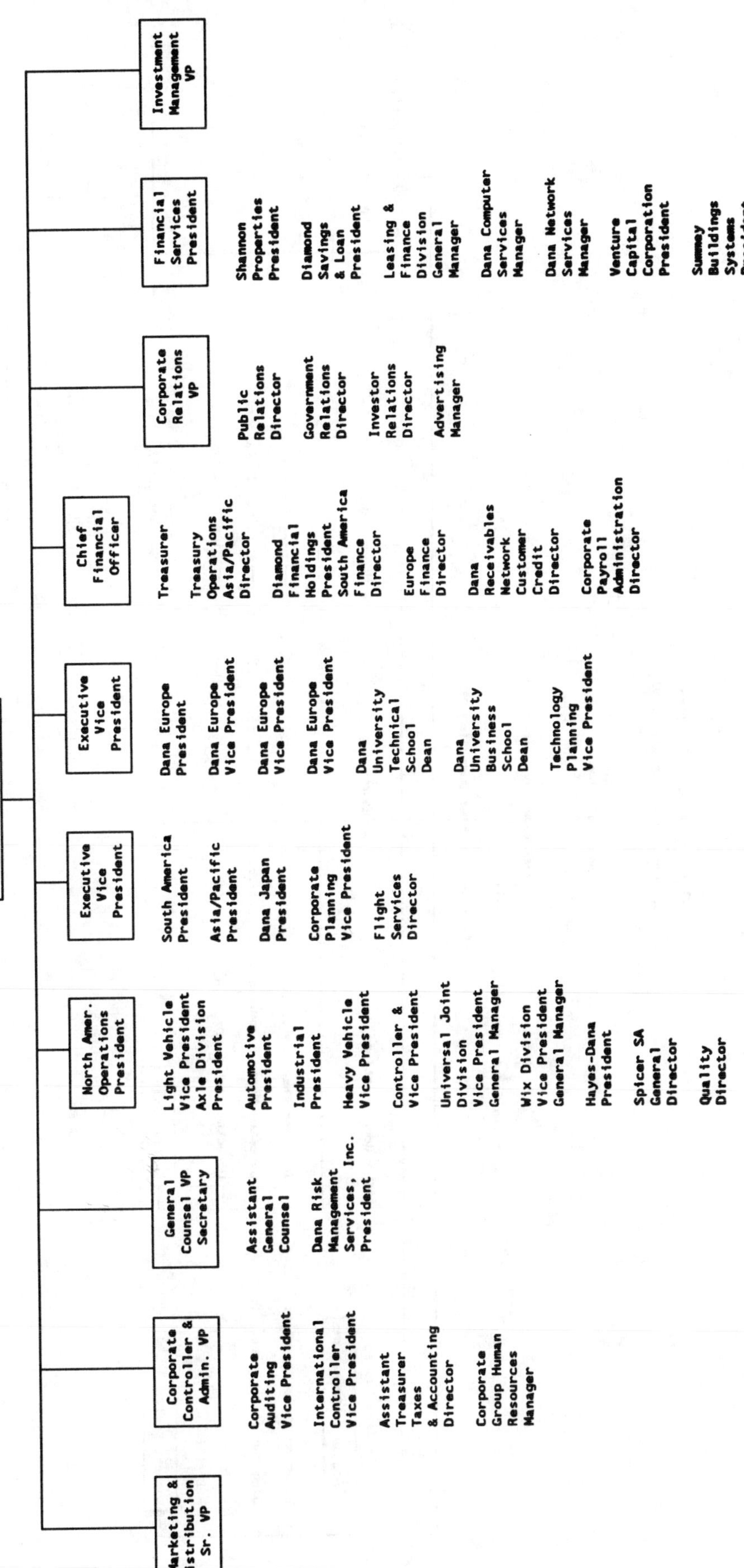
DANA CORP.
Source: Company update, 1991
Chairman of the Board President Chief Executive Officer Chief Operating Officer
Marketing & Distribution Sr. VP
Corporate Controller & Admin. VP
Corporate Auditing Vice President
International Controller Vice President
Assistant Treasurer Taxes & Accounting Director
Corporate Group Human Resources Manager
General Counsel VP Secretary
Assistant General Counsel
Dana Risk Management Services, Inc. President
North Amer. Operations President
Light Vehicle Vice President Axle Division President
Automotive President
Industrial President
Heavy Vehicle Vice President
Controller & Vice President
Universal Joint Division Vice President General Manager
Wix Division Vice President General Manager
Hayes-Dana President
Spicer SA General Director
Quality Director
Executive Vice President
South America President
Asia/Pacific President
Dana Japan President
Corporate Planning Vice President
Flight Services Director
Executive Vice President
Dana Europe President
Dana Europe Vice President
Dana Europe Vice President
Dana Europe Vice President
Dana University Technical School Dean
Dana University Business School Dean
Technology Planning Vice President
Chief Financial Officer
Treasurer
Treasury Operations Asia/Pacific Director
Diamond Financial Holdings President
South America Finance Director
Europe Finance Director
Dana Receivables Network Customer Credit Director
Corporate Payroll Administration Director
Corporate Relations VP
Public Relations Director
Government Relations Director
Investor Relations Director
Advertising Manager
Financial Services President
Shannon Properties President
Diamond Savings & Loan President
Leasing & Finance Division General Manager
Dana Computer Services Manager
Dana Network Services Manager
Venture Capital Corporation President
Summey Buildings Systems President
Investment Management VP

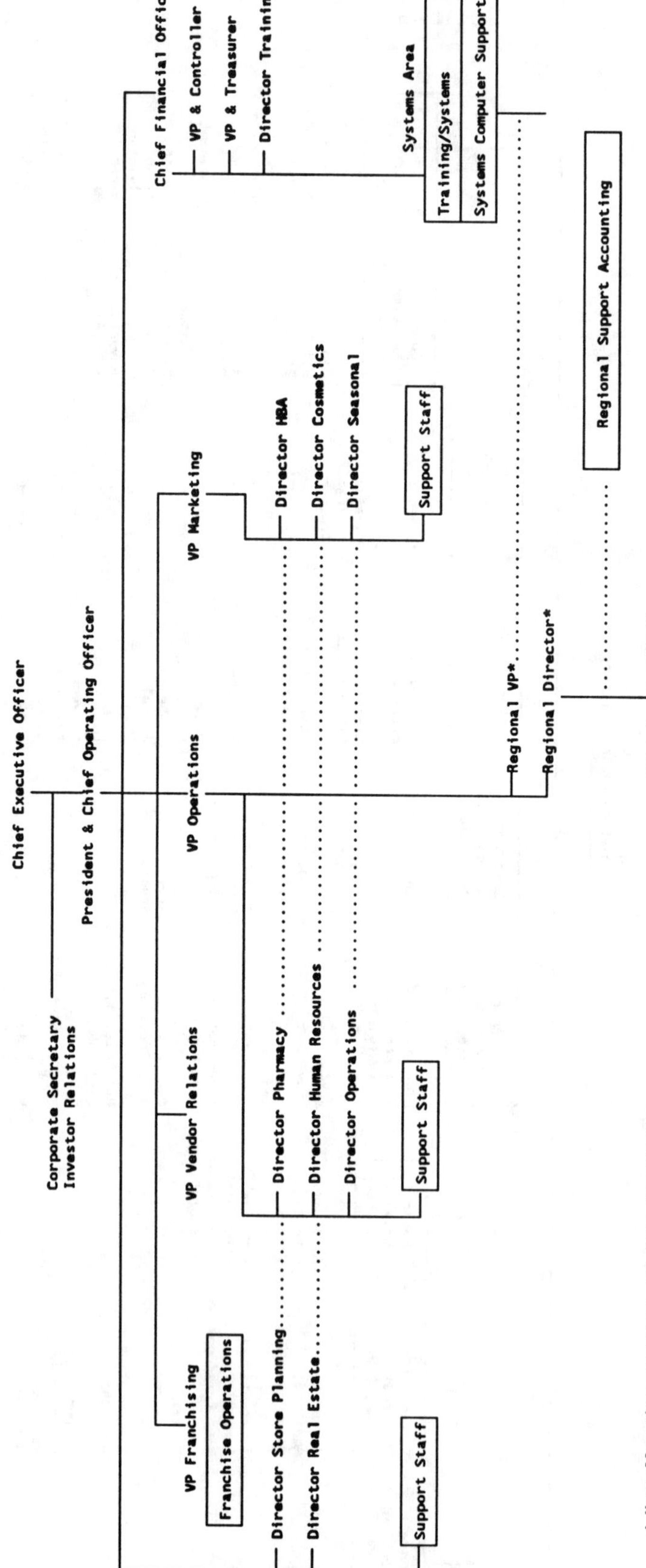
Drug Emporium
Source: Company update, 1991
Shareholders
Board of Directors
Chairman of the Board
Chief Executive Officer
Corporate Secretary
Investor Relations
President & Chief Operating Officer
VP Franchising
Franchise Operations
VP Vendor Relations
VP Operations
VP Marketing
Chief Financial Officer
VP & Controller
VP & Treasurer
Director Training
Director Store Planning
Director Real Estate
Support Staff
Director Pharmacy
Director Human Resources
Director Operations
Support Staff
Director HBA
Director Cosmetics
Director Seasonal
Support Staff
Systems Area
Training/Systems
Systems Computer Support
Regional VP*
Regional Director*
District Manager**
Store Manager
Regional Support Accounting
* Not all market operators are Vice Presidents.
Some Joint-Venture operators are officers of
a separate incorporation.
** Not all regions have district managers.
NOTE: VP's & Directors are accountable to CFO.

E.I. DU PONT DE NEMOURS

Source: SITE SELECTION
35: 1186+ (October 1990)

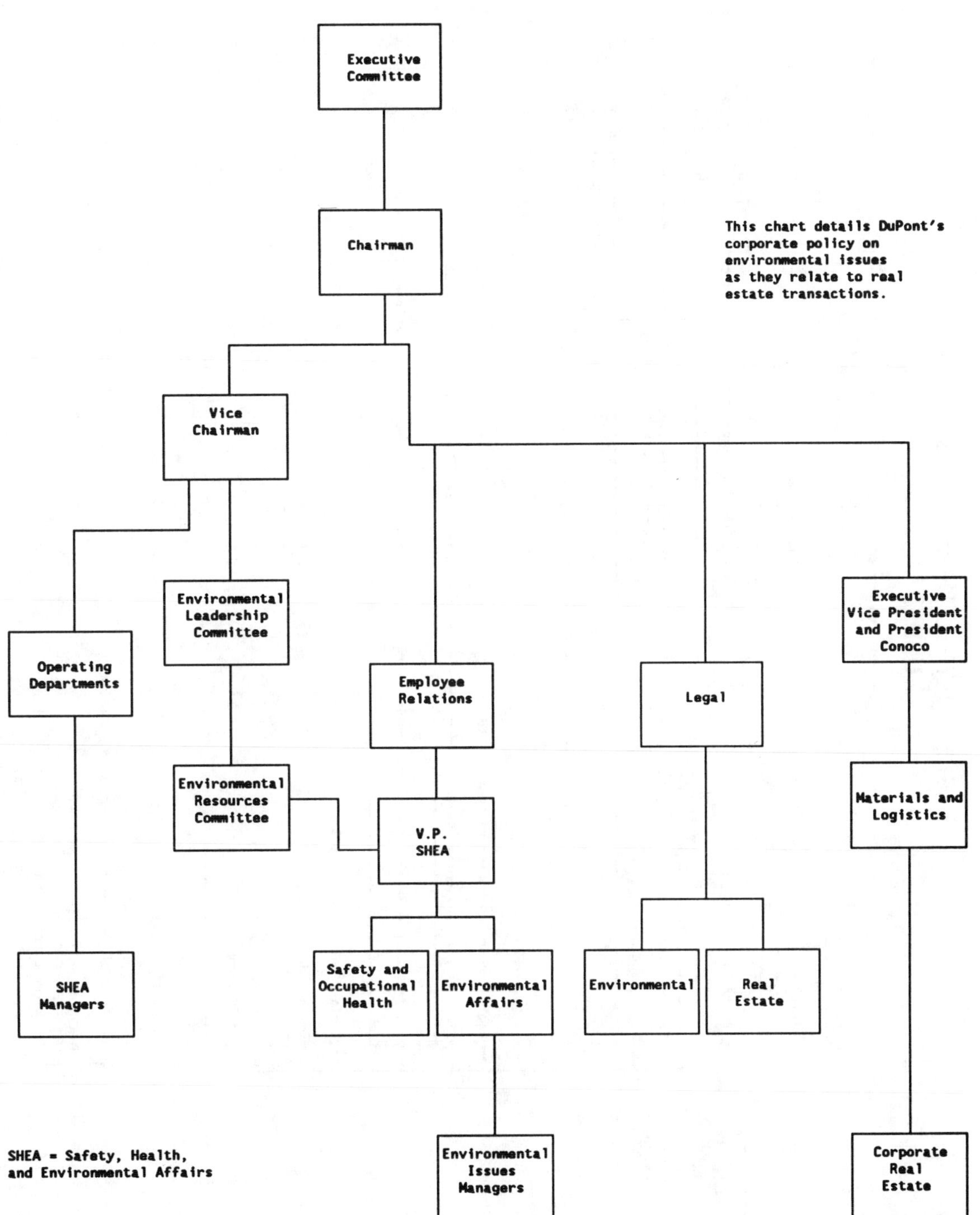

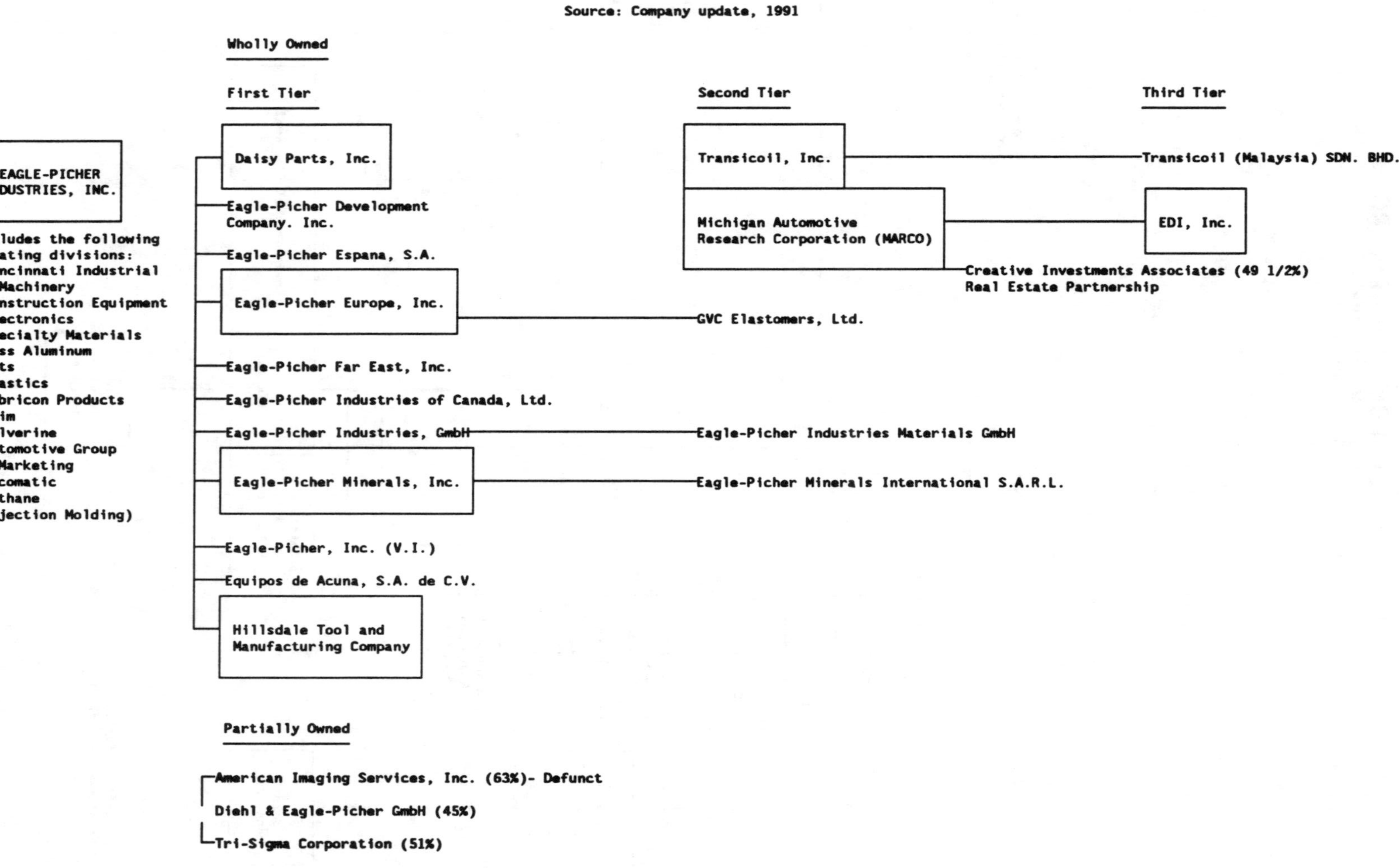
EAGLE-PICHER INDUSTRIES, INC.
SUBSIDIARIES
Source: Company update, 1991
Wholly Owned
First Tier
Second Tier
Third Tier
EAGLE-PICHER INDUSTRIES, INC.
(includes the following operating divisions:
Cincinnati Industrial Machinery
Construction Equipment
Electronics
Specialty Materials
Ross Aluminum
Mats
Plastics
Fabricon Products
Trim
Wolverine
Automotive Group
Marketing
Orcomatic
Orthane
Injection Molding)
Daisy Parts, Inc.
Eagle-Picher Development Company. Inc.
Eagle-Picher Espana, S.A.
Eagle-Picher Europe, Inc.
Eagle-Picher Far East, Inc.
Eagle-Picher Industries of Canada, Ltd.
Eagle-Picher Industries, GmbH
Eagle-Picher Minerals, Inc.
Eagle-Picher, Inc. (V.I.)
Equipos de Acuna, S.A. de C.V.
Hillsdale Tool and Manufacturing Company
Transicoil, Inc.
Michigan Automotive Research Corporation (MARCO)
GVC Elastomers, Ltd.
Eagle-Picher Industries Materials GmbH
Eagle-Picher Minerals International S.A.R.L.
Transicoil (Malaysia) SDN. BHD.
EDI, Inc.
Creative Investments Associates (49 1/2%)
Real Estate Partnership
Partially Owned
American Imaging Services, Inc. (63%)- Defunct
Diehl & Eagle-Picher GmbH (45%)
Tri-Sigma Corporation (51%)

EDPER/HEES (Canada)
Source: FINANCIAL POST
1+ (February 9, 1991)

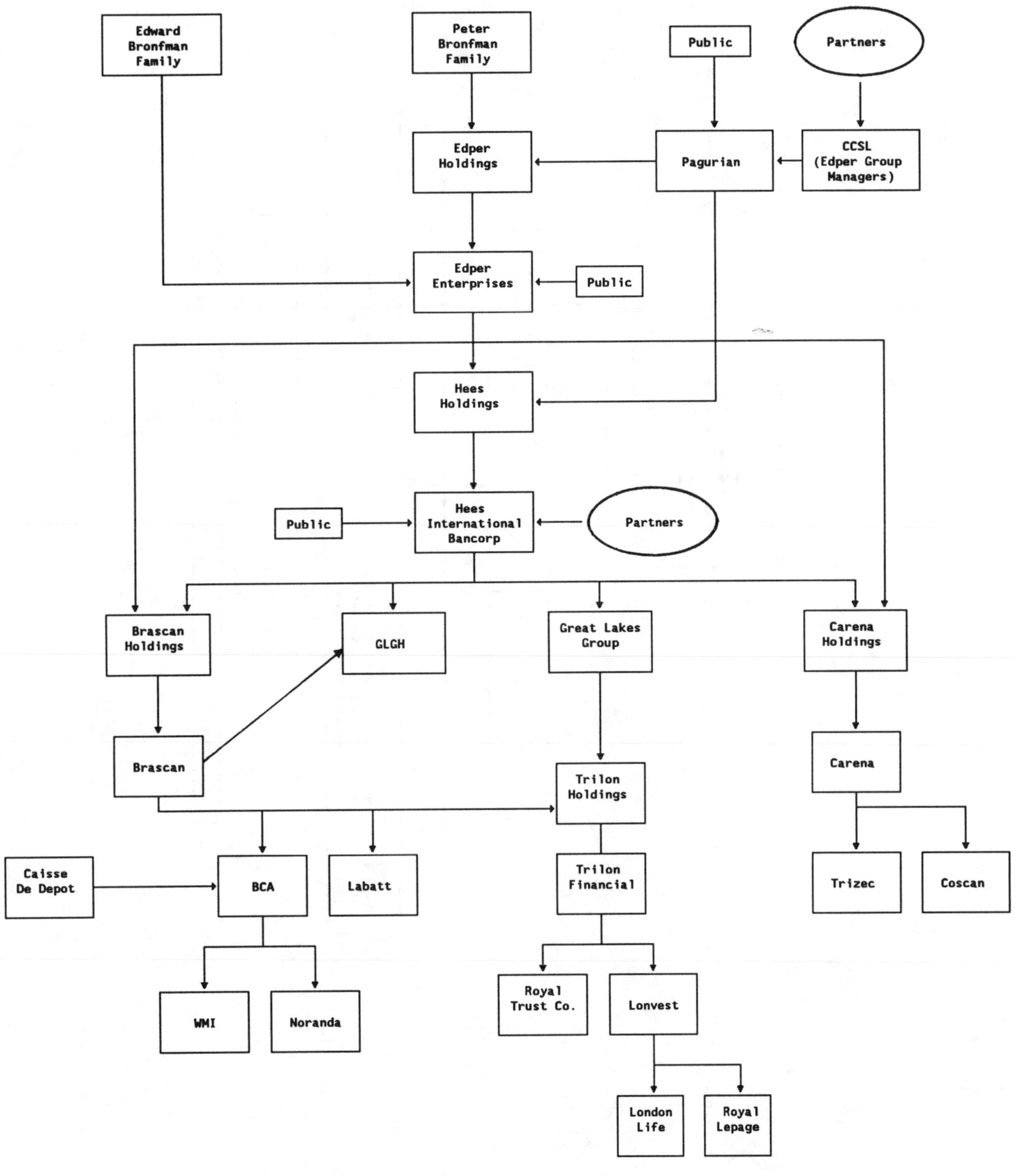

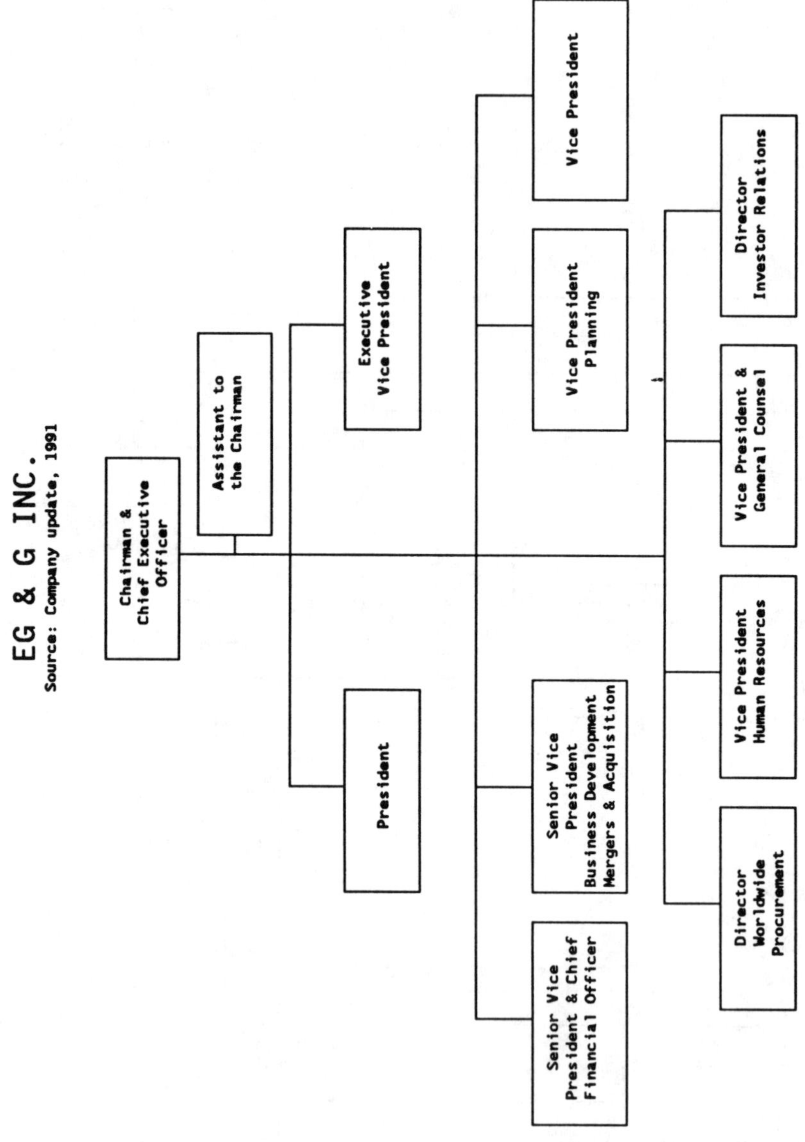
EG & G INC.
Source: Company update, 1991
Chairman & Chief Executive Officer
Assistant to the Chairman
President
Executive Vice President
Senior Vice President & Chief Financial Officer
Senior Vice President Business Development Mergers & Acquisition
Vice President Planning
Vice President
Director Worldwide Procurement
Vice President Human Resources
Vice President & General Counsel
Director Investor Relations

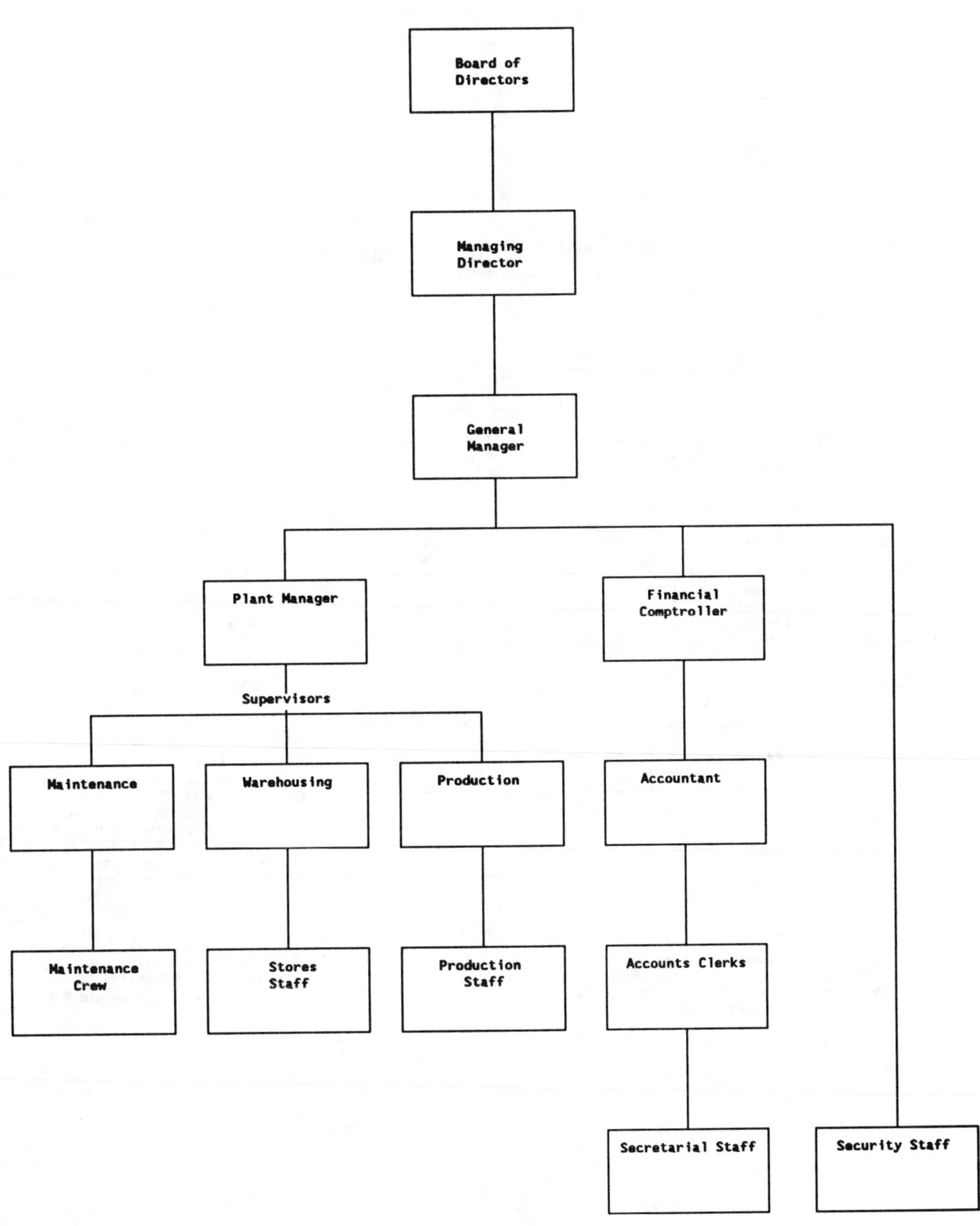
ELECTRIC ARC (JAMAICA) LTD.
Source: WORLD DEVELOPMENT
18: 91+ (January 1991)
Board of Directors
Managing Director
General Manager
Plant Manager
Financial Comptroller
Supervisors
Maintenance
Warehousing
Production
Accountant
Maintenance Crew
Stores Staff
Production Staff
Accounts Clerks
Secretarial Staff
Security Staff

ELF AQUITAINE (France)

Source: RESEARCH TECHNOLOGY MANAGEMENT
34: 33+ (Sept.-Oct. 1991)

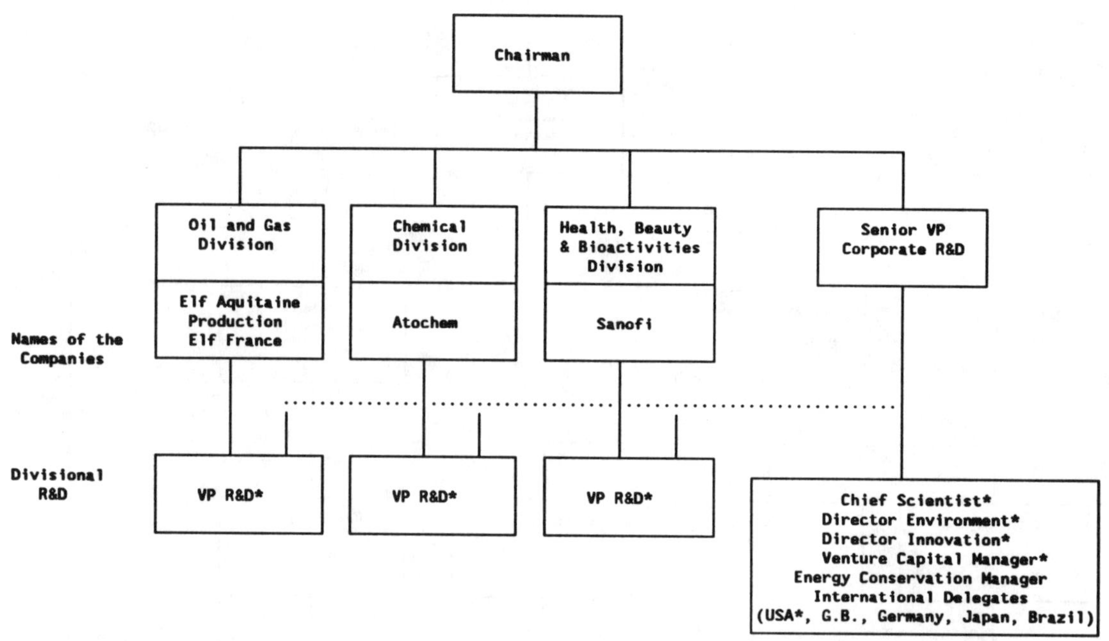

Each vice president of R&D is under the authority of his own division's president while at the same time reporting to the Senior VP of Corporate R&D.

*Individuals are members of the Group Research Committee chaired by the Senior VP Corporate R&D.

EQUITABLE RESOURCES, INC.

Source: Annual report, 1990

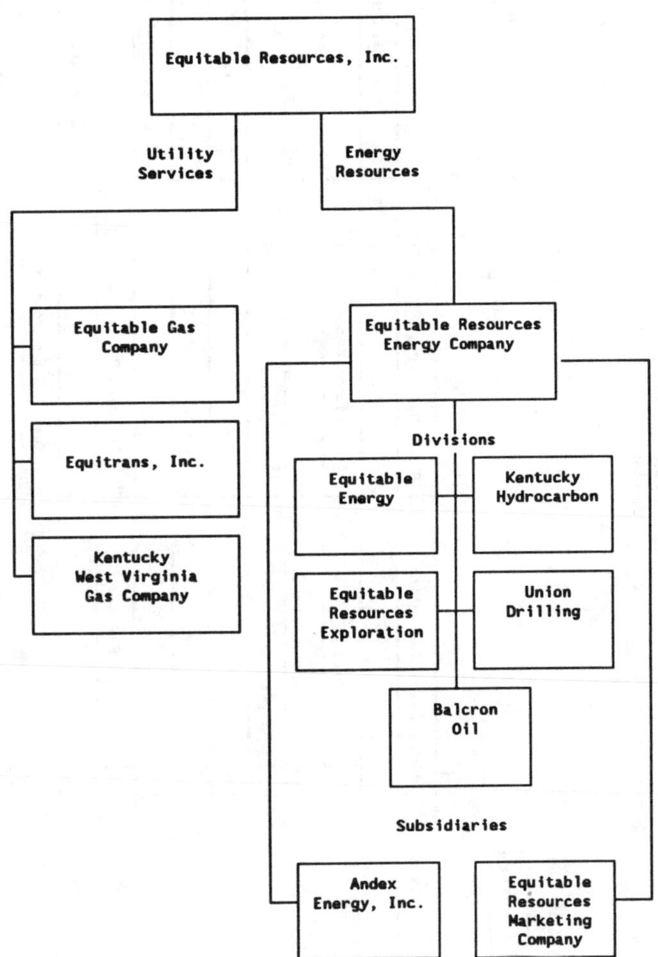

Equitable Resources, Inc. conducts business through two segments: Energy Resources explores for, develops and produces natural gas and oil; Utility Services purchases, gathers, transports, stores, and distributes natural gas.

ETHYL CORP.

Source: Company update, 1991

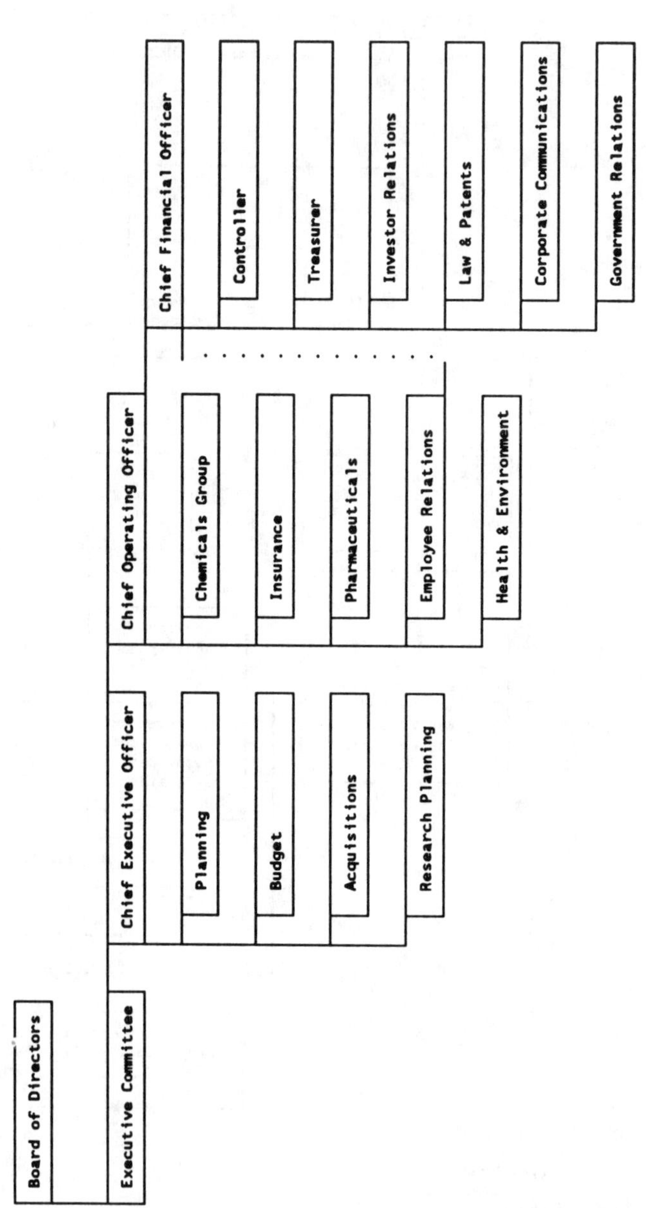

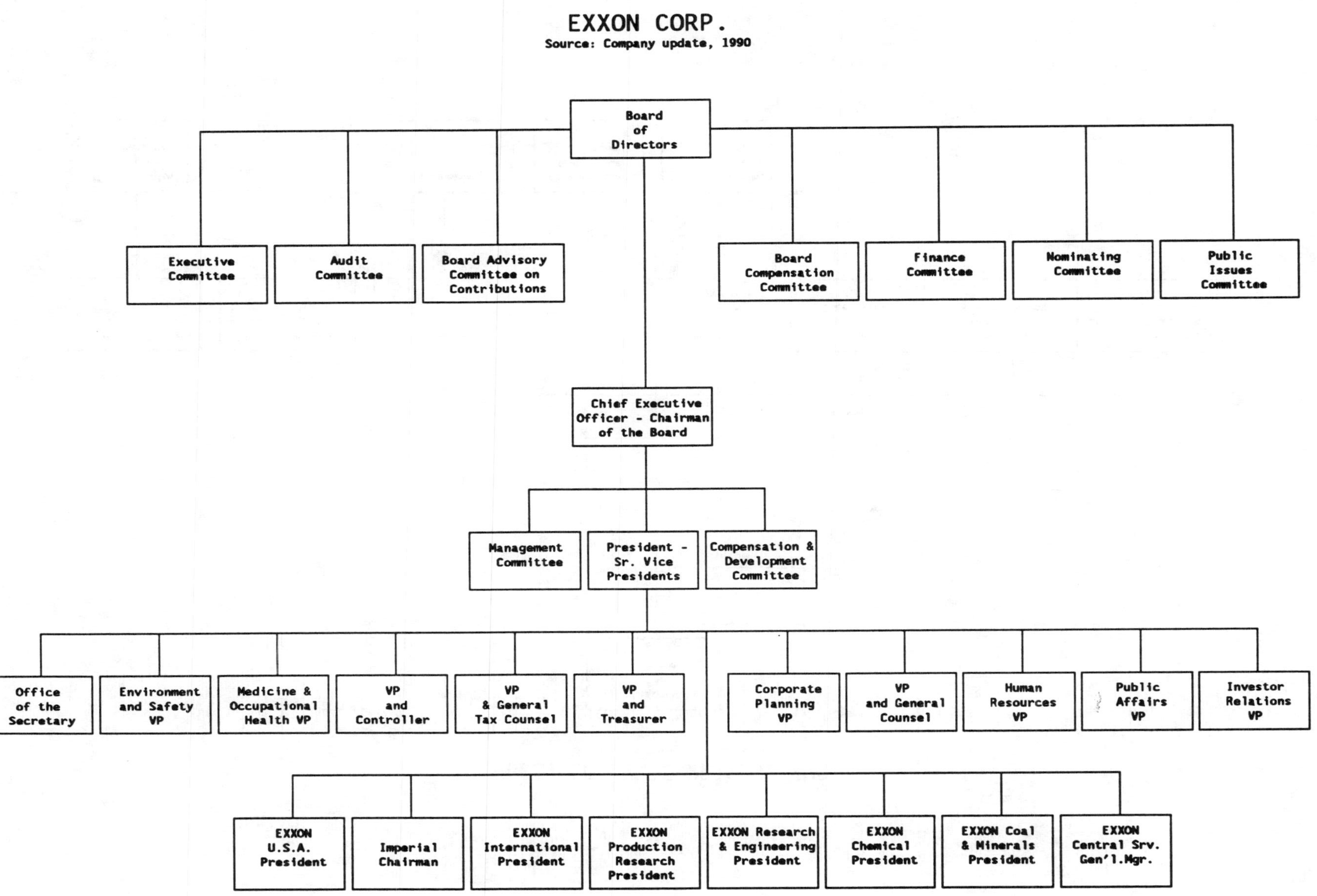
EXXON CORP.
Source: Company update, 1990
Board of Directors
Executive Committee
Audit Committee
Board Advisory Committee on Contributions
Board Compensation Committee
Finance Committee
Nominating Committee
Public Issues Committee
Chief Executive Officer - Chairman of the Board
Management Committee
President - Sr. Vice Presidents
Compensation & Development Committee
Office of the Secretary
Environment and Safety VP
Medicine & Occupational Health VP
VP and Controller
VP & General Tax Counsel
VP and Treasurer
Corporate Planning VP
VP and General Counsel
Human Resources VP
Public Affairs VP
Investor Relations VP
EXXON U.S.A. President
Imperial Chairman
EXXON International President
EXXON Production Research President
EXXON Research & Engineering President
EXXON Chemical President
EXXON Coal & Minerals President
EXXON Central Srv. Gen'l.Mgr.

FLEETWOOD ENTERPRISES, INC.

Source: Company update, 1991

FORD MOTOR CO.

Source: Company update, 1991

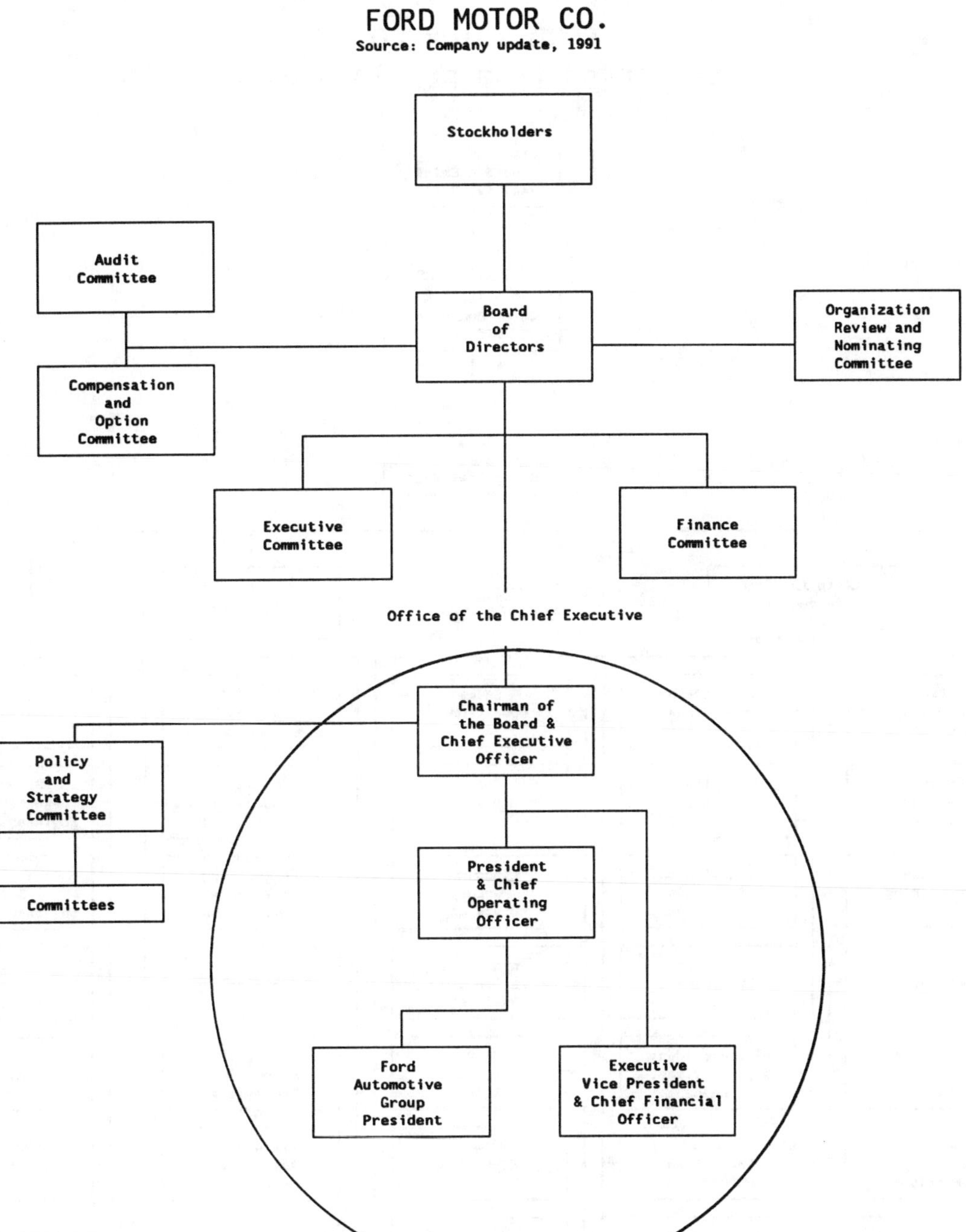

Continued on next page

FORD MOTOR CO.
Continued from previous page

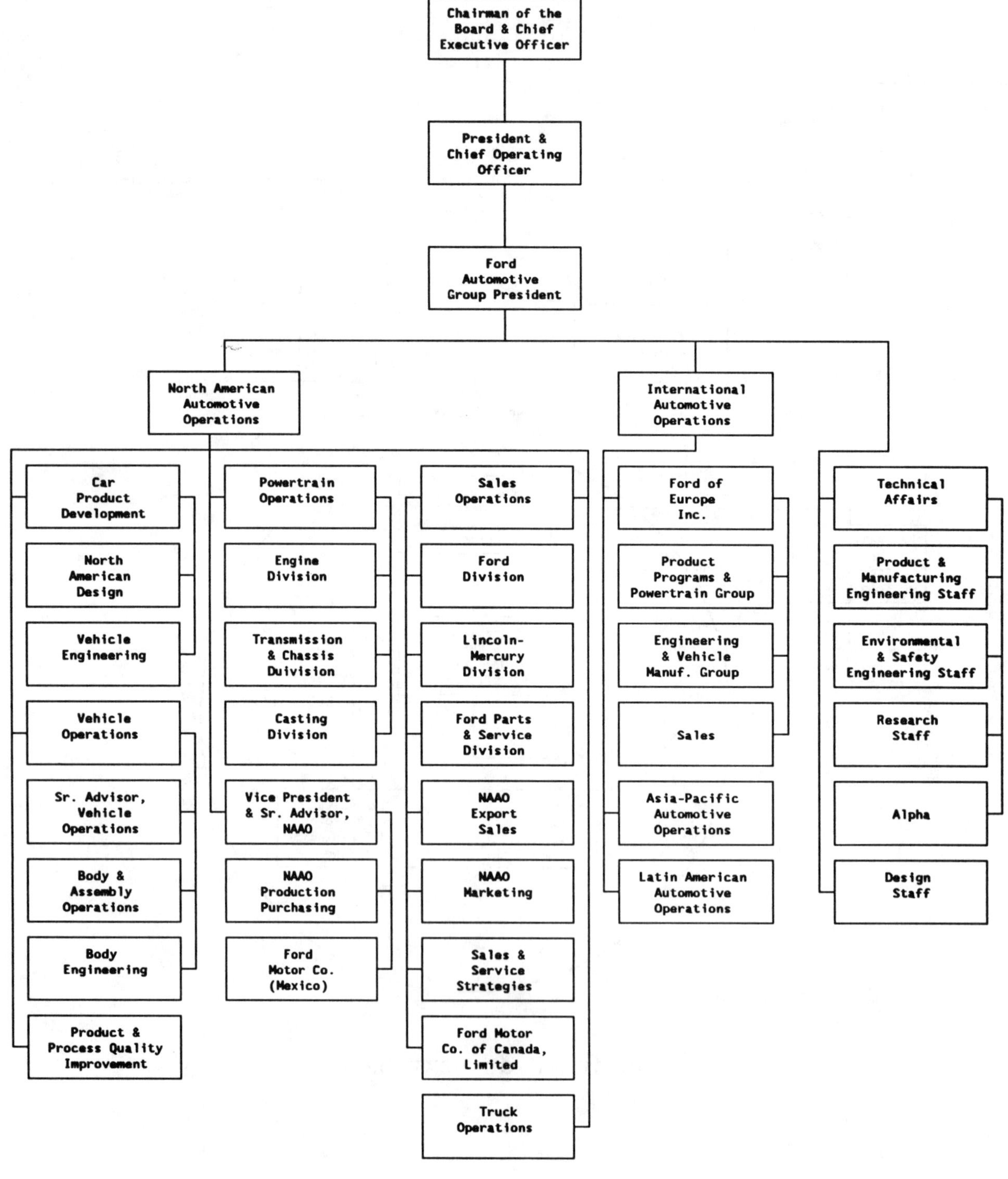

Continued on next page

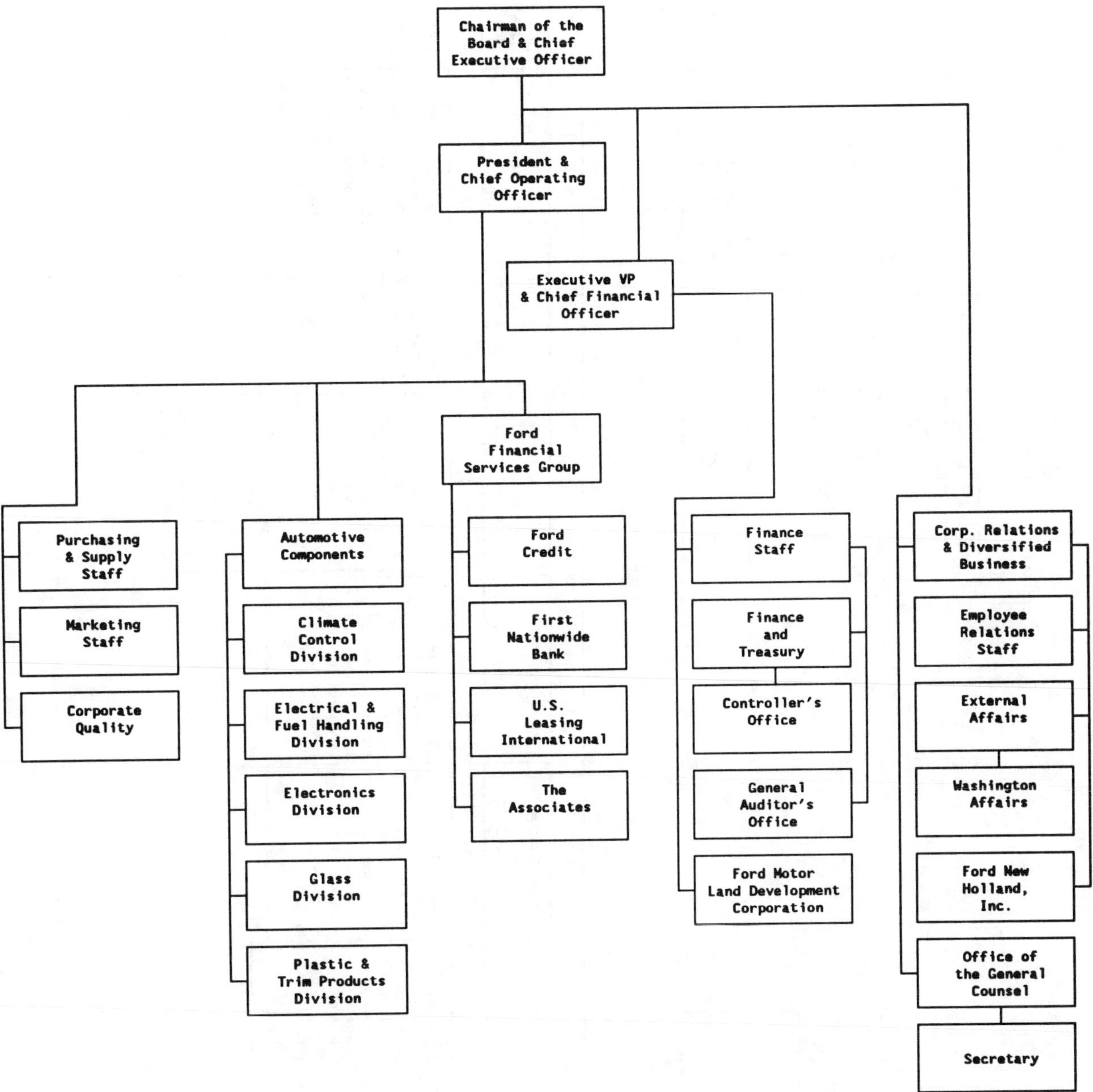
FORD MOTOR CO.
Continued from previous page
Chairman of the Board & Chief Executive Officer
President & Chief Operating Officer
Executive VP & Chief Financial Officer
Ford Financial Services Group
Purchasing & Supply Staff
Marketing Staff
Corporate Quality
Automotive Components
Climate Control Division
Electrical & Fuel Handling Division
Electronics Division
Glass Division
Plastic & Trim Products Division
Ford Credit
First Nationwide Bank
U.S. Leasing International
The Associates
Finance Staff
Finance and Treasury
Controller's Office
General Auditor's Office
Ford Motor Land Development Corporation
Corp. Relations & Diversified Business
Employee Relations Staff
External Affairs
Washington Affairs
Ford New Holland, Inc.
Office of the General Counsel
Secretary

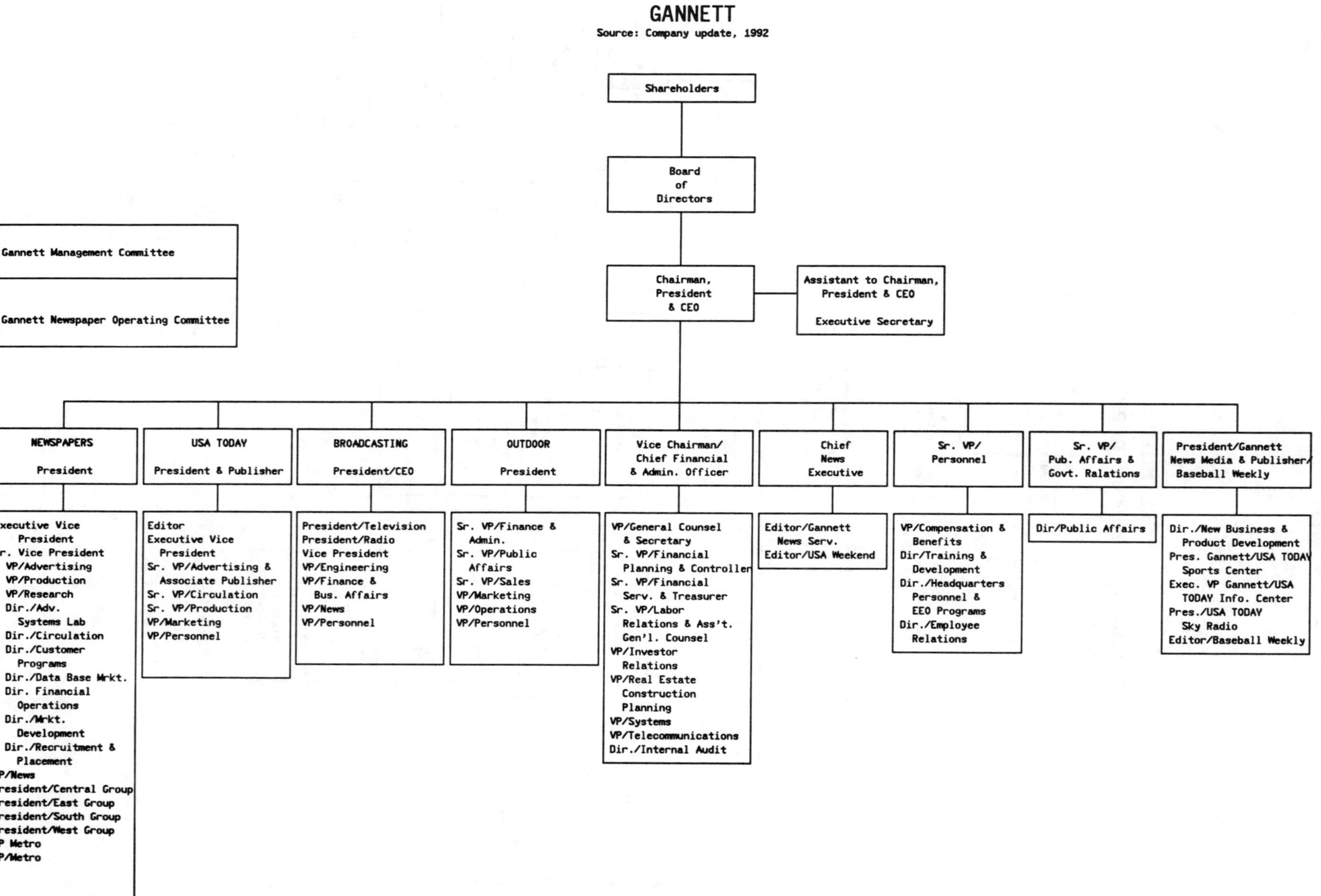
GANNETT
Source: Company update, 1992
Shareholders
Board of Directors
Chairman, President & CEO
Assistant to Chairman, President & CEO
Executive Secretary
Gannett Management Committee
Gannett Newspaper Operating Committee
NEWSPAPERS
President
Executive Vice President
Sr. Vice President
VP/Advertising
VP/Production
VP/Research
Dir./Adv. Systems Lab
Dir./Circulation
Dir./Customer Programs
Dir./Data Base Mrkt.
Dir. Financial Operations
Dir./Mrkt. Development
Dir./Recruitment & Placement
VP/News
President/Central Group
President/East Group
President/South Group
President/West Group
VP Metro
VP/Metro
USA TODAY
President & Publisher
Editor
Executive Vice President
Sr. VP/Advertising & Associate Publisher
Sr. VP/Circulation
Sr. VP/Production
VP/Marketing
VP/Personnel
BROADCASTING
President/CEO
President/Television
President/Radio
Vice President
VP/Engineering
VP/Finance & Bus. Affairs
VP/News
VP/Personnel
OUTDOOR
President
Sr. VP/Finance & Admin.
Sr. VP/Public Affairs
Sr. VP/Sales
VP/Marketing
VP/Operations
VP/Personnel
Vice Chairman/ Chief Financial & Admin. Officer
VP/General Counsel & Secretary
Sr. VP/Financial Planning & Controller
Sr. VP/Financial Serv. & Treasurer
Sr. VP/Labor Relations & Ass't. Gen'l. Counsel
VP/Investor Relations
VP/Real Estate Construction Planning
VP/Systems
VP/Telecommunications
Dir./Internal Audit
Chief News Executive
Editor/Gannett News Serv.
Editor/USA Weekend
Sr. VP/ Personnel
VP/Compensation & Benefits
Dir/Training & Development
Dir./Headquarters Personnel & EEO Programs
Dir./Employee Relations
Sr. VP/ Pub. Affairs & Govt. Ralations
Dir/Public Affairs
President/Gannett News Media & Publisher/ Baseball Weekly
Dir./New Business & Product Development
Pres. Gannett/USA TODAY Sports Center
Exec. VP Gannett/USA TODAY Info. Center
Pres./USA TODAY Sky Radio
Editor/Baseball Weekly

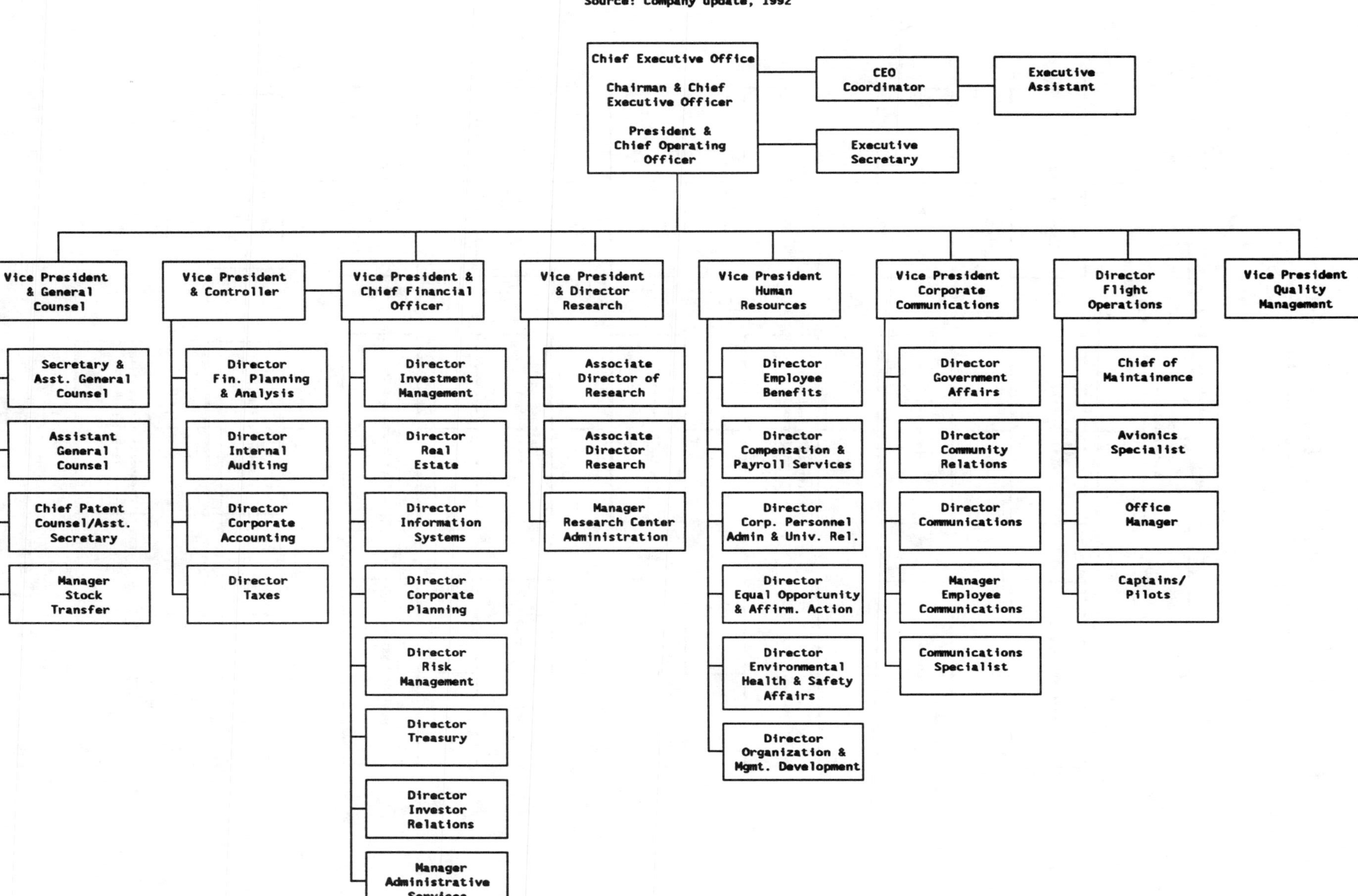
GENCORP
Source: Company update, 1992
Chief Executive Office
Chairman & Chief Executive Officer
President & Chief Operating Officer
CEO Coordinator
Executive Assistant
Executive Secretary
Vice President & General Counsel
Secretary & Asst. General Counsel
Assistant General Counsel
Chief Patent Counsel/Asst. Secretary
Manager Stock Transfer
Vice President & Controller
Director Fin. Planning & Analysis
Director Internal Auditing
Director Corporate Accounting
Director Taxes
Vice President & Chief Financial Officer
Director Investment Management
Director Real Estate
Director Information Systems
Director Corporate Planning
Director Risk Management
Director Treasury
Director Investor Relations
Manager Administrative Services
Vice President & Director Research
Associate Director of Research
Associate Director Research
Manager Research Center Administration
Vice President Human Resources
Director Employee Benefits
Director Compensation & Payroll Services
Director Corp. Personnel Admin & Univ. Rel.
Director Equal Opportunity & Affirm. Action
Director Environmental Health & Safety Affairs
Director Organization & Mgmt. Development
Vice President Corporate Communications
Director Government Affairs
Director Community Relations
Director Communications
Manager Employee Communications
Communications Specialist
Director Flight Operations
Chief of Maintainence
Avionics Specialist
Office Manager
Captains/Pilots
Vice President Quality Management

GENERAL ELECTRIC CO.

Source: Company update, 1991

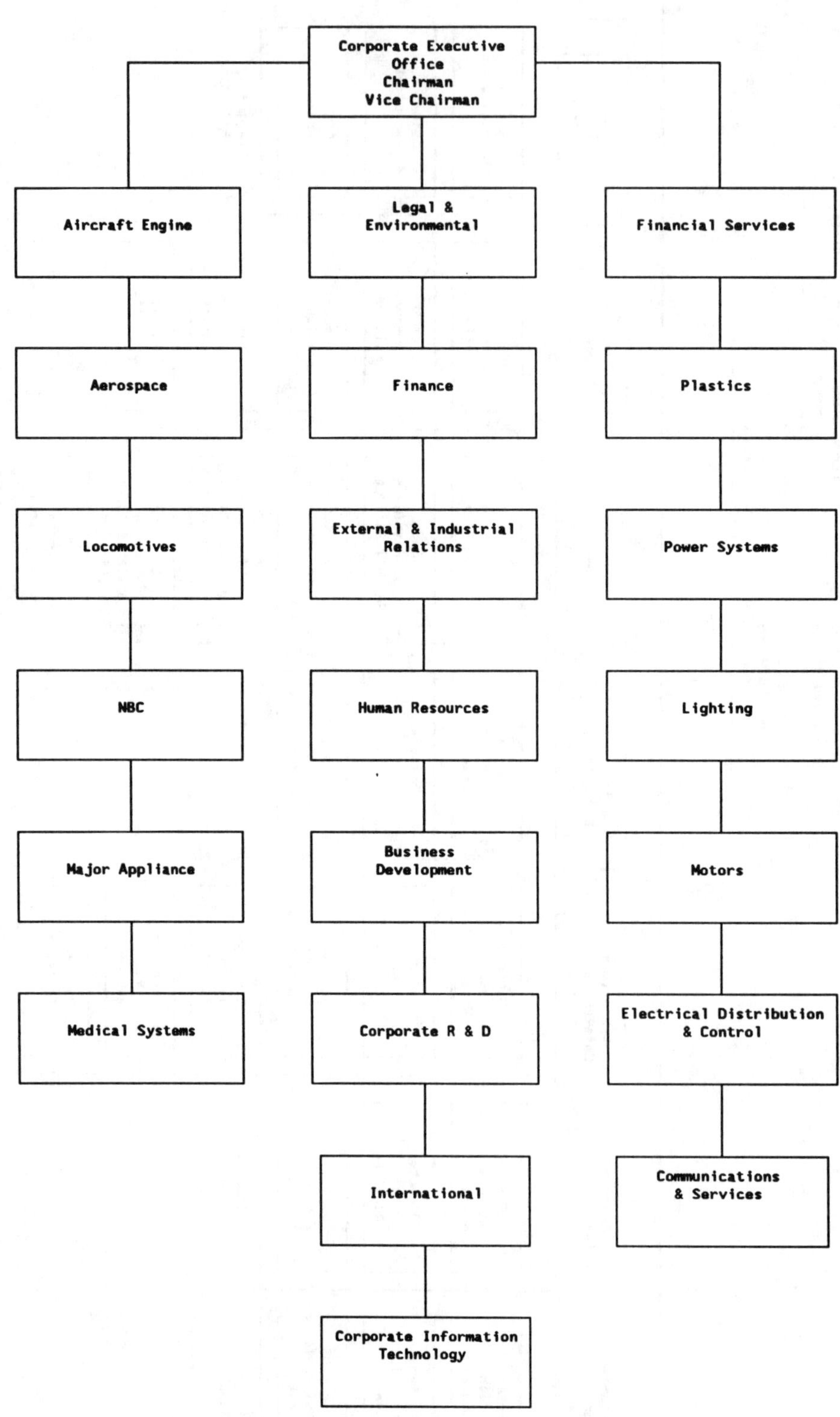

GENERAL MOTORS CORP.

Source: Annual report, 1991

- Chairman
  - Legal Staff
  - Vice Chairman
    - Electronics Data Systems Corp.
    - GM Hughes Electronics Corp.
      - Hughes Aircraft Company
      - Delco Electronics Corp.
    - Technical Staff Group
  - President
    - Chevrolet, Pontiac, GM of Canada Group
    - Saturn Corporation
    - Buick, Oldsmobile, Cadillac Group
    - Powertrain Division
    - Truck and Bus Group
    - Materials Management
    - Executive VP
      - Power Prod. & Defense Ops. Group
      - Automotive Components Group
      - Service Parts Operation
  - Vice Chairman
    - Internatl. Export, African, & Mideast Ops.
    - Asia & Pacific Operations
    - General Motors Europe
    - Group Lotus, plc.
    - Latin American Operations
  - Executive VP
    - Operating Staffs Group
    - Public Affairs & Mkgt. Group
  - Executive VP
    - GM Acceptance Corp.
    - Finance Group
  - Quality & Reliability Staff

GENERAL MOTORS
BUICK, OLDSMOBILE, CADILLAC GROUP
CADILLAC MOTOR CAR DIVISION

Source: B O C Supplier Council, 1991

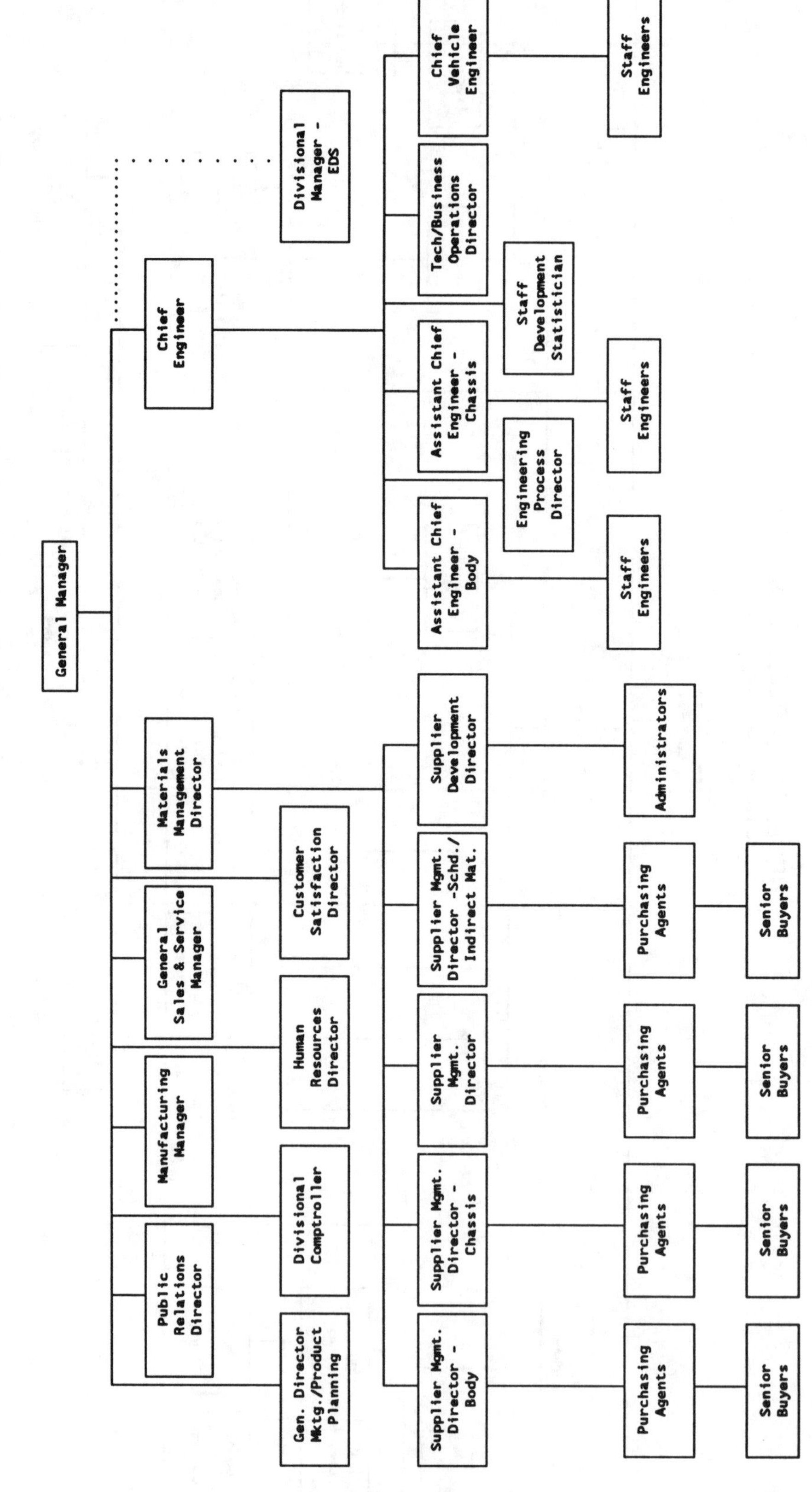

GENERAL MOTORS
BUICK, OLDSMOBILE, CADILLAC GROUP
TYPICAL MANUFACTURING STRUCTURE
Source: B O C Supplier Council, 1991

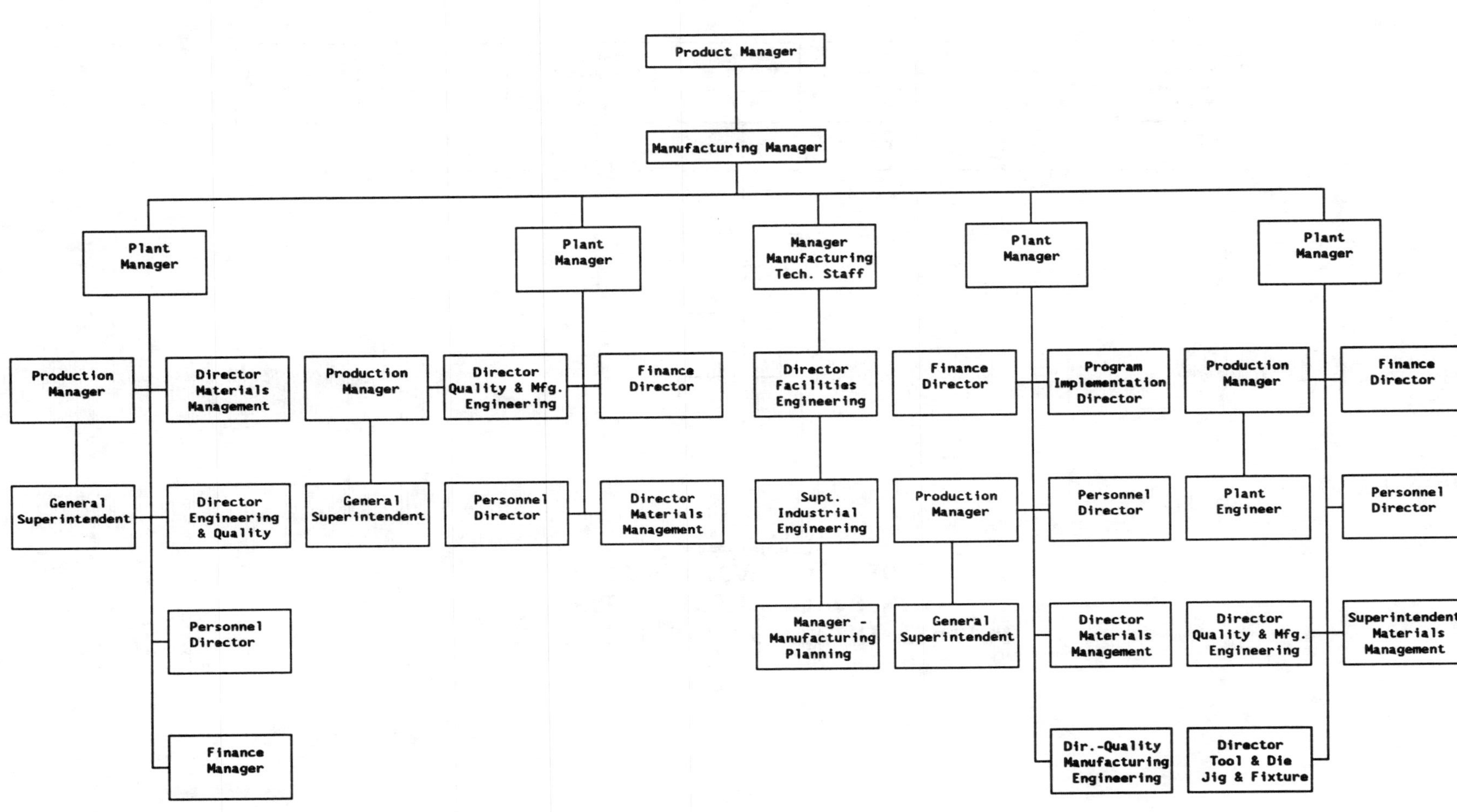

GENERAL SERVICES ADMINISTRATION
REAL PROPERTY MANAGEMENT
NATIONAL CAPITAL REGION

Source: BUILDINGS
85: 40+ (July 1991)

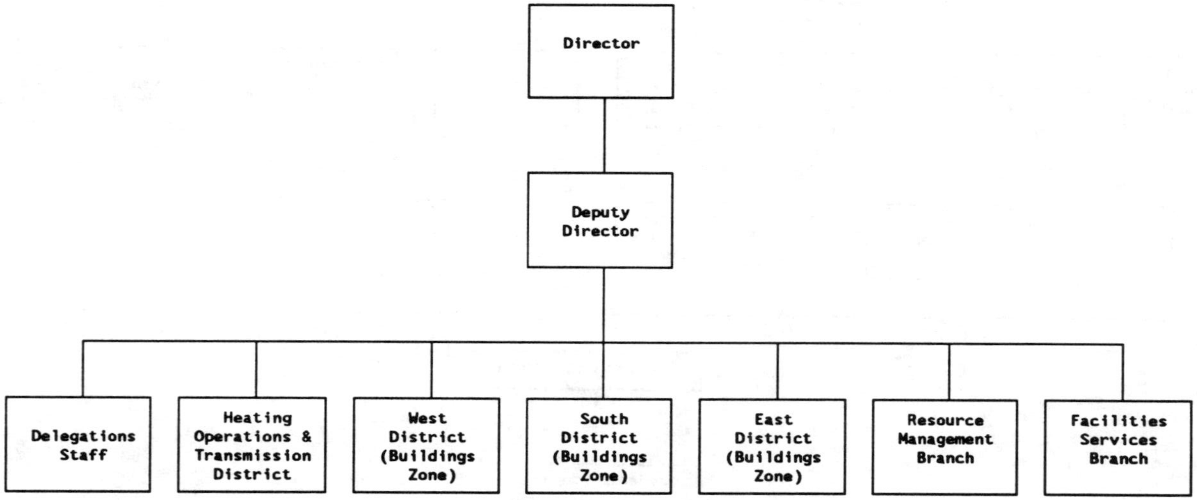

Director
Deputy Director
Delegations Staff
Heating Operations & Transmission District
West District (Buildings Zone)
South District (Buildings Zone)
East District (Buildings Zone)
Resource Management Branch
Facilities Services Branch

GENESCO INC.

Source: Company update, 1991

- Chairman & Chief Executve Officer
  - Administrative Assistant
  - President, Chief Operating Officer
    - President, The Greif Companies
    - Chairman, Johnston & Murphy
    - Vice President, Footwear Administration
    - President, Jarman
    - Vice President, Footwear Human Resources
    - President, Journeys
    - Director, MIS
    - President, Laredo/Code West
    - President, Mitre Sports
  - Director, Internal Audit
  - VP, Finance & Chief Financial Officer
  - Vice President, Law, Corporate Secretary
  - Vice President, Human Resources
  - Director, Corporate Relations

GEVAERT GROUPE (Belgium)

Source: Annual report, 1990

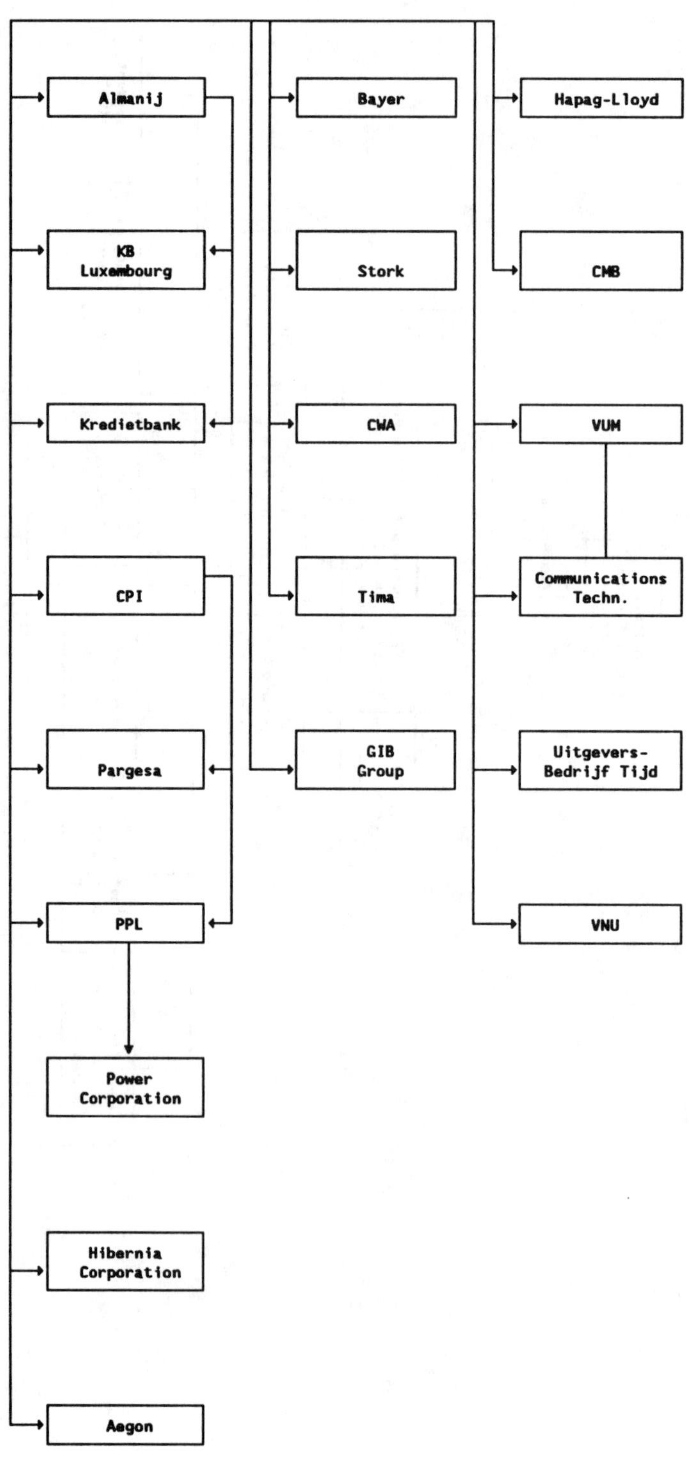

THE GITANO GROUP, INC.

Source: Annual report, 1990

Gitano seeks to move from being a sales driven organization with many small specialized divisions to an account management structure. The first phase of this strategic reorganization concluded in March 1991, with twelve womenswear divisions combining into one business unit.--Annual report, 1991

GKN plc. (United Kingdom)

Source: Annual report, 1990

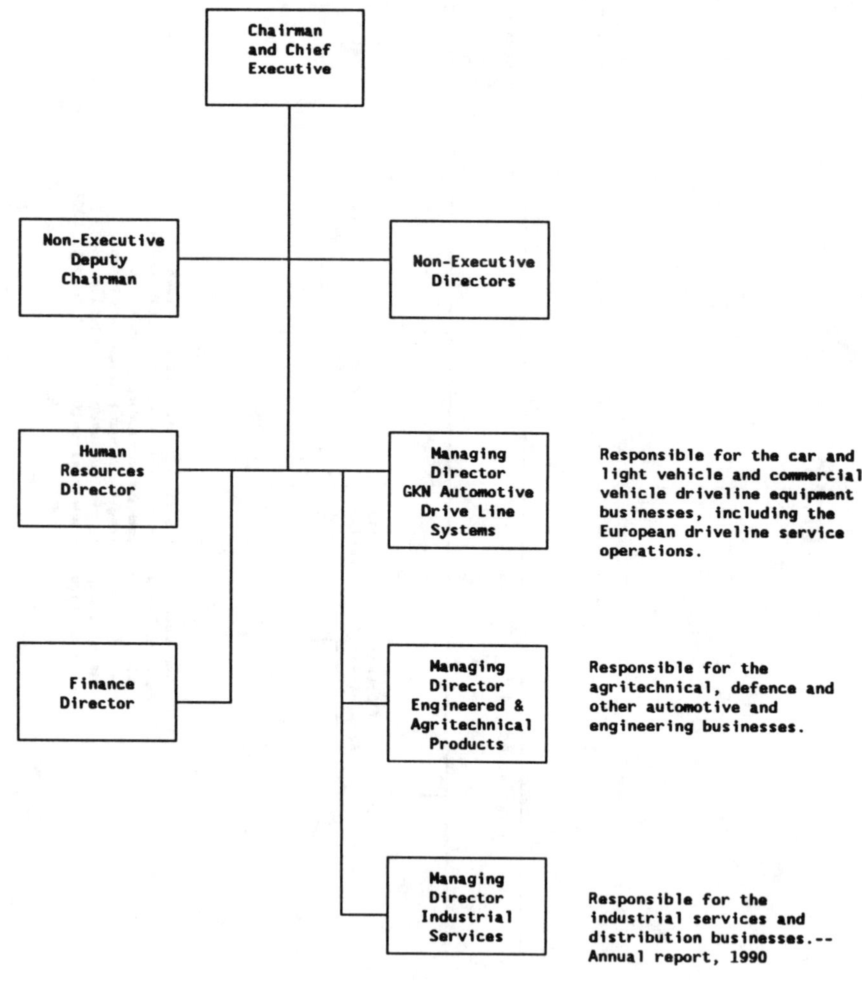

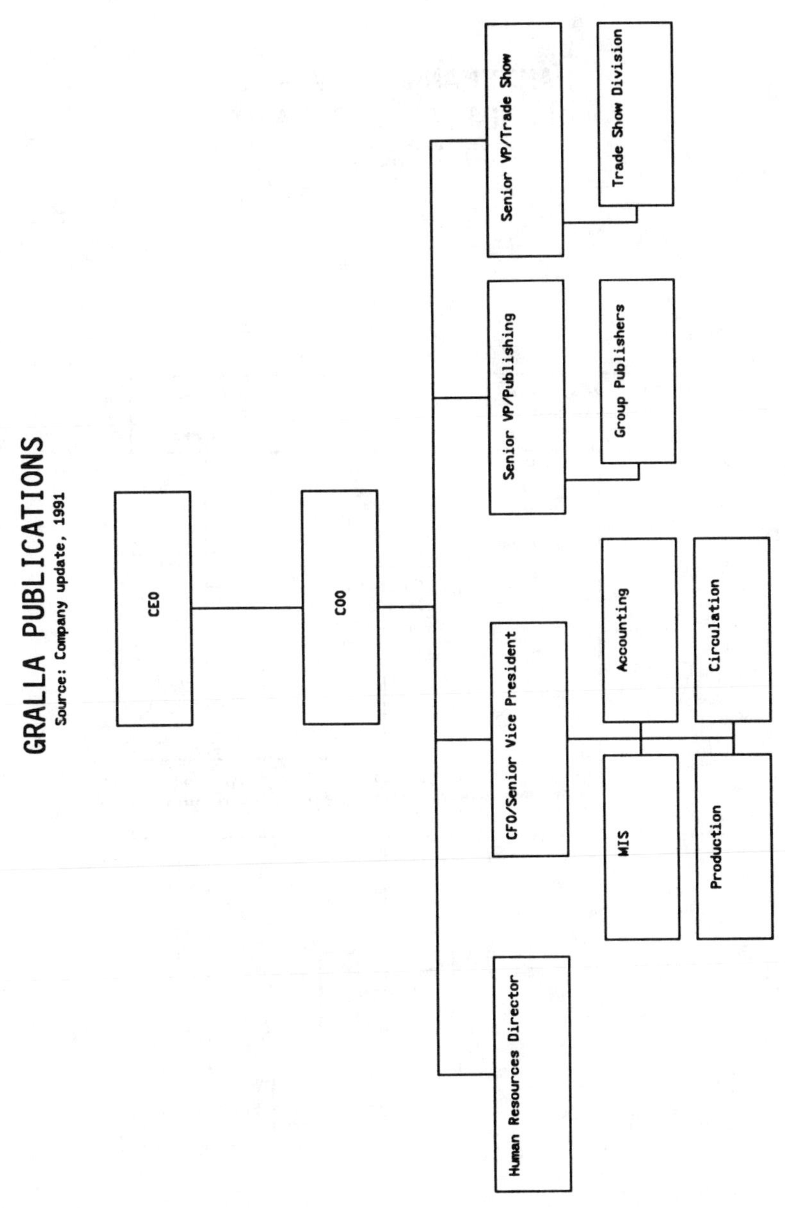
GRALLA PUBLICATIONS
Source: Company update, 1991
CEO
COO
Senior VP/Trade Show
Trade Show Division
Senior VP/Publishing
Group Publishers
CFO/Senior Vice President
Accounting
Circulation
MIS
Production
Human Resources Director

HAHNEMANN UNIVERSITY
HOSPITAL LABORATORY

Source: MEDICAL LABORATORY OBSERVER
20: 55+ (March 1988)

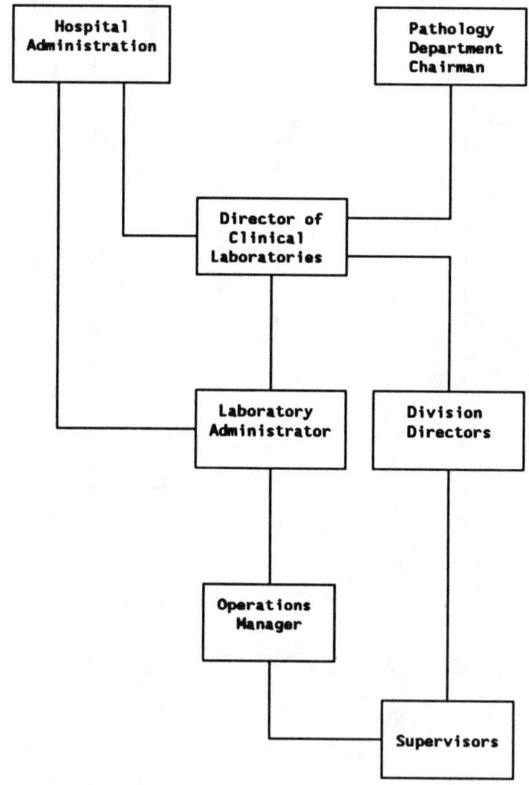

HARNISCHFEGER INDUSTRIES, INC.

Source: Annual report, 1990

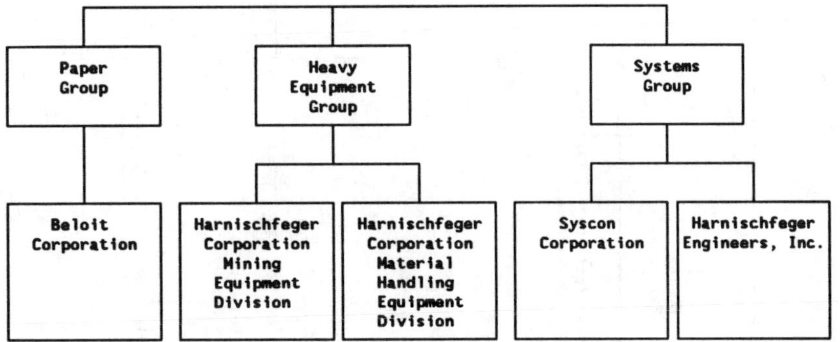

Harnischfeger Industries, Inc. is a holding company for subsidiaries involved in papermaking machinery manufacturing (Beloit Corp.); surface mining and material handling equipment manufacturing (Harnischfeger Corp.); and systems integration services (Harnischfeger Engineers, Inc. and Syscon Corp.).--Annual report, 1990

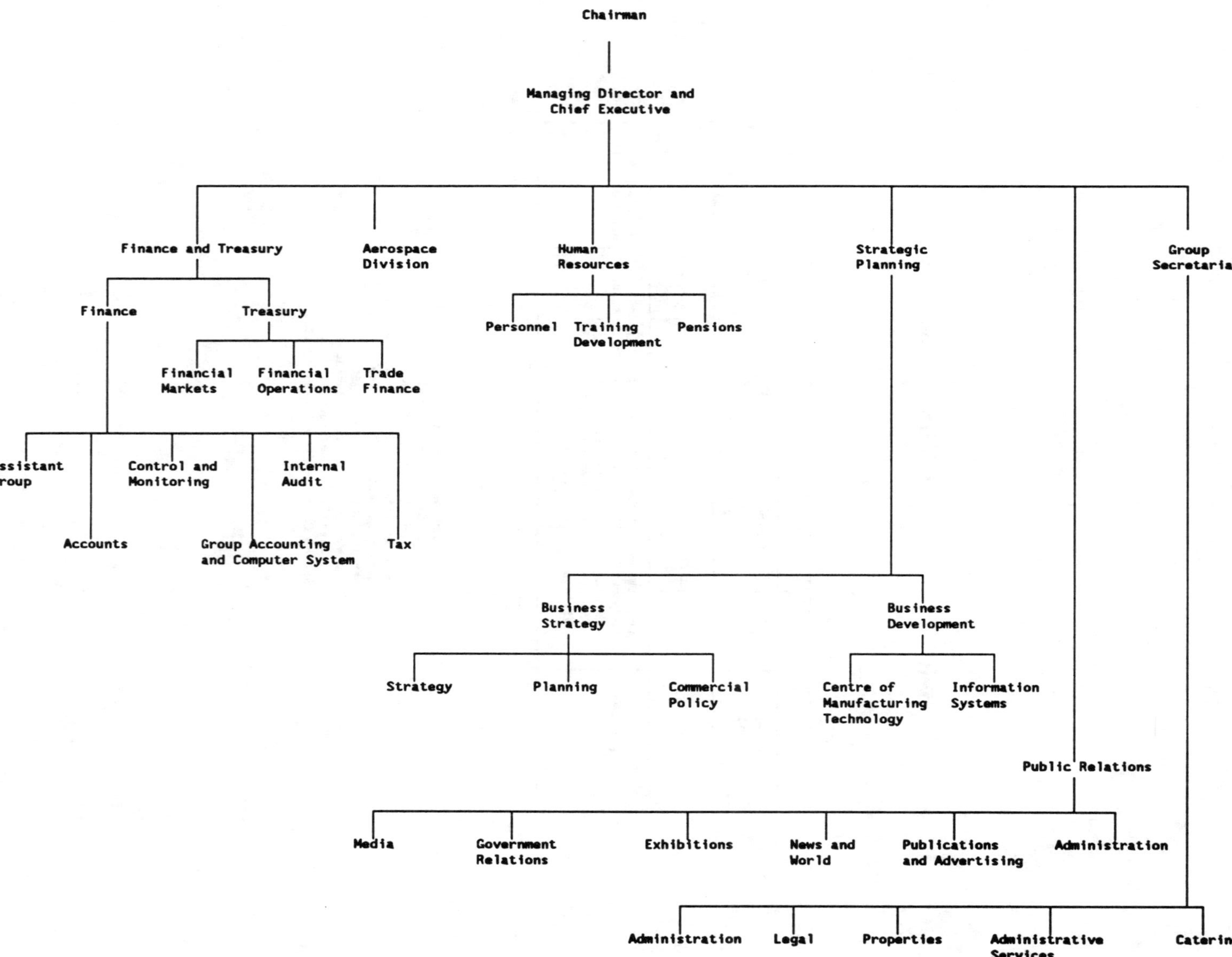
HAWKER SIDDELEY GROUP (England)
Source: Company update, 1991
Chairman
Managing Director and Chief Executive
Finance and Treasury
Aerospace Division
Human Resources
Strategic Planning
Group Secretariat
Finance
Treasury
Personnel
Training Development
Pensions
Financial Markets
Financial Operations
Trade Finance
Assistant Group
Control and Monitoring
Internal Audit
Accounts
Group Accounting and Computer System
Tax
Business Strategy
Business Development
Strategy
Planning
Commercial Policy
Centre of Manufacturing Technology
Information Systems
Public Relations
Media
Government Relations
Exhibitions
News and World
Publications and Advertising
Administration
Administration
Legal
Properties
Administrative Services
Catering

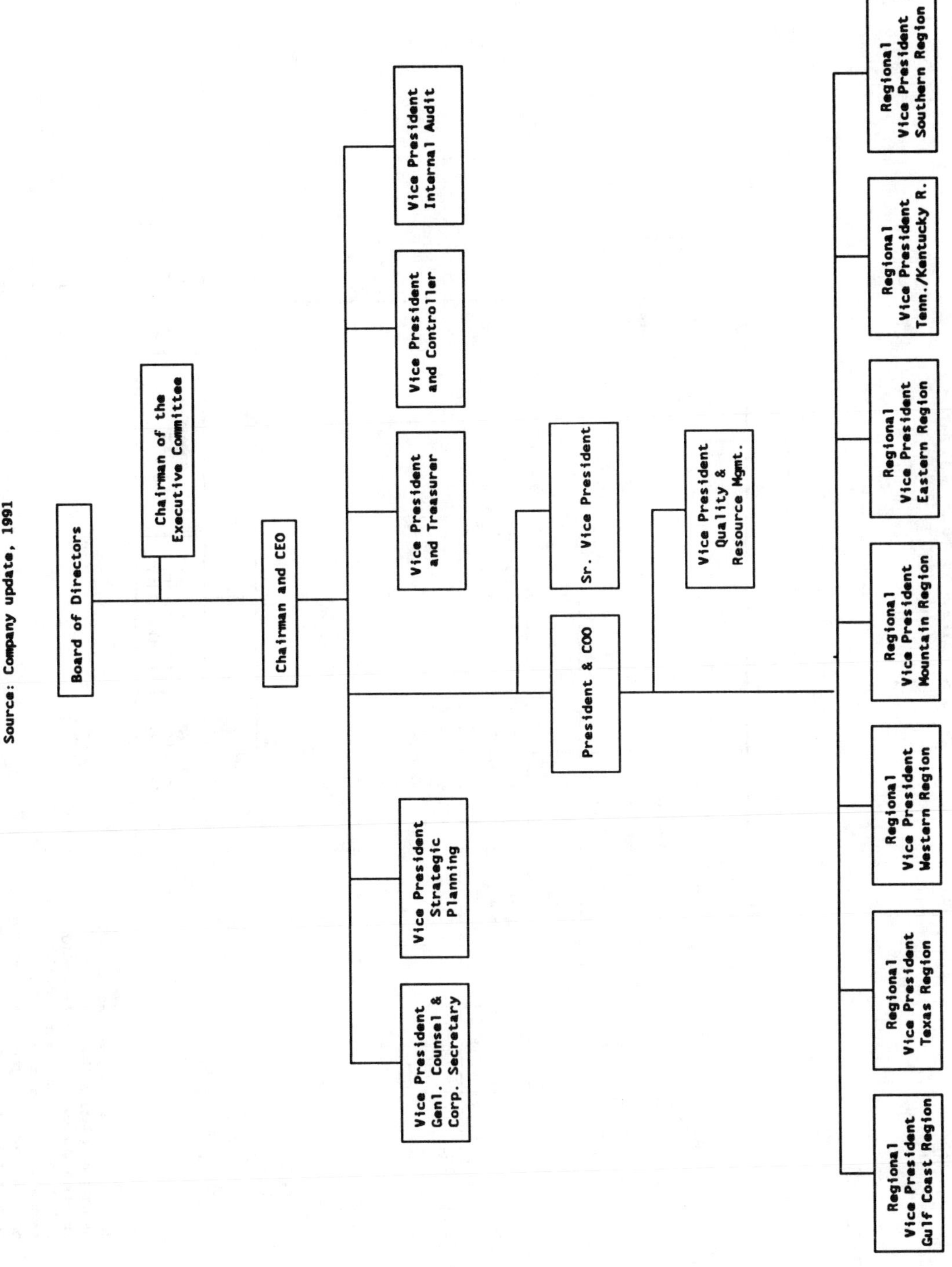
HEALTHTRUST INC. - The Hospital Co.
Source: Company update, 1991
Board of Directors
Chairman of the Executive Committee
Chairman and CEO
Vice President Treasurer
Vice President and Controller
Vice President Internal Audit
Vice President Strategic Planning
Vice President Genl. Counsel & Corp. Secretary
Sr. Vice President
President & COO
Vice President Quality & Resource Mgmt.
Regional Vice President Southern Region
Regional Vice President Tenn./Kentucky R.
Regional Vice President Eastern Region
Regional Vice President Mountain Region
Regional Vice President Western Region
Regional Vice President Texas Region
Regional Vice President Gulf Coast Region

HEIL CO.

Source: NATIONALITY PRODUCTIVITY REVIEW
9:179+ (Spring 1990)

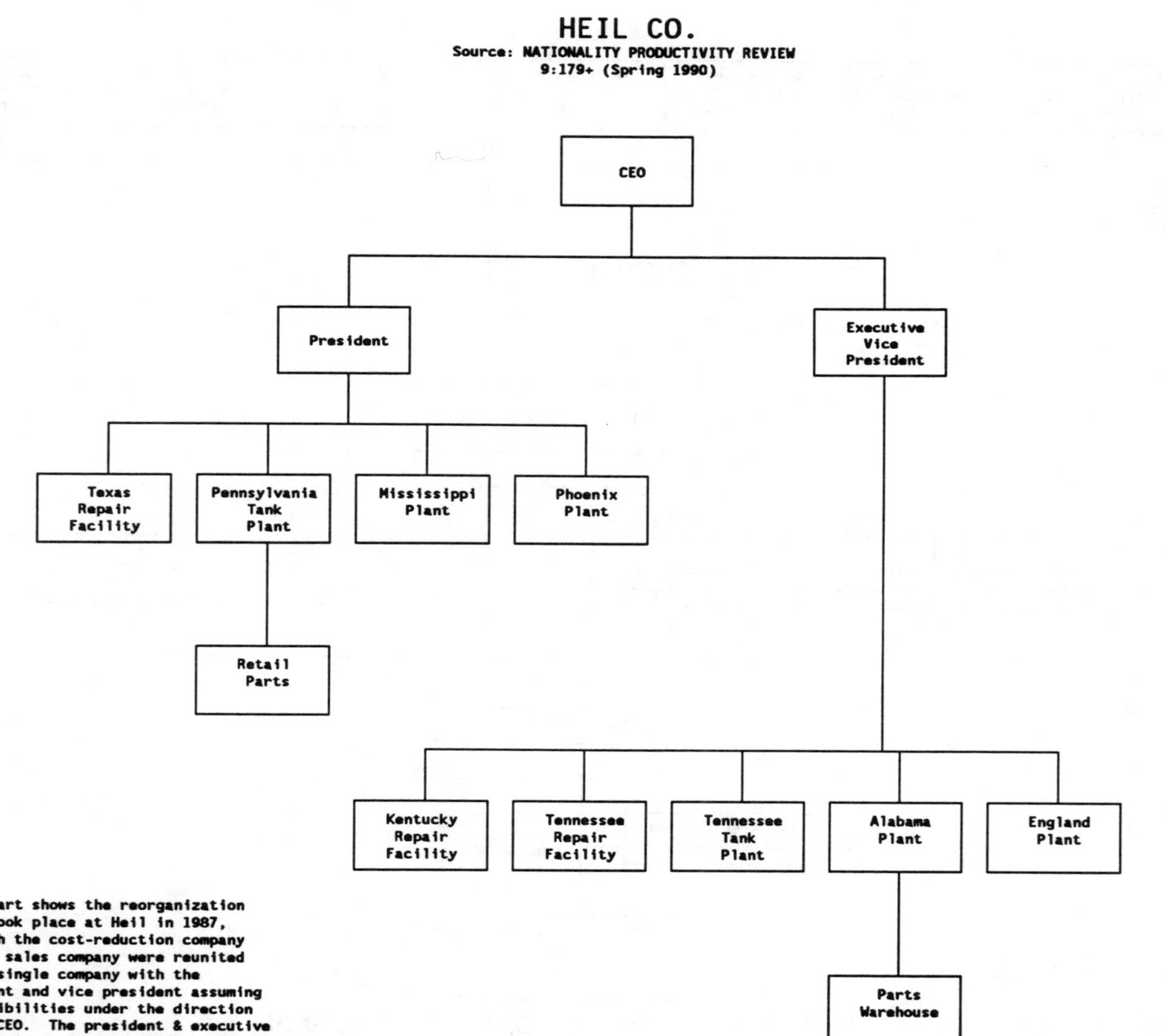

This chart shows the reorganization which took place at Heil in 1987, in which the cost-reduction company and the sales company were reunited into a single company with the president and vice president assuming responsibilities under the direction of the CEO. The president & executive vice president divided the responsibility for various operating components of the company.

HENRY FORD HEALTH SYSTEM (Detroit, Michigan)

Source: MODERN HEALTHCARE
20: 33+ (December 17, 1990)

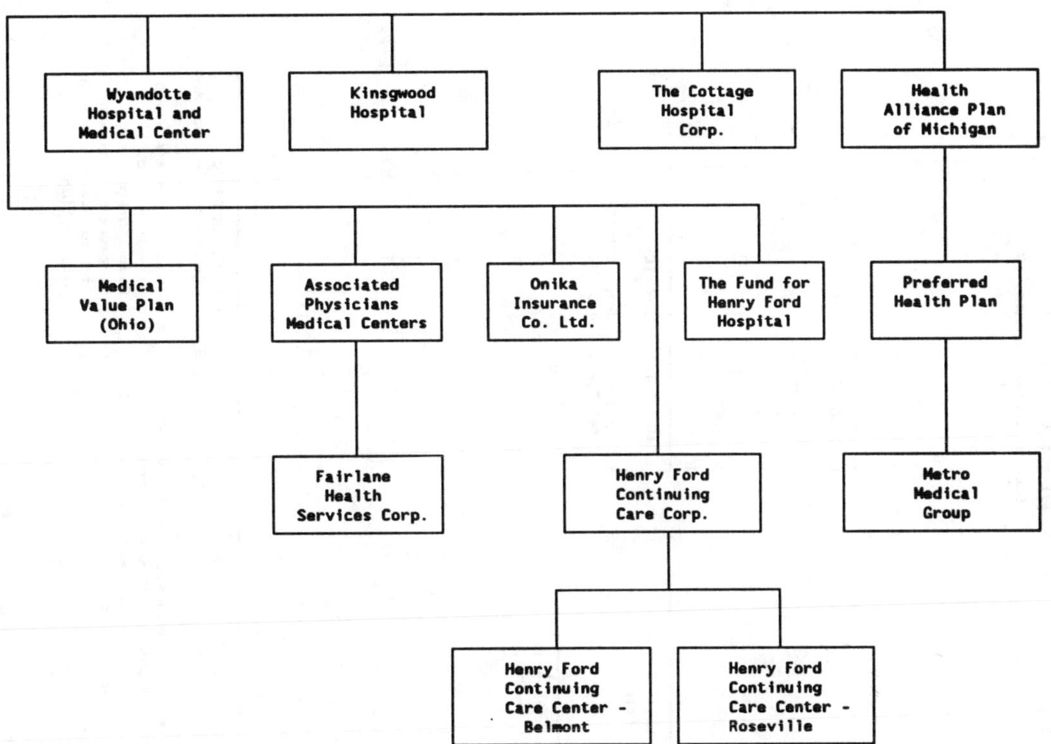

Wyandotte Hospital and Medical Center, Kingswood Hospital, Cottage Hospital Corp., and Health Alliance Plan of Michigan are affiliates of the Henry Ford Health System are are members of the system's obligated group. The other entities are divisions within the system.

HEWLETT-PACKARD CO.

Source: Company update, 1991

BOARD OF DIRECTORS

Chairman

Chief Financial Officer
Senior Vice President

Personnel
Director

Internal Audit
Director

HP Laboratories
Director

Administration
Vice President

CHIEF EXECUTIVE OFFICE

President and Chief Executive Officer
Chief Operating Officer

U.S. Field Operations

Europe/Middle East/
Africa Operations

Intercontinental Operations

BUSINESS DEVELOPMENT
Executive Vice President

Circuit Technology Group
Corporate Development
Corporate Education
Corporate Engineering
Corporate Manufacturing
Corporate Quality

MEASUREMENT SYSTEMS
Executive Vice President

Test and Measurement Organization
Electronic Instruments Group
Microwave and Communications Group
Analytical Group
Medical Group
Component Group

COMPUTER PRODUCTS
Executive Vice President

Printing Systems Group
Ink-Jet Products
Mass Storage Group
Personal Systems Group
Personal Computer Group
Distribution

COMPUTER SYSTEMS
Executive Vice President

Networked Systems Group
Information Architecture Group
Worldwide Customer Support Operations
Computer Manufacturing

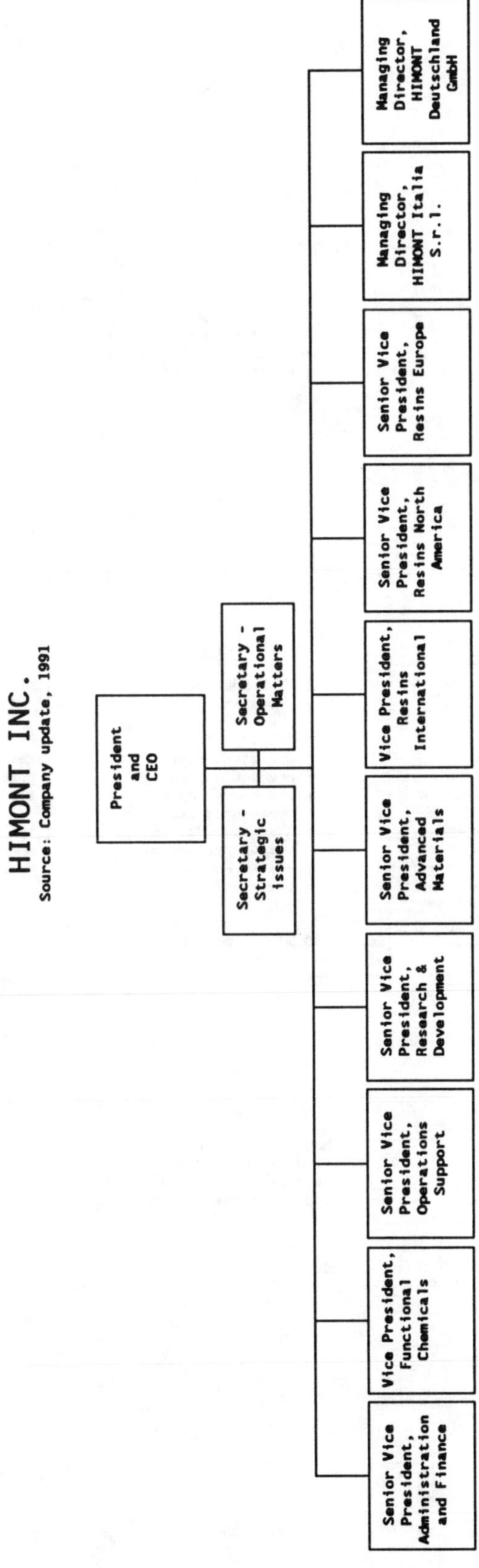
HIMONT INC.
Source: Company update, 1991
President and CEO
Secretary - Strategic issues
Secretary - Operational Matters
Senior Vice President, Administration and Finance
Vice President, Functional Chemicals
Senior Vice President, Operations Support
Senior Vice President, Research & Development
Senior Vice President, Advanced Materials
Vice President, Resins International
Senior Vice President, Resins North America
Senior Vice President, Resins Europe
Managing Director, HIMONT Italia S.r.l.
Managing Director, HIMONT Deutschland GmbH

HONDA (Japan)

Source: AUTOMOTIVE INDUSTRIES
170: 71+ (November 1990)

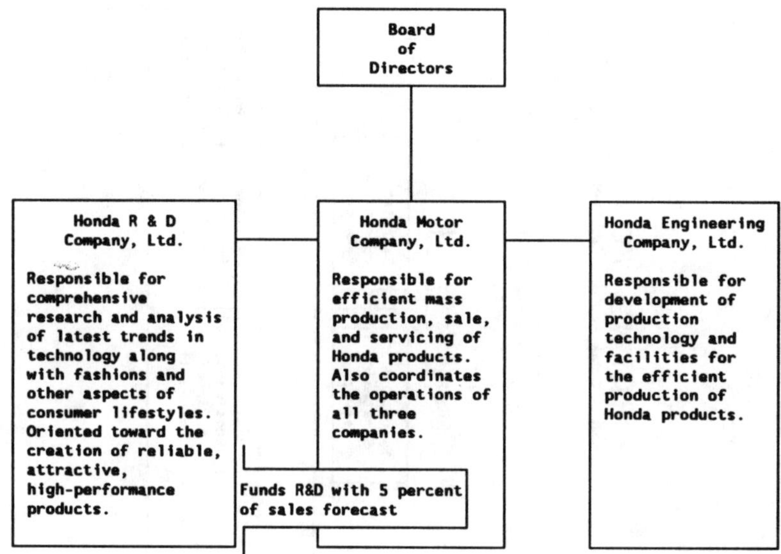

Board
of
Directors
Honda R & D
Company, Ltd.
Responsible for comprehensive research and analysis of latest trends in technology along with fashions and other aspects of consumer lifestyles. Oriented toward the creation of reliable, attractive, high-performance products.
Honda Motor
Company, Ltd.
Responsible for efficient mass production, sale, and servicing of Honda products. Also coordinates the operations of all three companies.
Honda Engineering
Company, Ltd.
Responsible for development of production technology and facilities for the efficient production of Honda products.
Funds R&D with 5 percent of sales forecast

Honda's cross-functional focus insures a broad depth of experience, understanding, and a minimum of repetition.

HOSPITAL CORP. OF AMERICA

Source: Company update, 1991

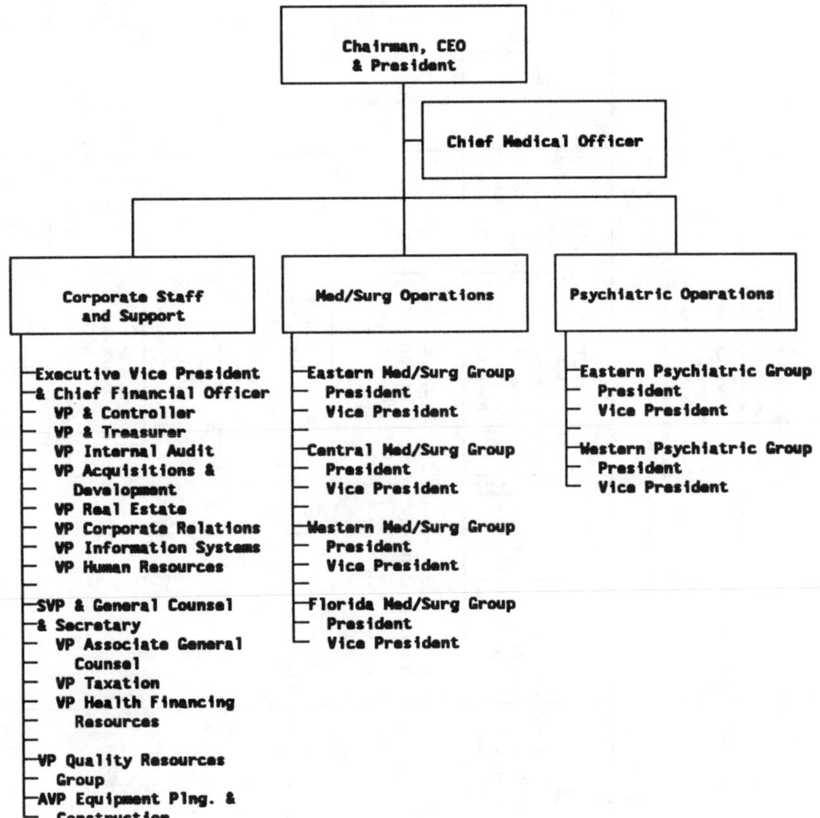
Chairman, CEO
& President
Chief Medical Officer
Corporate Staff
and Support
Med/Surg Operations
Psychiatric Operations
Executive Vice President
& Chief Financial Officer
VP & Controller
VP & Treasurer
VP Internal Audit
VP Acquisitions &
Development
VP Real Estate
VP Corporate Relations
VP Information Systems
VP Human Resources
SVP & General Counsel
& Secretary
VP Associate General
Counsel
VP Taxation
VP Health Financing
Resources
VP Quality Resources
Group
AVP Equipment Plng. &
Construction
Eastern Med/Surg Group
President
Vice President
Central Med/Surg Group
President
Vice President
Western Med/Surg Group
President
Vice President
Florida Med/Surg Group
President
Vice President
Eastern Psychiatric Group
President
Vice President
Western Psychiatric Group
President
Vice President

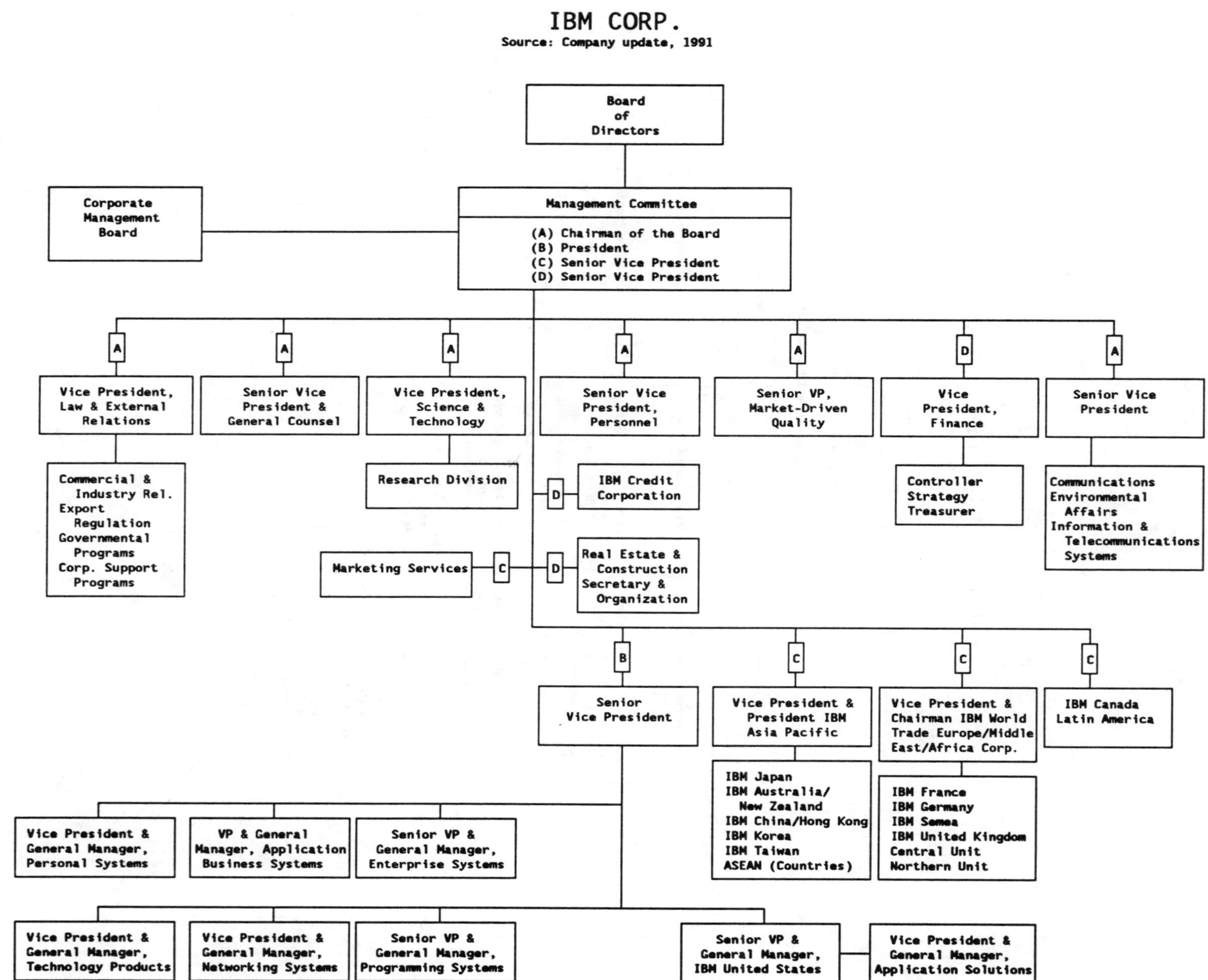
IBM CORP.
Source: Company update, 1991
Board of Directors
Corporate Management Board
Management Committee
(A) Chairman of the Board
(B) President
(C) Senior Vice President
(D) Senior Vice President
A
Vice President, Law & External Relations
Commercial & Industry Rel.
Export Regulation
Governmental Programs
Corp. Support Programs
A
Senior Vice President & General Counsel
A
Vice President, Science & Technology
Research Division
A
Senior Vice President, Personnel
A
Senior VP, Market-Driven Quality
D
Vice President, Finance
Controller
Strategy
Treasurer
A
Senior Vice President
Communications
Environmental Affairs
Information & Telecommunications Systems
D
IBM Credit Corporation
Marketing Services
C
D
Real Estate & Construction
Secretary & Organization
B
Senior Vice President
C
Vice President & President IBM Asia Pacific
IBM Japan
IBM Australia/New Zealand
IBM China/Hong Kong
IBM Korea
IBM Taiwan
ASEAN (Countries)
C
Vice President & Chairman IBM World Trade Europe/Middle East/Africa Corp.
IBM France
IBM Germany
IBM Semea
IBM United Kingdom
Central Unit
Northern Unit
C
IBM Canada
Latin America
Vice President & General Manager, Personal Systems
VP & General Manager, Application Business Systems
Senior VP & General Manager, Enterprise Systems
Vice President & General Manager, Technology Products
Vice President & General Manager, Networking Systems
Senior VP & General Manager, Programming Systems
Senior VP & General Manager, IBM United States
Vice President & General Manager, Application Solutions

INTERNATIONAL MONETARY FUND

Source: INTERNATIONAL JOURNAL OF PUBLIC ADMINISTRATION 9:P1+ (January 1987)

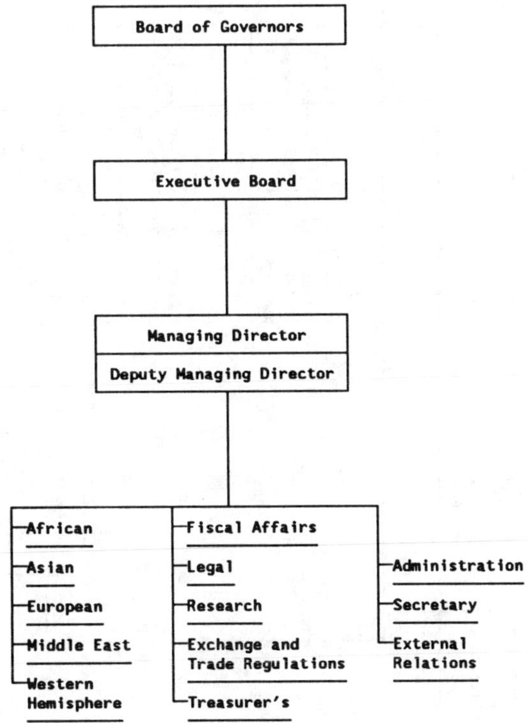

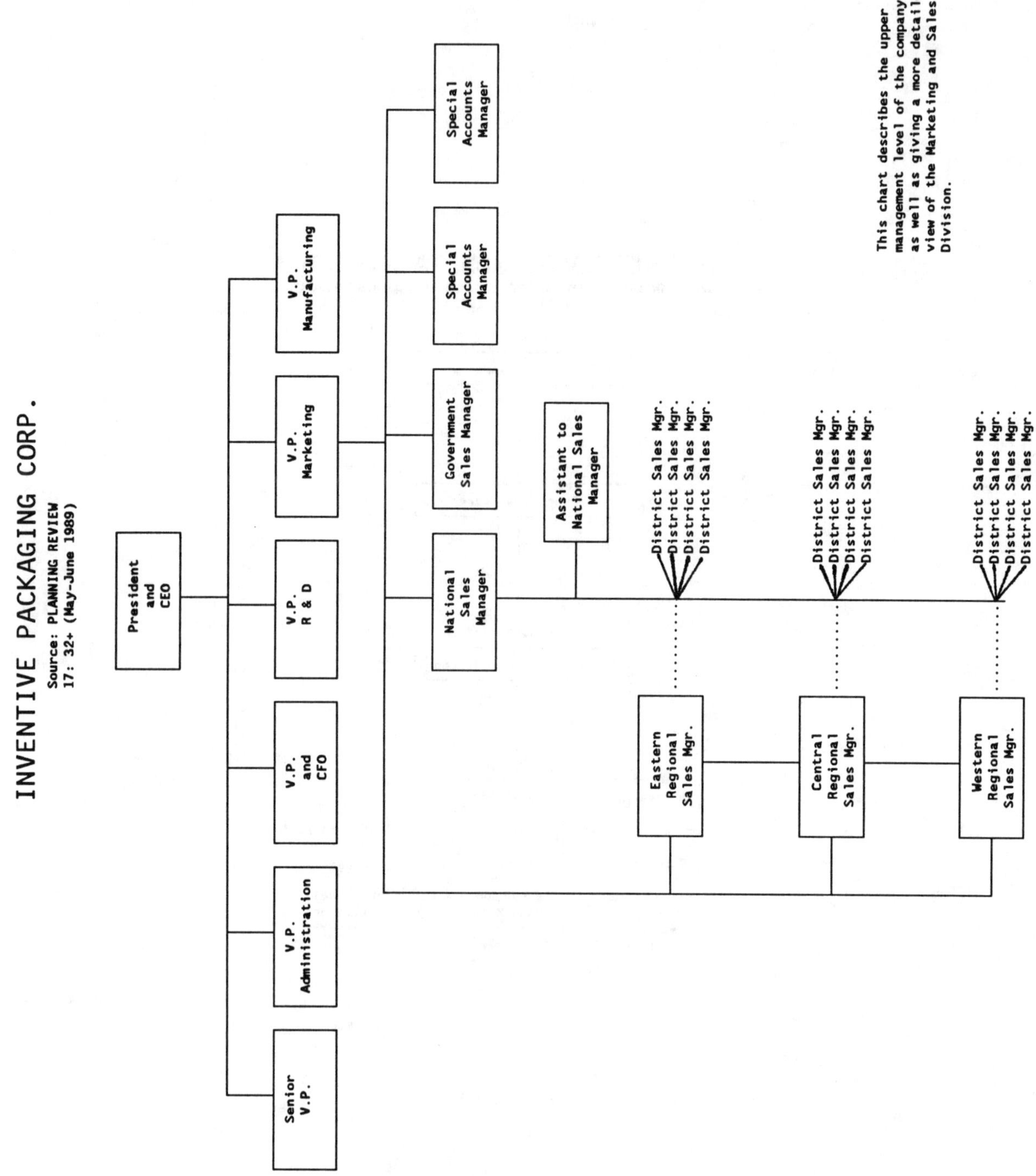
INVENTIVE PACKAGING CORP.
Source: PLANNING REVIEW
17: 32+ (May-June 1989)
President and CEO
Senior V.P.
V.P. Administration
V.P. and CFO
V.P. R & D
V.P. Marketing
V.P. Manufacturing
National Sales Manager
Government Sales Manager
Special Accounts Manager
Special Accounts Manager
Assistant to National Sales Manager
District Sales Mgr.
District Sales Mgr.
District Sales Mgr.
District Sales Mgr.
District Sales Mgr.
District Sales Mgr.
District Sales Mgr.
District Sales Mgr.
District Sales Mgr.
District Sales Mgr.
District Sales Mgr.
District Sales Mgr.
Eastern Regional Sales Mgr.
Central Regional Sales Mgr.
Western Regional Sales Mgr.
This chart describes the upper management level of the company as well as giving a more detailed view of the Marketing and Sales Division.

JAPAN FINE CERAMICS CENTER

Source: BUSINESS JAPAN
34: 53+ (April 1989)

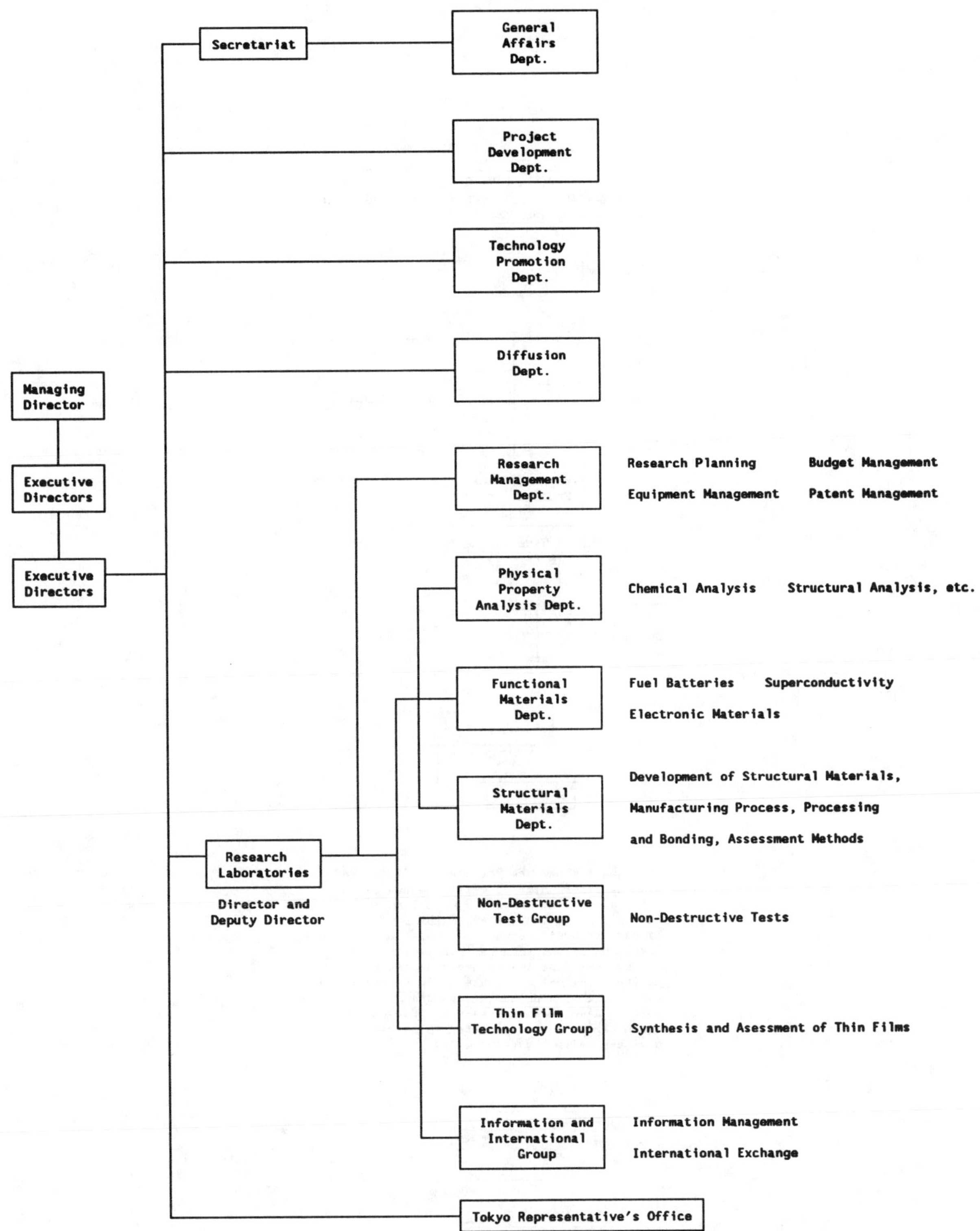
Secretariat
General Affairs Dept.
Project Development Dept.
Technology Promotion Dept.
Diffusion Dept.
Managing Director
Executive Directors
Executive Directors
Research Management Dept.
Research Planning
Budget Management
Equipment Management
Patent Management
Physical Property Analysis Dept.
Chemical Analysis
Structural Analysis, etc.
Functional Materials Dept.
Fuel Batteries
Superconductivity
Electronic Materials
Structural Materials Dept.
Development of Structural Materials,
Manufacturing Process, Processing
and Bonding, Assessment Methods
Research Laboratories
Director and Deputy Director
Non-Destructive Test Group
Non-Destructive Tests
Thin Film Technology Group
Synthesis and Asessment of Thin Films
Information and International Group
Information Management
International Exchange
Tokyo Representative's Office

JOHNS HOPKINS HOSPITAL

Source: HOSPITAL & HEALTH SERVICES ADMINISTRATION
109+ (March/April 1986)

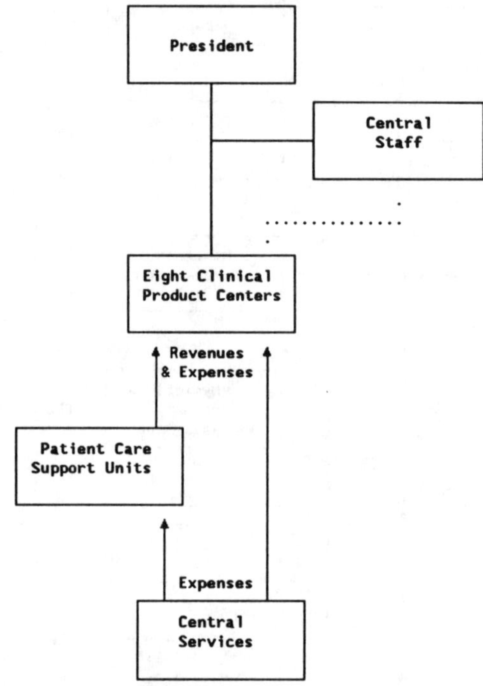

This chart shows the President's Office and central staff which in effect behave as an informal holding company. Reporting to this central administration are eight product centers or business units. These centers are fashioned around surgery, pediatrics, etc. The support departments are depicted as patient care units because their revenues and expenses are reported through the business units. Also shown are services departments whose expenses are allocated to both primary business units & support units.

KANSALLIS-OSAKE-PANKKI (Finland)

Source: Annual report, 1991

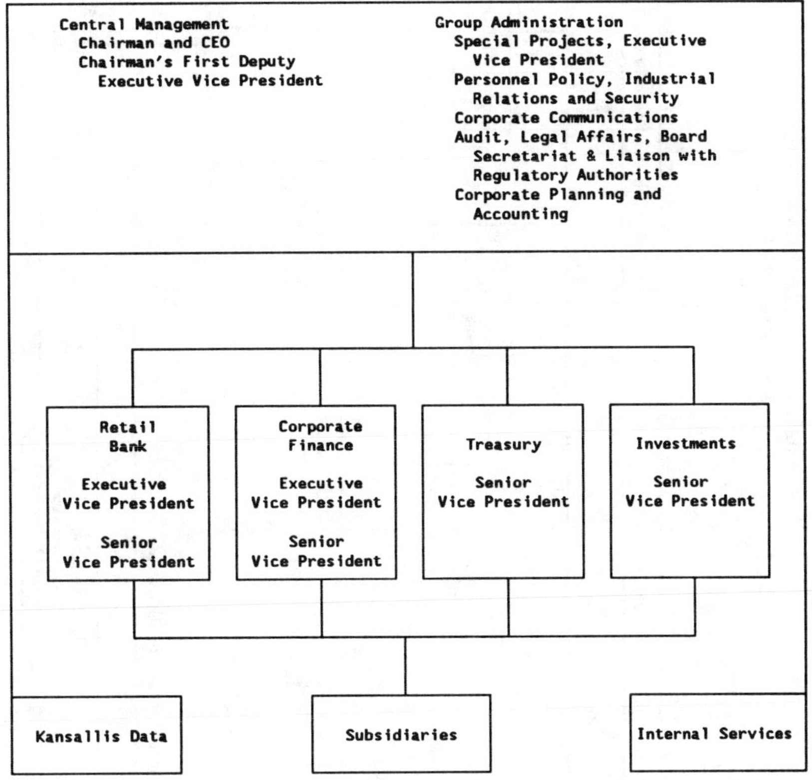

This chart depicts the new corporate structure that was adopted at the beginning of 1991, in which Central Management is assisted by Group Administration.

KAO CORP. (Japan)
PRODUCTION DIVISION

Source: Company update, 1991

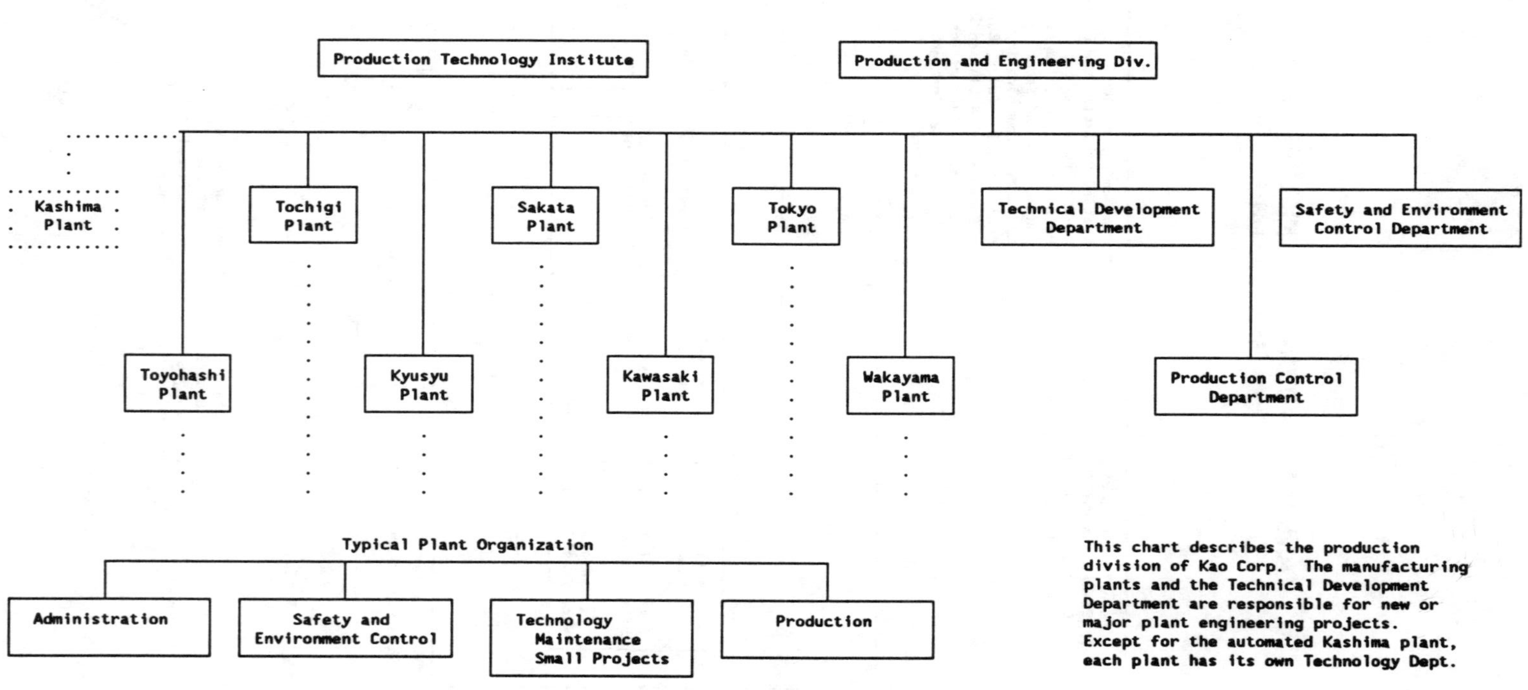

This chart describes the production division of Kao Corp. The manufacturing plants and the Technical Development Department are responsible for new or major plant engineering projects. Except for the automated Kashima plant, each plant has its own Technology Dept.

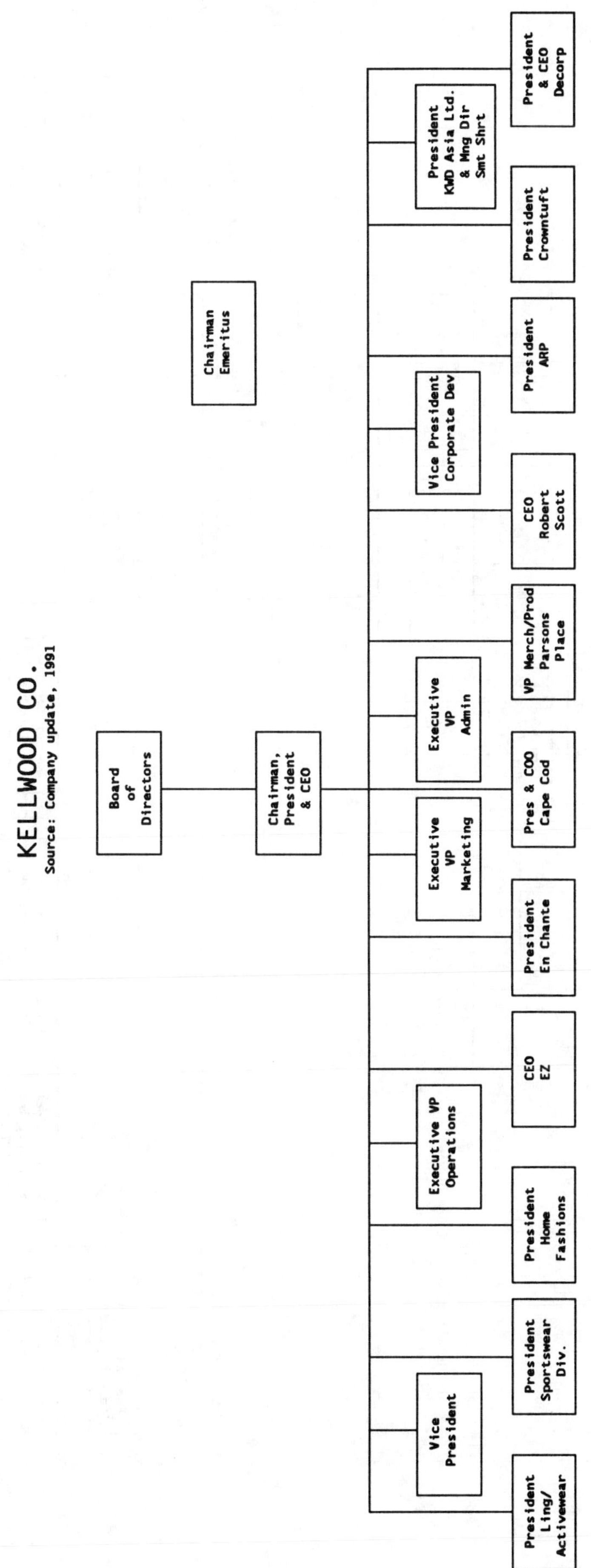
KELLWOOD CO.
Source: Company update, 1991
Board of Directors
Chairman, President & CEO
Chairman Emeritus
Vice President
Executive VP Operations
Executive VP Marketing
Executive VP Admin
Vice President Corporate Dev
President KWD Asia Ltd. & Mng Dir Smt Shrt
President Ling/ Activewear
President Sportswear Div.
President Home Fashions
CEO EZ
President En Chante
Pres & COO Cape Cod
VP Merch/Prod Parsons Place
CEO Robert Scott
President ARP
President Crowntuft
President & CEO Decorp

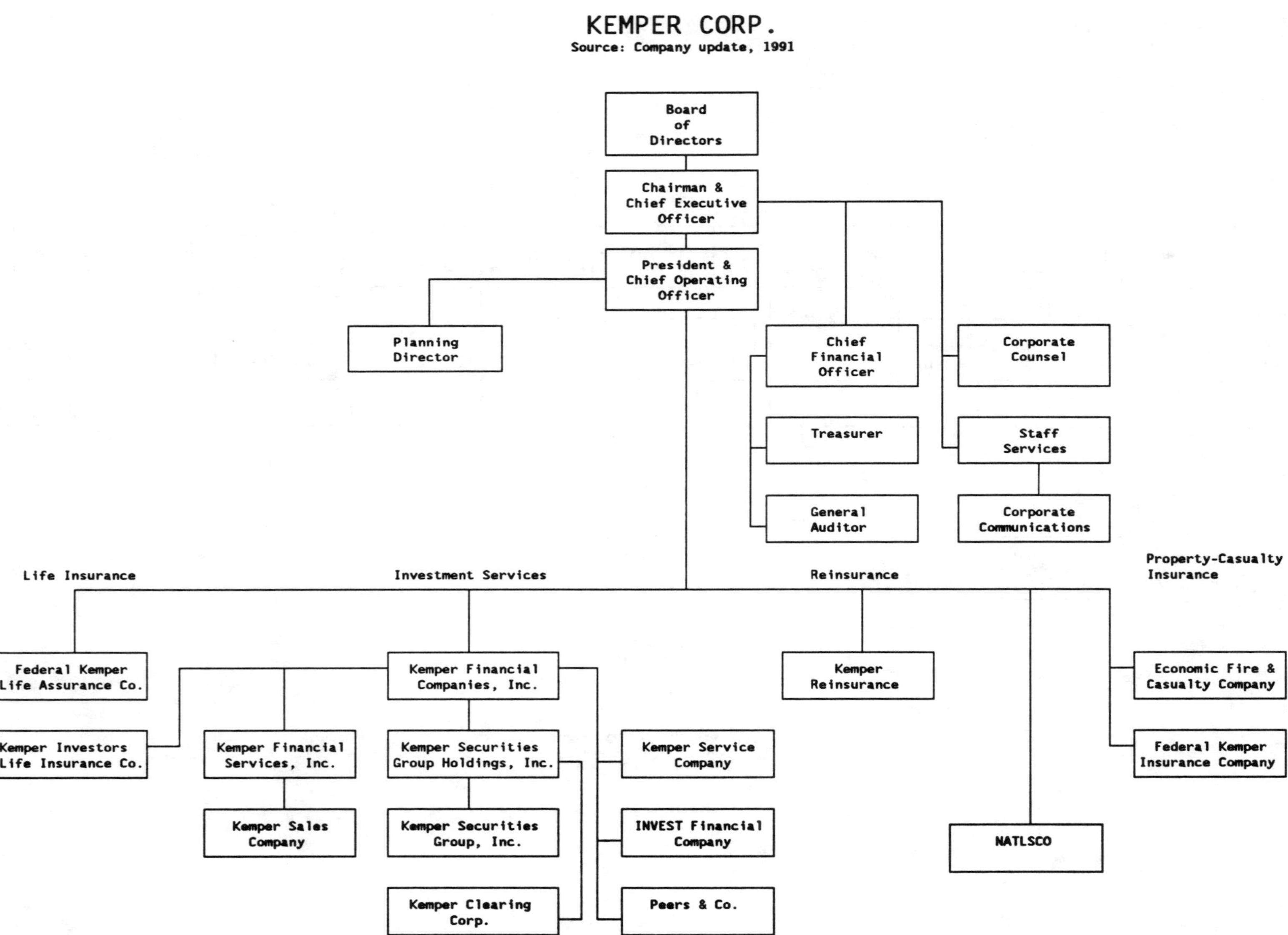
KEMPER CORP.
Source: Company update, 1991
Board of Directors
Chairman & Chief Executive Officer
President & Chief Operating Officer
Planning Director
Chief Financial Officer
Treasurer
General Auditor
Corporate Counsel
Staff Services
Corporate Communications
Life Insurance
Investment Services
Reinsurance
Property-Casualty Insurance
Federal Kemper Life Assurance Co.
Kemper Investors Life Insurance Co.
Kemper Financial Companies, Inc.
Kemper Financial Services, Inc.
Kemper Sales Company
Kemper Securities Group Holdings, Inc.
Kemper Securities Group, Inc.
Kemper Clearing Corp.
Kemper Service Company
INVEST Financial Company
Peers & Co.
Kemper Reinsurance
NATLSCO
Economic Fire & Casualty Company
Federal Kemper Insurance Company

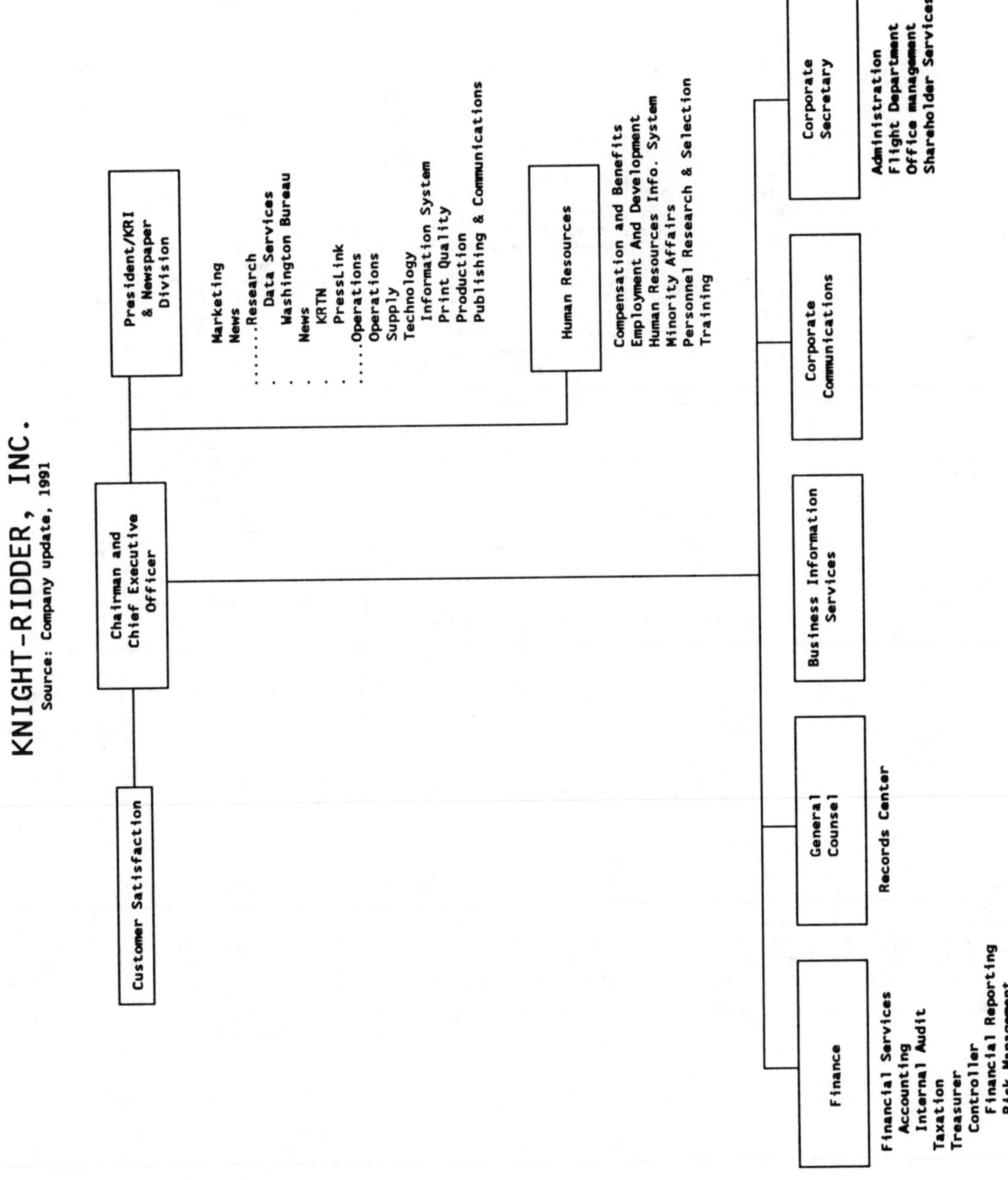
KNIGHT-RIDDER, INC.
Source: Company update, 1991
Customer Satisfaction
Chairman and Chief Executive Officer
President/KRI & Newspaper Division
Marketing
News
Research
Data Services
Washington Bureau
News
KRTN
PressLink
Operations
Operations
Supply
Technology
Information System
Print Quality
Production
Publishing & Communications
Human Resources
Compensation and Benefits
Employment And Development
Human Resources Info. System
Minority Affairs
Personnel Research & Selection
Training
Finance
Financial Services
Accounting
Internal Audit
Taxation
Treasurer
Controller
Financial Reporting
Risk Management
General Counsel
Records Center
Business Information Services
Corporate Communications
Corporate Secretary
Administration
Flight Department
Office management
Shareholder Services

LEGGETT & PLATT INC.

Source: Company update, 1991

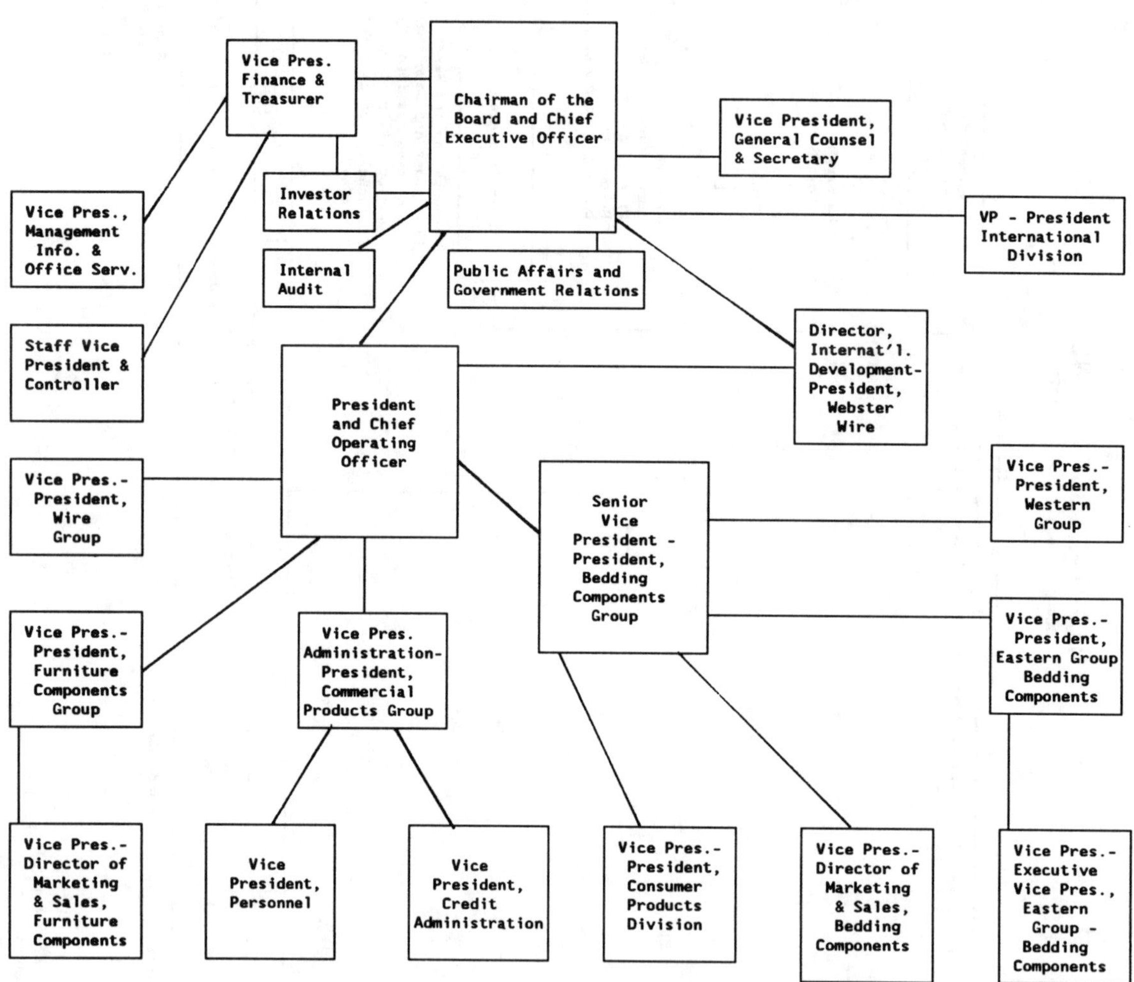

LEX SERVICE PLC (Great Britain)

Source: ELECTRONIC BUSINESS
13: 42+ (June 1, 1987)

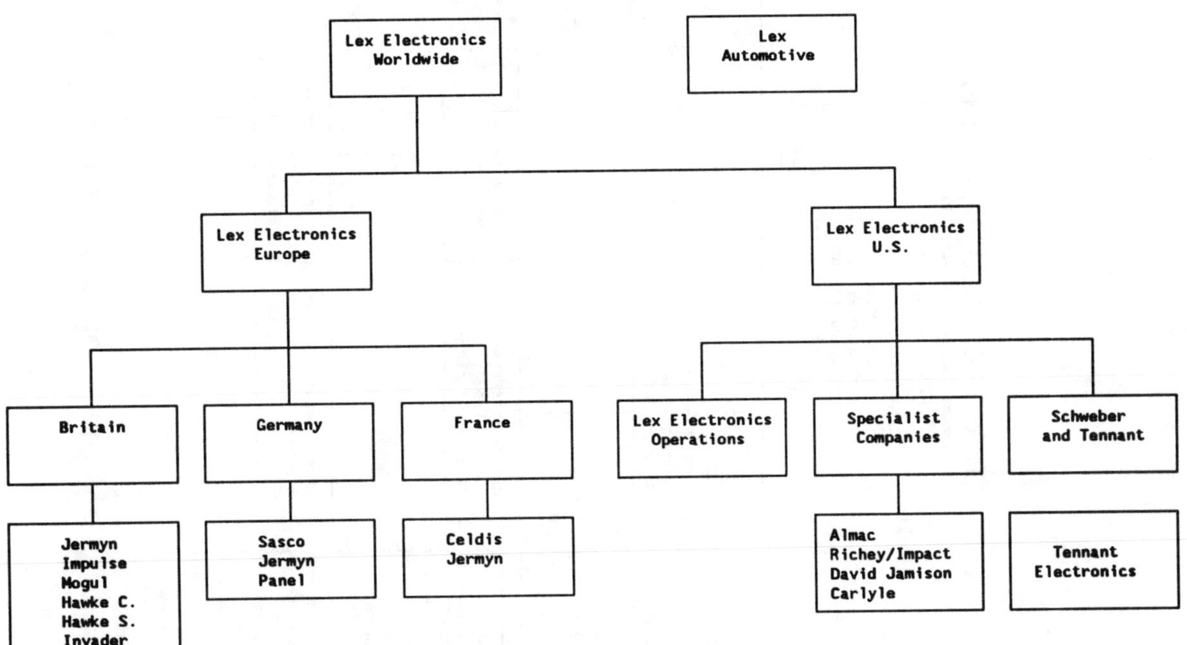

This chart focuses on the electronics distribution business, Lex Electronics, of Lex Service Plc which also has an automotive distribution & leasing line in Britain. While each distributor remains independent as a sales & marketing center, the strategy of Lex Electronics is to combine the logistics & central marketing functions. Lex Electronics Operations (LEO) was set up in the U.S. market to perform this function.

LONE STAR TECHNOLOGIES, INC.

Source: Company update, 1991

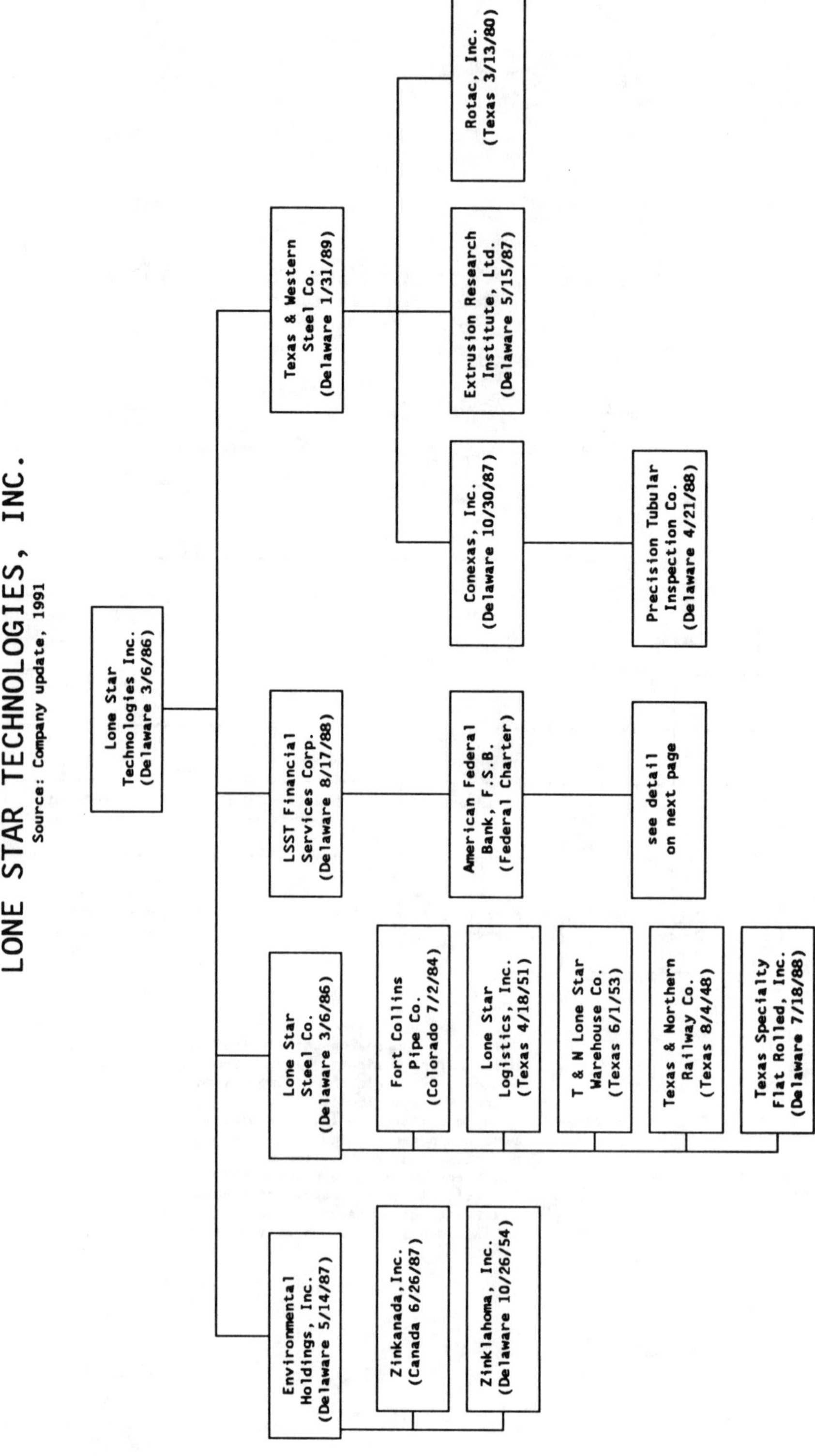

Continued on next page

LONE STAR TECHNOLOGIES INC.
Continued from previous page

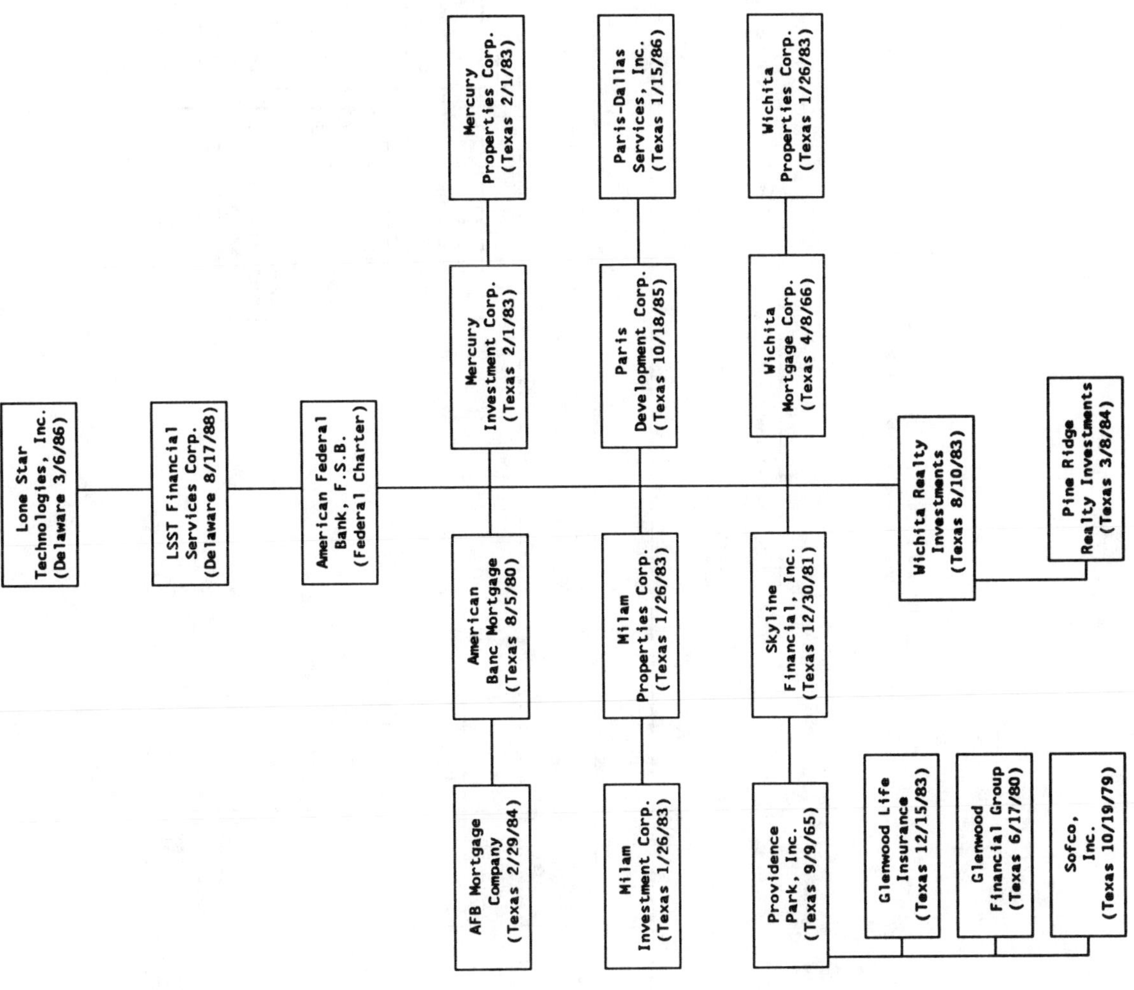
Lone Star Technologies, Inc. (Delaware 3/6/86)
LSST Financial Services Corp. (Delaware 8/17/88)
American Federal Bank, F.S.B. (Federal Charter)
Mercury Investment Corp. (Texas 2/1/83)
Mercury Properties Corp. (Texas 2/1/83)
American Banc Mortgage (Texas 8/5/80)
AFB Mortgage Company (Texas 2/29/84)
Paris Development Corp. (Texas 10/18/85)
Paris-Dallas Services, Inc. (Texas 1/15/86)
Milam Properties Corp. (Texas 1/26/83)
Milam Investment Corp. (Texas 1/26/83)
Wichita Mortgage Corp. (Texas 4/8/66)
Wichita Properties Corp. (Texas 1/26/83)
Skyline Financial, Inc. (Texas 12/30/81)
Providence Park, Inc. (Texas 9/9/65)
Glenwood Life Insurance (Texas 12/15/83)
Glenwood Financial Group (Texas 6/17/80)
Sofco, Inc. (Texas 10/19/79)
Wichita Realty Investments (Texas 8/10/83)
Pine Ridge Realty Investments (Texas 3/8/84)

LONGVIEW FIBRE CO.

Source: Company update, 1991

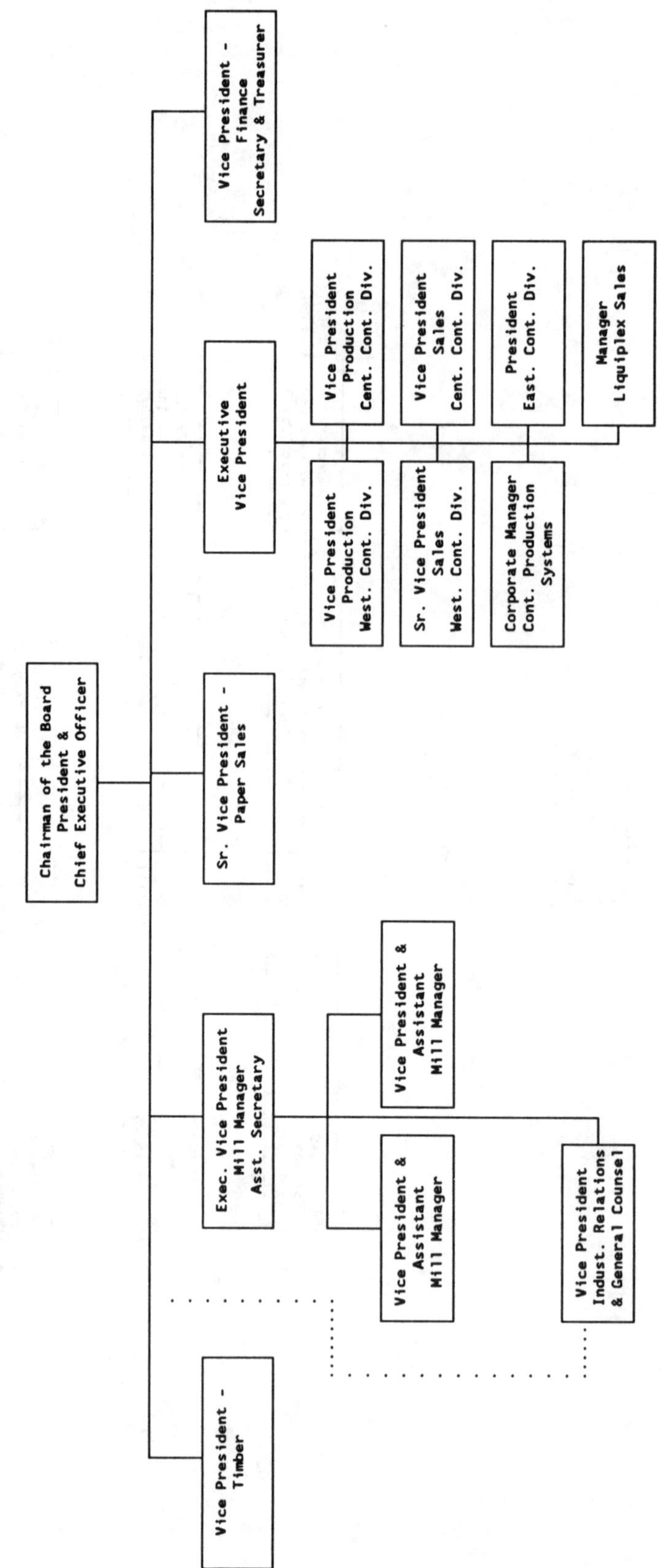

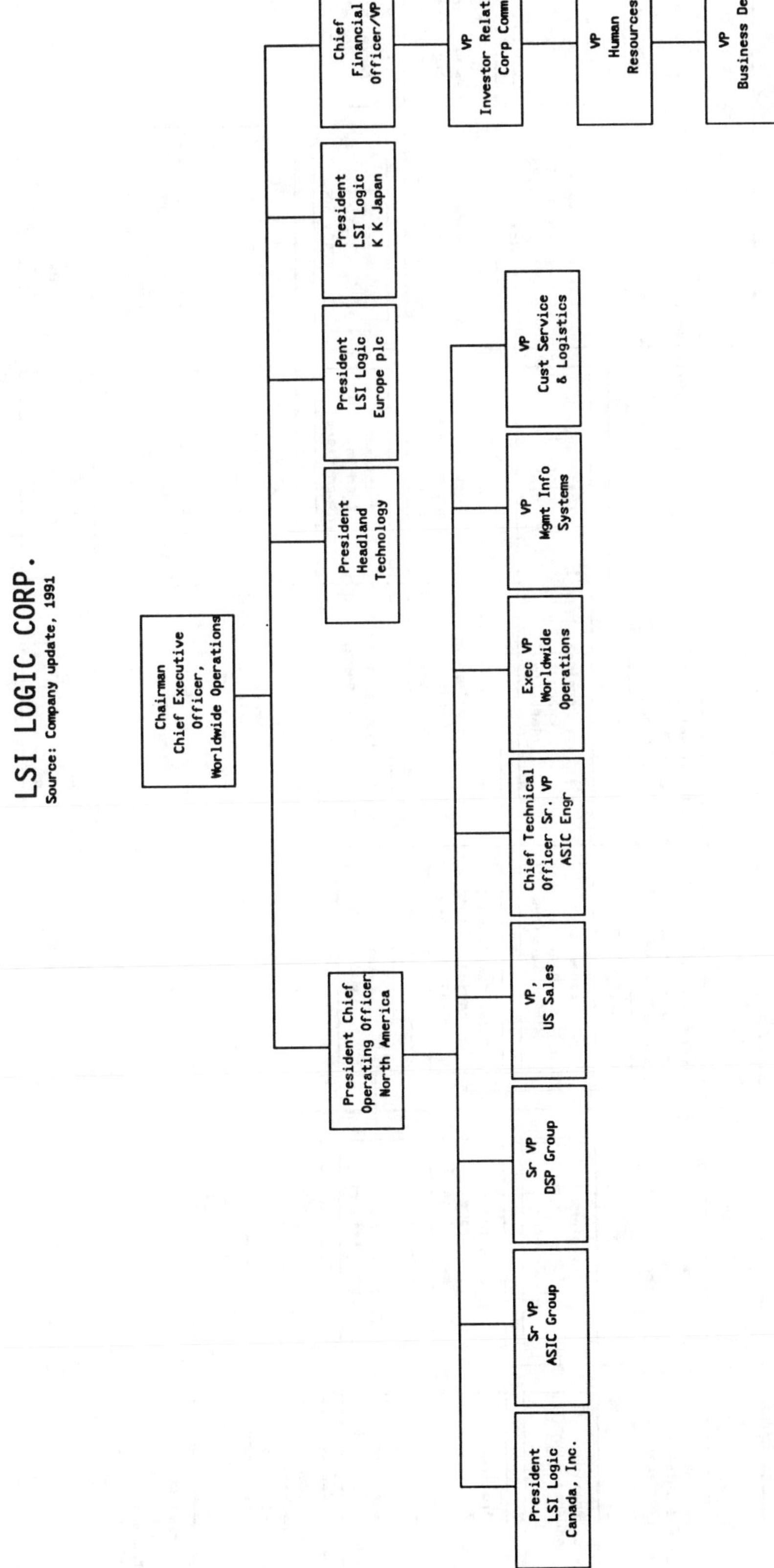
LSI LOGIC CORP.
Source: Company update, 1991
Chairman Chief Executive Officer, Worldwide Operations
President Headland Technology
President LSI Logic Europe plc
President LSI Logic K K Japan
Chief Financial Officer/VP
VP Investor Relations Corp Comm
VP Human Resources
VP Business Dev
President Chief Operating Officer North America
President LSI Logic Canada, Inc.
Sr VP ASIC Group
Sr VP DSP Group
VP, US Sales
Chief Technical Officer Sr. VP ASIC Engr
Exec VP Worldwide Operations
VP Mgmt Info Systems
VP Cust Service & Logistics

M.A. HANNA CO.

Source: Company update, 1991

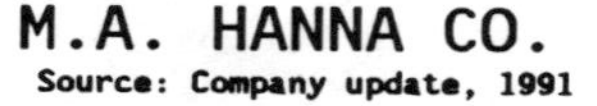

Chairman & CEO
Vice President, Finance & Chief Financial Officer
Vice President and Treasurer
Vice President Taxes
Comptroller
President & GM Hanna Insurance Svs.
President Beneplan Strategies, Inc.
Vice President and Secretary
Assistant General Counsel
Director Corporate Real Estate
Sr. Director Corporate Dev. & Public Affairs
Chief Pilot
Vice President Marine Services & Special Projects
General Manager Marine Services
Chief Executive & Operating Officer Synthecolor, S.A.
Director Internal Audit
President & COO Iron Ore Co. of Canada
Vice President Energy Resources
General Manager Midland Southwest
President & GM Colowyo Coal Company
Director Operating Analysis
Vice President Ore Sales
Controller Iron Ore Company of Canada
President & COO
Chairman Colonial Rubber
President Burton Rubber Processing Inc.
President & GM Day International
General Manager Southwest Chemical Svs.
President Bruck Plastics
President Fiberchem, Inc.
President & CEO Cadillac Plastic Chemical Co.
President PMS Consolidated
President & CEO Avecor, Inc.
President & COO Allied Color Industries, Inc.
Vice President, Total Quality Planning & Technical Serv.
Manager Research & Development
Vice President Human Resources & Industrial Relations
Director Employee Benefits
Dir. Excellence in Hr. Management & Org. Development
Dir., Pay-for-Performance Sys. & Compensation
Office Manager

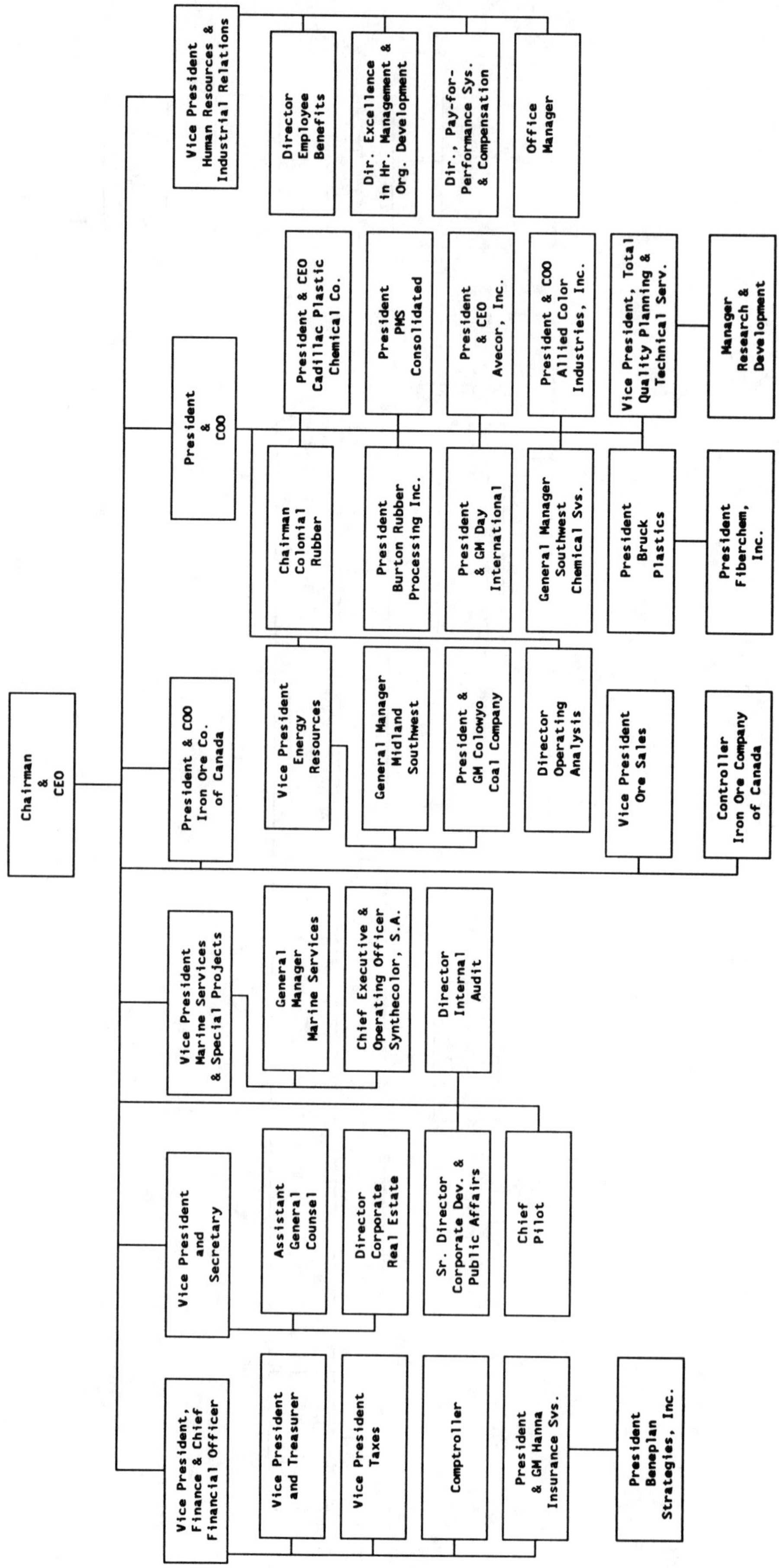

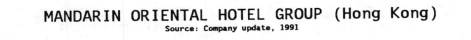

MANDARIN ORIENTAL HOTEL GROUP (Hong Kong)
Source: Company update, 1991
Managing Director

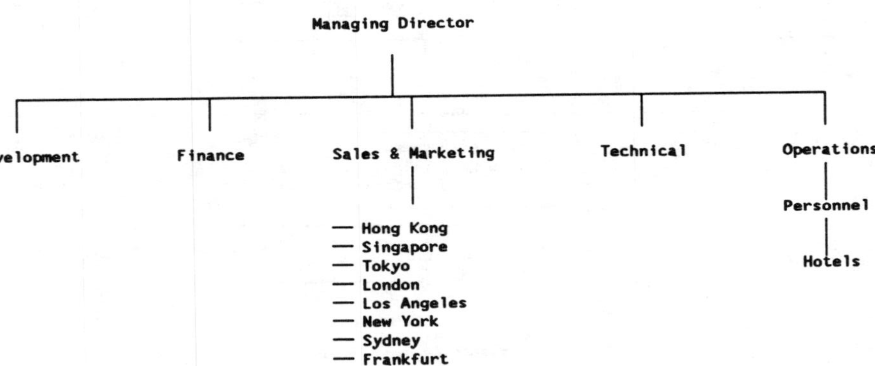
Development
Finance
Sales & Marketing
Technical
Operations
Hong Kong
Singapore
Tokyo
London
Los Angeles
New York
Sydney
Frankfurt
Personnel
Hotels

MARINER HOTEL CORP.

Source: Company update, 1991

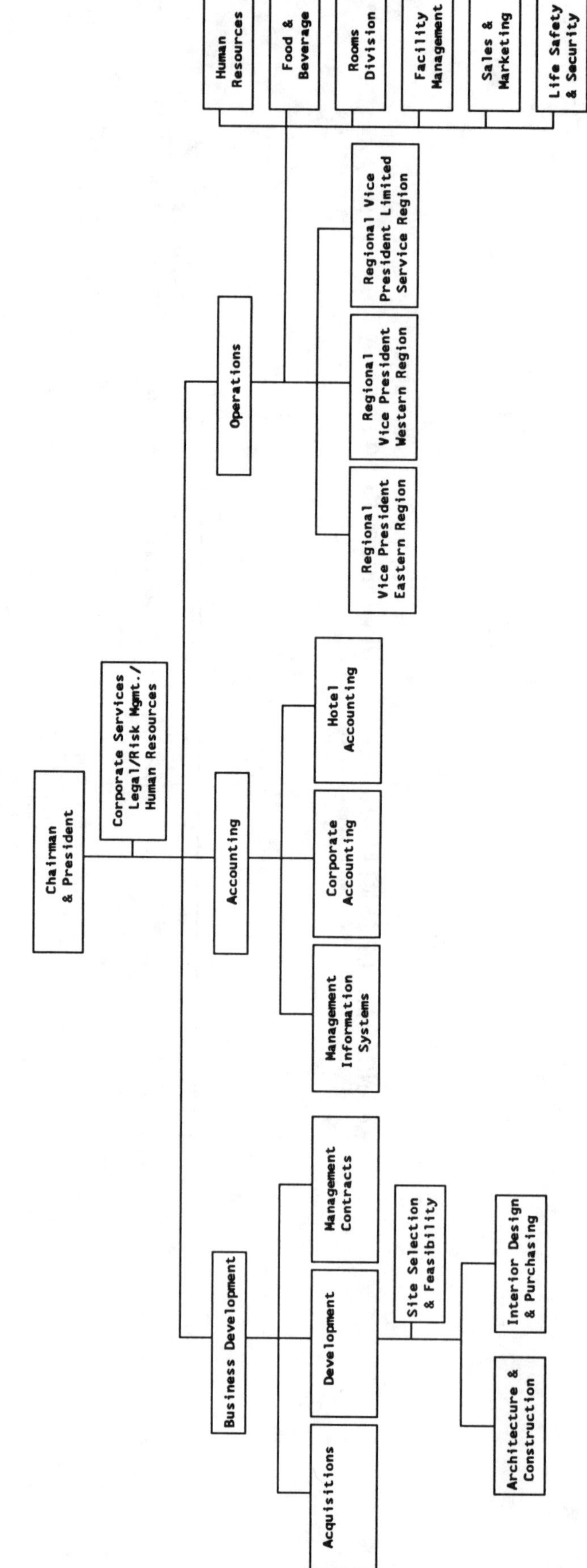

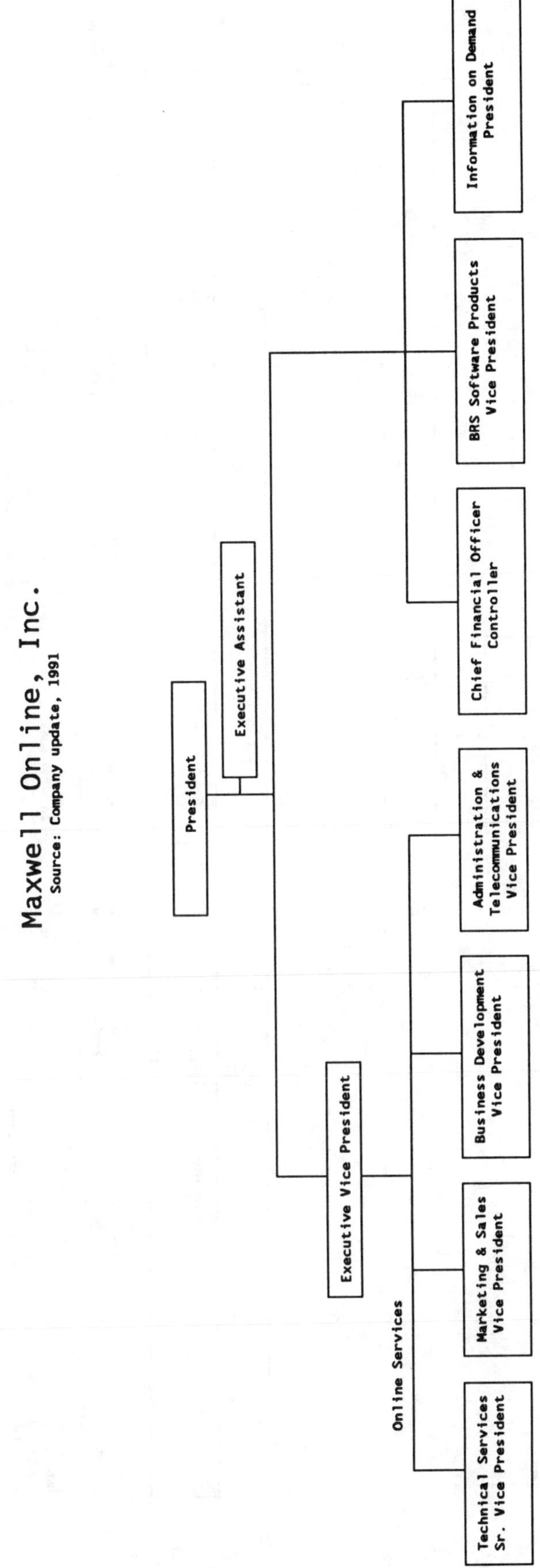
Maxwell Online, Inc.
Source: Company update, 1991
President
Executive Assistant
Executive Vice President
Online Services
Technical Services
Sr. Vice President
Marketing & Sales
Vice President
Business Development
Vice President
Administration &
Telecommunications
Vice President
Chief Financial Officer
Controller
BRS Software Products
Vice President
Information on Demand
President

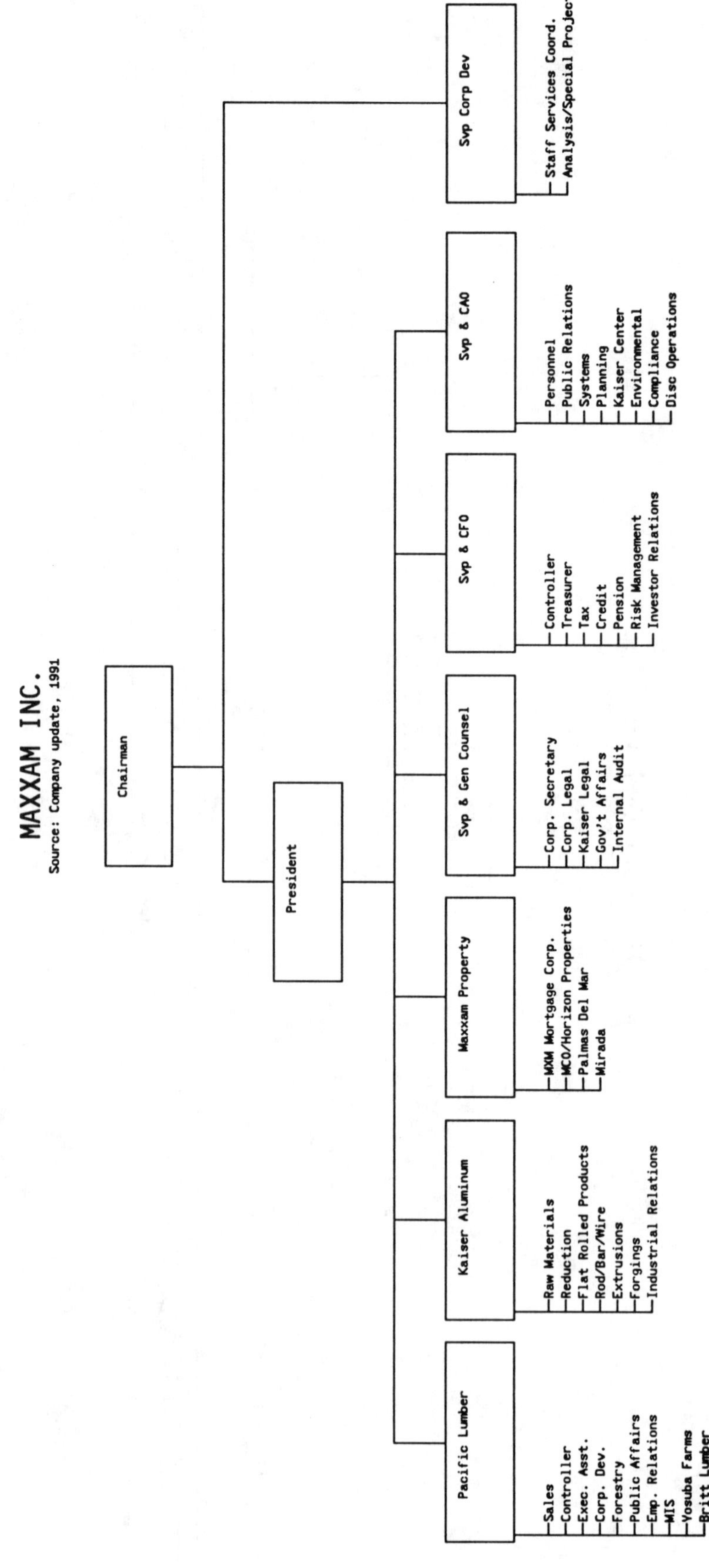
MAXXAM INC.
Source: Company update, 1991
Chairman
President
Svp Corp Dev
Staff Services Coord.
Analysis/Special Projects
Svp & CAO
Personnel
Public Relations
Systems
Planning
Kaiser Center
Environmental
Compliance
Disc Operations
Svp & CFO
Controller
Treasurer
Tax
Credit
Pension
Risk Management
Investor Relations
Svp & Gen Counsel
Corp. Secretary
Corp. Legal
Kaiser Legal
Gov't Affairs
Internal Audit
Maxxam Property
MXM Mortgage Corp.
MCO/Horizon Properties
Palmas Del Mar
Mirada
Kaiser Aluminum
Raw Materials
Reduction
Flat Rolled Products
Rod/Bar/Wire
Extrusions
Forgings
Industrial Relations
Pacific Lumber
Sales
Controller
Exec. Asst.
Corp. Dev.
Forestry
Public Affairs
Emp. Relations
MIS
Yosuba Farms
Britt Lumber

THE MAY INSTITUTE

Source: JOURNAL OF ORGANIZATIONAL BEHAVIORAL MANAGEMENT 5:99+ (Fall/Winter 1983)

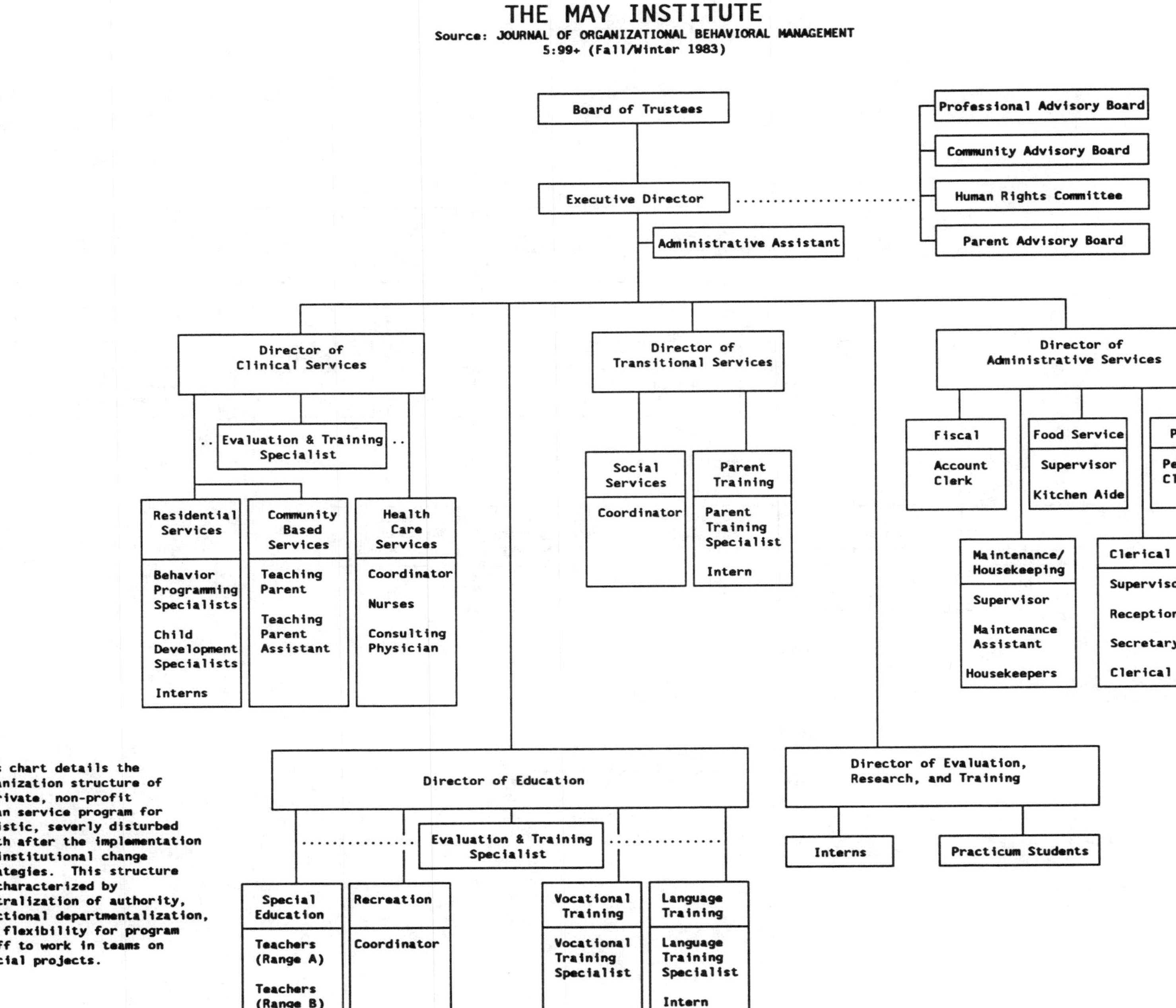

This chart details the organization structure of a private, non-profit human service program for autistic, severly disturbed youth after the implementation of institutional change strategies. This structure is characterized by centralization of authority, functional departmentalization, and flexibility for program staff to work in teams on special projects.

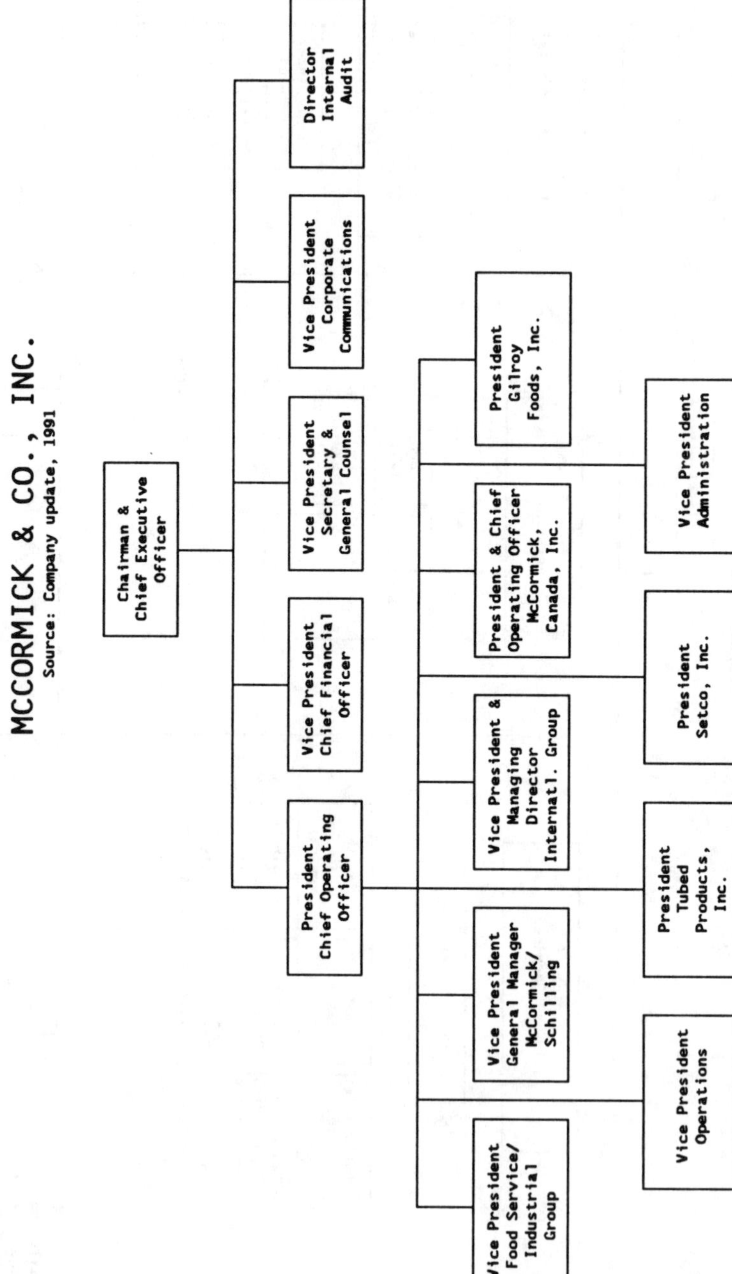
MCCORMICK & CO., INC.
Source: Company update, 1991
Chairman & Chief Executive Officer
President Chief Operating Officer
Vice President Chief Financial Officer
Vice President Secretary & General Counsel
Vice President Corporate Communications
Director Internal Audit
Vice President Food Service/ Industrial Group
Vice President General Manager McCormick/ Schilling
Vice President & Managing Director Internatl. Group
President & Chief Operating Officer McCormick, Canada, Inc.
President Gilroy Foods, Inc.
Vice President Operations
President Tubed Products, Inc.
President Setco, Inc.
Vice President Administration

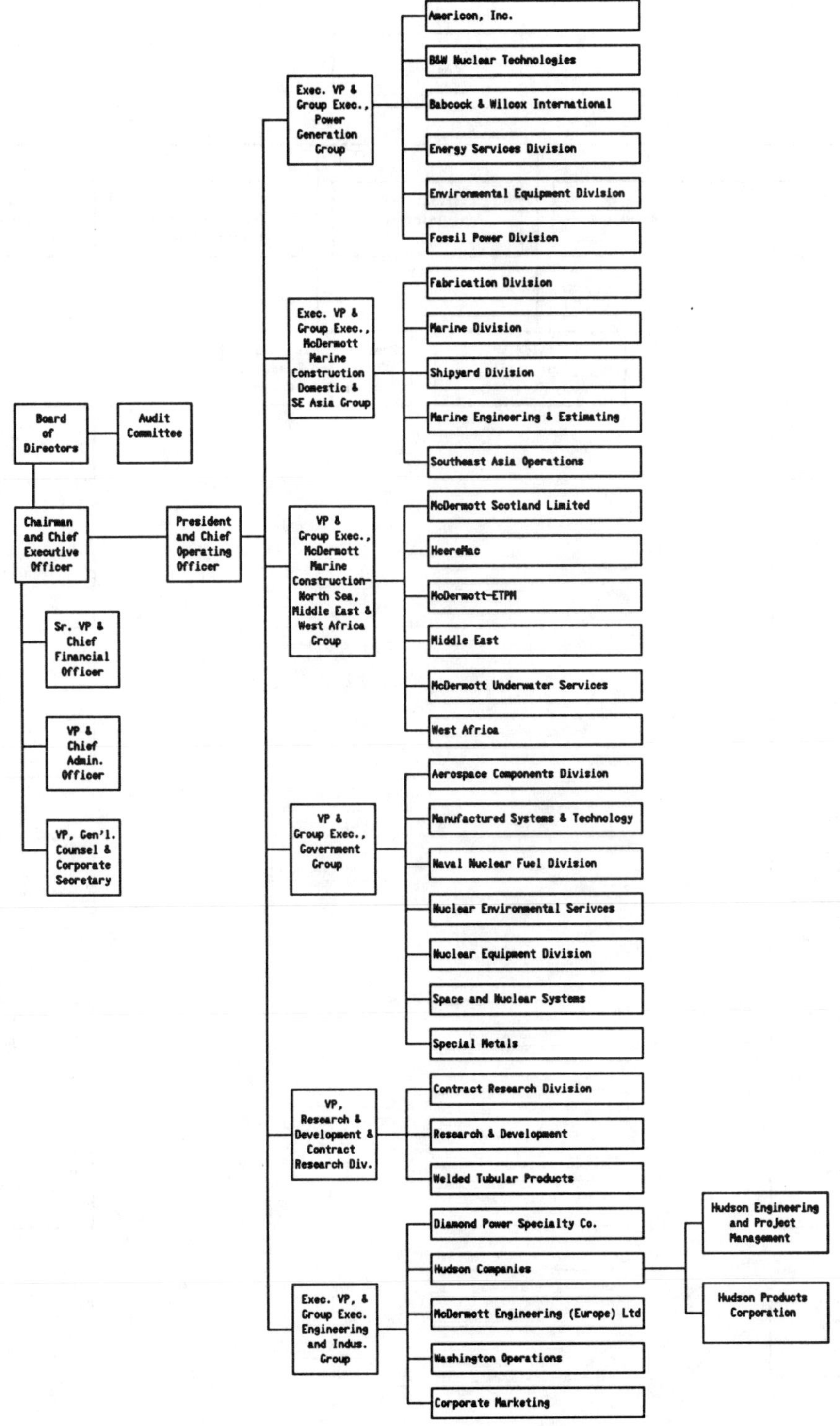
MCDERMOTT INTERNATIONAL, INC.
Source: Company update, 1991
Board of Directors
Audit Committee
Chairman and Chief Executive Officer
President and Chief Operating Officer
Sr. VP & Chief Financial Officer
VP & Chief Admin. Officer
VP, Gen'l. Counsel & Corporate Secretary
Exec. VP & Group Exec., Power Generation Group
Americon, Inc.
B&W Nuclear Technologies
Babcock & Wilcox International
Energy Services Division
Environmental Equipment Division
Fossil Power Division
Exec. VP & Group Exec., McDermott Marine Construction Domestic & SE Asia Group
Fabrication Division
Marine Division
Shipyard Division
Marine Engineering & Estimating
Southeast Asia Operations
VP & Group Exec., McDermott Marine Construction-North Sea, Middle East & West Africa Group
McDermott Scotland Limited
HeereMac
McDermott-ETPM
Middle East
McDermott Underwater Services
West Africa
VP & Group Exec., Government Group
Aerospace Components Division
Manufactured Systems & Technology
Naval Nuclear Fuel Division
Nuclear Environmental Serivces
Nuclear Equipment Division
Space and Nuclear Systems
Special Metals
VP, Research & Development & Contract Research Div.
Contract Research Division
Research & Development
Welded Tubular Products
Exec. VP, & Group Exec. Engineering and Indus. Group
Diamond Power Specialty Co.
Hudson Companies
McDermott Engineering (Europe) Ltd
Washington Operations
Corporate Marketing
Hudson Engineering and Project Management
Hudson Products Corporation

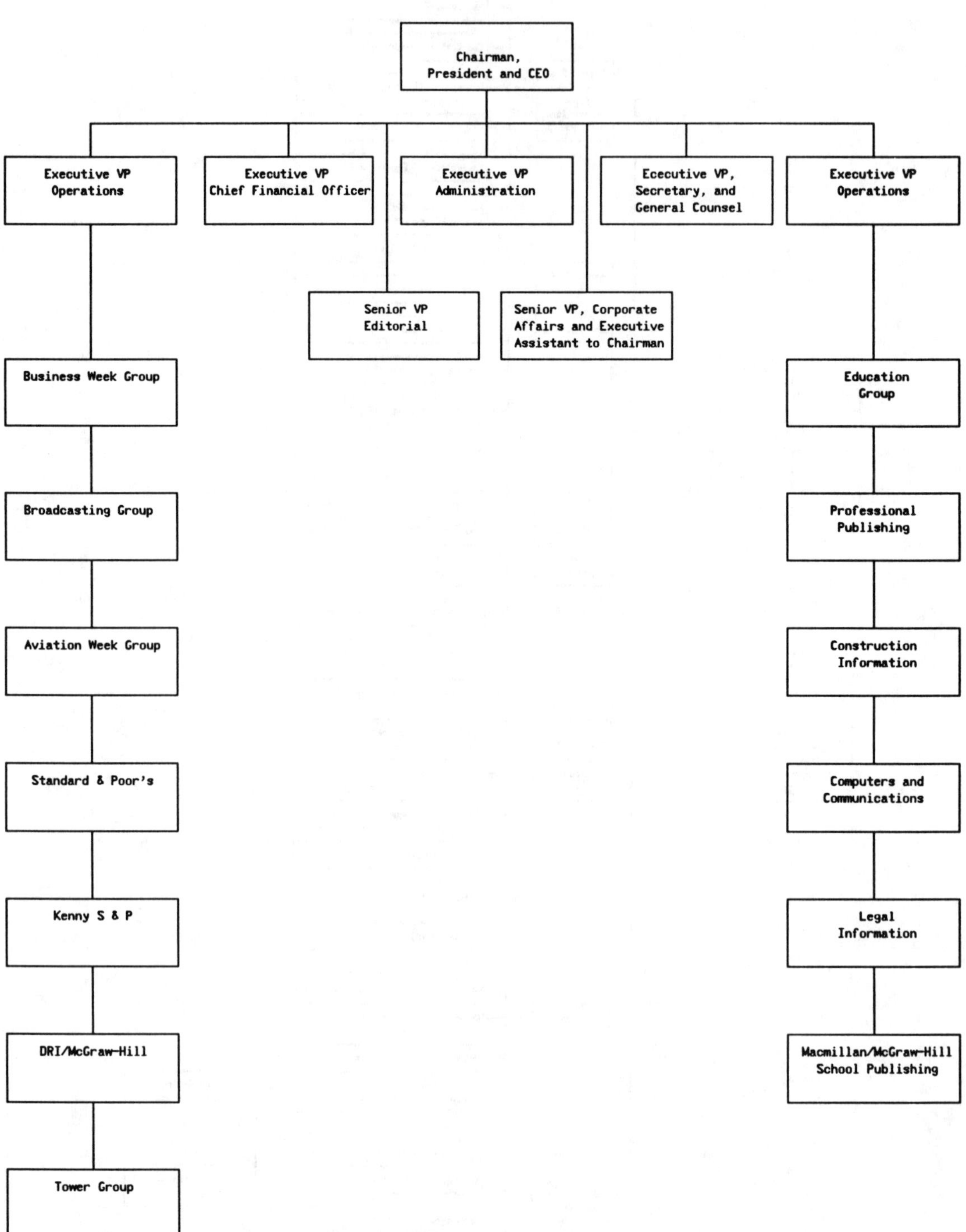
MCGRAW-HILL, INC.
Source: Company update, 1991
Chairman, President and CEO
Executive VP Operations
Executive VP Chief Financial Officer
Executive VP Administration
Ececutive VP, Secretary, and General Counsel
Executive VP Operations
Senior VP Editorial
Senior VP, Corporate Affairs and Executive Assistant to Chairman
Business Week Group
Broadcasting Group
Aviation Week Group
Standard & Poor's
Kenny S & P
DRI/McGraw-Hill
Tower Group
Education Group
Professional Publishing
Construction Information
Computers and Communications
Legal Information
Macmillan/McGraw-Hill School Publishing

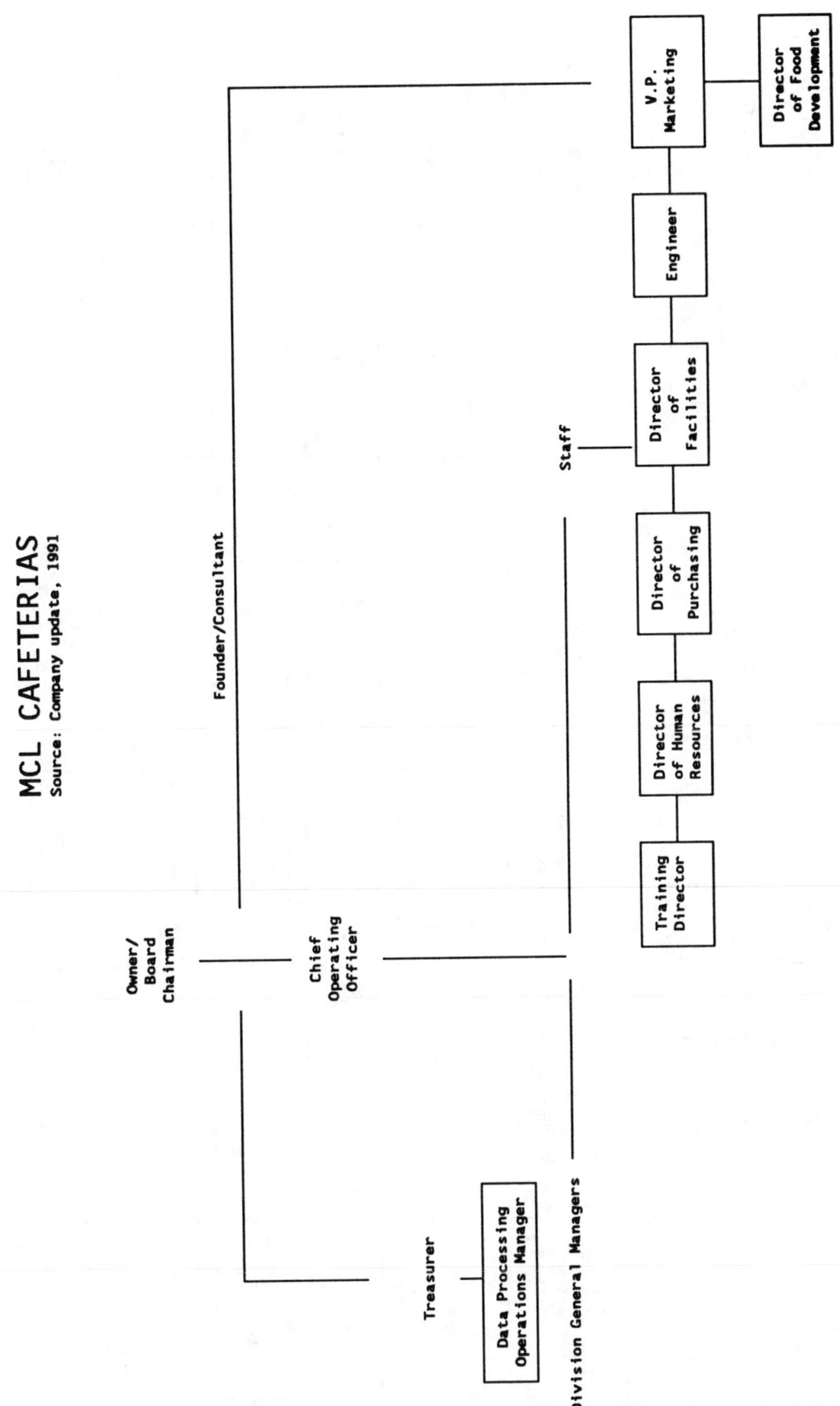
MCL CAFETERIAS
Source: Company update, 1991
Owner/ Board Chairman
Founder/Consultant
Treasurer
Data Processing Operations Manager
Chief Operating Officer
Staff
Division General Managers
Training Director
Director of Human Resources
Director of Purchasing
Director of Facilities
Engineer
V.P. Marketing
Director of Food Development

MERRILL LYNCH AND CO., INC.

Source: LONGE RANGE PLANNING
23: 27 (April 1990)

- Global System
  - Application Services
    - Structured Envir. Arch.
    - Corporate Data Platform
    - Structured Envir. Devel.
  - Strategic Business Systems
  - Admin/Par
  - International
    - London
    - Toronto
    - Tokyo
    - Asia/Pacific
  - Secur. Proc Syst. Group
    - Trades & Clearing
    - Finc'l./ Admin.
    - Custody Proc.
    - Secur. Proc.
    - Global Cust.
    - Global Secur.
    - Finc'l Svc.
- Capital Mkts Syst. (dashed line to CMG Mgmt.)
  - Equity
    - Equity
    - Trading Tech Support
    - FX
  - Fixed Income
    - Gov't. Secur./ Money Mkts.
    - Mtg. Backed/ Futures
    - Munis/ Mert
  - Computer Analytics
    - Analytics
    - Institutional
    - Infoshare
    - IBK
    - Branch Office Automation
  - SISD/SIOD
  - CMG Telecomm
- CMG Mgmt.

The Information Systems Division (Global System) is housed within the Operations System and Telecommunications Sector, one of five major groups within Merril Lynch.

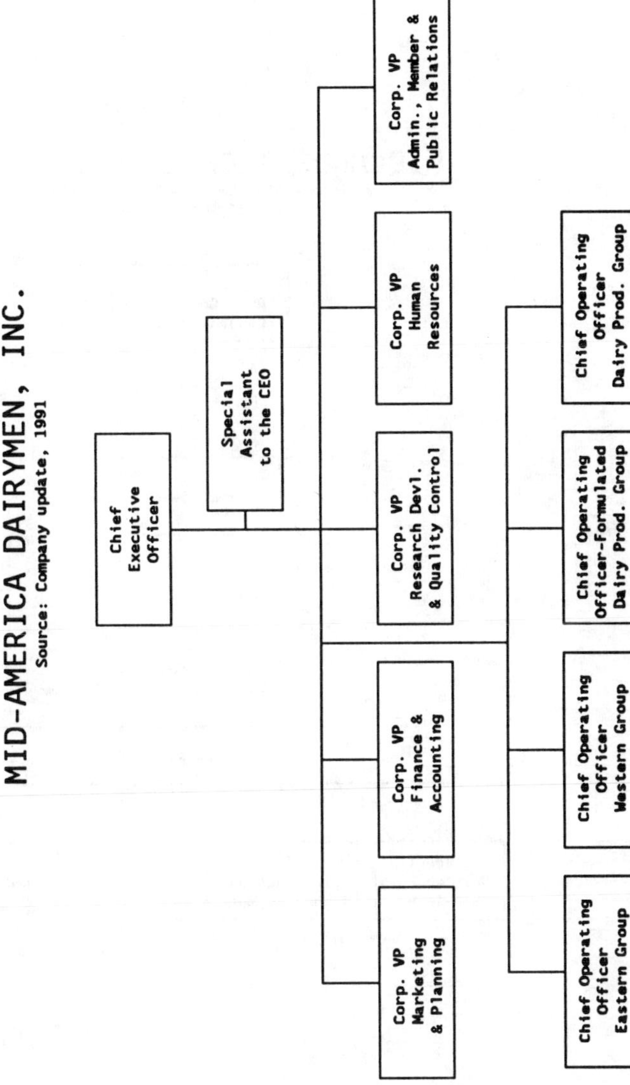
MID-AMERICA DAIRYMEN, INC.
Source: Company update, 1991
Chief Executive Officer
Special Assistant to the CEO
Corp. VP Marketing & Planning
Corp. VP Finance & Accounting
Corp. VP Research Devl. & Quality Control
Corp. VP Human Resources
Corp. VP Admin., Member & Public Relations
Chief Operating Officer Eastern Group
Chief Operating Officer Western Group
Chief Operating Officer-Formulated Dairy Prod. Group
Chief Operating Officer Dairy Prod. Group

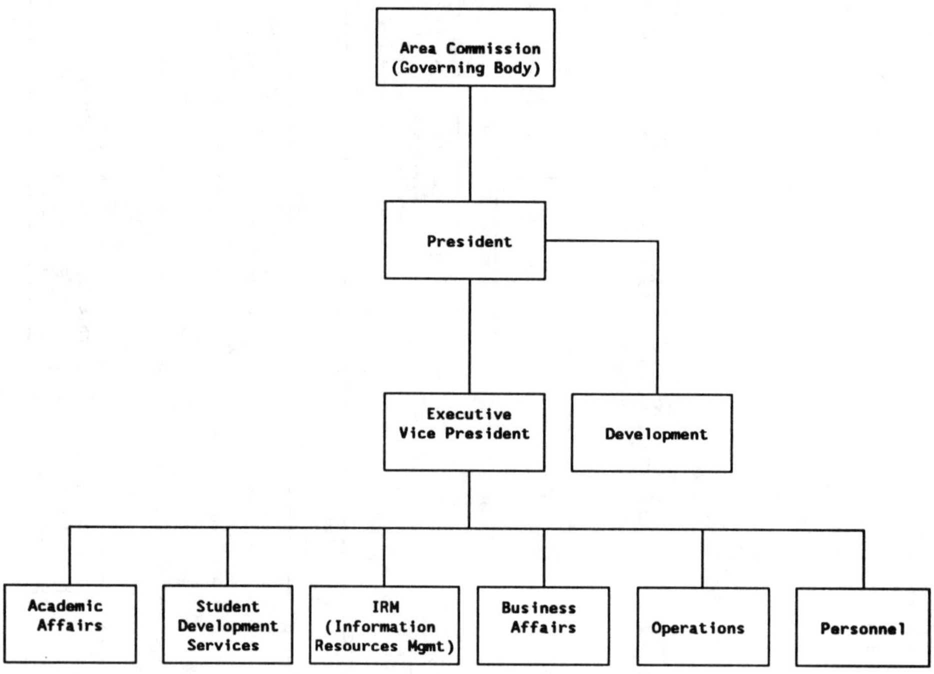
MIDLANDS TECHNICAL COLLEGE
Source: INFORMATION MGMT. REVIEW
1: 9-22 (Winter 1986)
Area Commission
(Governing Body)
President
Executive
Vice President
Development
Academic
Affairs
Student
Development
Services
IRM
(Information
Resources Mgmt)
Business
Affairs
Operations
Personnel

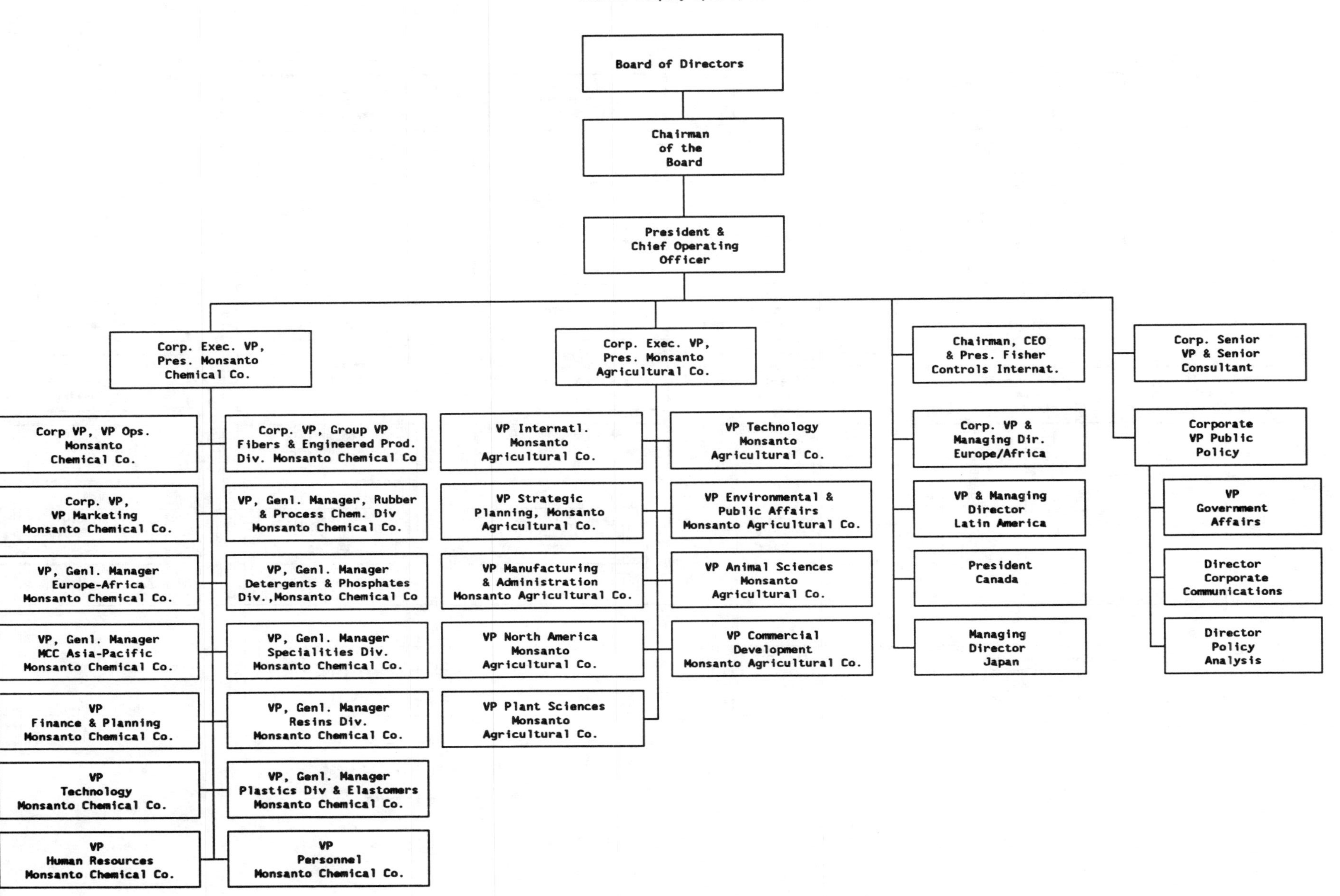
MONSANTO CO.
Source: Company update, 1991
Board of Directors
Chairman of the Board
President & Chief Operating Officer
Corp. Exec. VP, Pres. Monsanto Chemical Co.
Corp VP, VP Ops. Monsanto Chemical Co.
Corp. VP, VP Marketing Monsanto Chemical Co.
VP, Genl. Manager Europe-Africa Monsanto Chemical Co.
VP, Genl. Manager MCC Asia-Pacific Monsanto Chemical Co.
VP Finance & Planning Monsanto Chemical Co.
VP Technology Monsanto Chemical Co.
VP Human Resources Monsanto Chemical Co.
Corp. VP, Group VP Fibers & Engineered Prod. Div. Monsanto Chemical Co
VP, Genl. Manager, Rubber & Process Chem. Div Monsanto Chemical Co.
VP, Genl. Manager Detergents & Phosphates Div.,Monsanto Chemical Co
VP, Genl. Manager Specialities Div. Monsanto Chemical Co.
VP, Genl. Manager Resins Div. Monsanto Chemical Co.
VP, Genl. Manager Plastics Div & Elastomers Monsanto Chemical Co.
VP Personnel Monsanto Chemical Co.
Corp. Exec. VP, Pres. Monsanto Agricultural Co.
VP Internatl. Monsanto Agricultural Co.
VP Strategic Planning, Monsanto Agricultural Co.
VP Manufacturing & Administration Monsanto Agricultural Co.
VP North America Monsanto Agricultural Co.
VP Plant Sciences Monsanto Agricultural Co.
VP Technology Monsanto Agricultural Co.
VP Environmental & Public Affairs Monsanto Agricultural Co.
VP Animal Sciences Monsanto Agricultural Co.
VP Commercial Development Monsanto Agricultural Co.
Chairman, CEO & Pres. Fisher Controls Internat.
Corp. VP & Managing Dir. Europe/Africa
VP & Managing Director Latin America
President Canada
Managing Director Japan
Corp. Senior VP & Senior Consultant
Corporate VP Public Policy
VP Government Affairs
Director Corporate Communications
Director Policy Analysis

Continued on next page

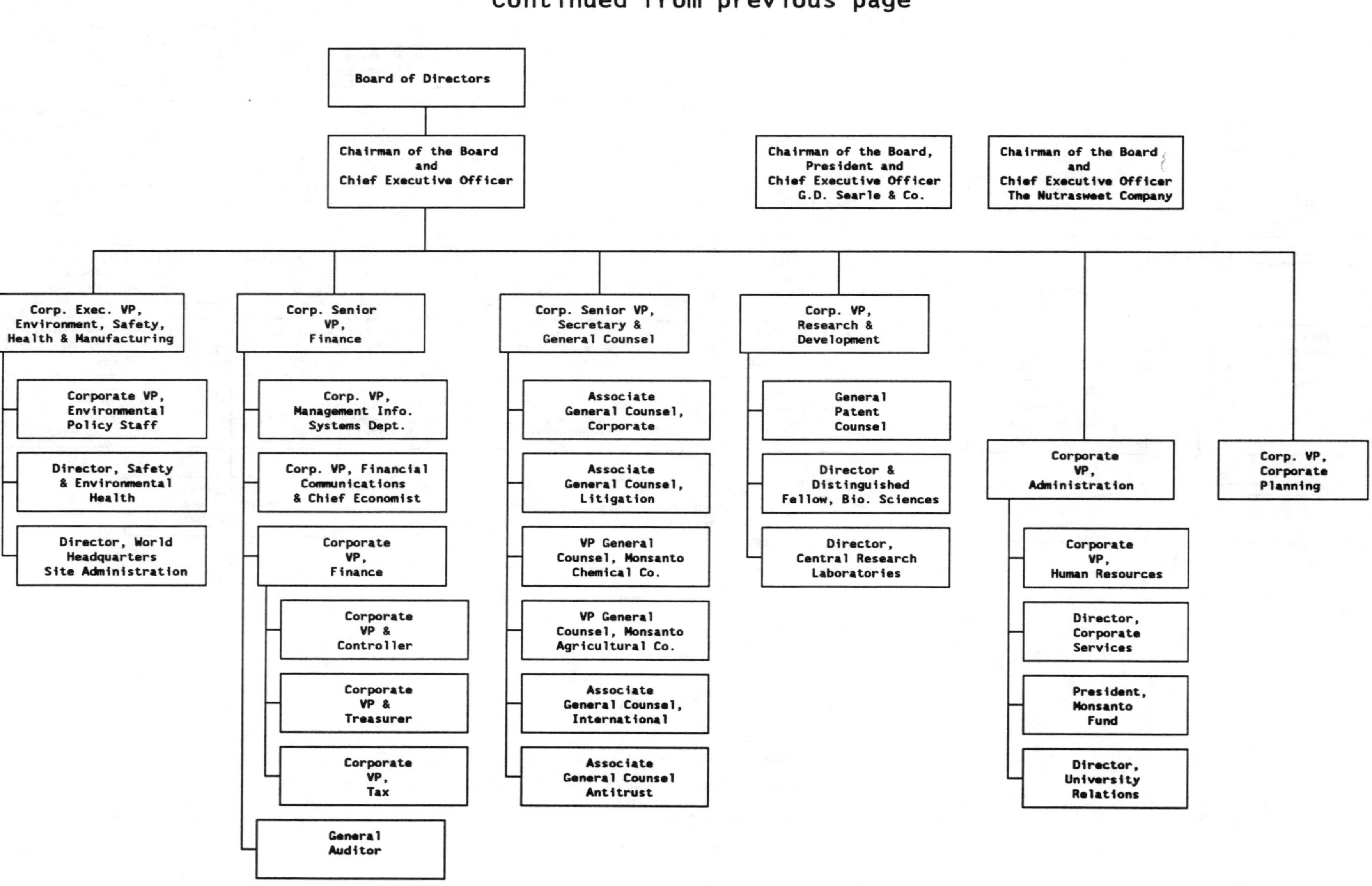
MONSANTO CO.
Continued from previous page
Board of Directors
Chairman of the Board and Chief Executive Officer
Chairman of the Board, President and Chief Executive Officer G.D. Searle & Co.
Chairman of the Board and Chief Executive Officer The Nutrasweet Company
Corp. Exec. VP, Environment, Safety, Health & Manufacturing
Corporate VP, Environmental Policy Staff
Director, Safety & Environmental Health
Director, World Headquarters Site Administration
Corp. Senior VP, Finance
Corp. VP, Management Info. Systems Dept.
Corp. VP, Financial Communications & Chief Economist
Corporate VP, Finance
Corporate VP & Controller
Corporate VP & Treasurer
Corporate VP, Tax
General Auditor
Corp. Senior VP, Secretary & General Counsel
Associate General Counsel, Corporate
Associate General Counsel, Litigation
VP General Counsel, Monsanto Chemical Co.
VP General Counsel, Monsanto Agricultural Co.
Associate General Counsel, International
Associate General Counsel Antitrust
Corp. VP, Research & Development
General Patent Counsel
Director & Distinguished Fellow, Bio. Sciences
Director, Central Research Laboratories
Corporate VP, Administration
Corporate VP, Human Resources
Director, Corporate Services
President, Monsanto Fund
Director, University Relations
Corp. VP, Corporate Planning

MURPHY OIL CORP. & SUBSIDIARIES

Source: Company update, 1991

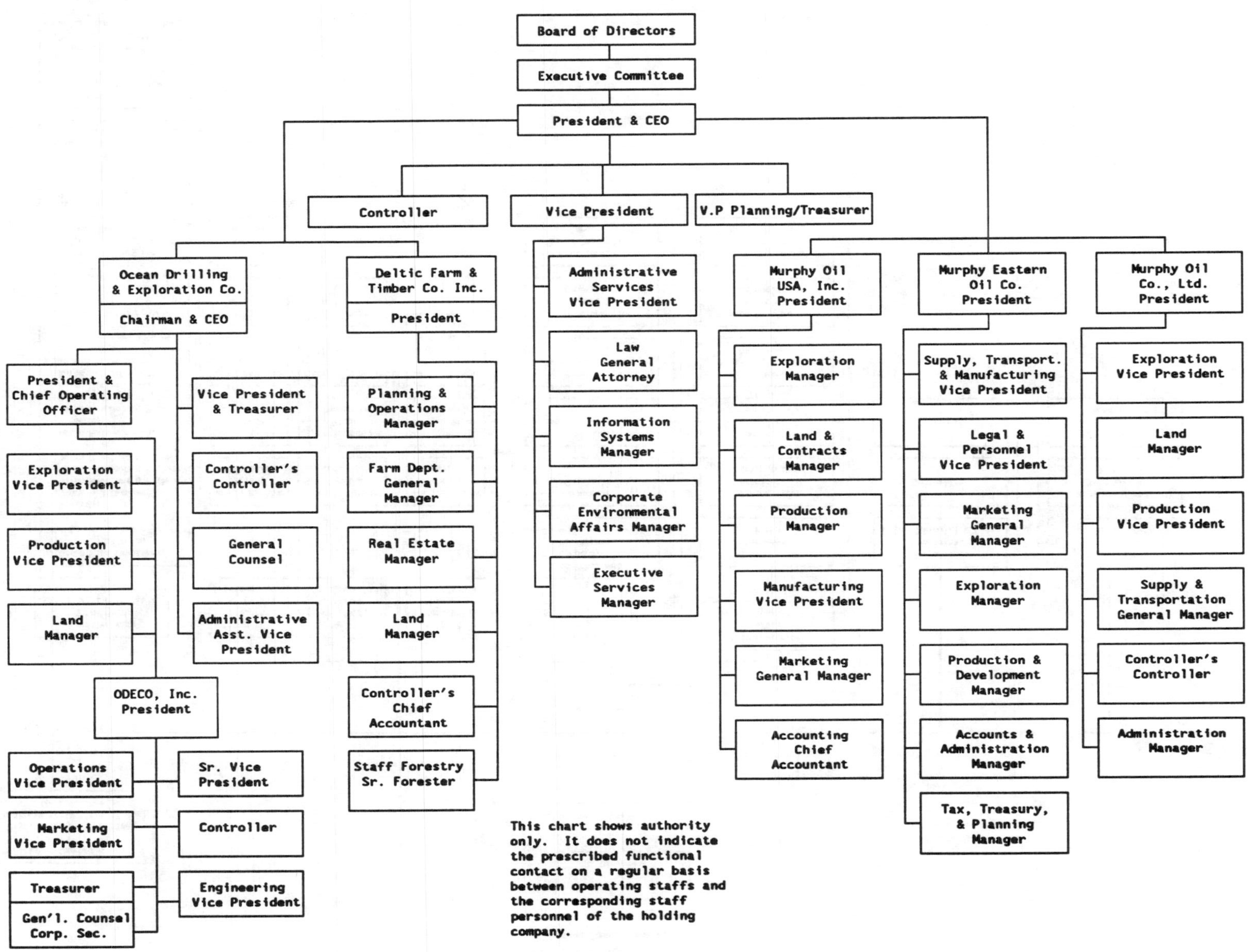

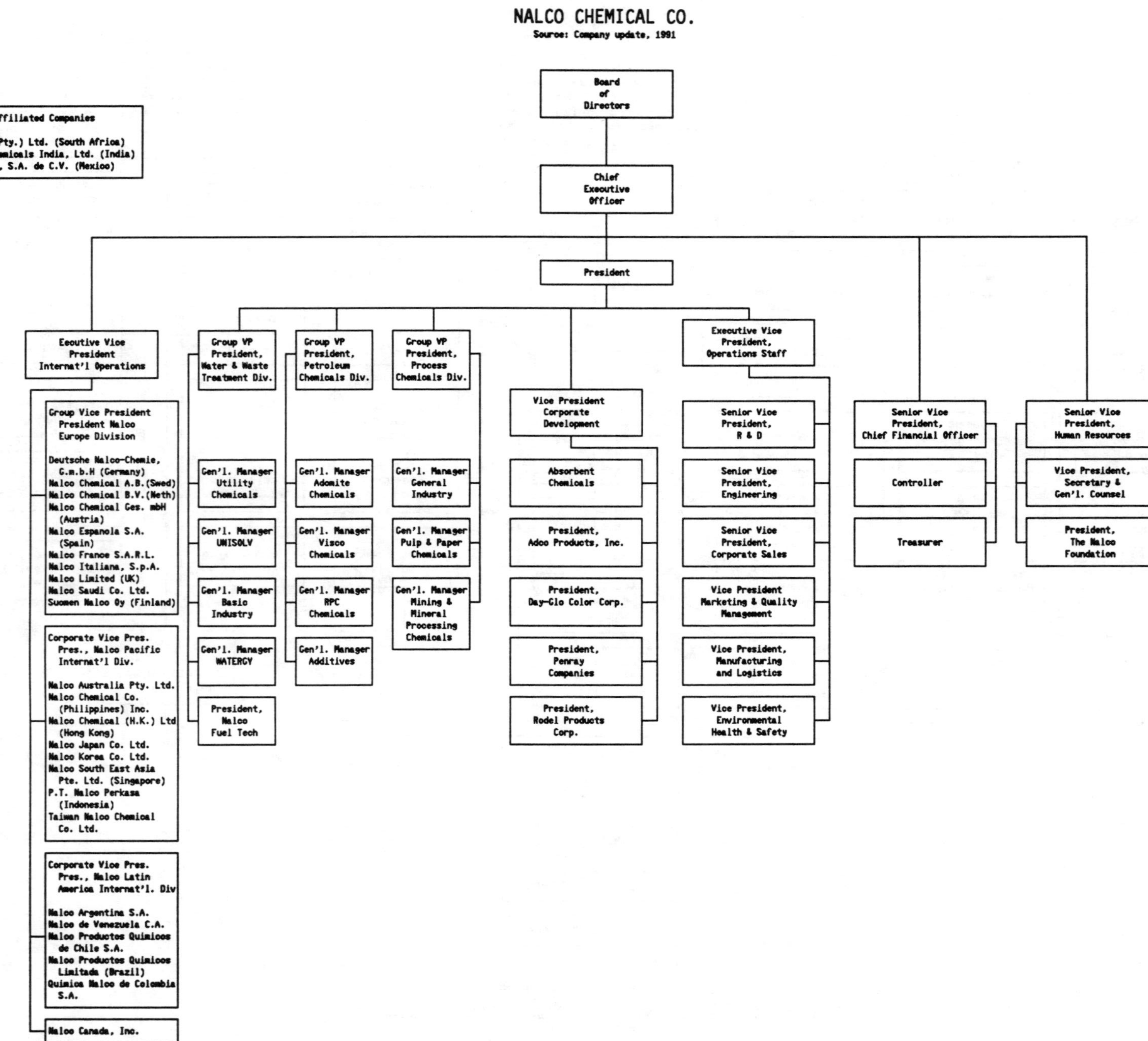
NALCO CHEMICAL CO.
Source: Company update, 1991
Affiliated Companies
Anikem (Pty.) Ltd. (South Africa)
Nalco Chemicals India, Ltd. (India)
Nalcomex, S.A. de C.V. (Mexico)
Board of Directors
Chief Executive Officer
President
Eecutive Vice President Internat'l Operations
Group Vice President President Nalco Europe Division
Deutsche Nalco-Chemie, G.m.b.H (Germany)
Nalco Chemical A.B.(Swed)
Nalco Chemical B.V.(Neth)
Nalco Chemical Ges. mbH (Austria)
Nalco Espanola S.A. (Spain)
Nalco France S.A.R.L.
Nalco Italiana, S.p.A.
Nalco Limited (UK)
Nalco Saudi Co. Ltd.
Suomen Nalco Oy (Finland)
Corporate Vice Pres. Pres., Nalco Pacific Internat'l Div.
Nalco Australia Pty. Ltd.
Nalco Chemical Co. (Philippines) Inc.
Nalco Chemical (H.K.) Ltd (Hong Kong)
Nalco Japan Co. Ltd.
Nalco Korea Co. Ltd.
Nalco South East Asia Pte. Ltd. (Singapore)
P.T. Nalco Perkasa (Indonesia)
Taiwan Nalco Chemical Co. Ltd.
Corporate Vice Pres. Pres., Nalco Latin America Internat'l. Div
Nalco Argentina S.A.
Nalco de Venezuela C.A.
Nalco Productos Quimicos de Chile S.A.
Nalco Productos Quimicos Limitada (Brazil)
Quimica Nalco de Colombia S.A.
Nalco Canada, Inc.
Group VP President, Water & Waste Treatment Div.
Gen'l. Manager Utility Chemicals
Gen'l. Manager UNISOLV
Gen'l. Manager Basic Industry
Gen'l. Manager WATERGY
President, Nalco Fuel Tech
Group VP President, Petroleum Chemicals Div.
Gen'l. Manager Adomite Chemicals
Gen'l. Manager Visco Chemicals
Gen'l. Manager RPC Chemicals
Gen'l. Manager Additives
Group VP President, Process Chemicals Div.
Gen'l. Manager General Industry
Gen'l. Manager Pulp & Paper Chemicals
Gen'l. Manager Mining & Mineral Processing Chemicals
Vice President Corporate Development
Absorbent Chemicals
President, Adco Products, Inc.
President, Day-Glo Color Corp.
President, Penray Companies
President, Rodel Products Corp.
Executive Vice President, Operations Staff
Senior Vice President, R & D
Senior Vice President, Engineering
Senior Vice President, Corporate Sales
Vice President Marketing & Quality Management
Vice President, Manufacturing and Logistics
Vice President, Environmental Health & Safety
Senior Vice President, Chief Financial Officer
Controller
Treasurer
Senior Vice President, Human Resources
Vice President, Secretary & Gen'l. Counsel
President, The Nalco Foundation

NATIONAL CITY CORP.

Source: Annual report, 1990

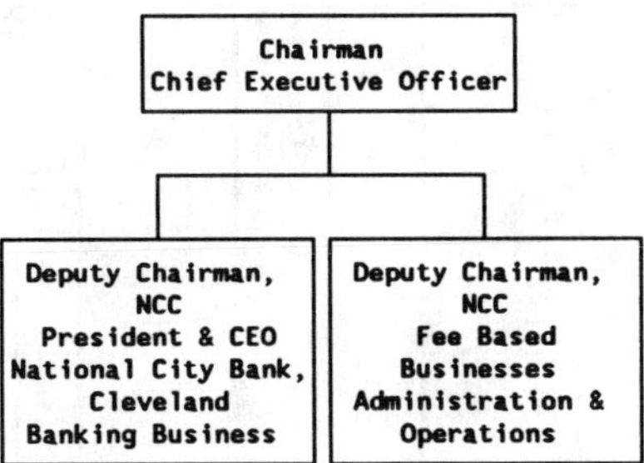

NATIONAL SERVICE INDUSTRIES, INC.

Source: Company update, 1991

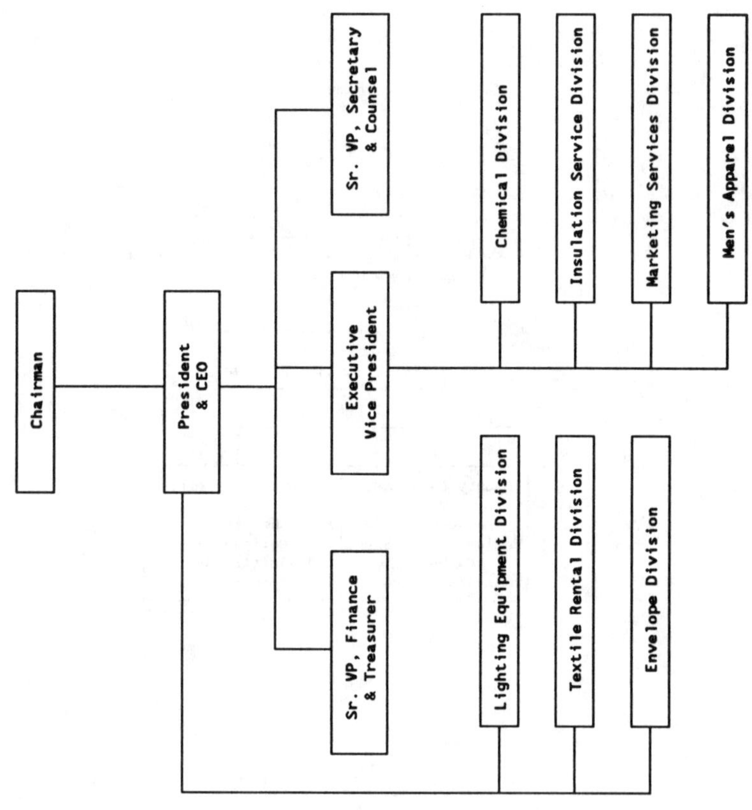

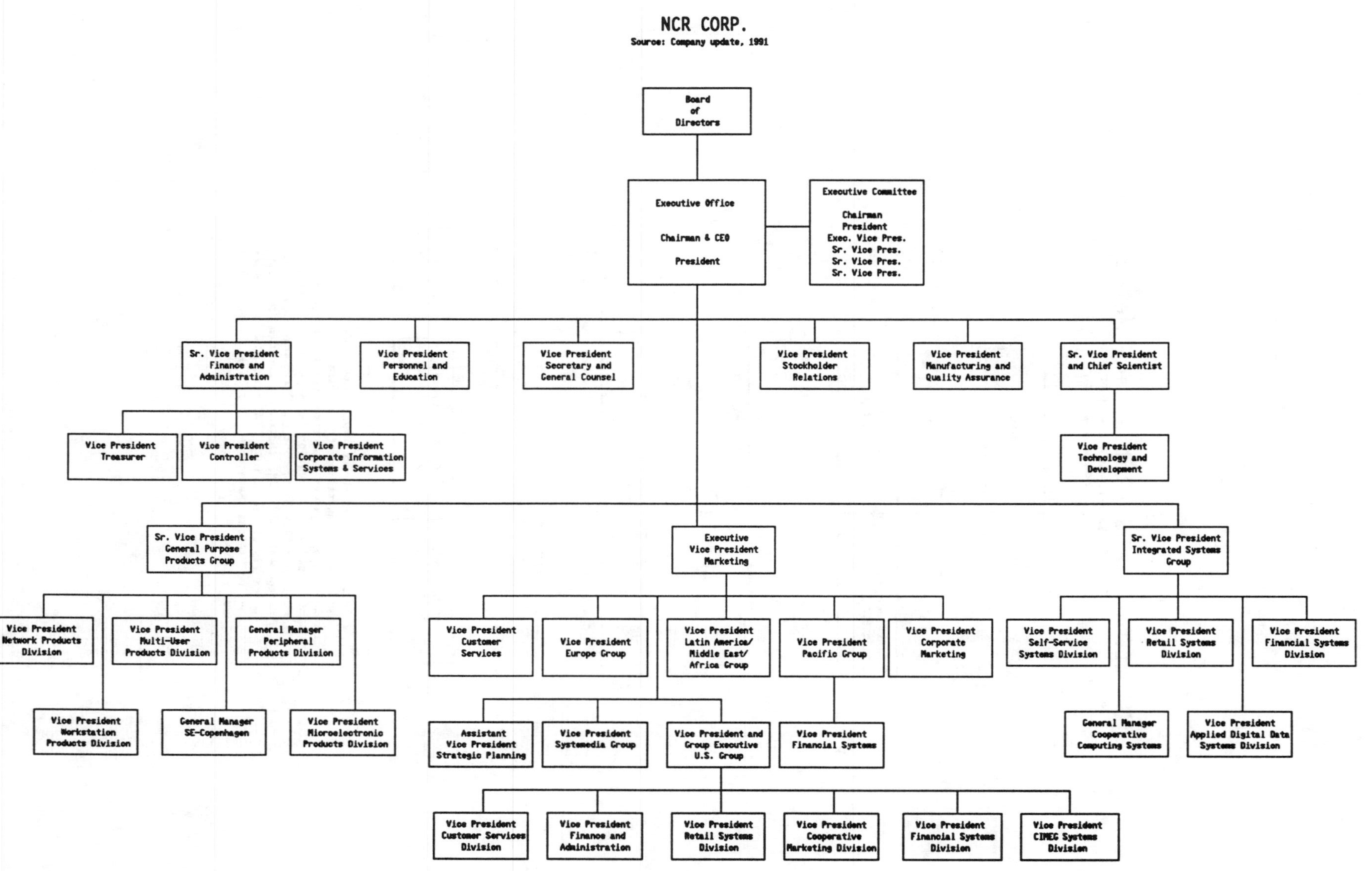
NCR CORP.
Source: Company update, 1991
Board of Directors
Executive Office
Chairman & CEO
President
Executive Committee
Chairman
President
Exec. Vice Pres.
Sr. Vice Pres.
Sr. Vice Pres.
Sr. Vice Pres.
Sr. Vice President Finance and Administration
Vice President Personnel and Education
Vice President Secretary and General Counsel
Vice President Stockholder Relations
Vice President Manufacturing and Quality Assurance
Sr. Vice President and Chief Scientist
Vice President Treasurer
Vice President Controller
Vice President Corporate Information Systems & Services
Vice President Technology and Development
Sr. Vice President General Purpose Products Group
Executive Vice President Marketing
Sr. Vice President Integrated Systems Group
Vice President Network Products Division
Vice President Multi-User Products Division
General Manager Peripheral Products Division
Vice President Customer Services
Vice President Europe Group
Vice President Latin America/ Middle East/ Africa Group
Vice President Pacific Group
Vice President Corporate Marketing
Vice President Self-Service Systems Division
Vice President Retail Systems Division
Vice President Financial Systems Division
Vice President Workstation Products Division
General Manager SE-Copenhagen
Vice President Microelectronic Products Division
Assistant Vice President Strategic Planning
Vice President Systemedia Group
Vice President and Group Executive U.S. Group
Vice President Financial Systems
General Manager Cooperative Computing Systems
Vice President Applied Digital Data Systems Division
Vice President Customer Services Division
Vice President Finance and Administration
Vice President Retail Systems Division
Vice President Cooperative Marketing Division
Vice President Financial Systems Division
Vice President CIMEG Systems Division

NEDLLOYD LINES (Rotterdam, Netherlands)

Source: AMERICAN SHIPPER
32: 14+ (October 1990)

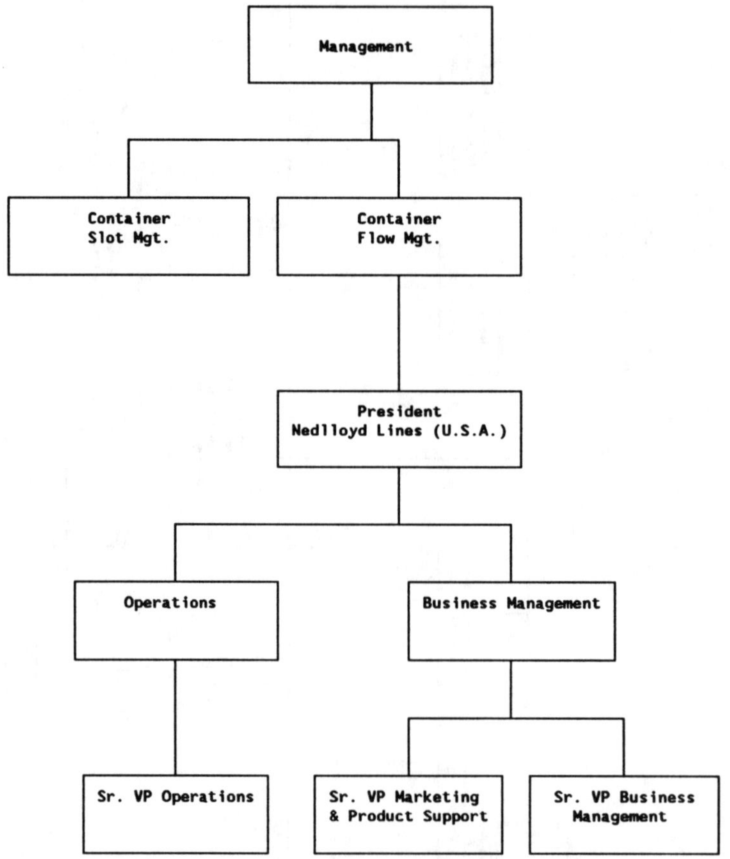

This chart shows the restructuring of Nedlloyd Lines in which the marketing of the overall transport service package was separated from the deployment of vessel slots, creating two separate divisions: Container Slot Management (CSM) and Container Flow Management (CFM). In the North American operation, primarily concerned with CFM, there are many regions, but no regional managers. This layer of management was removed.

NESTLE ENTERPRISES, INC.

Source: Annual report, 1989

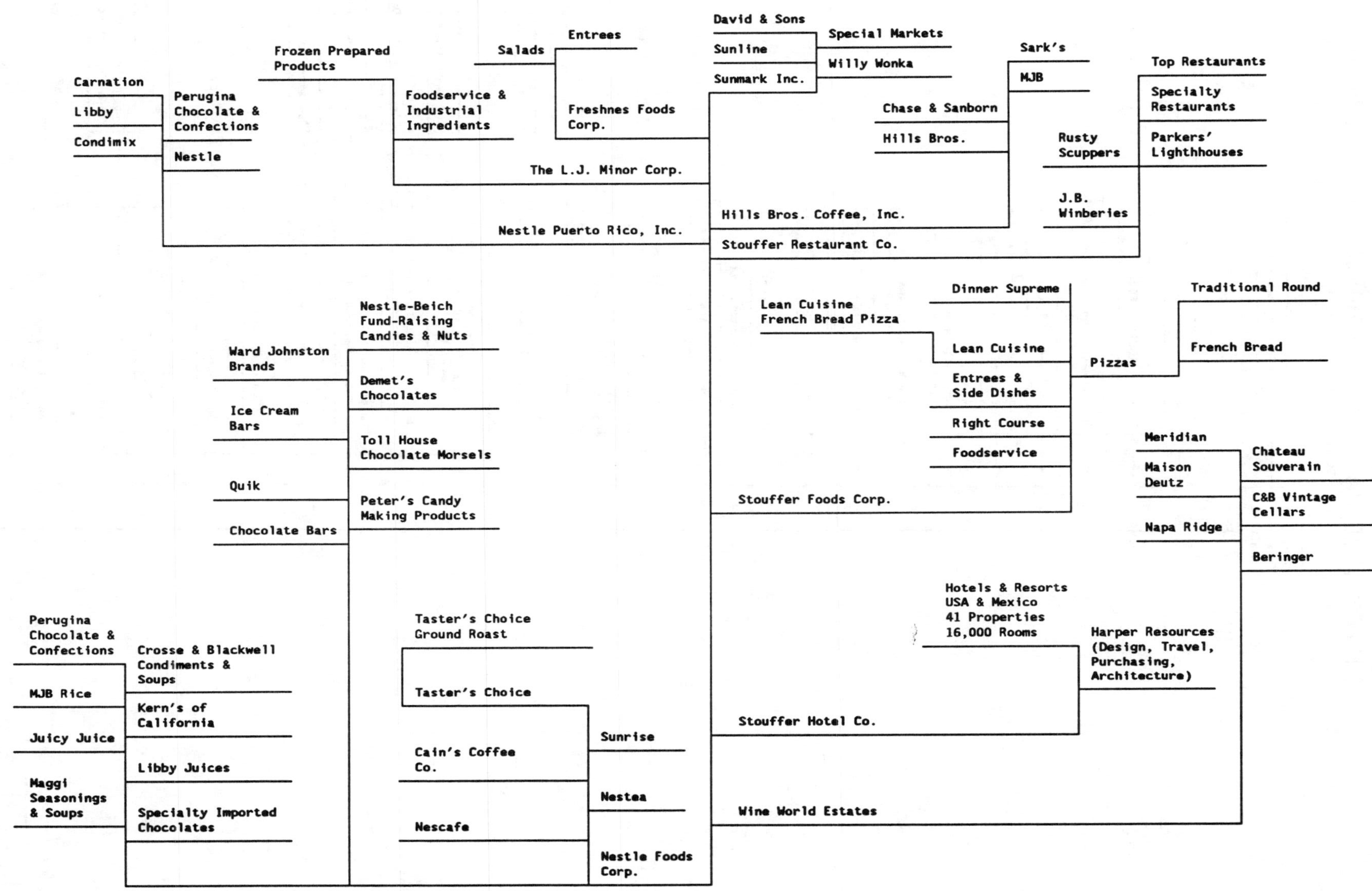

NIPPON TELEGRAPH AND TELEPHONE CORP. (Japan)

Source: Company update, 1991

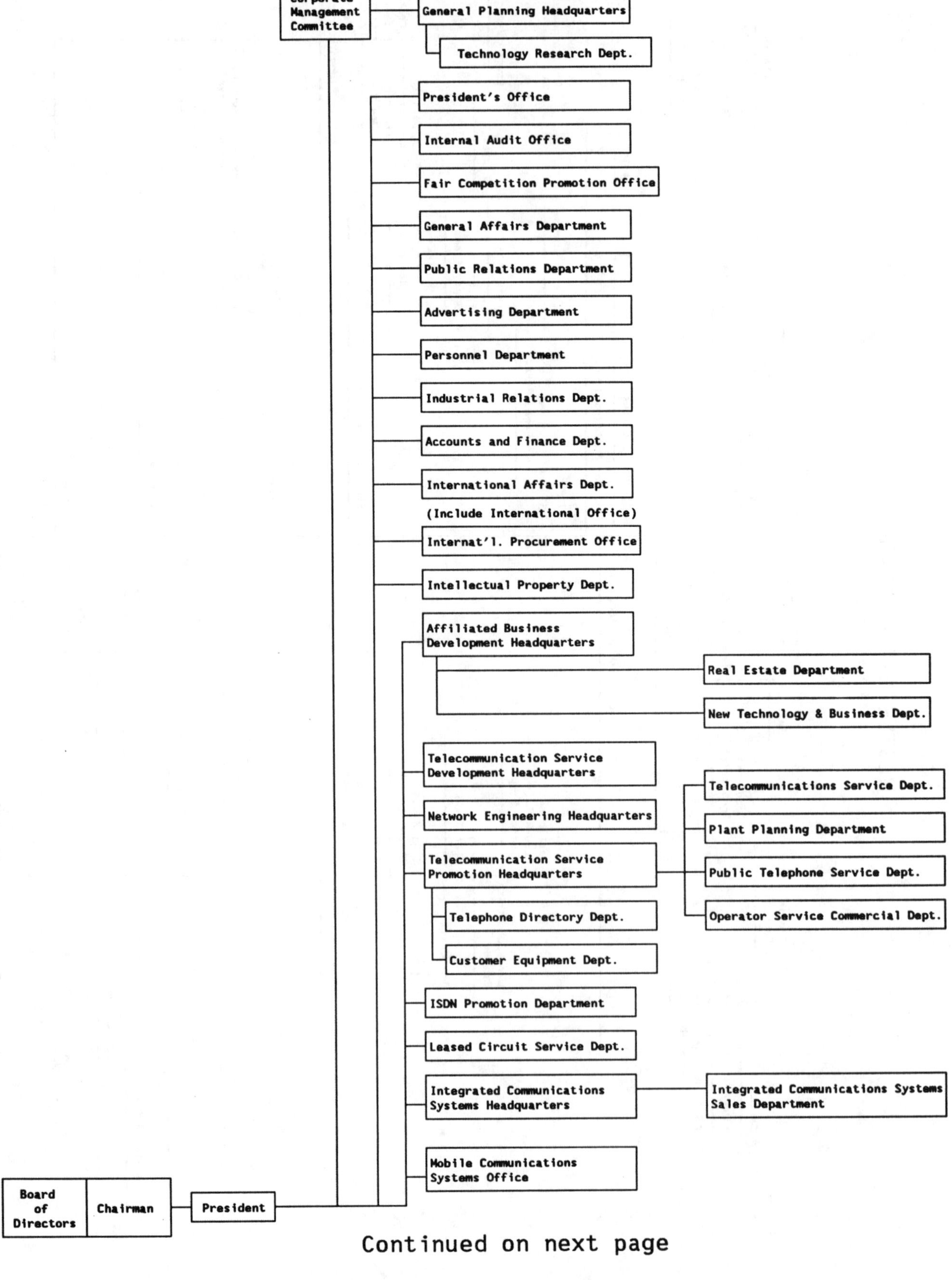
Corporate Management Committee
General Planning Headquarters
Technology Research Dept.
President's Office
Internal Audit Office
Fair Competition Promotion Office
General Affairs Department
Public Relations Department
Advertising Department
Personnel Department
Industrial Relations Dept.
Accounts and Finance Dept.
International Affairs Dept.
(Include International Office)
Internat'l. Procurement Office
Intellectual Property Dept.
Affiliated Business Development Headquarters
Real Estate Department
New Technology & Business Dept.
Telecommunication Service Development Headquarters
Network Engineering Headquarters
Telecommunication Service Promotion Headquarters
Telecommunications Service Dept.
Plant Planning Department
Public Telephone Service Dept.
Operator Service Commercial Dept.
Telephone Directory Dept.
Customer Equipment Dept.
ISDN Promotion Department
Leased Circuit Service Dept.
Integrated Communications Systems Headquarters
Integrated Communications Systems Sales Department
Mobile Communications Systems Office
Board of Directors
Chairman
President

Continued on next page

NIPPON TELEGRAPH AND TELEPHONE CORP. (Japan)
Continued from previous page

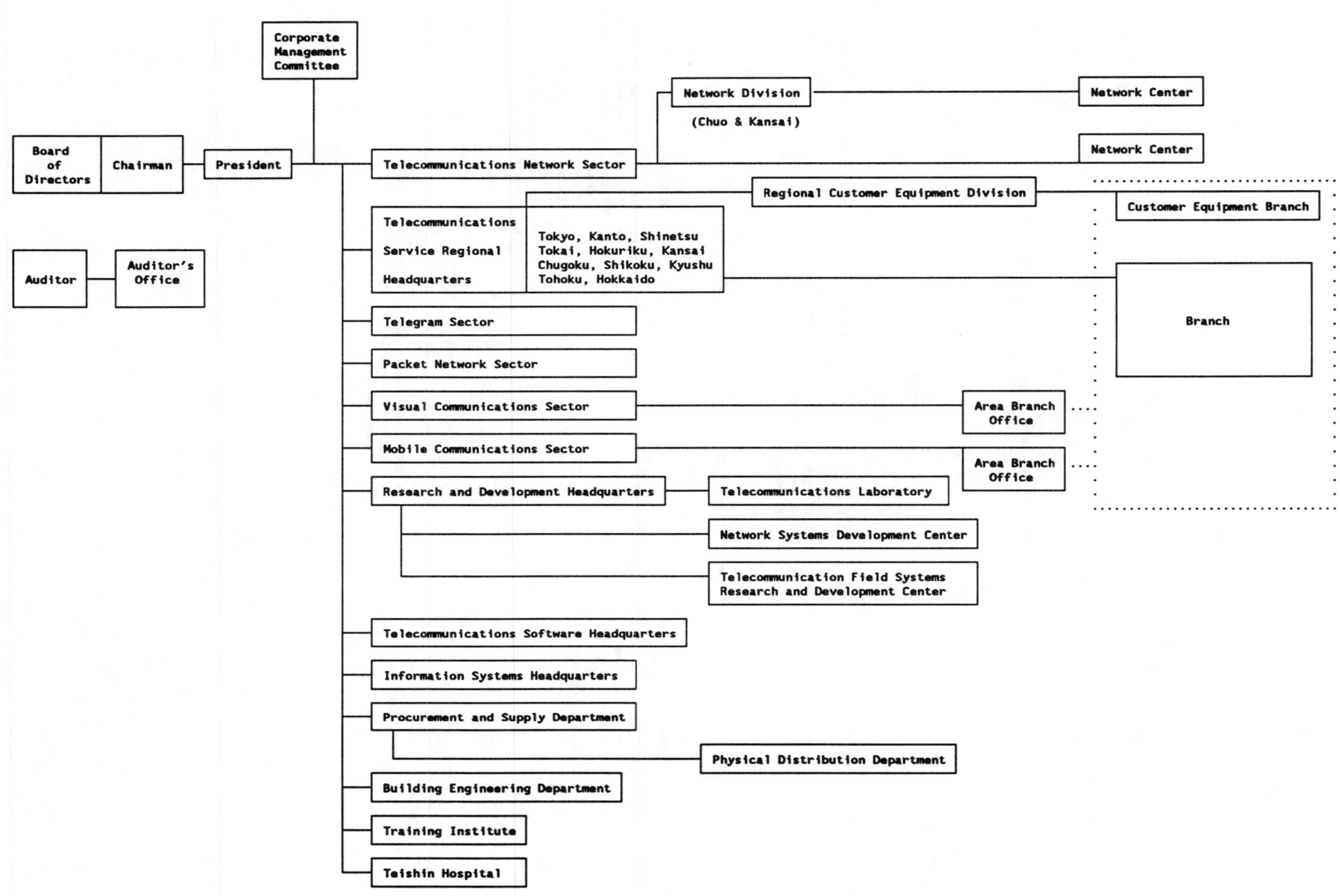

NYNEX CORP.

Source: "NYNEX Leader" (company inhouse newsletter)
8:6 (June 21, 1991)

NYNEX CORPORATE

Functions:

Executive
Legal
Finance
Human Resources
Planning
Quality
Ethics
Public Affairs
Corporate Communications

TELECOMMUNICATIONS GROUP

NYNEX Science & Technology, Inc.
New York Telephone
New England Telephone
Telesector Resources Group

WORLDWIDE SERVICES GROUP

NYNEX Information Resources Co.
NYNEX Business Information Systems Co.
NYNEX Mobile Communications Co.
AGS Computers, Inc.
The BIS Group Ltd.
NYNEX Computer Services Co.
NYNEX Development Co.
NYNEX Network Systems Co.
NYNEX International Co.

NYNEX Credit Co.
NYNEX Venture Co.
NYNEX Properties Co.
NYNEX Capital Funding Co.
NYNEX Trade Finance Co.
NYNEX Government Affairs Co.

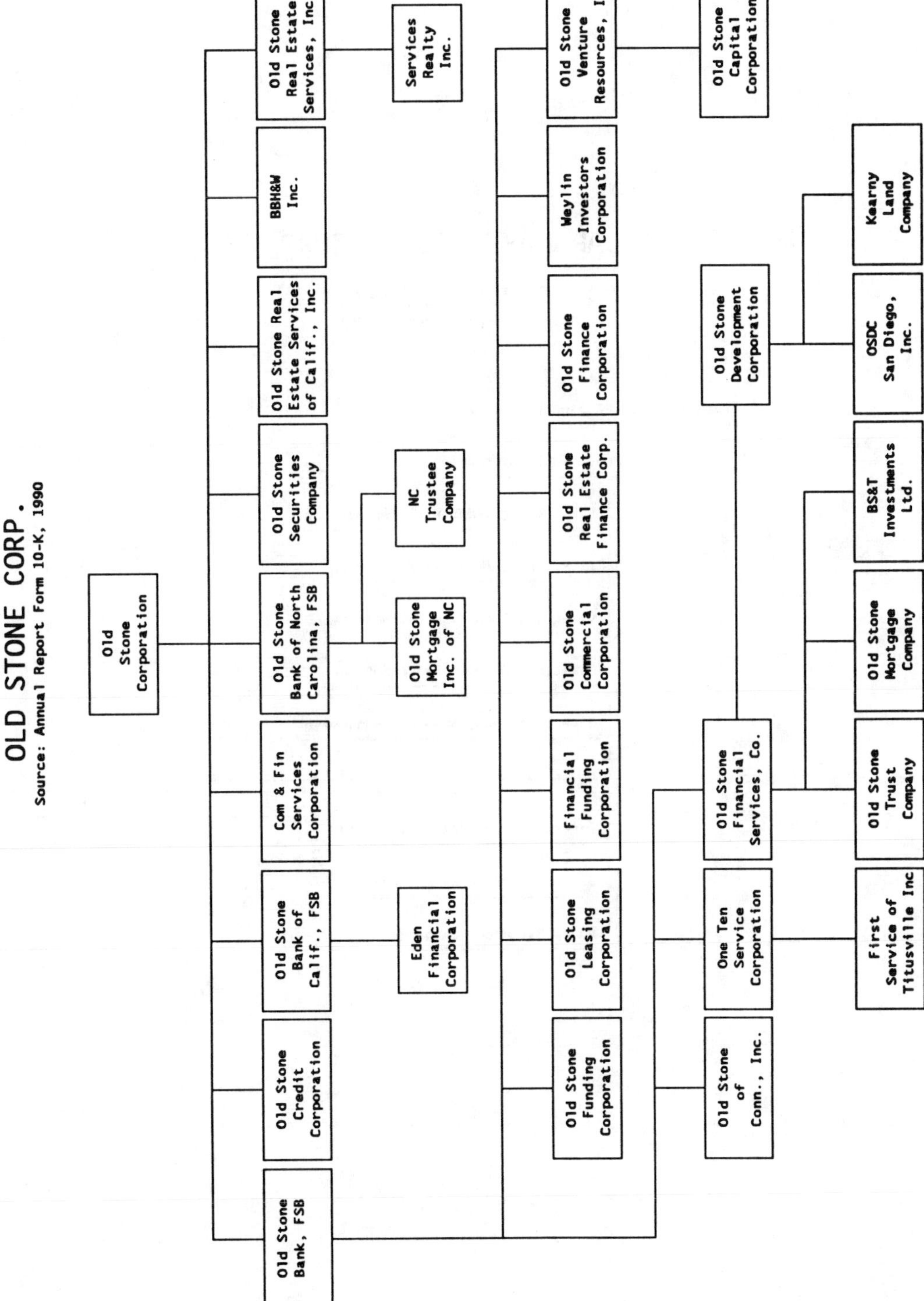
OLD STONE CORP.
Source: Annual Report Form 10-K, 1990
Old Stone Corporation
Old Stone Bank, FSB
Old Stone Credit Corporation
Old Stone Bank of Calif., FSB
Eden Financial Corporation
Com & Fin Services Corporation
Old Stone Bank of North Carolina, FSB
Old Stone Mortgage Inc. of NC
NC Trustee Company
Old Stone Securities Company
Old Stone Real Estate Services of Calif., Inc.
BBH&W Inc.
Old Stone Real Estate Services, Inc.
Services Realty Inc.
Old Stone Funding Corporation
Old Stone Leasing Corporation
Financial Funding Corporation
Old Stone Commercial Corporation
Old Stone Real Estate Finance Corp.
Old Stone Finance Corporation
Weylin Investors Corporation
Old Stone Venture Resources, Inc.
Old Stone Capital Corporation
Old Stone of Conn., Inc.
One Ten Service Corporation
First Service of Titusville Inc
Old Stone Financial Services, Co.
Old Stone Trust Company
Old Stone Mortgage Company
BS&T Investments Ltd.
Old Stone Development Corporation
OSDC San Diego, Inc.
Kearny Land Company

OSCAR MAYER FOODS CORP.

ENGINEERING DIVISION

Source: Company update, 1991

- Executive Vice President
  - Vice President, Engineering
    - Director of Industrial Engineering
    - Director of Facilities Planning
    - Director, Corporate Engineering
    - Director of Engineering Services
    - Vice President, Machine Development
    - New Products & Int'l Technical Services Manager
    - Director, Manufacturing Systems
    - Secondary Resources Manager
    - Human Resource Manager

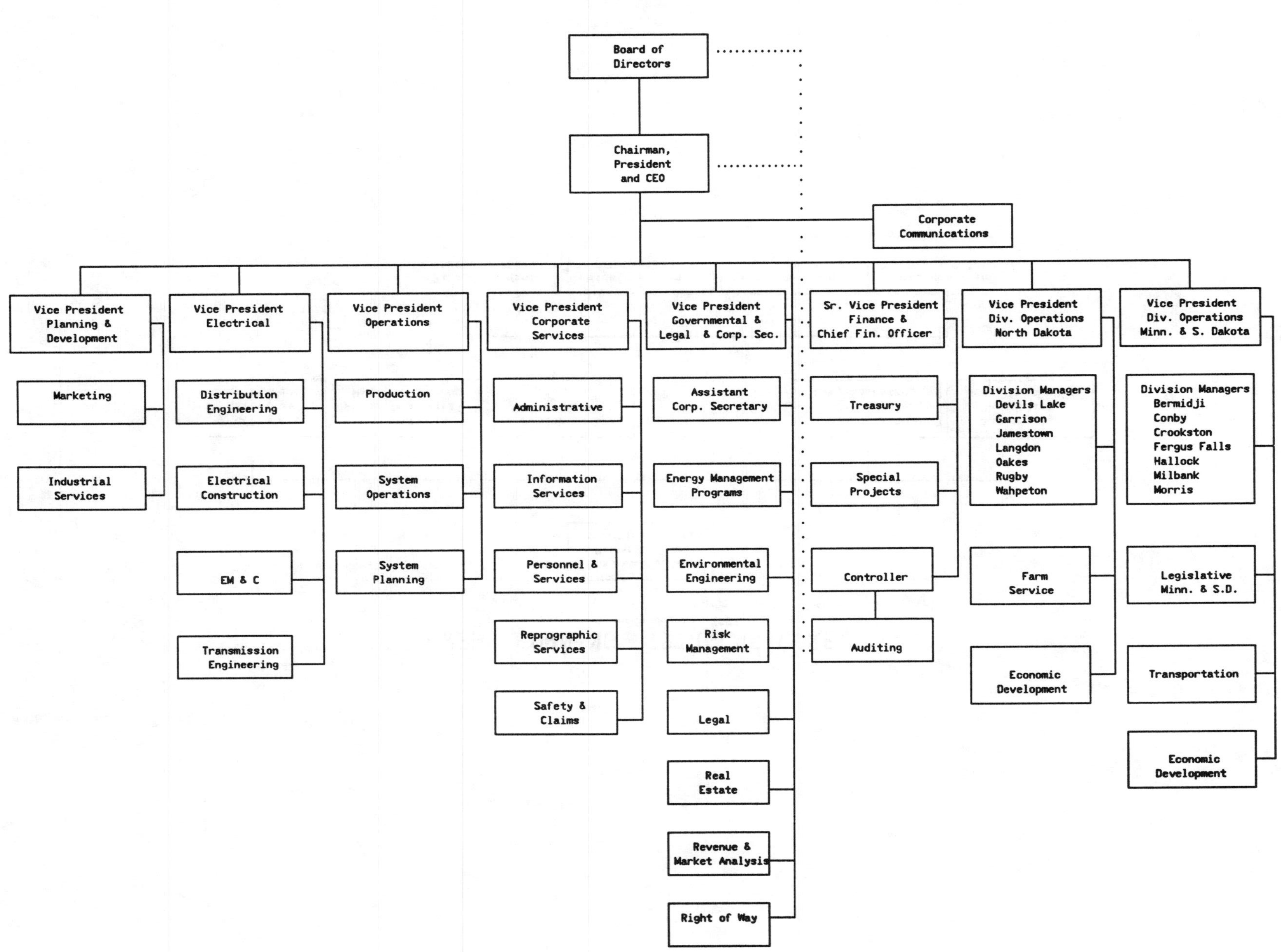
OTTER TAIL POWER CO.
Source: Company update, 1991
Board of Directors
Chairman, President and CEO
Corporate Communications
Vice President Planning & Development
Marketing
Industrial Services
Vice President Electrical
Distribution Engineering
Electrical Construction
EM & C
Transmission Engineering
Vice President Operations
Production
System Operations
System Planning
Vice President Corporate Services
Administrative
Information Services
Personnel & Services
Reprographic Services
Safety & Claims
Vice President Governmental & Legal & Corp. Sec.
Assistant Corp. Secretary
Energy Management Programs
Environmental Engineering
Risk Management
Legal
Real Estate
Revenue & Market Analysis
Right of Way
Sr. Vice President Finance & Chief Fin. Officer
Treasury
Special Projects
Controller
Auditing
Vice President Div. Operations North Dakota
Division Managers Devils Lake Garrison Jamestown Langdon Oakes Rugby Wahpeton
Farm Service
Economic Development
Vice President Div. Operations Minn. & S. Dakota
Division Managers Bermidji Conby Crookston Fergus Falls Hallock Milbank Morris
Legislative Minn. & S.D.
Transportation
Economic Development

OWENS-CORNING FIBERGLAS CORP.

Source: Company update, 1991

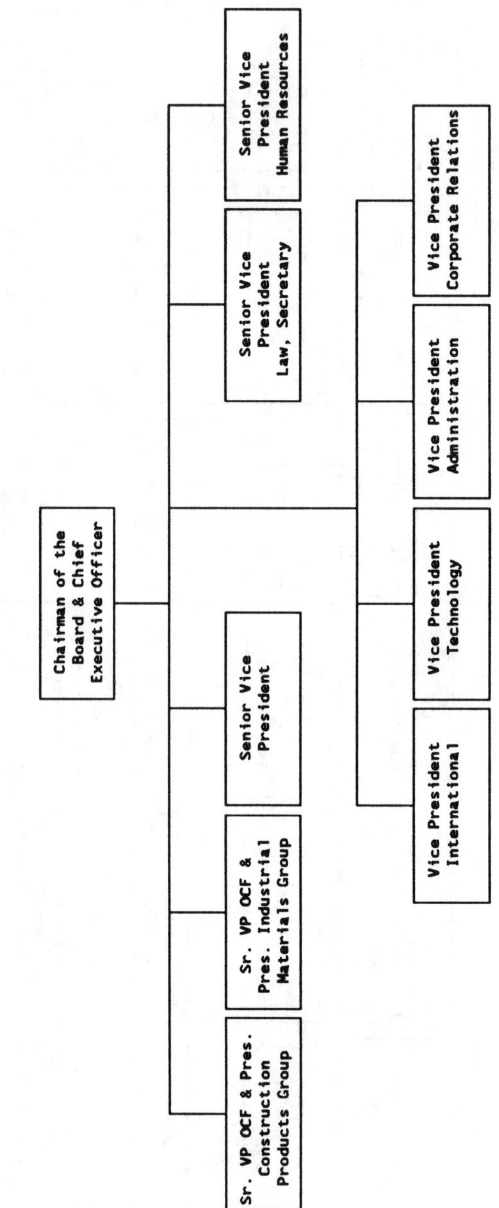

PACIFIC TELESIS GROUP

Source: Annual report, 1990

PARENT COMPANY
PACIFIC TELSIS

Pacific Telesis develops corporate policy for its family of companies. This includes planning strategic direction and human resources policy, ensuring management continuity, obtaining and allocating capital, monitoring subsidiary performance, providing legal counsel, promoting investor interest, and representing the corporation to external constituents.

BELL OPERATING COMPANIES

Customer Access to Network and Information Services: Pacific Bell, Nevada Bell	The companies provide local telephone services: specialized services including high-speed digital transmission and voice mail; and network access to toll, long distance, and information services.
Directory Publishing: Pacific Bell Directory	The company provides print directory advertising and related marketing services in California and Nevada.

PACTEL COMPANIES

Wireless Communications: PacTel Cellular, PacTel Paging, PacTel Teletrac	PacTel Cellular and PacTel Paging own, build, and operate cellular telephone and paging systems in the United States. PacTel Teletrac provides paging transmission for a company that offers vehicle location services.
Home Entertainment: Pac-Tel Cable	The company explores opportunities in the home entertainment industry. Its affiliates manage cable television operations in the United Kingdom.
International Operations: Pacific Telesis International	The company provices a variety of services directly and through affiliates in markets such as Germany, the United Kingdom, Japan, South Korea, and Thailand. Its offerings include wireless communications, access to value-added networks, and international long-distance telecommunications.

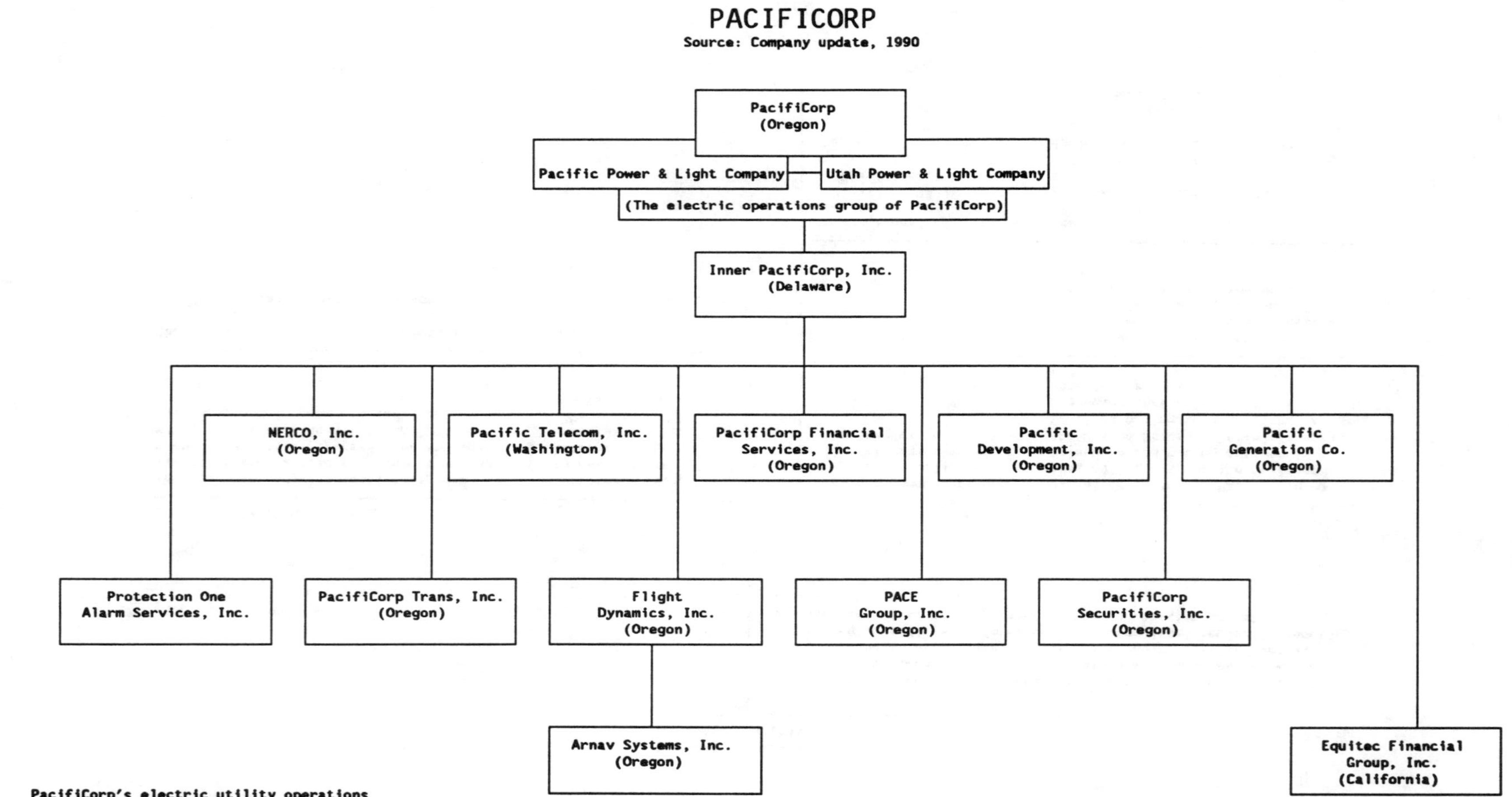
PACIFICORP
Source: Company update, 1990
PacifiCorp (Oregon)
Pacific Power & Light Company
Utah Power & Light Company
(The electric operations group of PacifiCorp)
Inner PacifiCorp, Inc. (Delaware)
NERCO, Inc. (Oregon)
Pacific Telecom, Inc. (Washington)
PacifiCorp Financial Services, Inc. (Oregon)
Pacific Development, Inc. (Oregon)
Pacific Generation Co. (Oregon)
Protection One Alarm Services, Inc.
PacifiCorp Trans, Inc. (Oregon)
Flight Dynamics, Inc. (Oregon)
PACE Group, Inc. (Oregon)
PacifiCorp Securities, Inc. (Oregon)
Arnav Systems, Inc. (Oregon)
Equitec Financial Group, Inc. (California)
PacifiCorp's electric utility operations are conducted under the assumed business names of Pacific Power & Light Company and Utah Power & Light Company; legally Pacific Power and Utah Power are not separate from PacifiCorp.

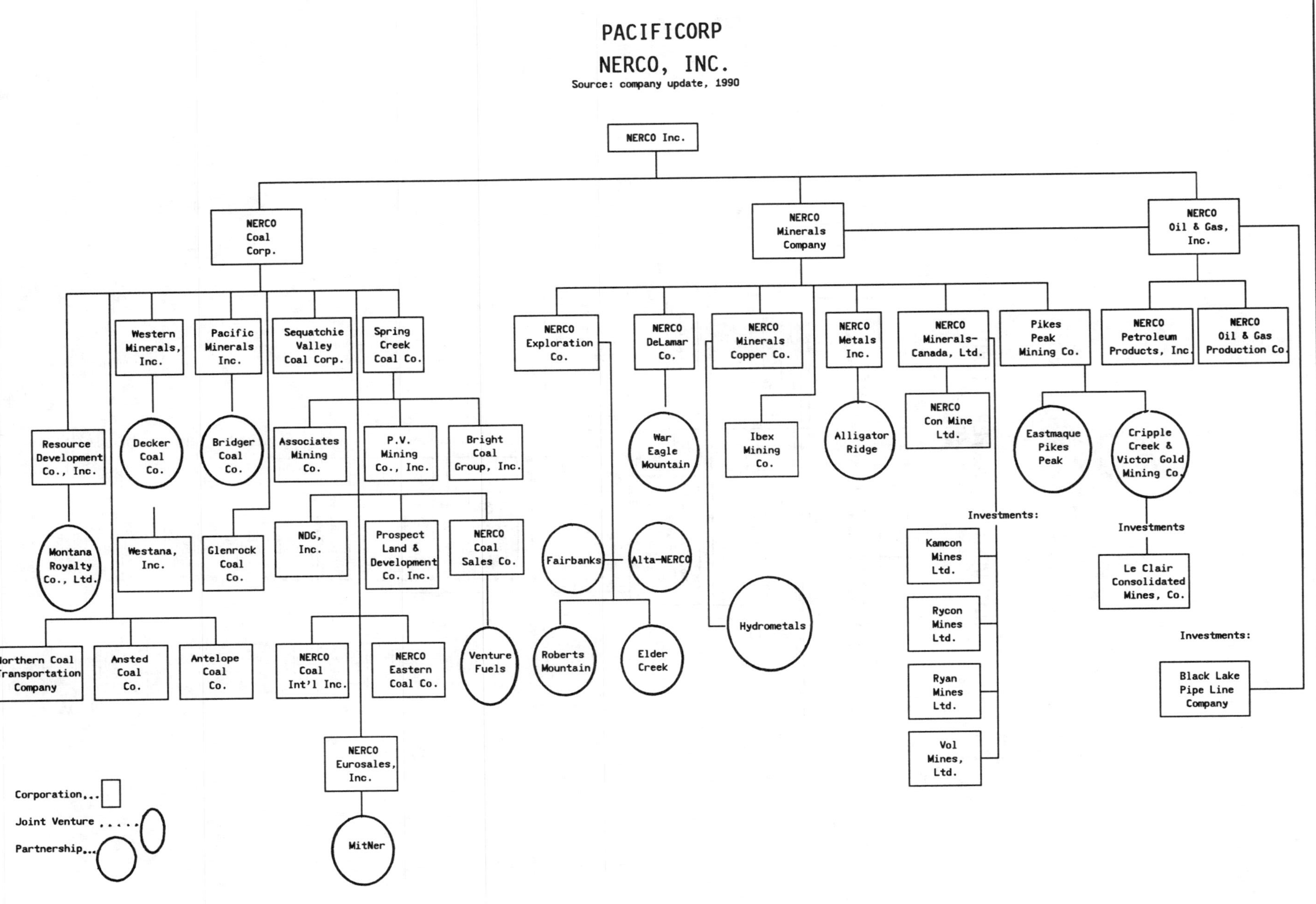
PACIFICORP
NERCO, INC.
Source: company update, 1990
NERCO Inc.
NERCO Coal Corp.
NERCO Minerals Company
NERCO Oil & Gas, Inc.
Resource Development Co., Inc.
Western Minerals, Inc.
Pacific Minerals Inc.
Sequatchie Valley Coal Corp.
Spring Creek Coal Co.
Decker Coal Co.
Bridger Coal Co.
Associates Mining Co.
P.V. Mining Co., Inc.
Bright Coal Group, Inc.
Montana Royalty Co., Ltd.
Westana, Inc.
Glenrock Coal Co.
NDG, Inc.
Prospect Land & Development Co. Inc.
NERCO Coal Sales Co.
Northern Coal Transportation Company
Ansted Coal Co.
Antelope Coal Co.
NERCO Coal Int'l Inc.
NERCO Eastern Coal Co.
Venture Fuels
NERCO Eurosales, Inc.
MitNer
NERCO Exploration Co.
NERCO DeLamar Co.
NERCO Minerals Copper Co.
NERCO Metals Inc.
NERCO Minerals-Canada, Ltd.
Pikes Peak Mining Co.
NERCO Petroleum Products, Inc.
NERCO Oil & Gas Production Co.
War Eagle Mountain
Ibex Mining Co.
Alligator Ridge
NERCO Con Mine Ltd.
Eastmaque Pikes Peak
Cripple Creek & Victor Gold Mining Co.
Fairbanks
Alta-NERCO
Roberts Mountain
Elder Creek
Hydrometals
Investments:
Kamcon Mines Ltd.
Rycon Mines Ltd.
Ryan Mines Ltd.
Vol Mines, Ltd.
Investments
Le Clair Consolidated Mines, Co.
Investments:
Black Lake Pipe Line Company
Corporation...
Joint Venture.....
Partnership...

PANHANDLE EASTERN CORP.

Source: Company update, 1991

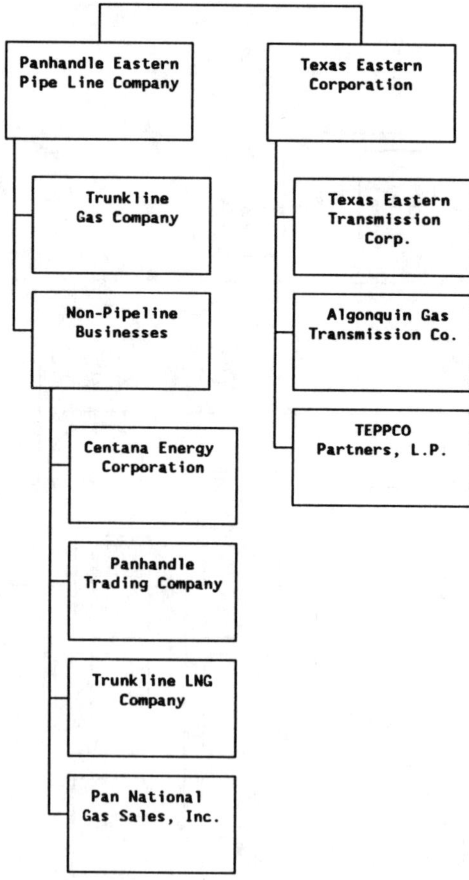

PARKER HANNIFIN CORP.

Source: Company update, 1991

Company organization is a strongly horizontal one, characterized by independent product divisions. These divisions are composed of small manufacturing plants, geographically dispersed in order to be close to consumers for better service.

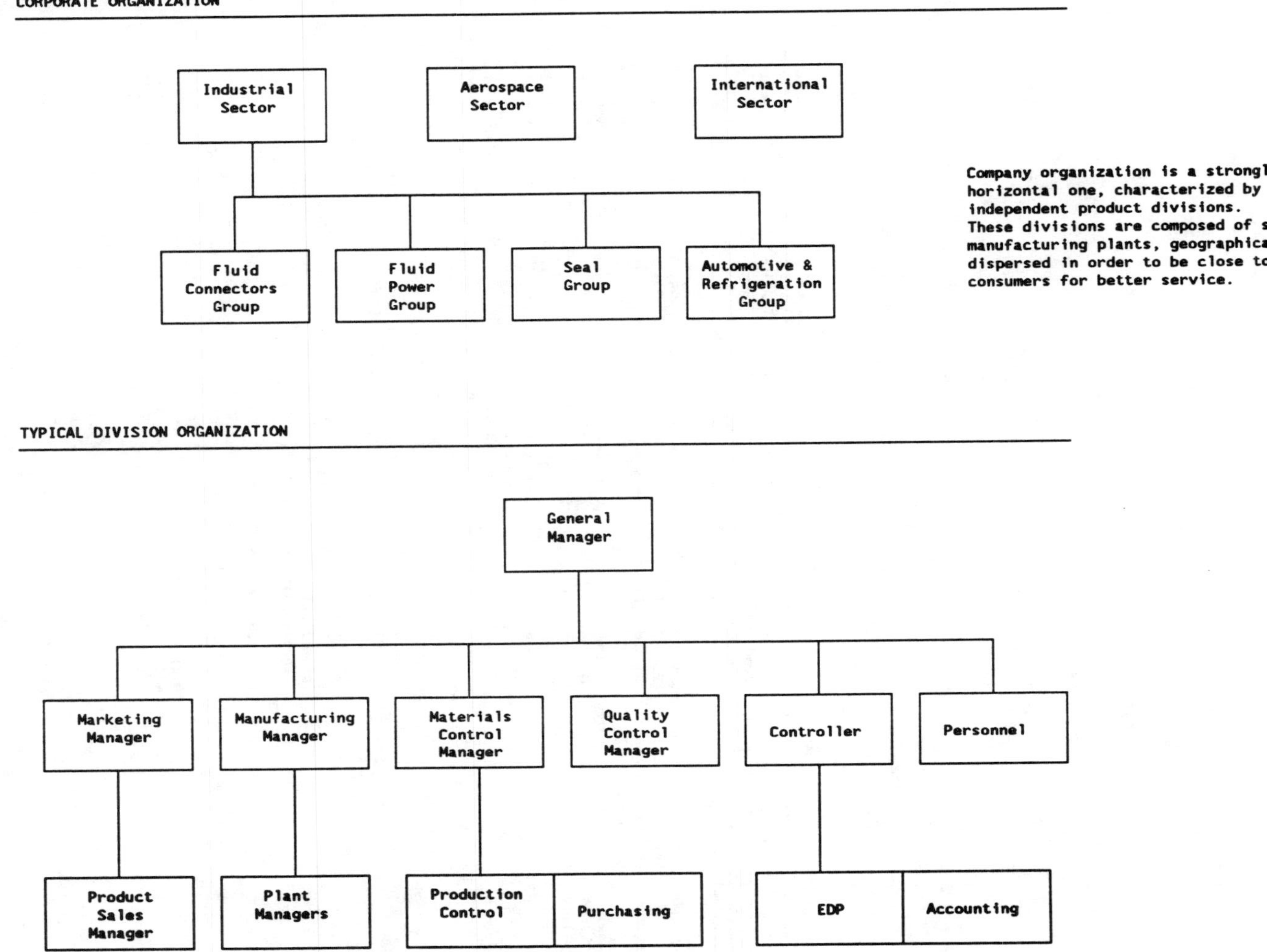

PFIZER INC.

Source: Company update, 1991

Pharmaceuticals Group

Domestic

- Pfizer Labs
- Roerig
- National Healthcare Operations

International

- Pfizer International (52 International Subsidiaries)

Hospital Products Group

- Howmedica
  - S.A. Benoist Girard & Cie.
  - Jaquet Orthopedie S.A.
  - Howmedica Faimon S.A
  - Climo S.A
- Deknatel
- Shiley Inc.
  - Stockert Instrumente G.m.b.H.
  - Dideco
  - Biomedical Sensors (Holdings) Ltd.
- Valleylab Inc.
- Schneider
- American Medical Systems Inc.
- Infusaid Inc.
- Pfizer Laser Systems

Consumer Products Group

- Consumer Health Care
- Oral Care
- Coty
- Consumer Products International

Animal Health Group

- Animal Health

Speciality Chemicals Group

- Specialty Chemicals
- Dairy & Brewery Products
- Oil Field Products
- C.A.L. (Flavors & Fragrances)

Speciality Minerals Group

- Minerals
- Quigley Company Inc.

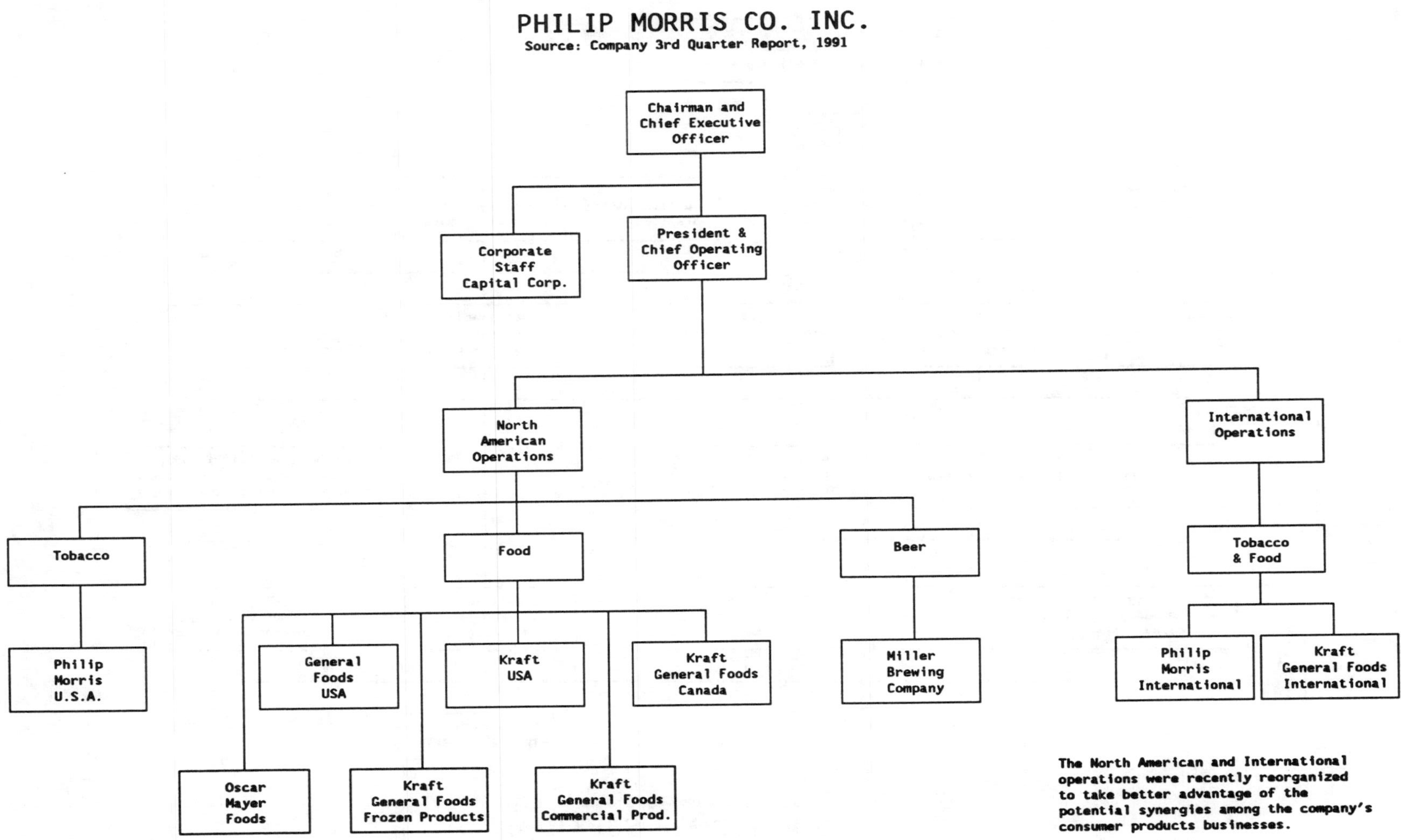
PHILIP MORRIS CO. INC.
Source: Company 3rd Quarter Report, 1991
Chairman and Chief Executive Officer
Corporate Staff Capital Corp.
President & Chief Operating Officer
North American Operations
International Operations
Tobacco
Food
Beer
Tobacco & Food
Philip Morris U.S.A.
General Foods USA
Kraft USA
Kraft General Foods Canada
Miller Brewing Company
Philip Morris International
Kraft General Foods International
Oscar Mayer Foods
Kraft General Foods Frozen Products
Kraft General Foods Commercial Prod.
The North American and International operations were recently reorganized to take better advantage of the potential synergies among the company's consumer products businesses.

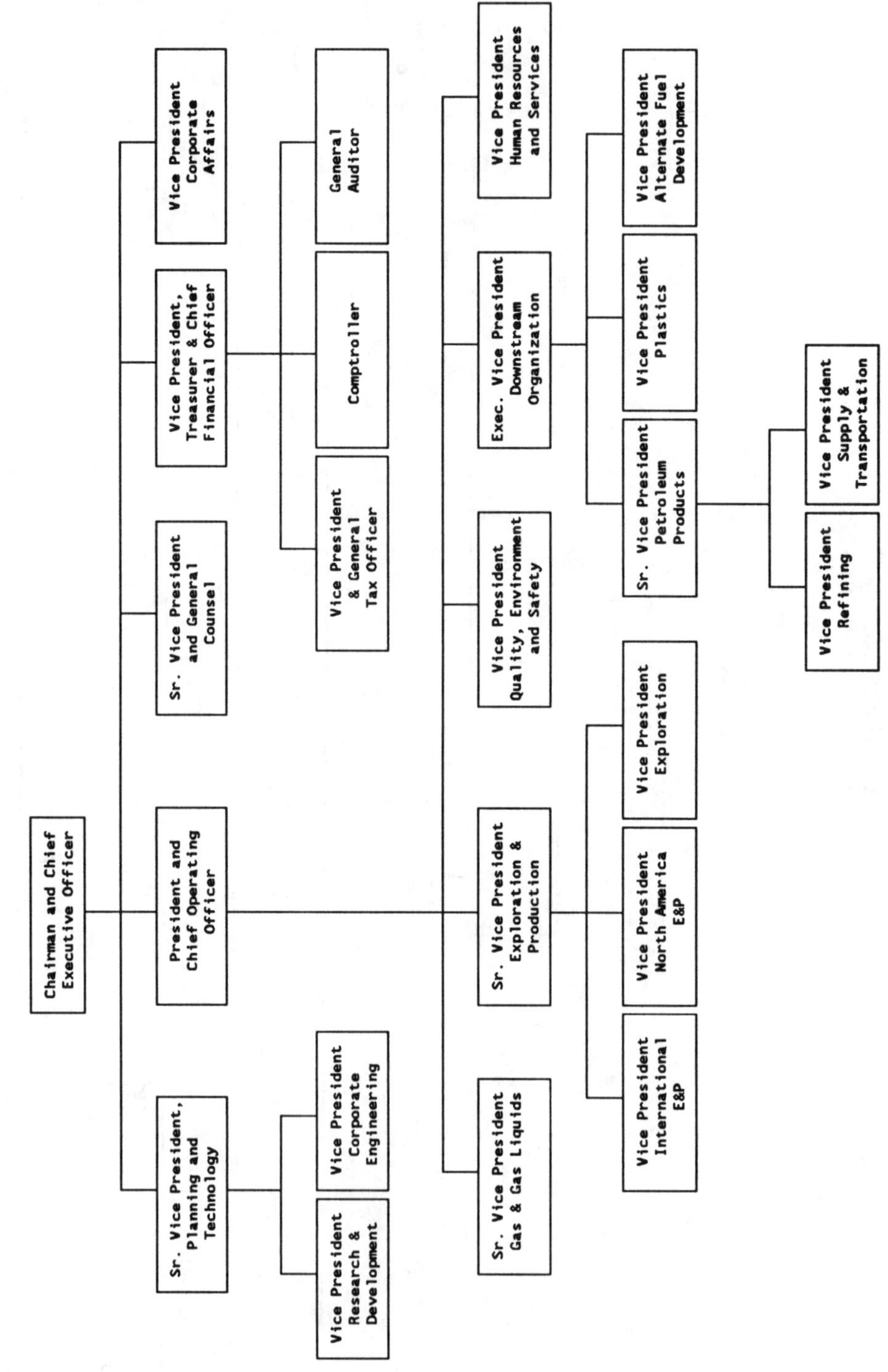
PHILLIPS PETROLEUM CO.
Source: Company update, 1991
Chairman and Chief Executive Officer
Sr. Vice President, Planning and Technology
President and Chief Operating Officer
Sr. Vice President and General Counsel
Vice President, Treasurer & Chief Financial Officer
Vice President Corporate Affairs
Vice President Research & Development
Vice President Corporate Engineering
Vice President & General Tax Officer
Comptroller
General Auditor
Sr. Vice President Gas & Gas Liquids
Sr. Vice President Exploration & Production
Vice President Quality, Environment and Safety
Exec. Vice President Downstream Organization
Vice President Human Resources and Services
Vice President International E&P
Vice President North America E&P
Vice President Exploration
Sr. Vice President Petroleum Products
Vice President Plastics
Vice President Alternate Fuel Development
Vice President Refining
Vice President Supply & Transportation

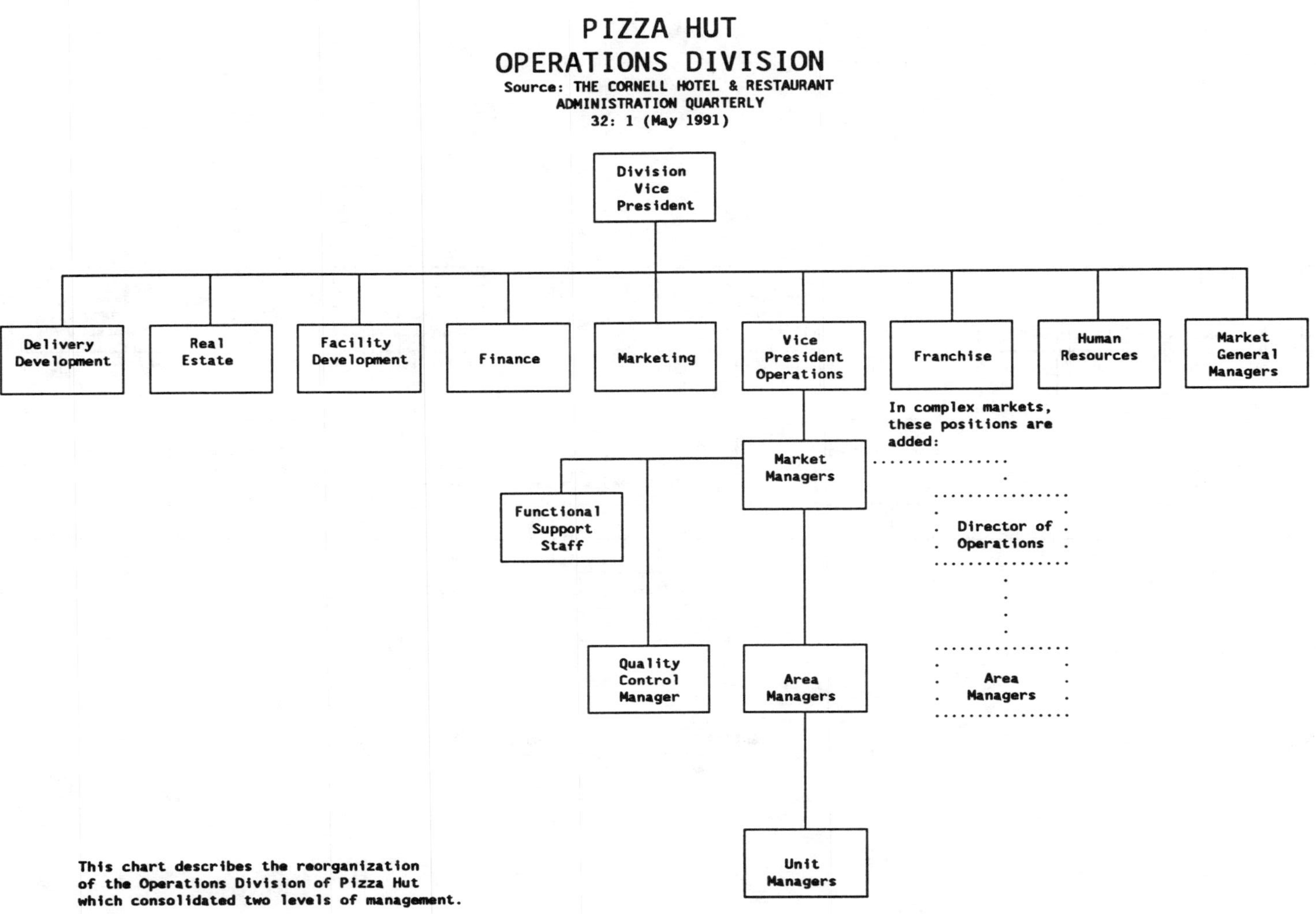
PIZZA HUT
OPERATIONS DIVISION
Source: THE CORNELL HOTEL & RESTAURANT ADMINISTRATION QUARTERLY 32: 1 (May 1991)
Division Vice President
Delivery Development
Real Estate
Facility Development
Finance
Marketing
Vice President Operations
Franchise
Human Resources
Market General Managers
Market Managers
Functional Support Staff
Quality Control Manager
Area Managers
Unit Managers
In complex markets, these positions are added:
Director of Operations
Area Managers
This chart describes the reorganization of the Operations Division of Pizza Hut which consolidated two levels of management.

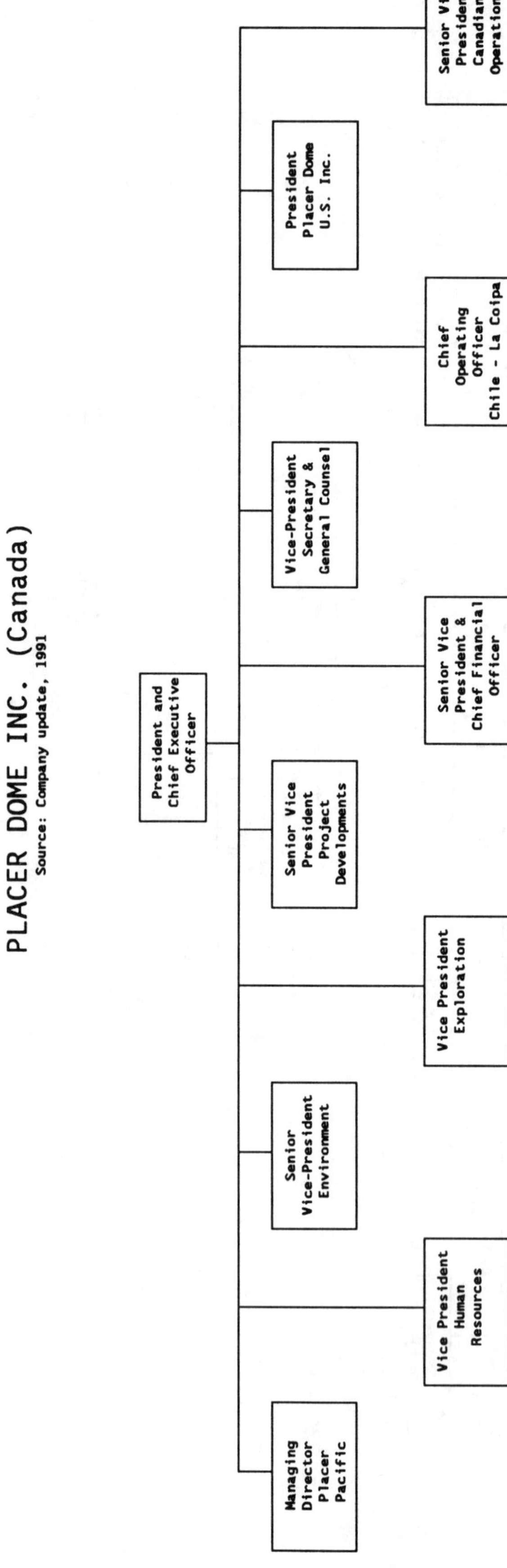
PLACER DOME INC. (Canada)
Source: Company update, 1991
President and Chief Executive Officer
Managing Director Placer Pacific
Vice President Human Resources
Senior Vice-President Environment
Vice President Exploration
Senior Vice President Project Developments
Senior Vice President & Chief Financial Officer
Vice-President Secretary & General Counsel
Chief Operating Officer Chile - La Coipa
President Placer Dome U.S. Inc.
Senior Vice President Canadian Operations

PPG INDUSTRIES, INC.

Source: Company update, 1991

- Board of Directors
  - Audit Committee
  - Nominating Committee
  - Officers-Directors Compensation Committee
  - Management Committee - Chairman
    - Chairman's Council - Chariman
    - Engineering Coordinating Committee - Chairman
    - Committee for Information Resources Management - Chairperson
    - Pension Investment Committee - Chairman
    - Research & Development Coordinating Committee - Chairman
    - Tax Committee - Chairman
    - Corporate Quality Council - Chairman
    - Biotechnology Coordinating Committe - Chairman
    - Ethics Committee - Chairman
    - European Management Council - Chairman
  - Compensation & Executive Development Committee - Chairman
    - Employee Benefits Committee - Chairman
  - Environmental Affairs Committee - Chairman

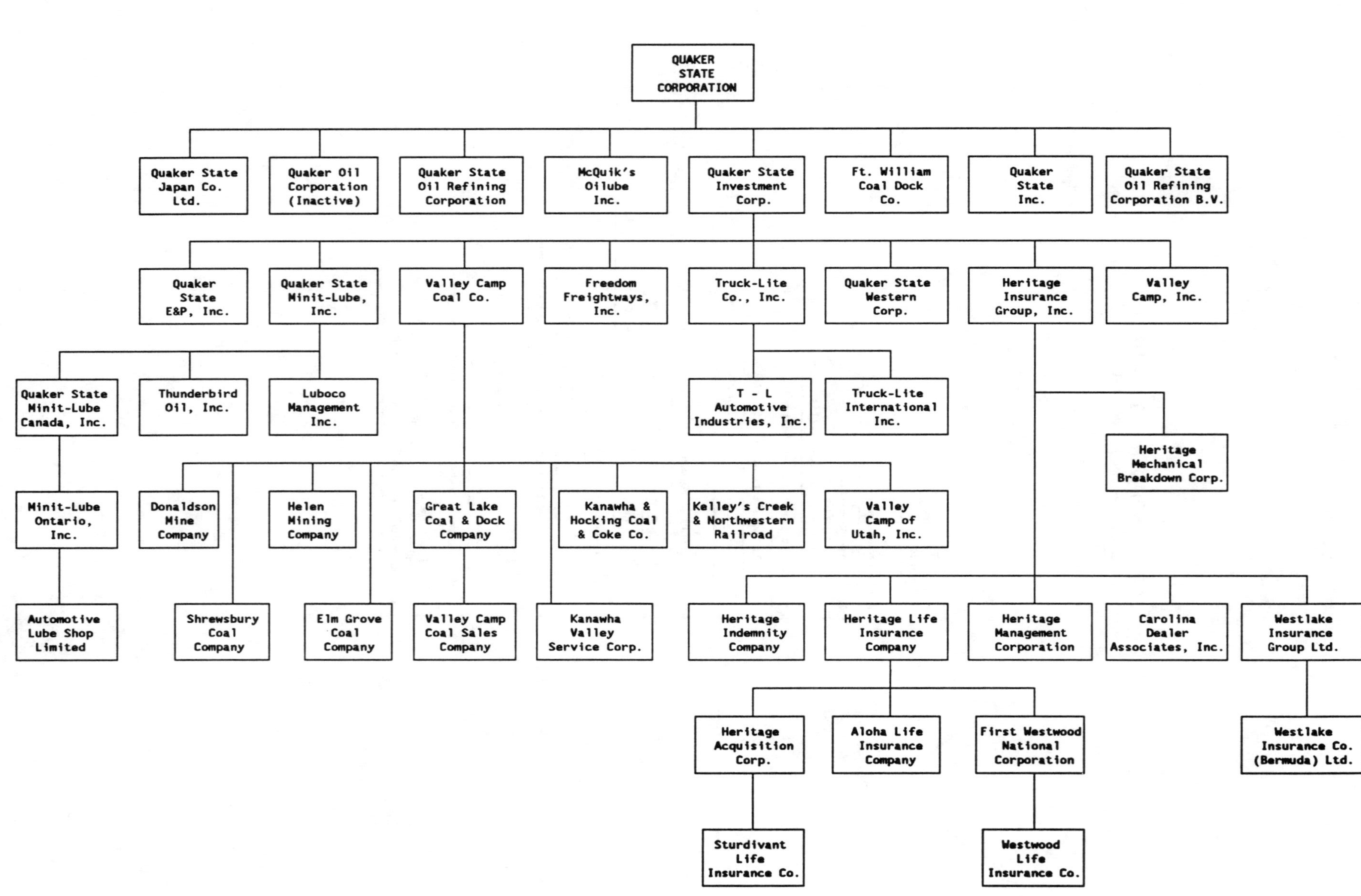
QUAKER STATE CORP.
Source: Company update, 1991
QUAKER STATE CORPORATION
Quaker State Japan Co. Ltd.
Quaker Oil Corporation (Inactive)
Quaker State Oil Refining Corporation
McQuik's Oilube Inc.
Quaker State Investment Corp.
Ft. William Coal Dock Co.
Quaker State Inc.
Quaker State Oil Refining Corporation B.V.
Quaker State E&P, Inc.
Quaker State Minit-Lube, Inc.
Valley Camp Coal Co.
Freedom Freightways, Inc.
Truck-Lite Co., Inc.
Quaker State Western Corp.
Heritage Insurance Group, Inc.
Valley Camp, Inc.
Quaker State Minit-Lube Canada, Inc.
Thunderbird Oil, Inc.
Luboco Management Inc.
T - L Automotive Industries, Inc.
Truck-Lite International Inc.
Heritage Mechanical Breakdown Corp.
Minit-Lube Ontario, Inc.
Donaldson Mine Company
Helen Mining Company
Great Lake Coal & Dock Company
Kanawha & Hocking Coal & Coke Co.
Kelley's Creek & Northwestern Railroad
Valley Camp of Utah, Inc.
Automotive Lube Shop Limited
Shrewsbury Coal Company
Elm Grove Coal Company
Valley Camp Coal Sales Company
Kanawha Valley Service Corp.
Heritage Indemnity Company
Heritage Life Insurance Company
Heritage Management Corporation
Carolina Dealer Associates, Inc.
Westlake Insurance Group Ltd.
Heritage Acquisition Corp.
Aloha Life Insurance Company
First Westwood National Corporation
Westlake Insurance Co. (Bermuda) Ltd.
Sturdivant Life Insurance Co.
Westwood Life Insurance Co.

REED INTERNATIONAL
Source: Annual report, 1991

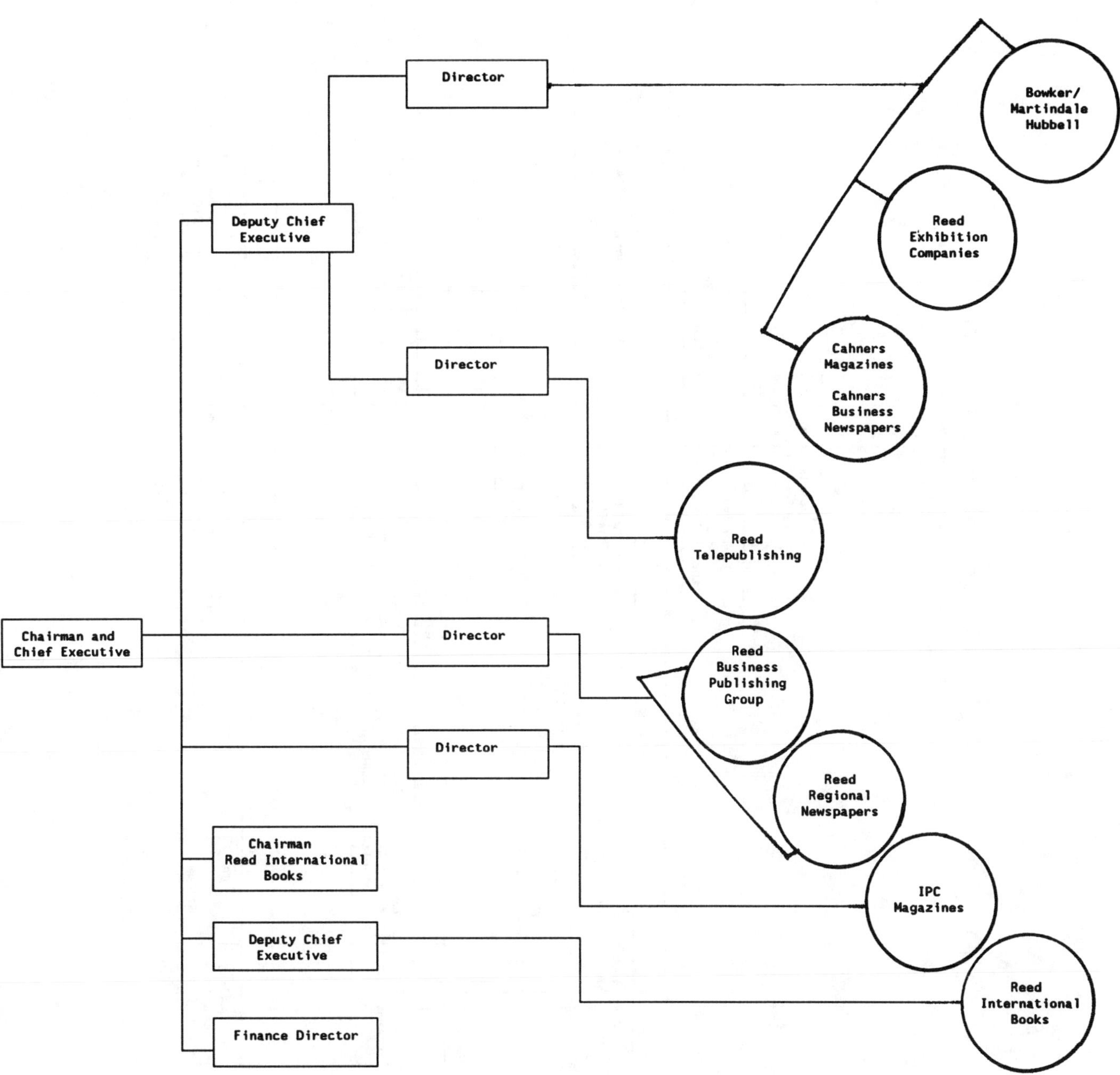

REYNOLDS METALS CO.

Source: Company update, 1991

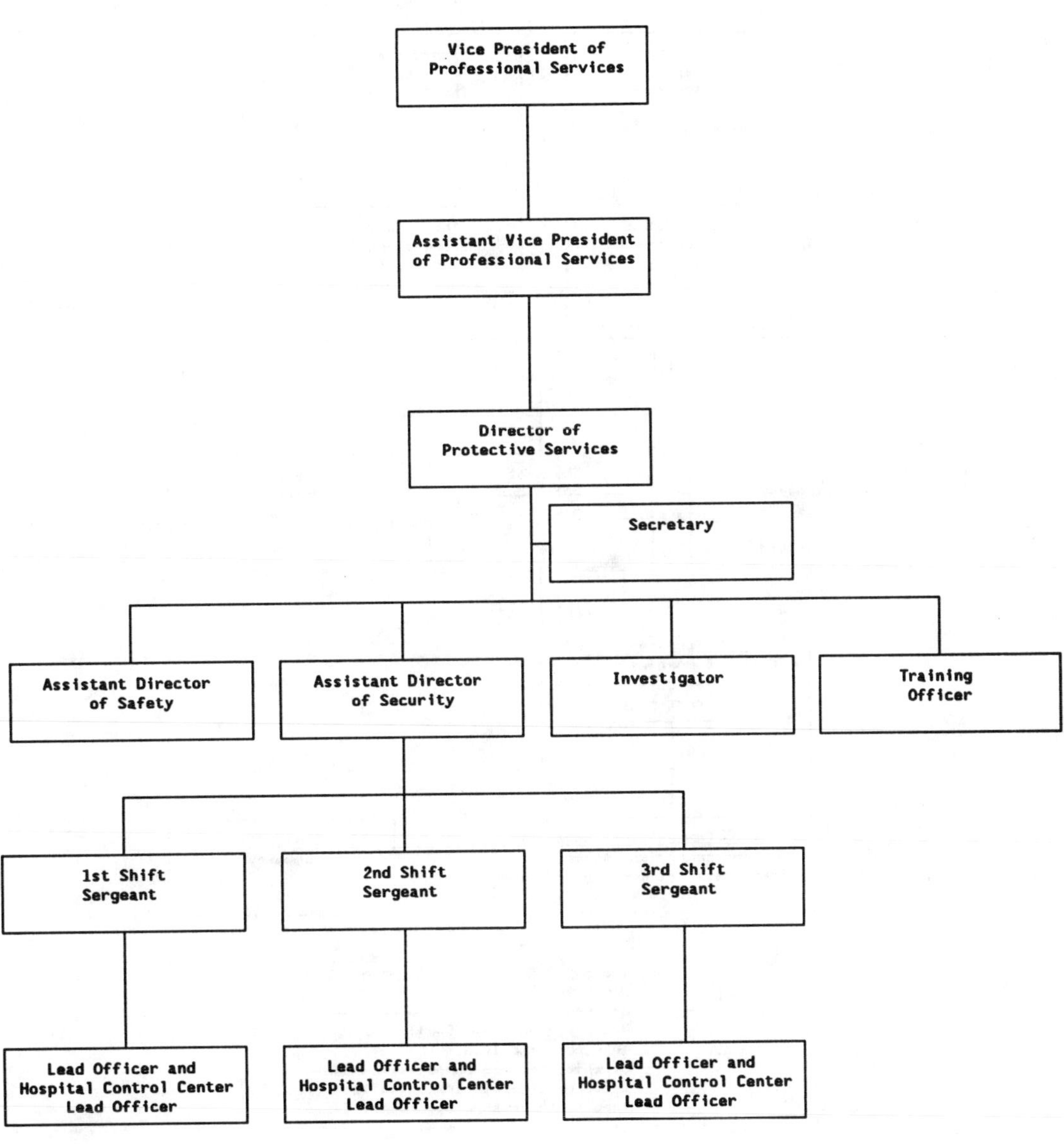
RIVERSIDE METHODIST HOSPITAL
DEPARTMENT OF PROTECTIVE SERVICES
Source: SECURITY MANAGEMENT
32: 173+ (September 1988)
Vice President of Professional Services
Assistant Vice President of Professional Services
Director of Protective Services
Secretary
Assistant Director of Safety
Assistant Director of Security
Investigator
Training Officer
1st Shift Sergeant
2nd Shift Sergeant
3rd Shift Sergeant
Lead Officer and Hospital Control Center Lead Officer
Lead Officer and Hospital Control Center Lead Officer
Lead Officer and Hospital Control Center Lead Officer

ROYAL DUTCH/SHELL GROUP OF COMPANIES (Netherlands)

Source: Annual report, 1990

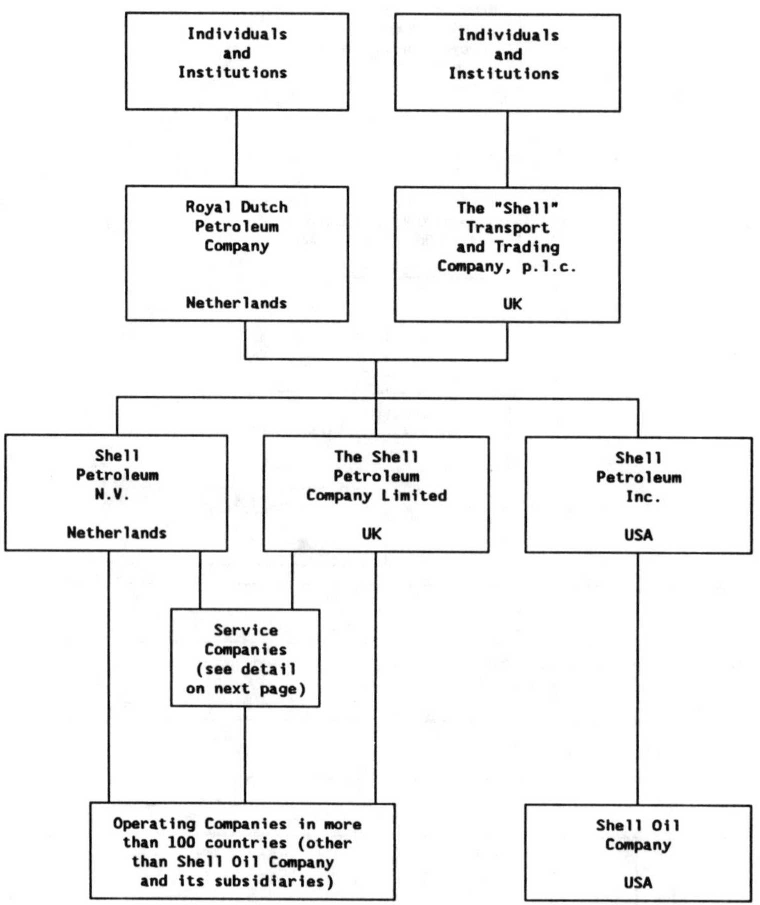

The Royal Dutch/Shell Group of Companies has grown out of an alliance between Royal Dutch Petroleum and the "Shell" Transport and Trading Co. plc., by which the two companies agreed to merge their interests while keeping their separate identities.

ROYAL DUTCH/SHELL GROUP OF COMPANIES (Netherlands)
SERVICE COMPANIES

Source: Company update, 1991

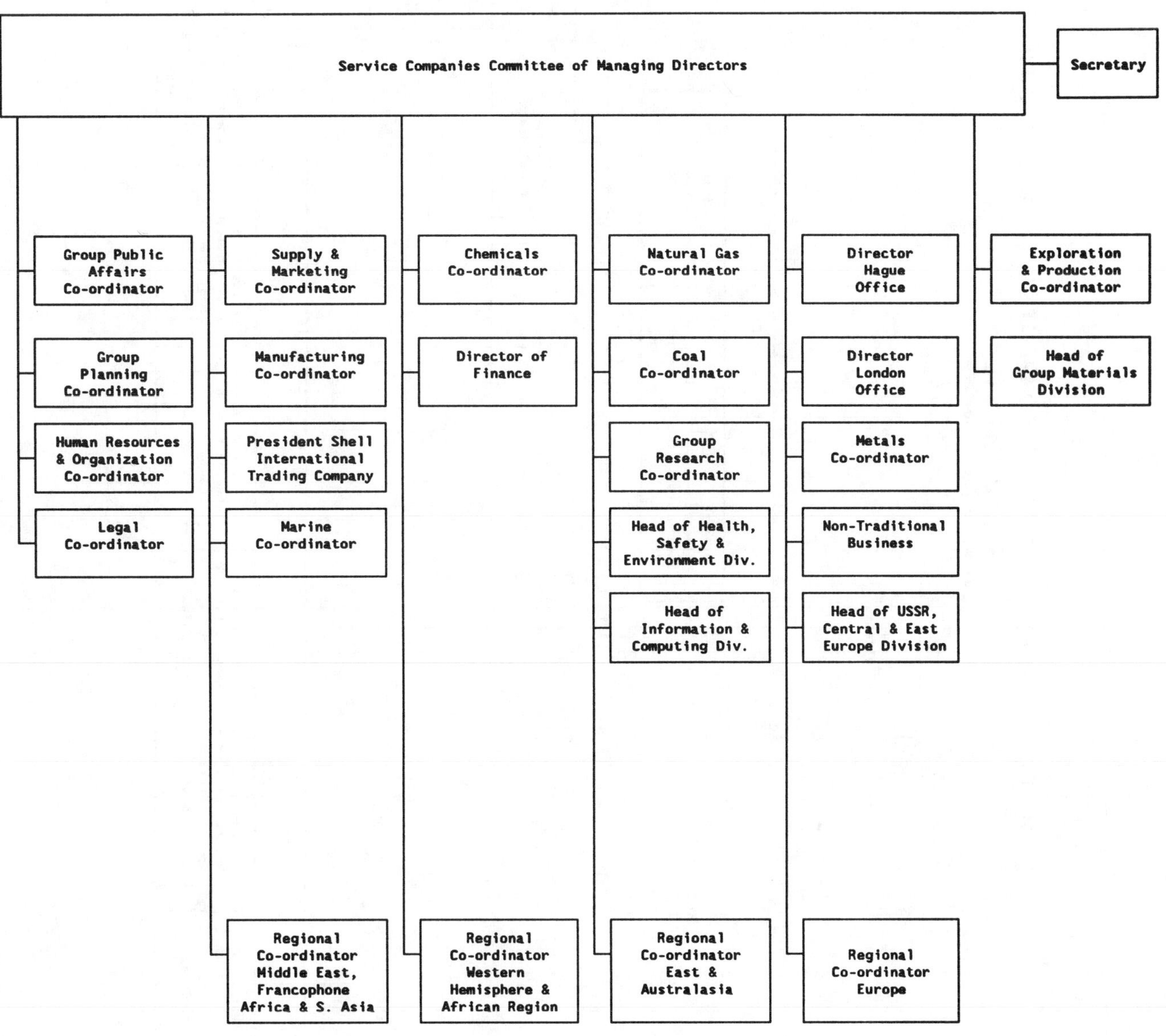

ROYAL DUTCH/SHELL GROUP OF COMPANIES (Netherlands)
SHELL U.K. OIL

Source: Company update, 1991

Managing Director

Corporate Office
- Director Finance & Information Services
- Director Personnel
  - Staff Planning and Resourcing
  - Personnel Strategy
  - Personnel Development
  - Office Manager
  - Job Evaluation
  - Regional Office Services
  - Personnel Glasgow R.O.
- Director Corporate Strategy

Director & General Manager Retail Division

Director & General Manager Commercial Division

Director & General Manager Special Markets Division

Director & General Manager Trading Division

Director & General Manager Supply & Distribution Division

Director & General Manager Shell Haven Refinery

Director & General Manager Stanlow Manufacturing Complex

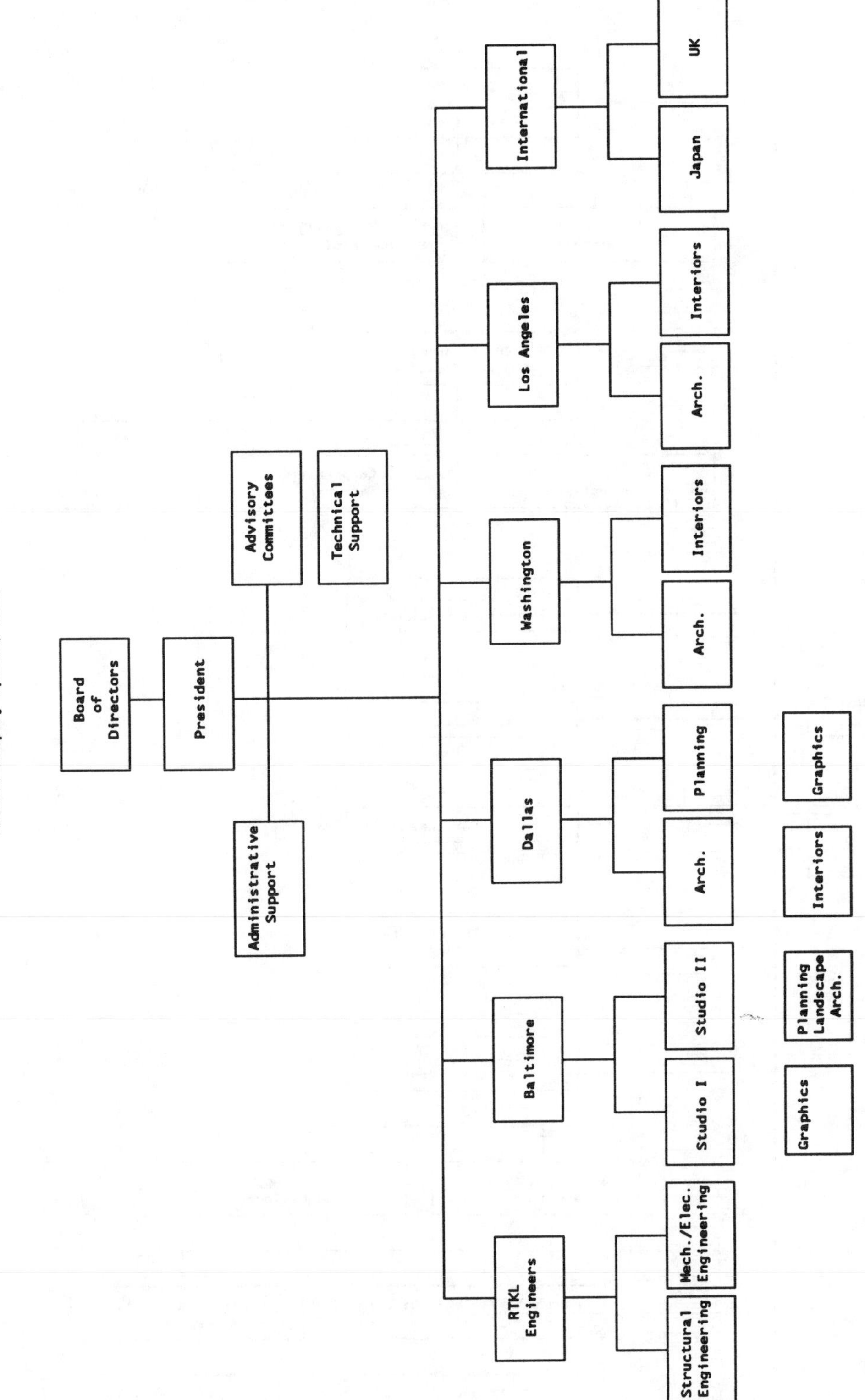
RTKL ASSOCIATES INC.
Source: Company update, 1991
Board of Directors
President
Advisory Committees
Technical Support
Administrative Support
RTKL Engineers
Structural Engineering
Mech./Elec. Engineering
Baltimore
Studio I
Studio II
Graphics
Planning Landscape Arch.
Dallas
Arch.
Planning
Interiors
Graphics
Washington
Arch.
Interiors
Los Angeles
Arch.
Interiors
International
Japan
UK

RUSSELL CORP.

Source: TEXTILE WORLD
140: 40+ (June 1990)

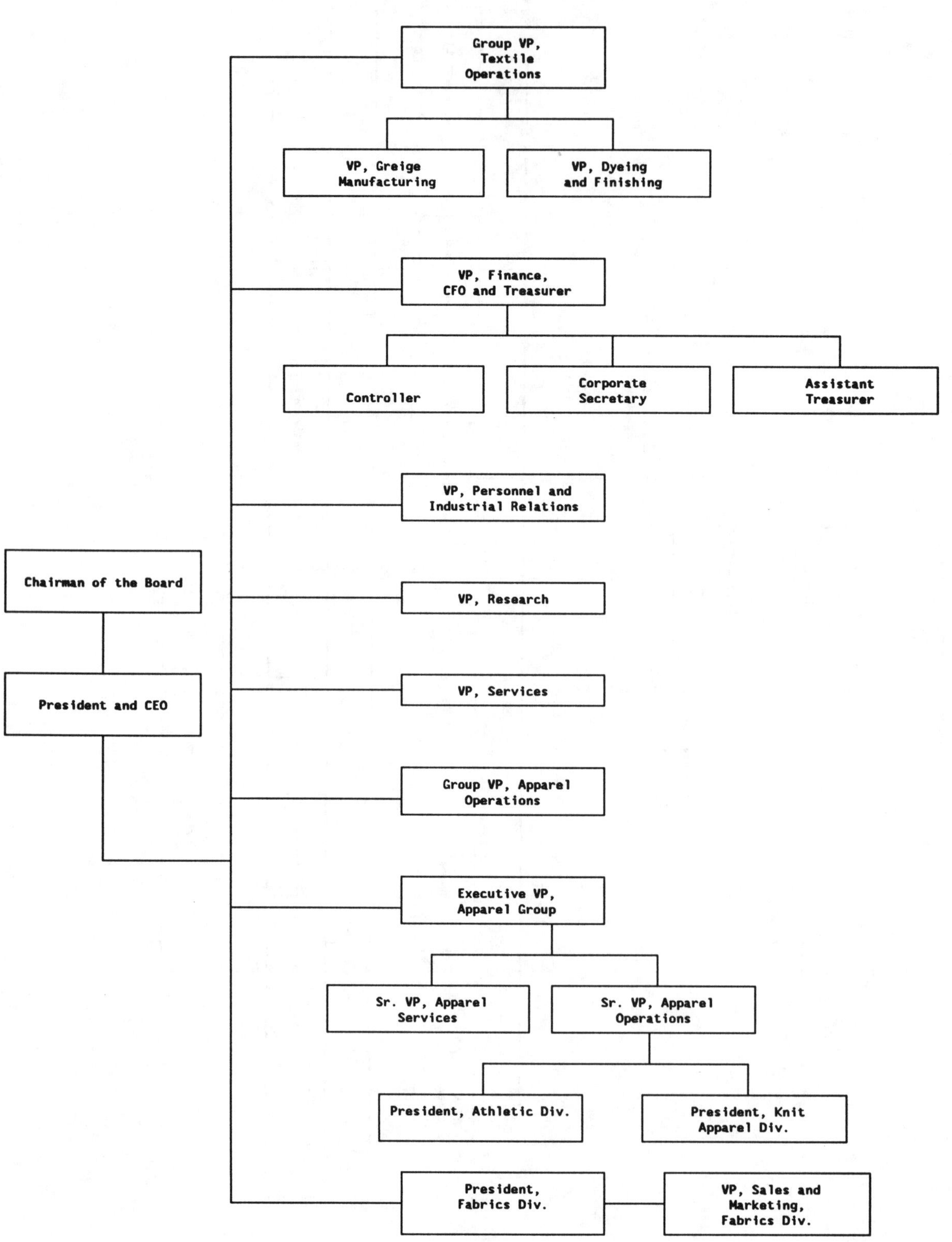

SAAB-SCANIA (Sweden)

Source: company update, 1991

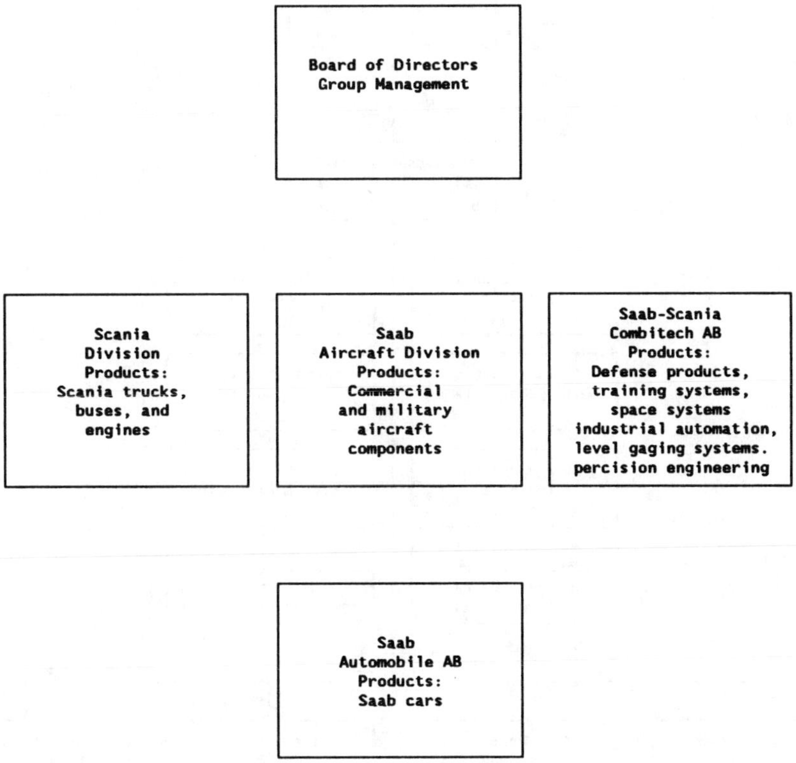

Board of Directors
Group Management

Scania
Division
Products:
Scania trucks,
buses, and
engines

Saab
Aircraft Division
Products:
Commercial
and military
aircraft
components

Saab-Scania
Combitech AB
Products:
Defense products,
training systems,
space systems
industrial automation,
level gaging systems.
percision engineering

Saab
Automobile AB
Products:
Saab cars

SAS INTERNATIONAL HOTELS (Belgium)

Source: Company update, 1991

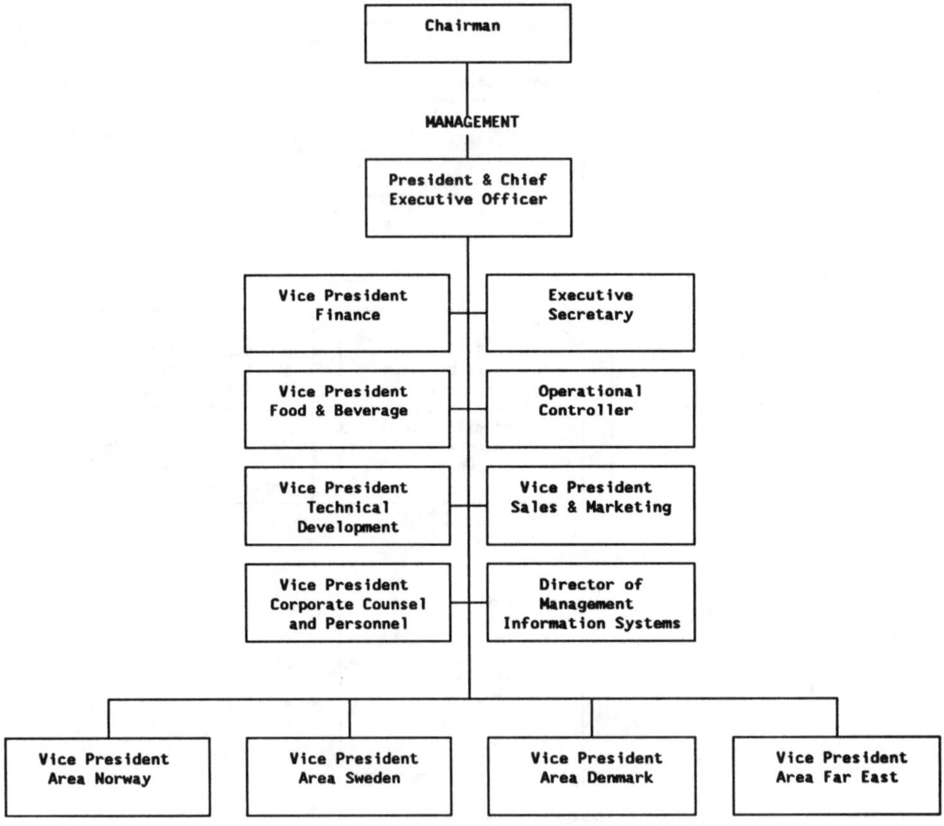

SCANDIC HOTEL AB

Source: "25 Years--This Is the Result"
1988

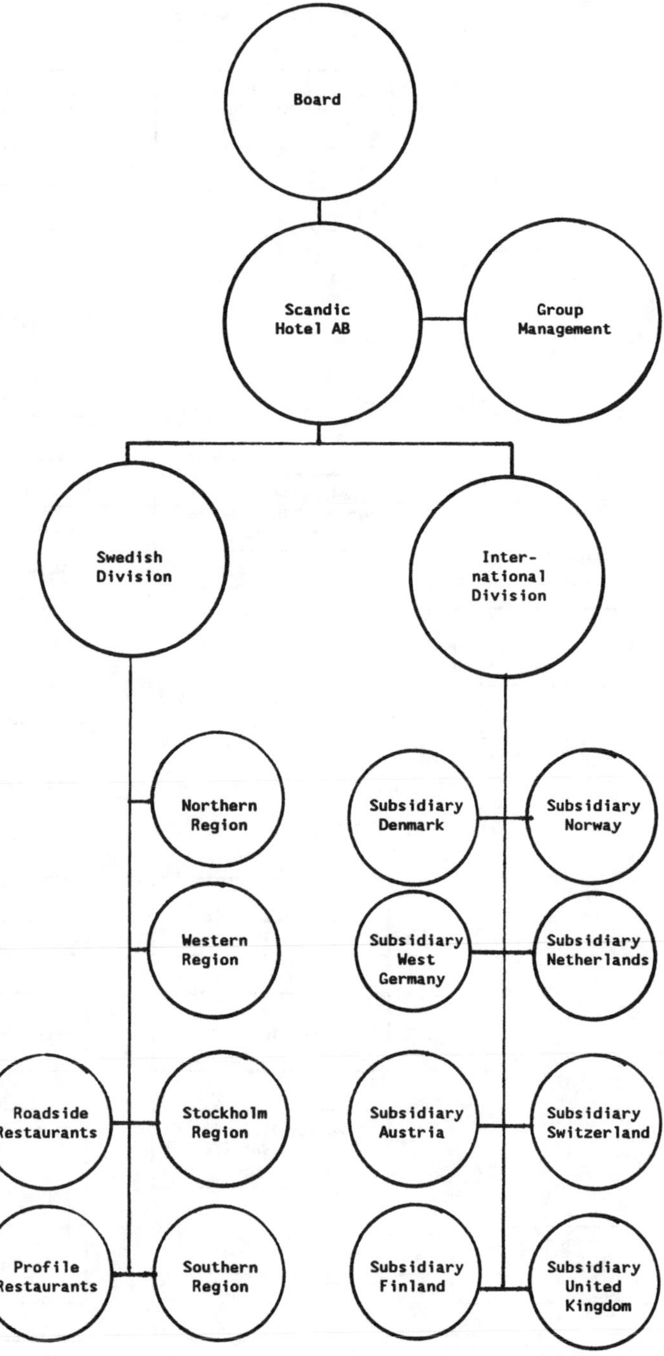

SCOTTISH & NEWCASTLE BREWERIES PLC (Scotland)

Source: Annual report, 1988

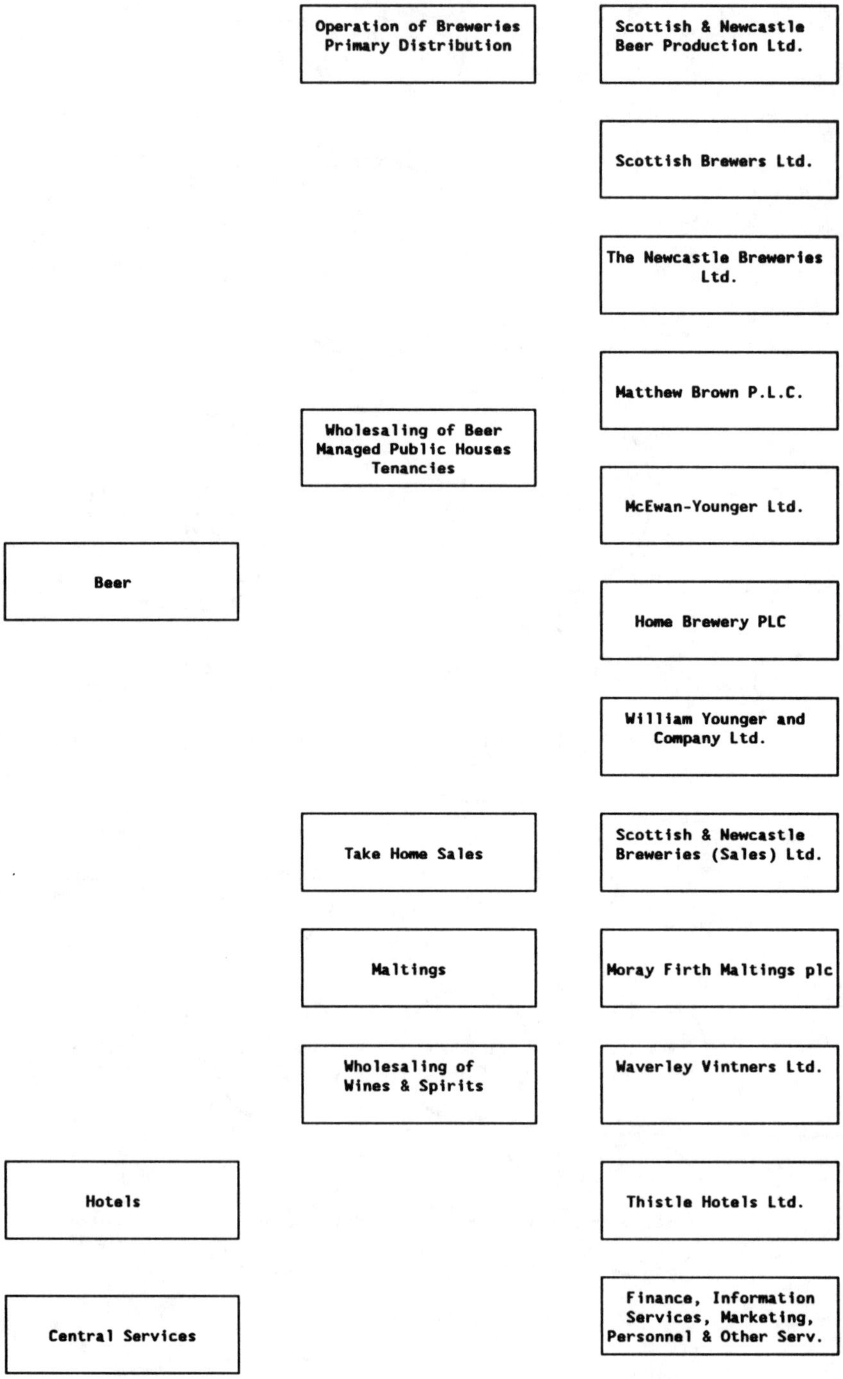

Operation of Breweries
Primary Distribution

Scottish & Newcastle
Beer Production Ltd.

Scottish Brewers Ltd.

The Newcastle Breweries
Ltd.

Matthew Brown P.L.C.

Wholesaling of Beer
Managed Public Houses
Tenancies

McEwan-Younger Ltd.

Beer

Home Brewery PLC

William Younger and
Company Ltd.

Take Home Sales

Scottish & Newcastle
Breweries (Sales) Ltd.

Maltings

Moray Firth Maltings plc

Wholesaling of
Wines & Spirits

Waverley Vintners Ltd.

Hotels

Thistle Hotels Ltd.

Central Services

Finance, Information
Services, Marketing,
Personnel & Other Serv.

SEARS, ROEBUCK AND CO.
CORPORATE OPERATIONS

Source: Annual report, 1988

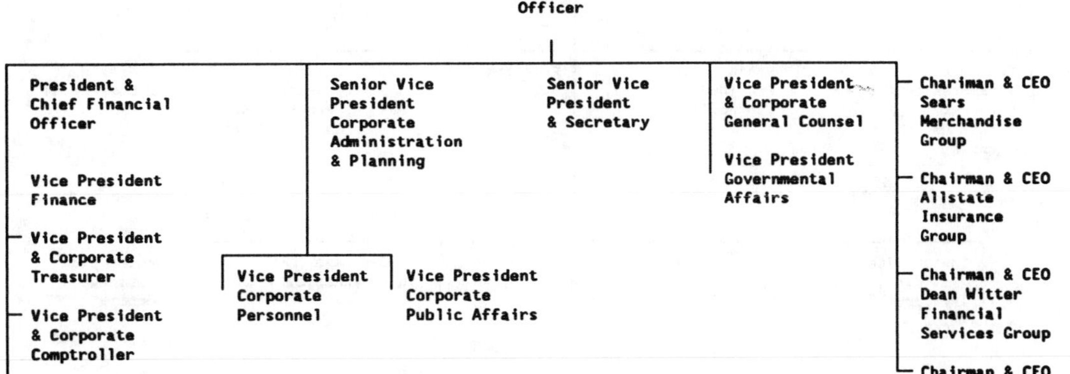

SEARS ROEBUCK AND CO.
ALLSTATE INSURANCE GROUP

Source: Annual Report, 1988

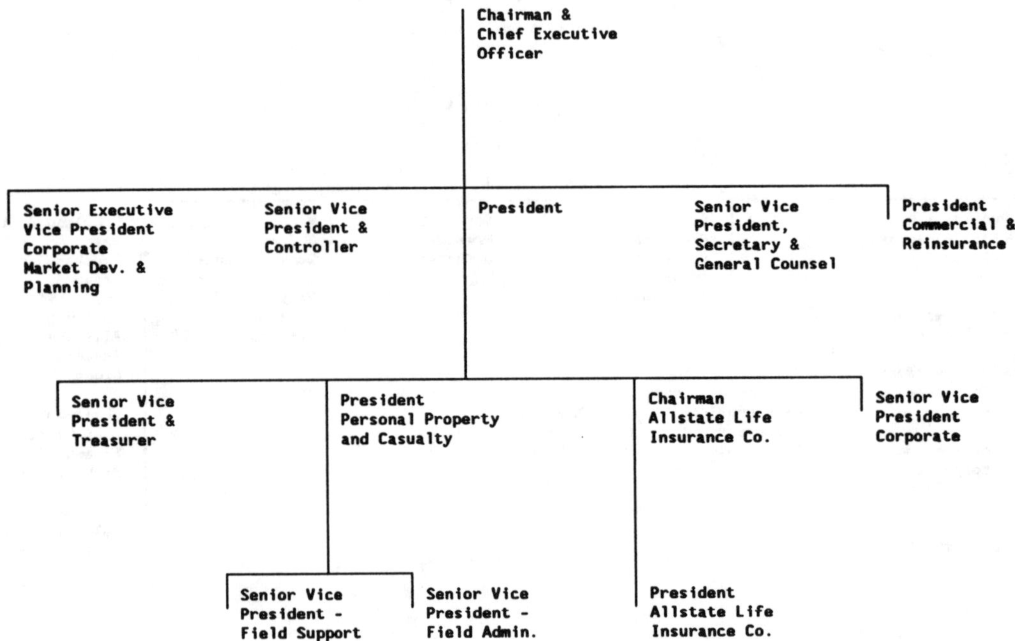

SEARS ROEBUCK AND CO.
COLDWELL BANKER REAL ESTATE GROUP

Source: Sears annual report, 1988

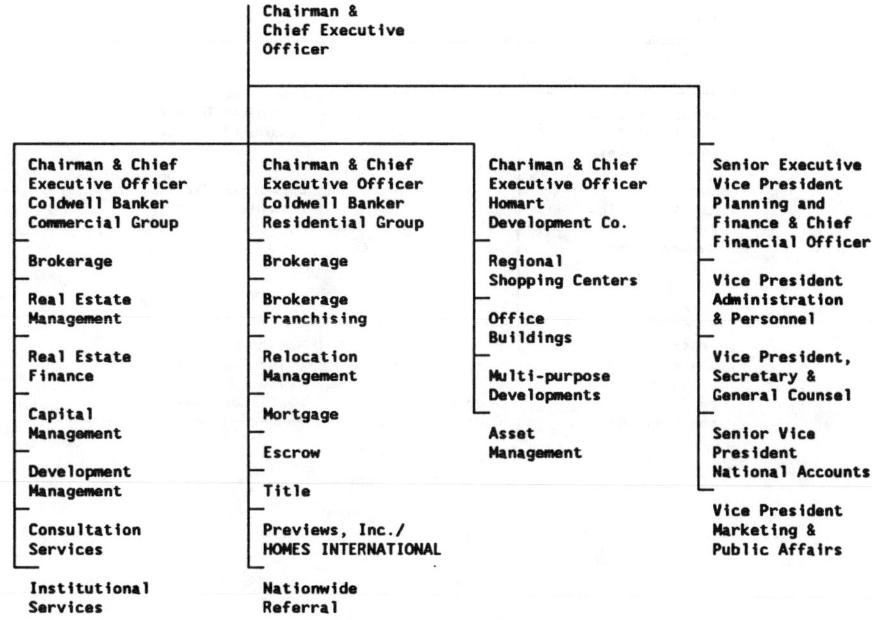

Chairman & Chief Executive Officer
Chairman & Chief Executive Officer Coldwell Banker Commercial Group
Brokerage
Real Estate Management
Real Estate Finance
Capital Management
Development Management
Consultation Services
Institutional Services
Chairman & Chief Executive Officer Coldwell Banker Residential Group
Brokerage
Brokerage Franchising
Relocation Management
Mortgage
Escrow
Title
Previews, Inc./ HOMES INTERNATIONAL
Nationwide Referral
Chariman & Chief Executive Officer Homart Development Co.
Regional Shopping Centers
Office Buildings
Multi-purpose Developments
Asset Management
Senior Executive Vice President Planning and Finance & Chief Financial Officer
Vice President Administration & Personnel
Vice President, Secretary & General Counsel
Senior Vice President National Accounts
Vice President Marketing & Public Affairs

SEARS ROEBUCK AND CO.
DEAN WITTER FINANCIAL SERVICES GROUP

Source: Sears annual report, 1988

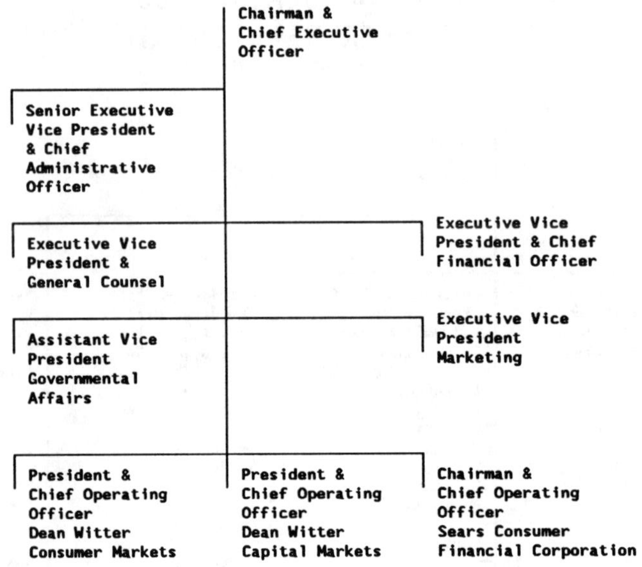

Dean Witter Financial Services Group conducts its securities related activities through the Consumer Markets and Capital Markets divisions. The Sears Consumer Financial Corp. division serves as the administrative umbrella for Discover Card Services, Sears Payment Systems, and mortgage and consumer lending.--
Sears Annual report, 1988.

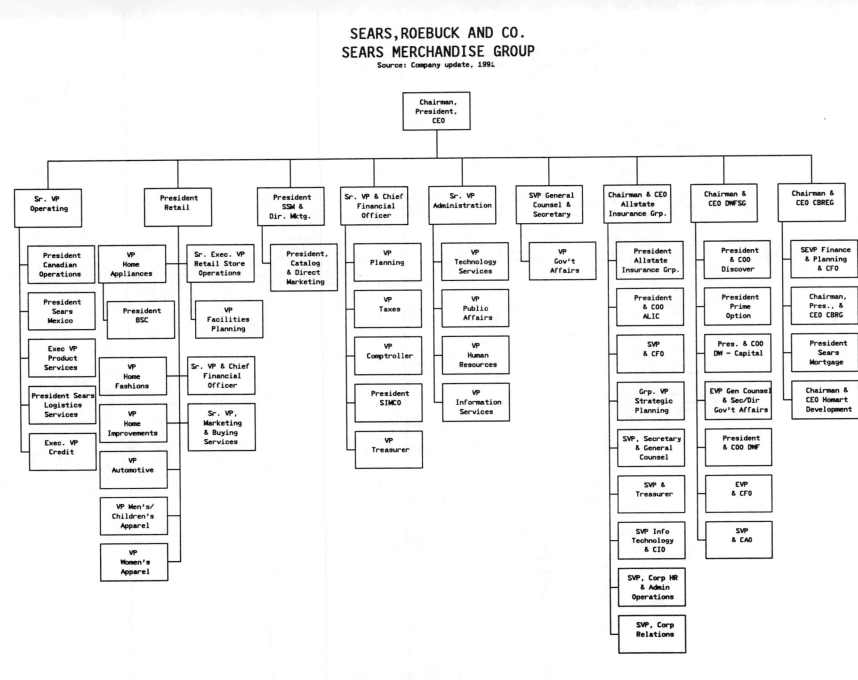

SEARS, ROEBUCK AND CO.
SEARS MERCHANDISE GROUP

Source: Company update, 1991

Chairman, President, CEO

- Sr. VP Operating
  - President Canadian Operations
  - President Sears Mexico
  - Exec VP Product Services
  - President Sears Logistics Services
  - Exec. VP Credit
- President Retail
  - Sr. Exec. VP Retail Store Operations
    - VP Home Appliances
      - President BSC
    - VP Facilities Planning
  - Sr. VP & Chief Financial Officer
  - Sr. VP, Marketing & Buying Services
  - VP Home Fashions
  - VP Home Improvements
  - VP Automotive
  - VP Men's/Children's Apparel
  - VP Women's Apparel
- President SSM & Dir. Mktg.
  - President, Catalog & Direct Marketing
- Sr. VP & Chief Financial Officer
  - VP Planning
  - VP Taxes
  - VP Comptroller
  - President SIMCO
  - VP Treasurer
- Sr. VP Administration
  - VP Technology Services
  - VP Public Affairs
  - VP Human Resources
  - VP Information Services
- SVP General Counsel & Secretary
  - VP Gov't Affairs
- Chairman & CEO Allstate Insurance Grp.
  - President Allstate Insurance Grp.
  - President & COO ALIC
  - SVP & CFO
  - Grp. VP Strategic Planning
  - SVP, Secretary & General Counsel
  - SVP & Treasurer
  - SVP Info Technology & CIO
  - SVP, Corp HR & Admin Operations
  - SVP, Corp Relations
- Chairman & CEO DWFSG
  - President & COO Discover
  - President Prime Option
  - Pres. & COO DW - Capital
  - EVP Gen Counsel & Sec/Dir Gov't Affairs
  - President & COO DWF
  - EVP & CFO
  - SVP & CAO
- Chairman & CEO CBREG
  - SEVP Finance & Planning & CFO
  - Chairman, Pres., & CEO CBRG
  - President Sears Mortgage
  - Chairman & CEO Homart Development

SEIBU DEPARTMENT STORES (Japan)

Source: Company update, 1991

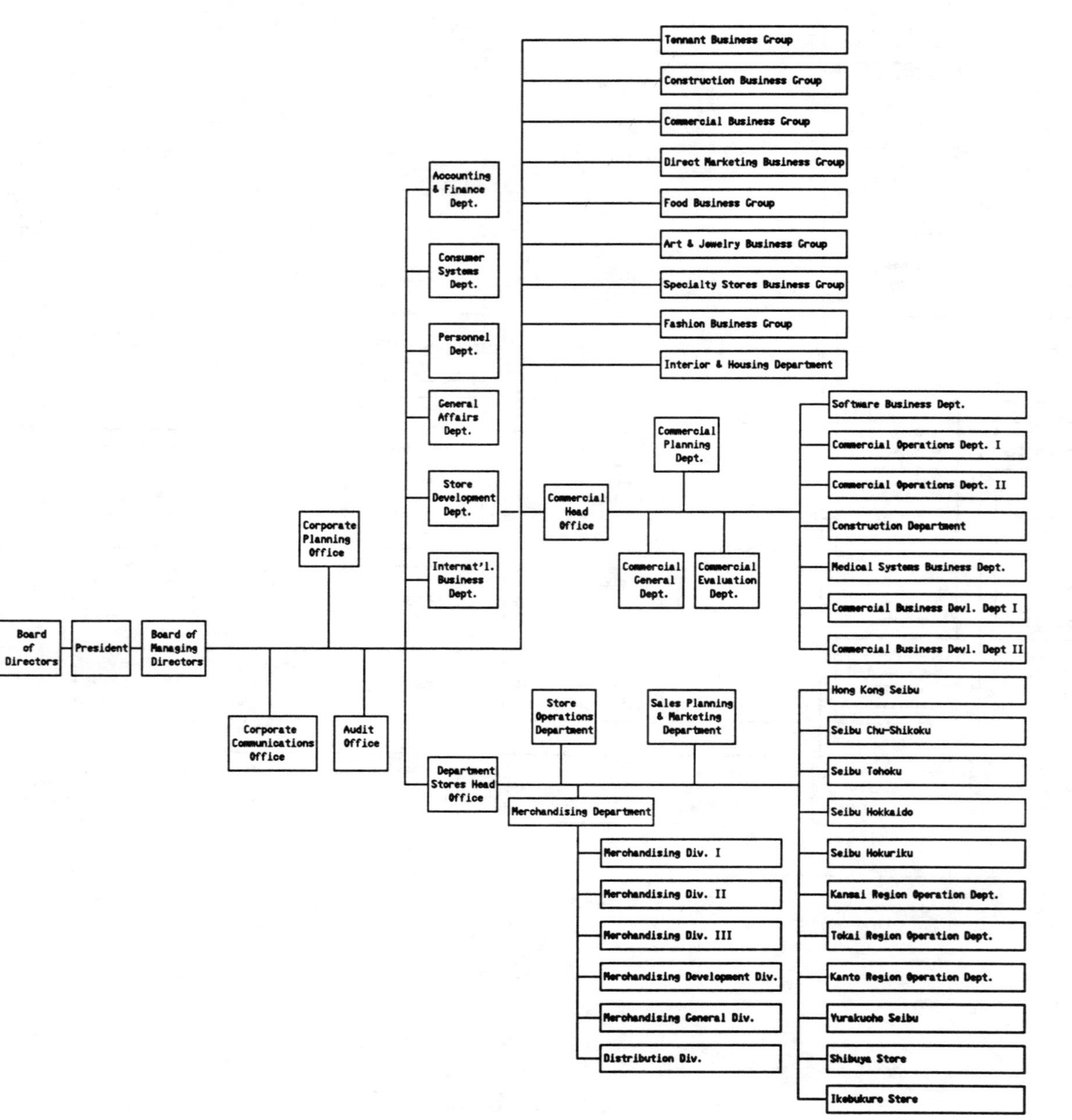

SIEMENS (Germany)

Source: Annual report, 1991

Managing Board
Corporate Executive
Committee

Groups

- Industrial and Building Systems
- Drives and Standard Products
- Automation
- Automotive Systems
- Power Generation (KWU)
- Power Transmission and Distribution
- Semiconductors
- Medical Engineering
- Public Communication Networks
- Passive Components and Electron Tubes
- Private Communication Systems
- Defense Electronics
- Transportation Systems

Special divisions

- Audio and Video Systems
- Electromechanical Components

Legally independent unit

- Osram GmH

Corporate divisions

- Corporate Finance
- Corporate Research and Development
- Corporate Personnel
- Corporate Production and Logistics
- Corporate Planning and Development

Central departments

- Corporate Relations
- Berlin Administration
- International Regions

Centralized services

- Domestic Regional Administration
- Berlin
- Munich
- Personnel

Regional organization
Regional offices, international Siemens companies, sales companies, representative offices, agencies

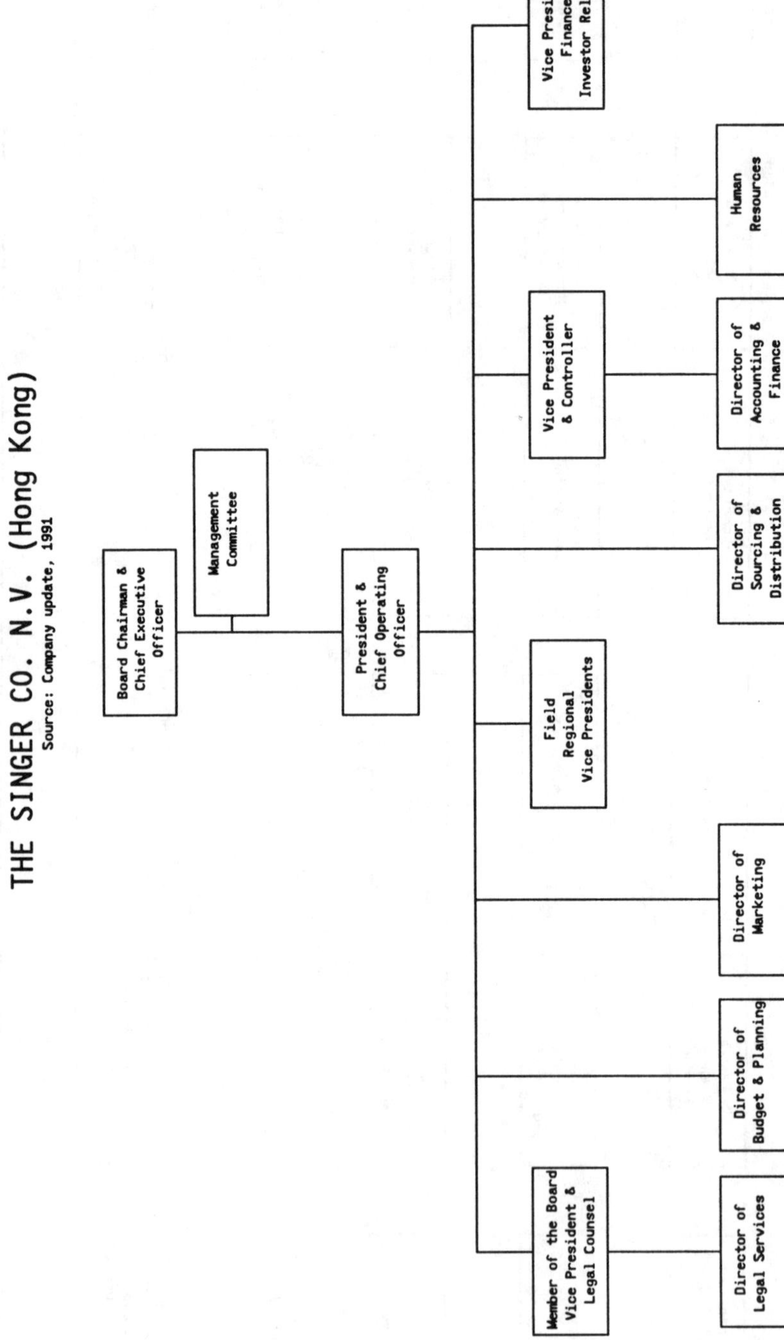
THE SINGER CO. N.V. (Hong Kong)
Source: Company update, 1991
Board Chairman & Chief Executive Officer
Management Committee
President & Chief Operating Officer
Vice President Finance & Investor Relations
Human Resources
Vice President & Controller
Director of Accounting & Finance
Director of Sourcing & Distribution
Field Regional Vice Presidents
Director of Marketing
Director of Budget & Planning
Member of the Board Vice President & Legal Counsel
Director of Legal Services

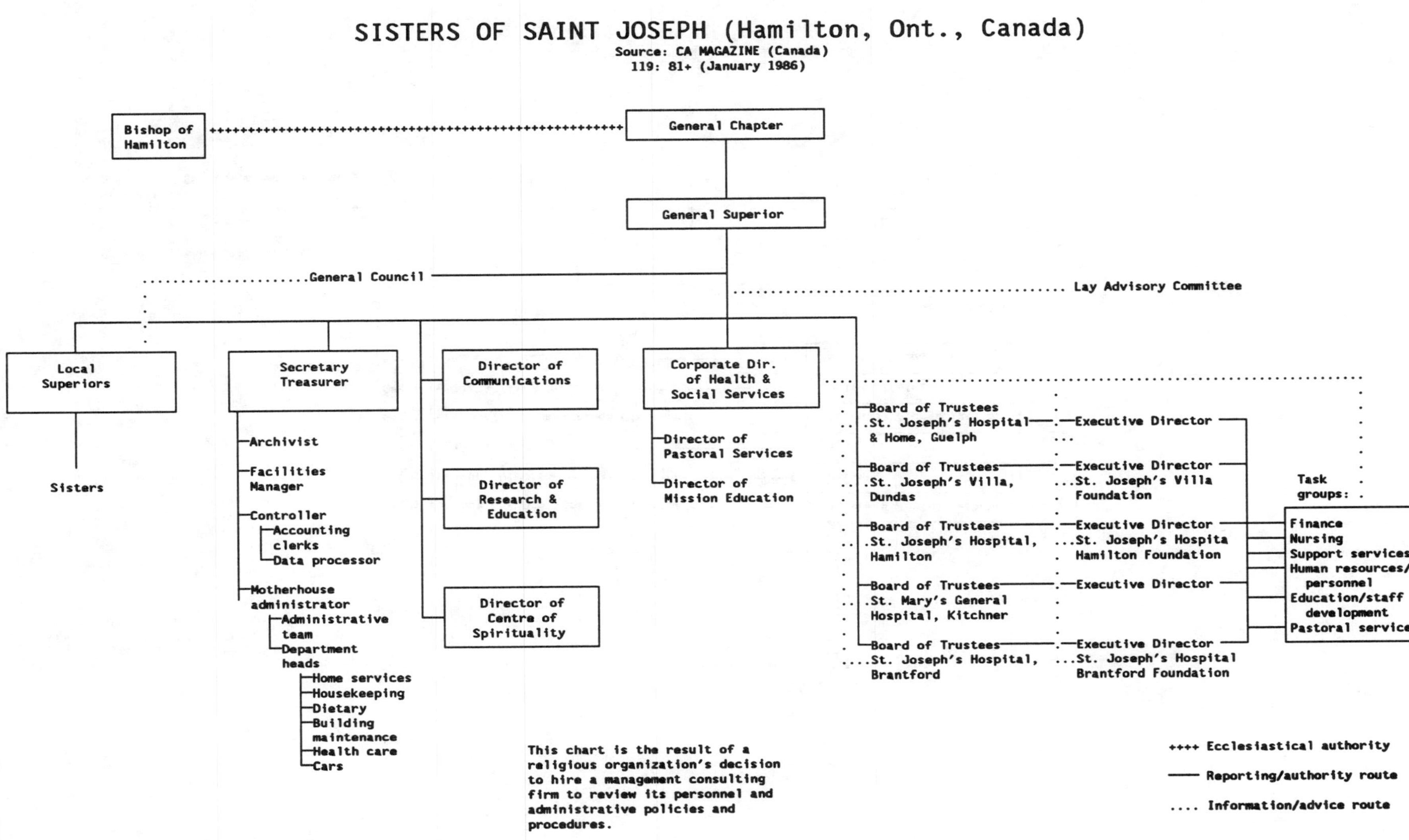
SISTERS OF SAINT JOSEPH (Hamilton, Ont., Canada)
Source: CA MAGAZINE (Canada)
119: 81+ (January 1986)
Bishop of Hamilton
General Chapter
General Superior
General Council
Lay Advisory Committee
Local Superiors
Sisters
Secretary Treasurer
Archivist
Facilities Manager
Controller
Accounting clerks
Data processor
Motherhouse administrator
Administrative team
Department heads
Home services
Housekeeping
Dietary
Building maintenance
Health care
Cars
Director of Communications
Director of Research & Education
Director of Centre of Spirituality
Corporate Dir. of Health & Social Services
Director of Pastoral Services
Director of Mission Education
Board of Trustees
St. Joseph's Hospital & Home, Guelph
Executive Director
Board of Trustees
St. Joseph's Villa, Dundas
Executive Director
St. Joseph's Villa Foundation
Board of Trustees
St. Joseph's Hospital, Hamilton
Executive Director
St. Joseph's Hospita Hamilton Foundation
Board of Trustees
St. Mary's General Hospital, Kitchner
Executive Director
Board of Trustees
St. Joseph's Hospital, Brantford
Executive Director
St. Joseph's Hospital Brantford Foundation
Task groups:
Finance
Nursing
Support services
Human resources/ personnel
Education/staff development
Pastoral service
This chart is the result of a religious organization's decision to hire a management consulting firm to review its personnel and administrative policies and procedures.
++++ Ecclesiastical authority
—— Reporting/authority route
.... Information/advice route

SKF GROUP (Sweden)

Source: Company update. 1991

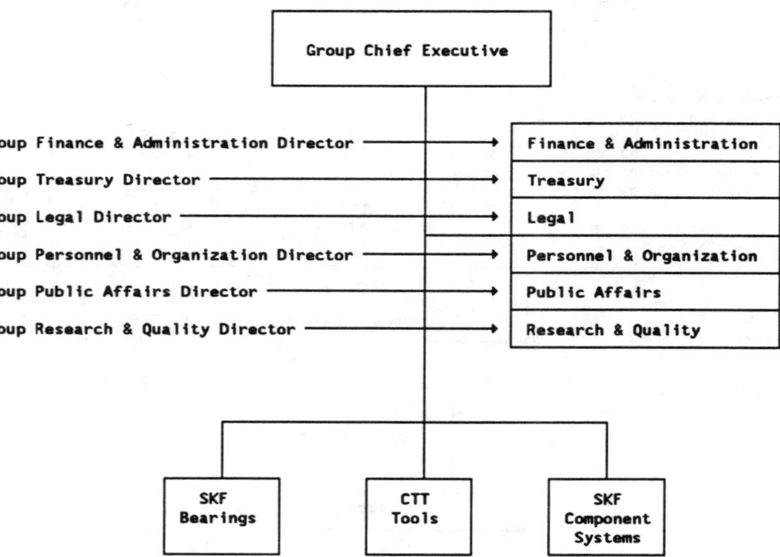

This chart shows the positions of the six staff units at Group level. Other areas of responsibility, such as Marketing, are delegated to the business areas (SKF Bearings, CTT Tools, and SKF Component Systems.)

SOUTHWESTERN BELL CORP.

Source: KANSAS CITY BUSINESS JOURNAL
7: 21+ (November 28, 1988)

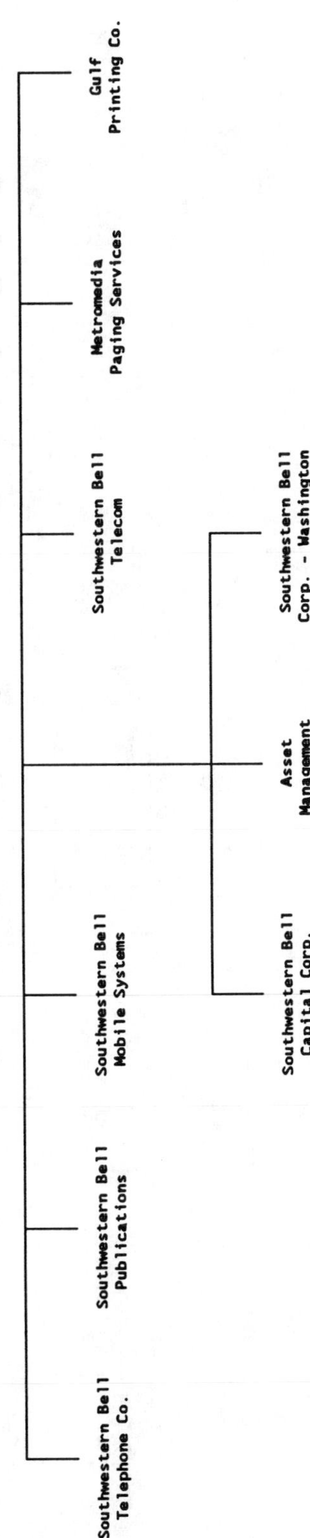

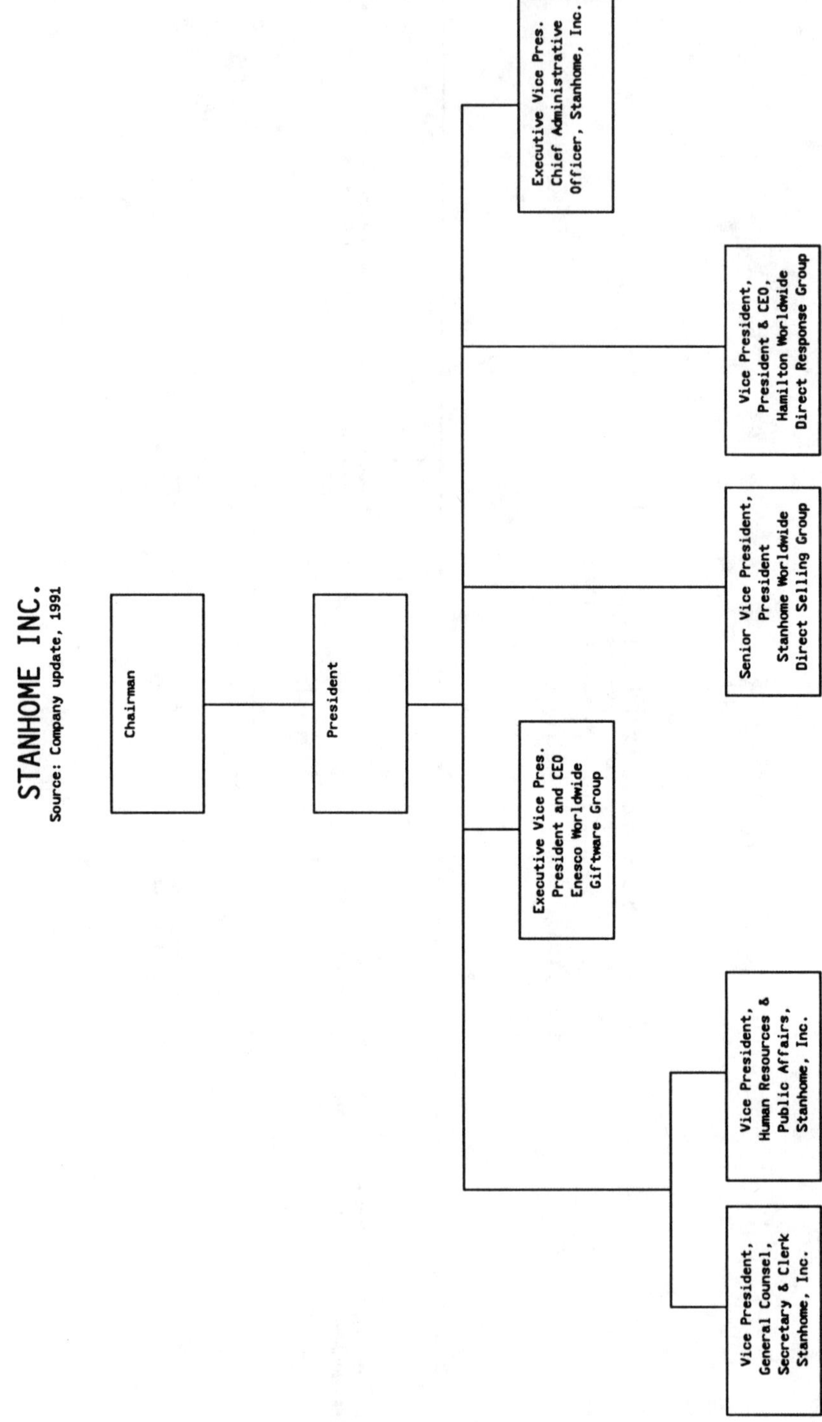
STANHOME INC.
Source: Company update, 1991
Chairman
President
Executive Vice Pres. President and CEO Enesco Worldwide Giftware Group
Executive Vice Pres. Chief Administrative Officer, Stanhome, Inc.
Vice President, General Counsel, Secretary & Clerk Stanhome, Inc.
Vice President, Human Resources & Public Affairs, Stanhome, Inc.
Senior Vice President, President Stanhome Worldwide Direct Selling Group
Vice President, President & CEO, Hamilton Worldwide Direct Response Group

STELCO INC. (Canada)

Source: Annual report, 1990

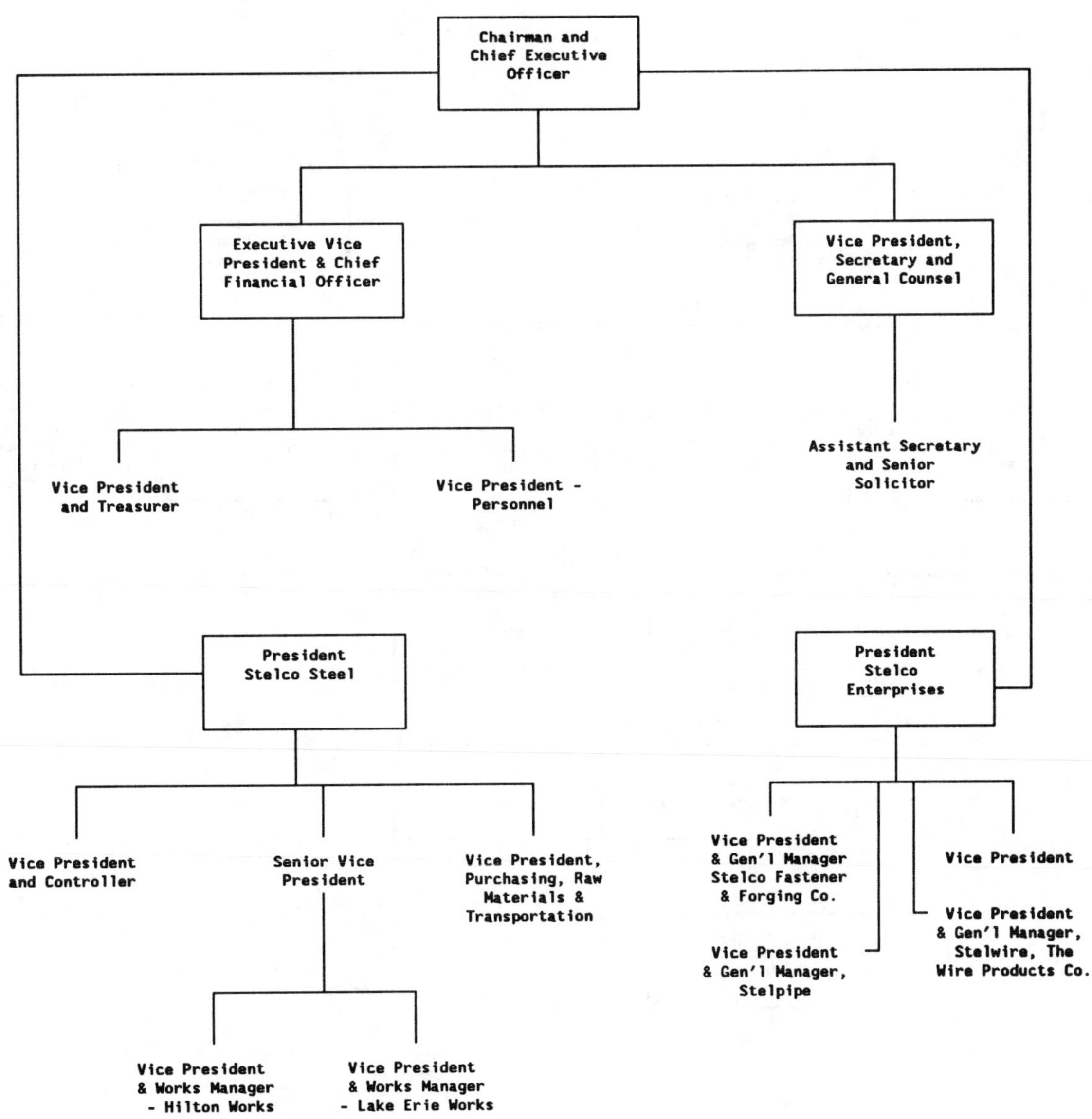

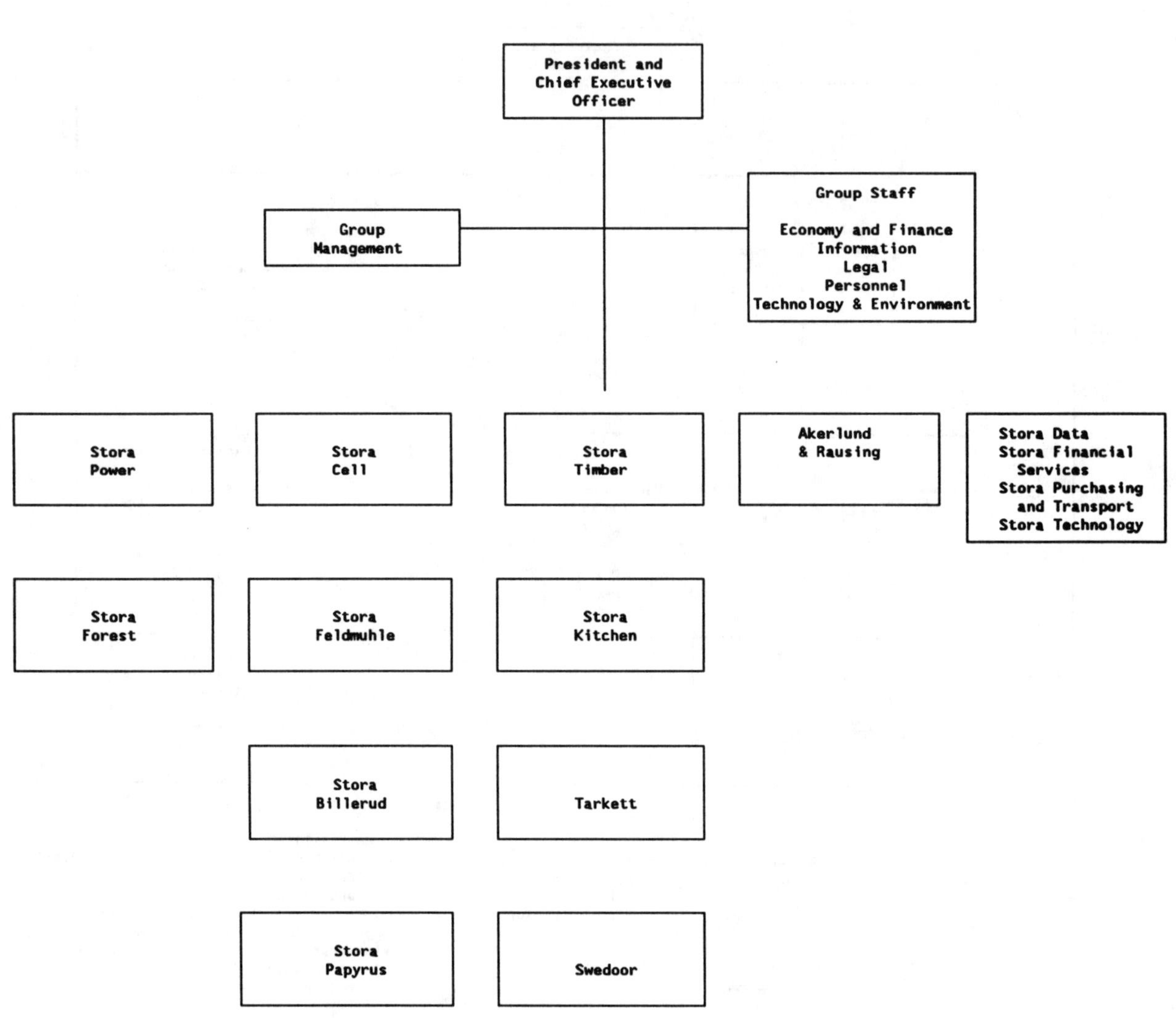
STORA KOPPARBERGS BERGSLAGS AB (Sweden)
Source: Company update, 1991
President and Chief Executive Officer
Group Management
Group Staff
Economy and Finance
Information
Legal
Personnel
Technology & Environment
Stora Power
Stora Cell
Stora Timber
Akerlund & Rausing
Stora Data
Stora Financial Services
Stora Purchasing and Transport
Stora Technology
Stora Forest
Stora Feldmuhle
Stora Kitchen
Stora Billerud
Tarkett
Stora Papyrus
Swedoor

SULZER (Switzerland)

Source: Company update, 1991

- Prasident der Konzernleitung

- Konzernstab Generalsekretariat und Information
- Konzernstabsbereich Finanz und Administration
- Konzernstab Finanz und Rechnungswesen
- Konzernstab Konzernrevision
- Konzernstab Recht
- Dienstleistungsbereich Liegenschaften
- Produktbereich Informatik

- Konzernstabsbereich Konzernentwicklung
- Konzernstab Unternehmensplanung
- Dienstleistungsbereich Sulzer-Innotec
- Konzernabteilung Industriele Elektronik
- Konzerngesellschaft ELMA Electronic AG Wetzikon

- Konzernstab Personal
- Konzernbereich Sulzer International
- Region Europa/Sudl. Afrika
- Region Nordamerika/Mexiko
- Region Asien/Australien
- Region Sudamerika/Afrika

Unternehmensbereich Sulzer Ruti

Funktionsbereiche

- Verkauf
- Technik
- Produktion
- Service
- Lizenzen und Logistik

Unternehmensbereich Sulzer Infra

Marktbereiche

- Sulzer Infra Schweiz
- Sulzer Infra Deutschland
- Sulzer Infra Frankreich
- Sulzer Infra Grossbritannien
- Sulzer Infra Niederlande
- Sulzer Infra Osterreich
- Sulzer Infra Spanien

Unternehmensbereich Sulzermedica

Bereiche

- Orthopadie
- Intermedics Herzschrittmacher
- Kreislaufimplantate

Unternehmensbereich Anlagentechnik

Produktbereiche

- Sulzer-Chemtech
- Pumpen

Unternehmensbereich Winterthur

Produktbereiche

- Thermische Energiesysteme
- Giessereien
- Kolbenkompressoren
- Lokomotiven und Getriebe
- Oberflachentechnik

Unternehmensbereich Escher Wyss

Produktbereiche

- Hydraulik
- Thermische Turbomaschinen
- Papiertechnik

SUMMA GROUP (Indonesia)
SUMMA INTERNATIONAL

Source: FAR EASTERN ECONOMIC REVIEW
148: 55+ (April 26, 1990)

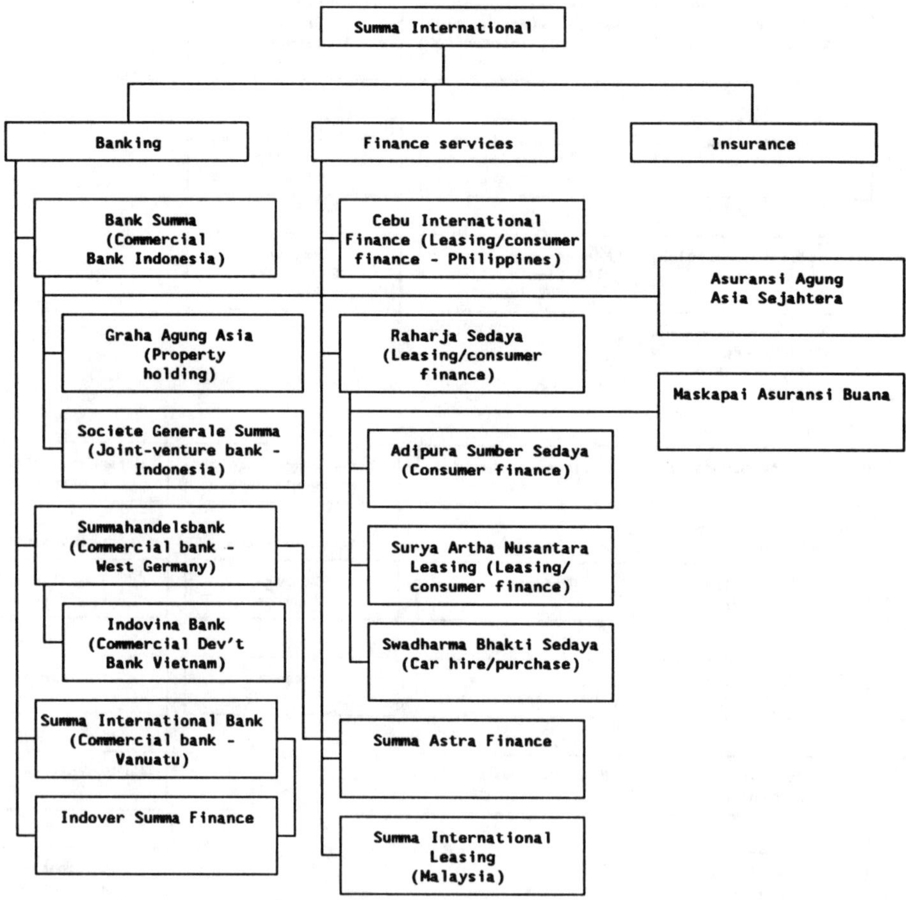

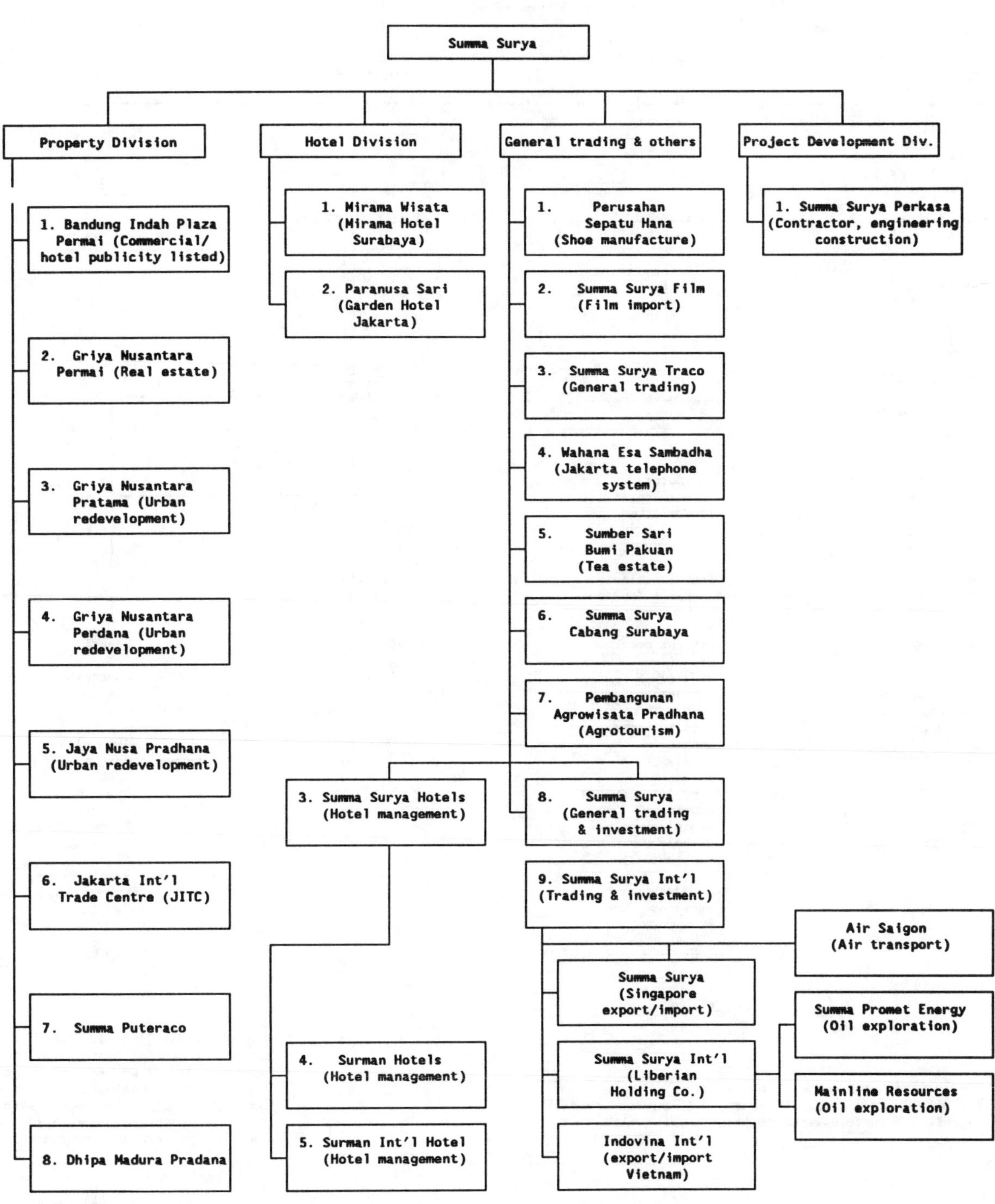
SUMMA GROUP (Indonesia)
SUMMA SURYA
Source: FAR EASTERN ECONOMIC REVIEW
148: 55+ (April 26, 1990
Summa Surya
Property Division
Hotel Division
General trading & others
Project Development Div.
1. Bandung Indah Plaza Permai (Commercial/ hotel publicity listed)
2. Griya Nusantara Permai (Real estate)
3. Griya Nusantara Pratama (Urban redevelopment)
4. Griya Nusantara Perdana (Urban redevelopment)
5. Jaya Nusa Pradhana (Urban redevelopment)
6. Jakarta Int'l Trade Centre (JITC)
7. Summa Puteraco
8. Dhipa Madura Pradana
1. Mirama Wisata (Mirama Hotel Surabaya)
2. Paranusa Sari (Garden Hotel Jakarta)
3. Summa Surya Hotels (Hotel management)
4. Surman Hotels (Hotel management)
5. Surman Int'l Hotel (Hotel management)
1. Perusahan Sepatu Hana (Shoe manufacture)
2. Summa Surya Film (Film import)
3. Summa Surya Traco (General trading)
4. Wahana Esa Sambadha (Jakarta telephone system)
5. Sumber Sari Bumi Pakuan (Tea estate)
6. Summa Surya Cabang Surabaya
7. Pembangunan Agrowisata Pradhana (Agrotourism)
8. Summa Surya (General trading & investment)
9. Summa Surya Int'l (Trading & investment)
Air Saigon (Air transport)
Summa Surya (Singapore export/import)
Summa Surya Int'l (Liberian Holding Co.)
Indovina Int'l (export/import Vietnam)
Summa Promet Energy (Oil exploration)
Mainline Resources (Oil exploration)
1. Summa Surya Perkasa (Contractor, engineering construction)

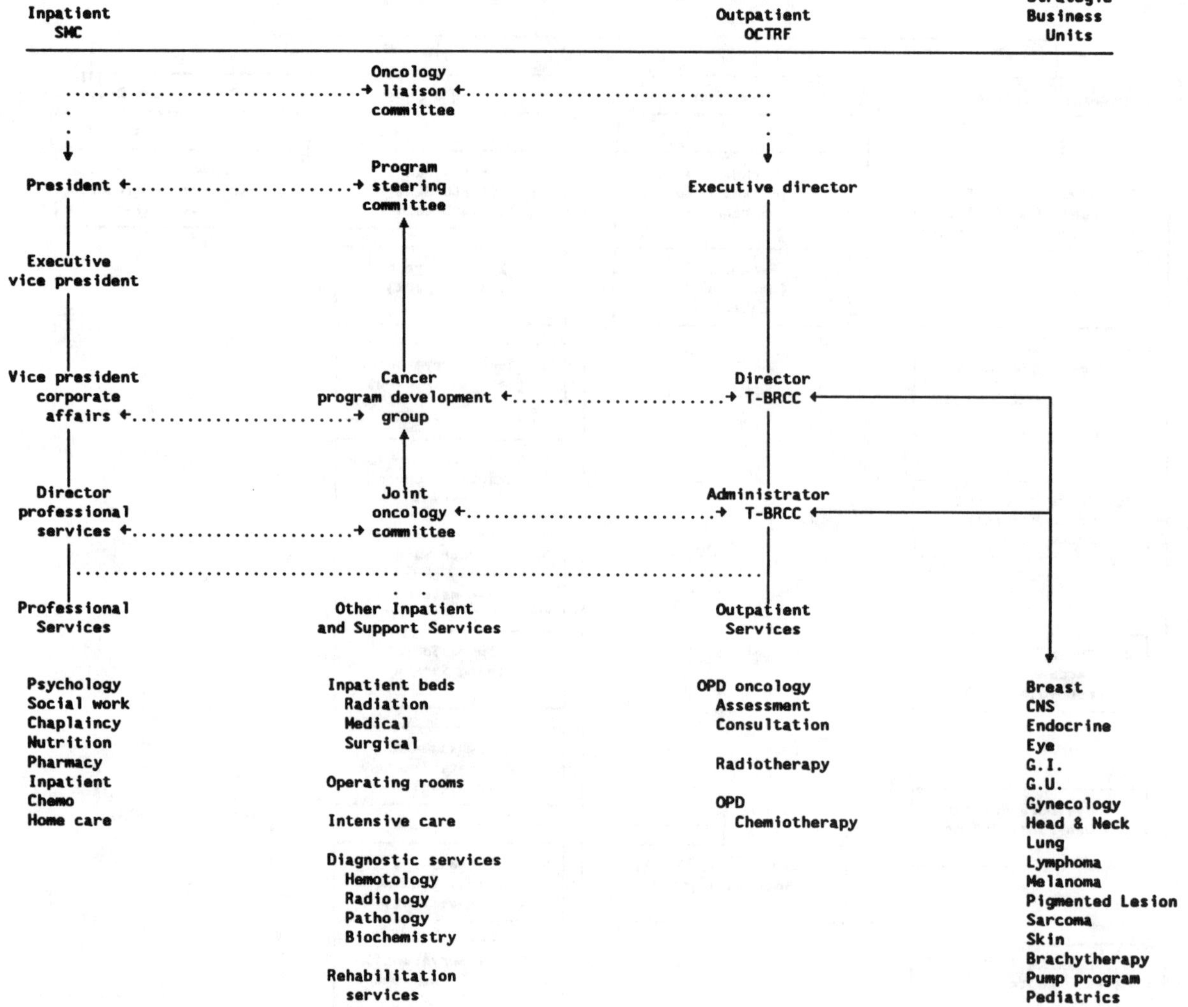

SMC = Sunnybrook Medical Centre
OCTRF = Ontario Cancer Treatment and Research Foundation
T-BRCC = Toronto-Bayview Regional Cancer Centre

This chart details the joint venture of Sunnybrook Medical Centre and Toronto-Bayview Regional Cancer Centre, of the Ontario Cancer Treatment and Research Foundation, to provide coordinated, integrated planning and marketing of comprehensive cancer services.

SWIFT TEXTILES INC.

Source: TEXTILE WORLD
139:48+ (June 1989)

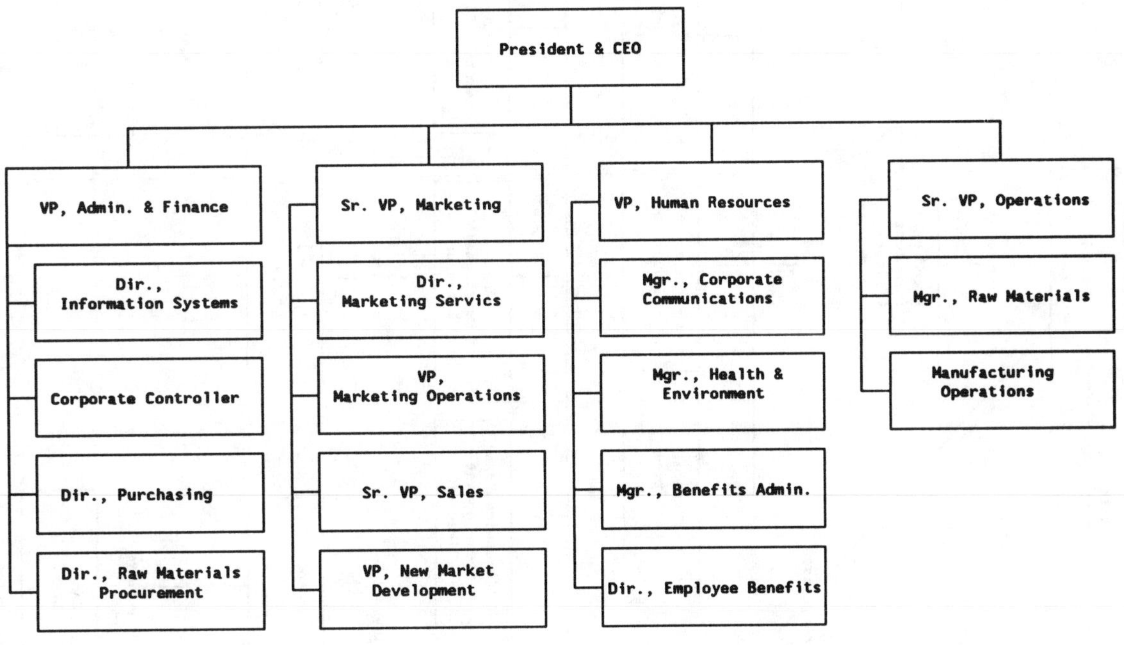

SYCAMORE GIRL SCOUT COUNCIL, INC.

Source: Volunteer Manual, 1990

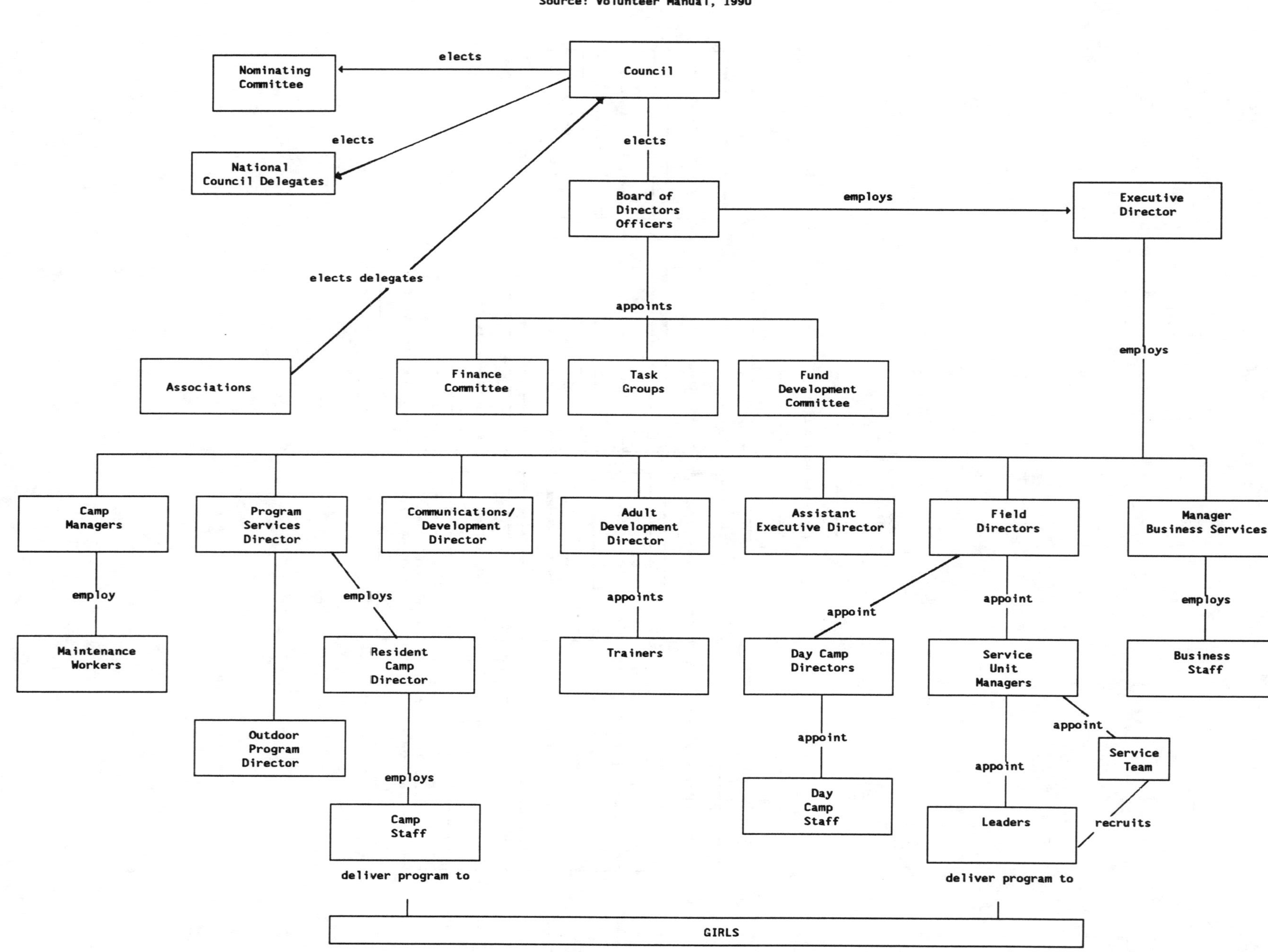

TAISEI CORP. (Japan)

Source: LONG RANGE PLANNING
23:53 (February 1990)

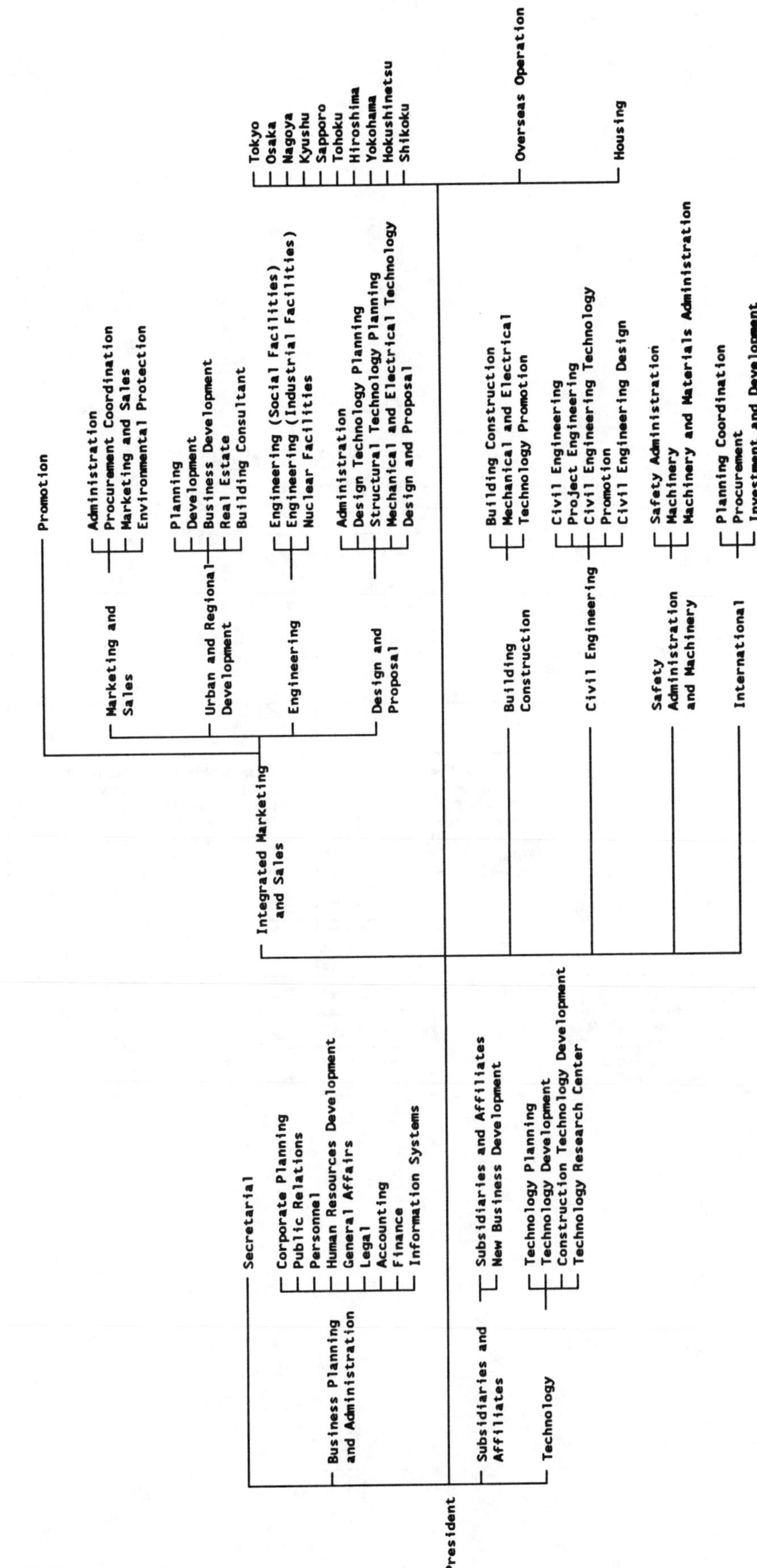

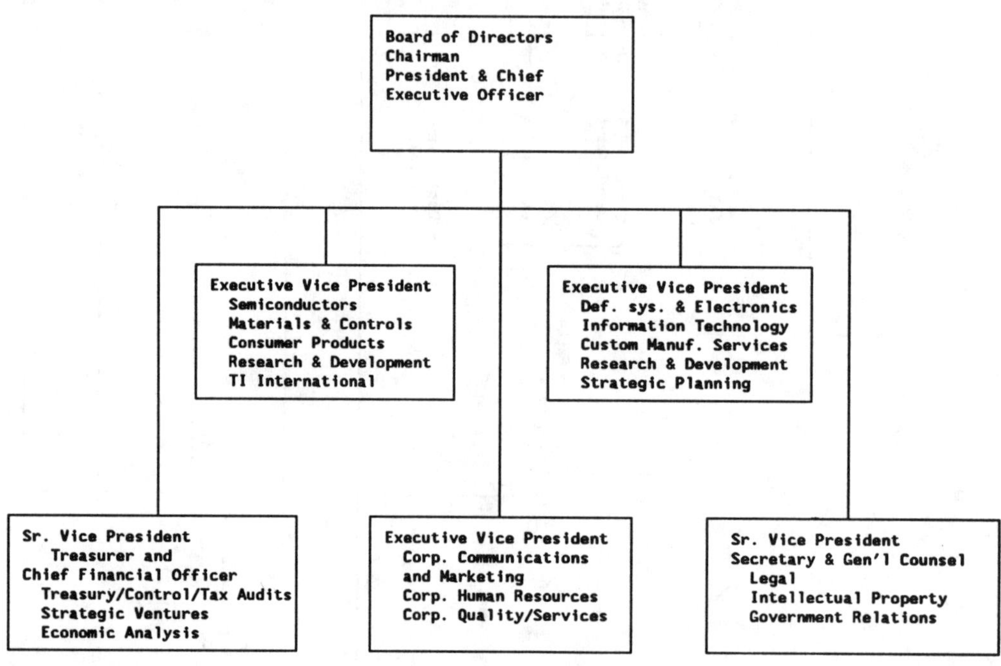
TEXAS INSTRUMENTS
Source: Company update, 1991
Board of Directors
Chairman
President & Chief
Executive Officer
Executive Vice President
Semiconductors
Materials & Controls
Consumer Products
Research & Development
TI International
Executive Vice President
Def. sys. & Electronics
Information Technology
Custom Manuf. Services
Research & Development
Strategic Planning
Sr. Vice President
Treasurer and
Chief Financial Officer
Treasury/Control/Tax Audits
Strategic Ventures
Economic Analysis
Executive Vice President
Corp. Communications
and Marketing
Corp. Human Resources
Corp. Quality/Services
Sr. Vice President
Secretary & Gen'l Counsel
Legal
Intellectual Property
Government Relations

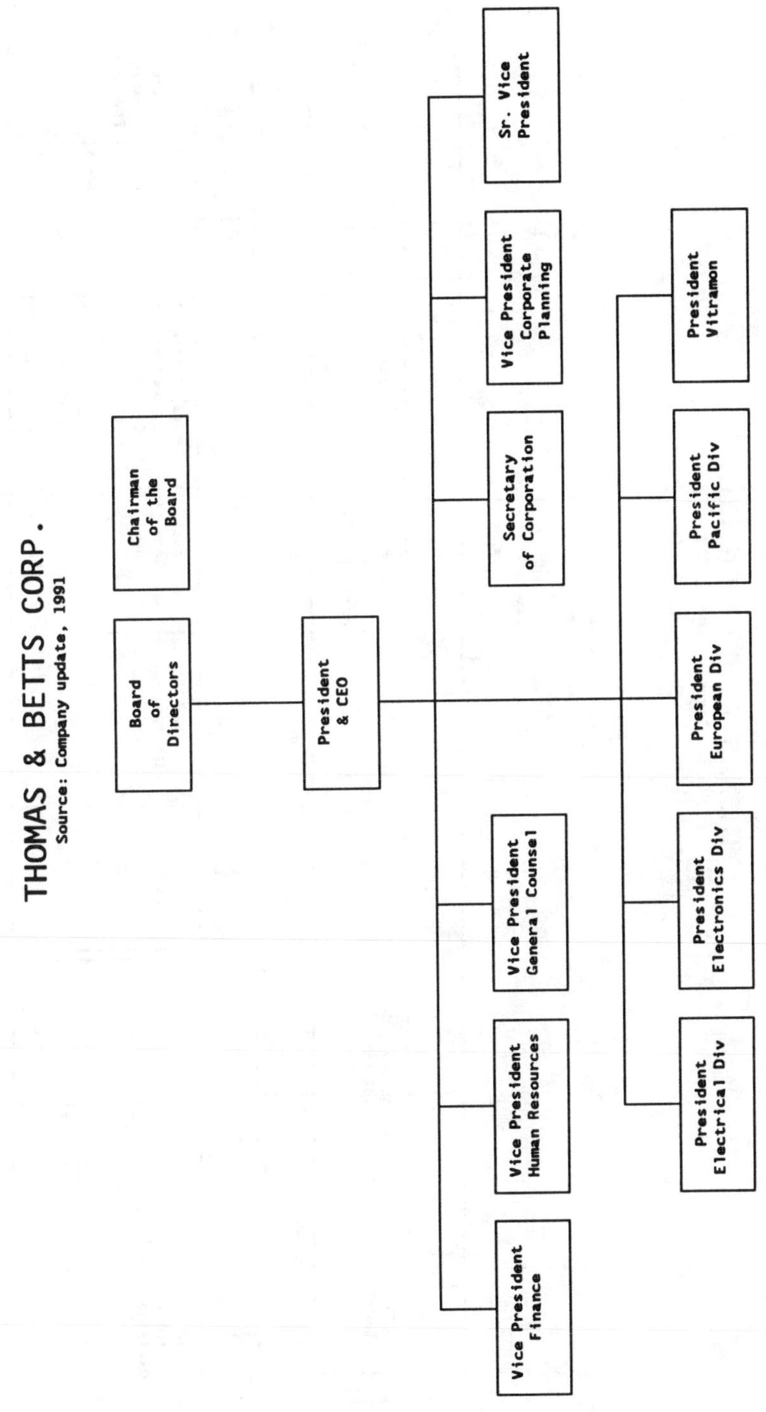
THOMAS & BETTS CORP.
Source: Company update, 1991
Board of Directors
Chairman of the Board
President & CEO
Vice President Finance
Vice President Human Resources
Vice President General Counsel
Secretary of Corporation
Vice President Corporate Planning
Sr. Vice President
President Electrical Div
President Electronics Div
President European Div
President Pacific Div
President Vitramon

THOMAS J. LIPTON CO.

Source: Company update, 1991

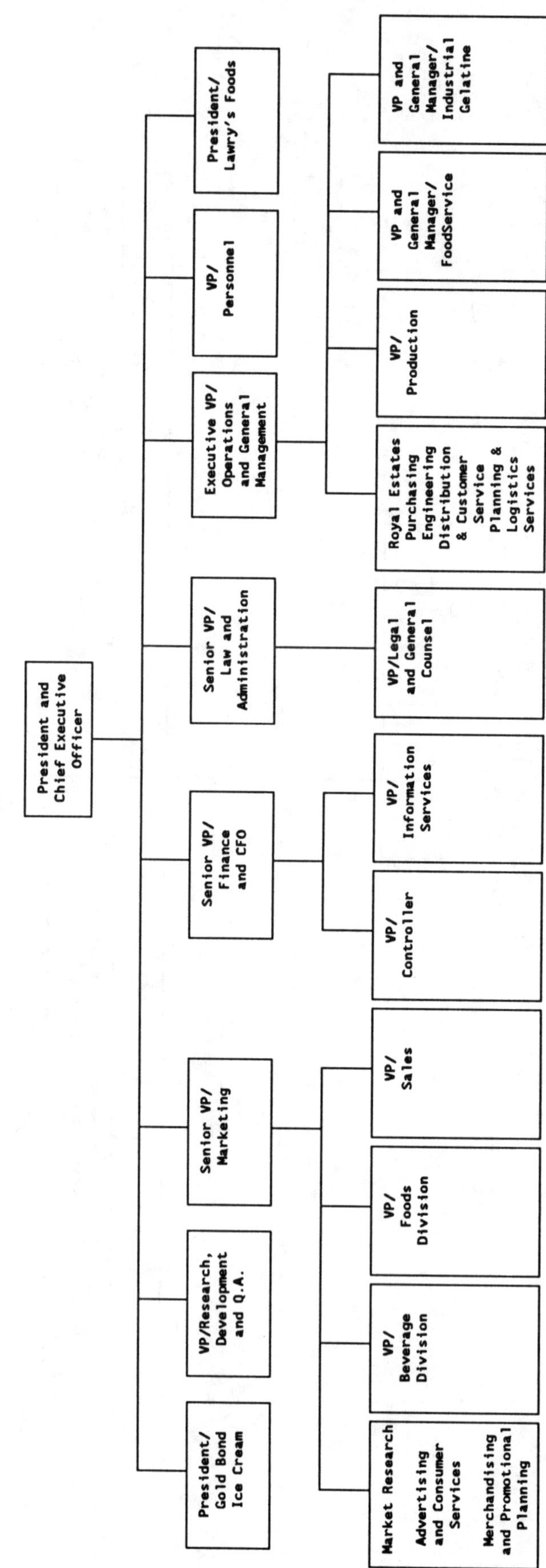

TOSHIBA CORP. (Japan)

Source: Company update, 1991

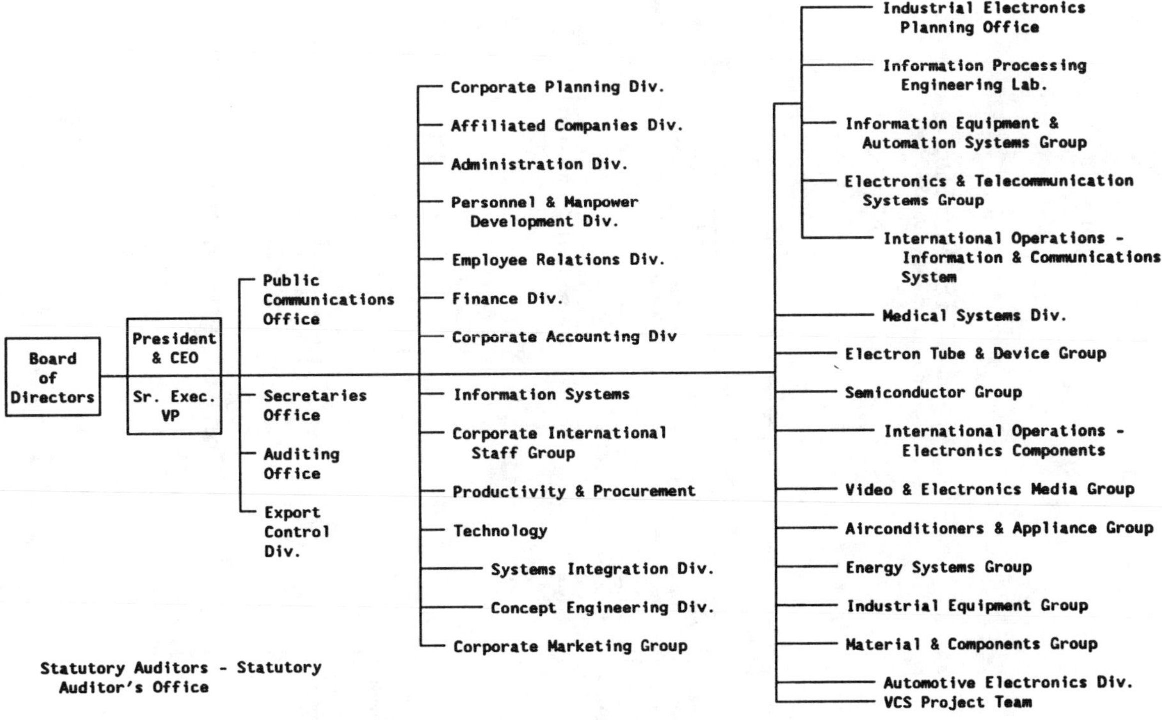

TRIBUNE CO.

Source: Company update, 1991

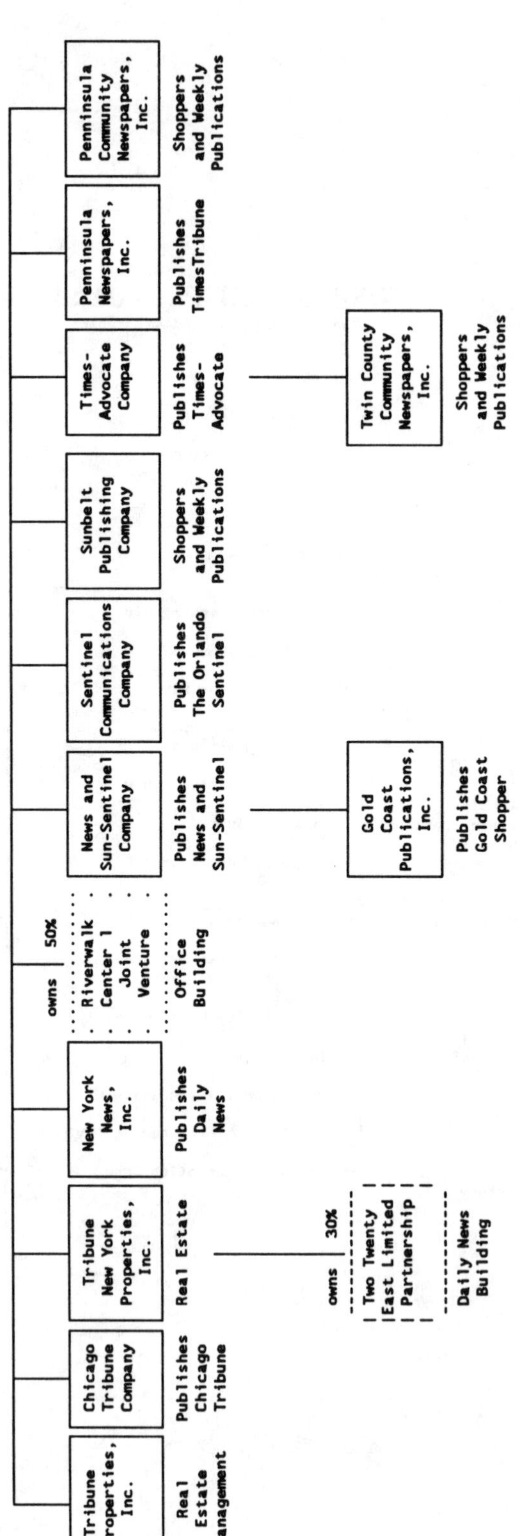

Continued on next page

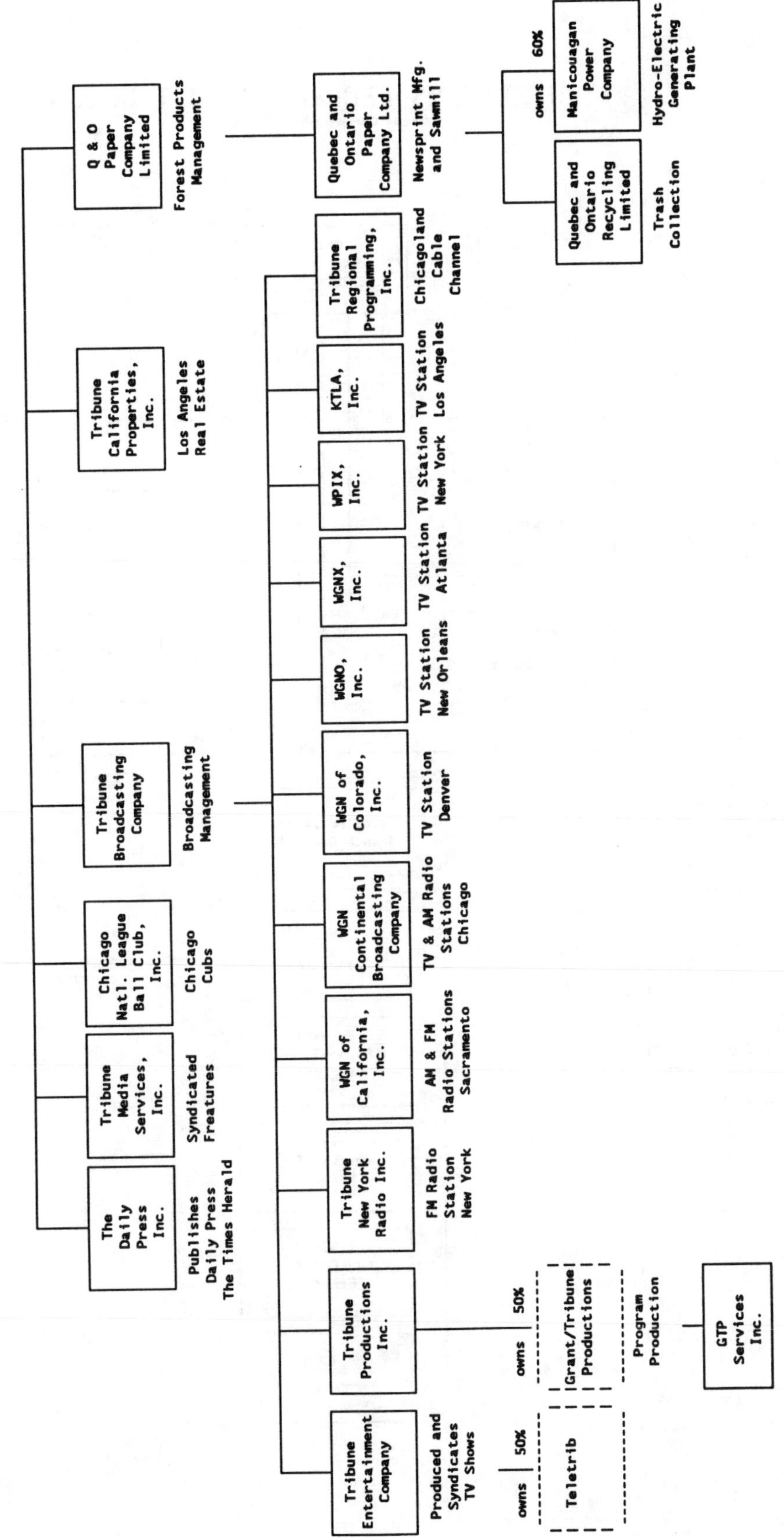
THE TRIBUNE CO.
Continued from previous page
The Daily Press Inc.
Publishes Daily Press The Times Herald
Tribune Media Services, Inc.
Syndicated Freatures
Chicago Natl. League Ball Club, Inc.
Chicago Cubs
Tribune Broadcasting Company
Broadcasting Management
Tribune California Properties, Inc.
Los Angeles Real Estate
Q & O Paper Company Limited
Forest Products Management
Tribune Entertainment Company
Produced and Syndicates TV Shows
owns 50%
Teletrib
Tribune Productions Inc.
owns 50%
Grant/Tribune Productions
Program Production
GTP Services Inc.
Tribune New York Radio Inc.
FM Radio Station New York
WGN of California, Inc.
AM & FM Radio Stations Sacramento
WGN Continental Broadcasting Company
TV & AM Radio Stations Chicago
WGN of Colorado, Inc.
TV Station Denver
WGNO, Inc.
TV Station New Orleans
WGNX, Inc.
TV Station Atlanta
WPIX, Inc.
TV Station New York
KTLA, Inc.
TV Station Los Angeles
Tribune Regional Programming, Inc.
Chicagoland Cable Channel
Quebec and Ontario Paper Company Ltd.
Newsprint Mfg. and Sawmill
Quebec and Ontario Recycling Limited
Trash Collection
owns 60%
Manicouagan Power Company
Hydro-Electric Generating Plant

TRW SYSTEMS FEDERAL CREDIT UNION

Source: Company update, 1991

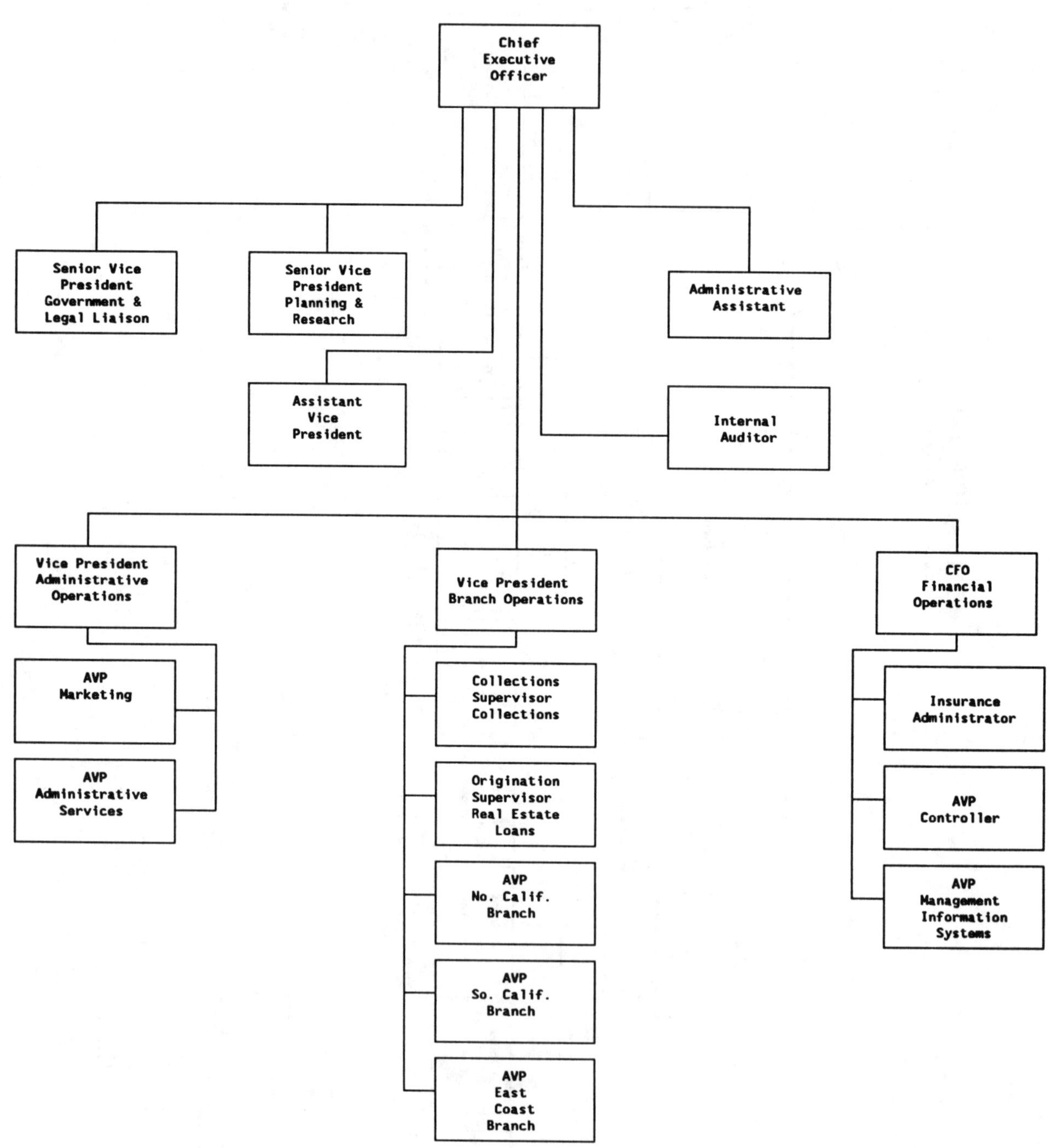

U.K. CUSTOMS AND EXCISE (United Kingdom)

Source: OPTIMUM (Canada)
20: 23 (1989/1990)

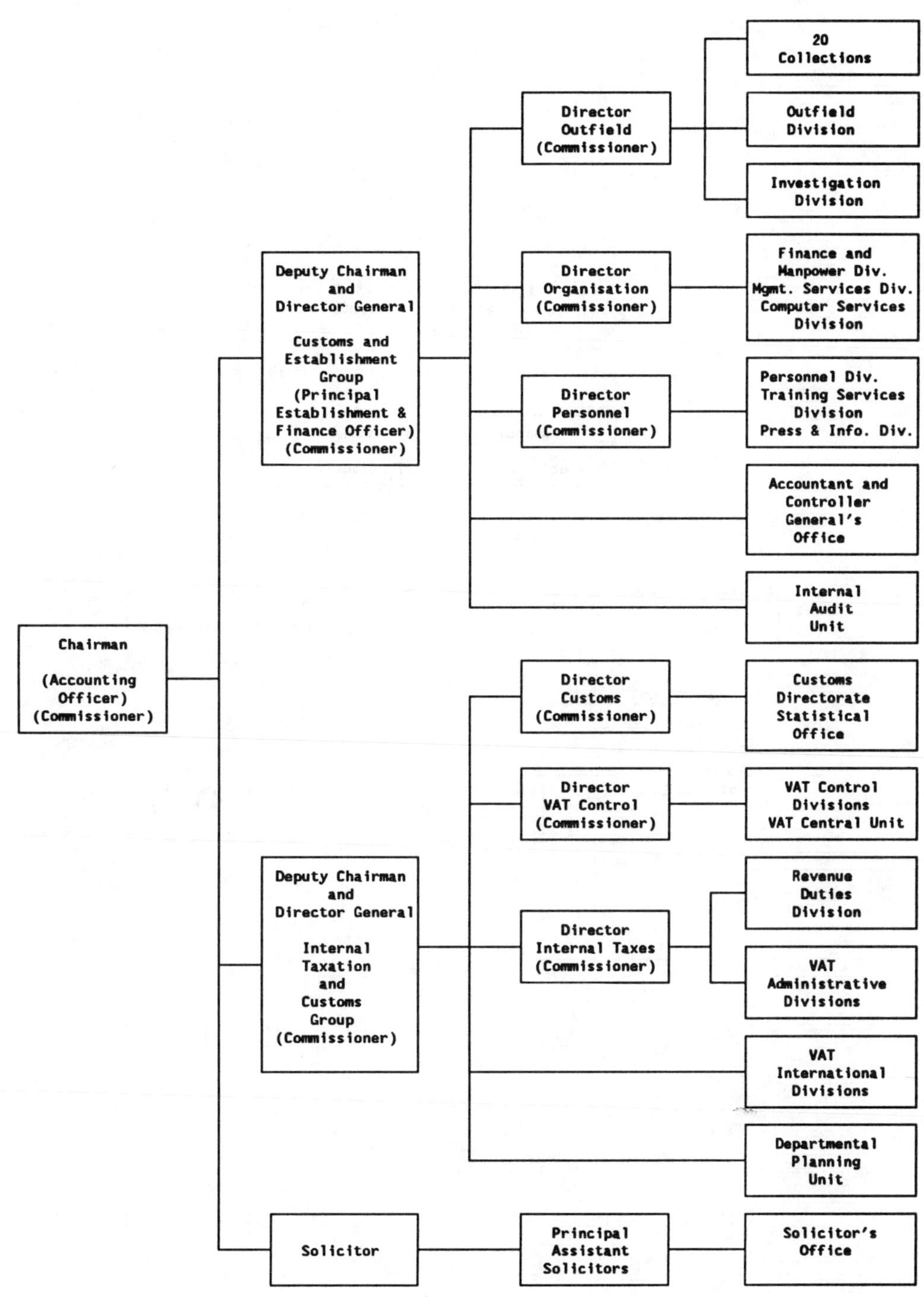

VAT = Value Added Tax

U.S. AIR FORCE
WEAPONS LABORATORY

Source: DEFENSE ELECTRONICS
23:39+ (January 1991)

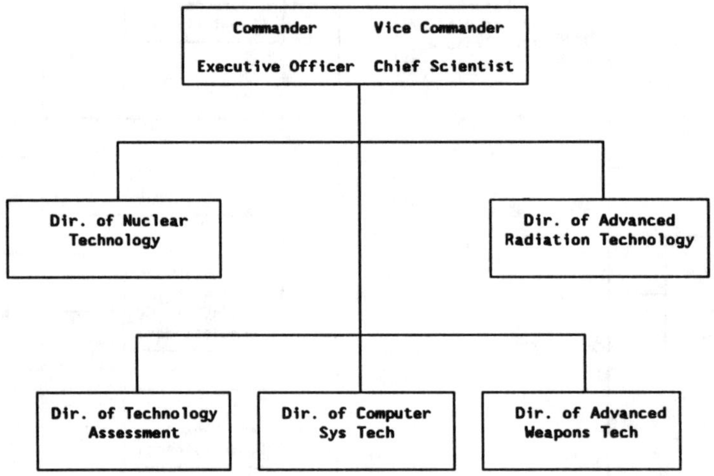

U.S. NATIONAL AERO-SPACE PLANE
NATIONAL PROGRAM OFFICE

Source: AVIATION WEEK
133: 38+ (October 29, 1990)

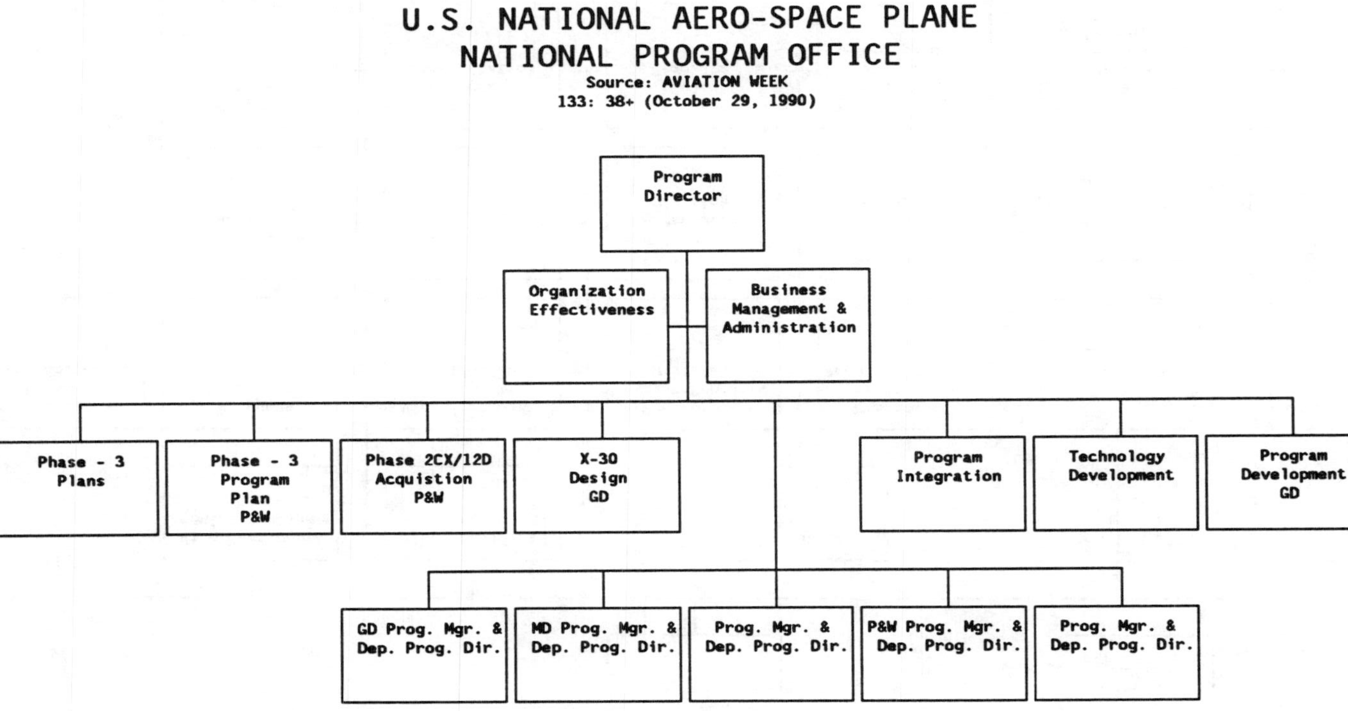

The National Program Office is an organization composed of the five prime contractors for the National Aero-Space Plane: General Dynamics, McDonnell Douglas, North American Aviation, Pratt & Whitney, and Rocketdyne.

UNIVERSAL FOODS CORP.

Source: Company update, 1991

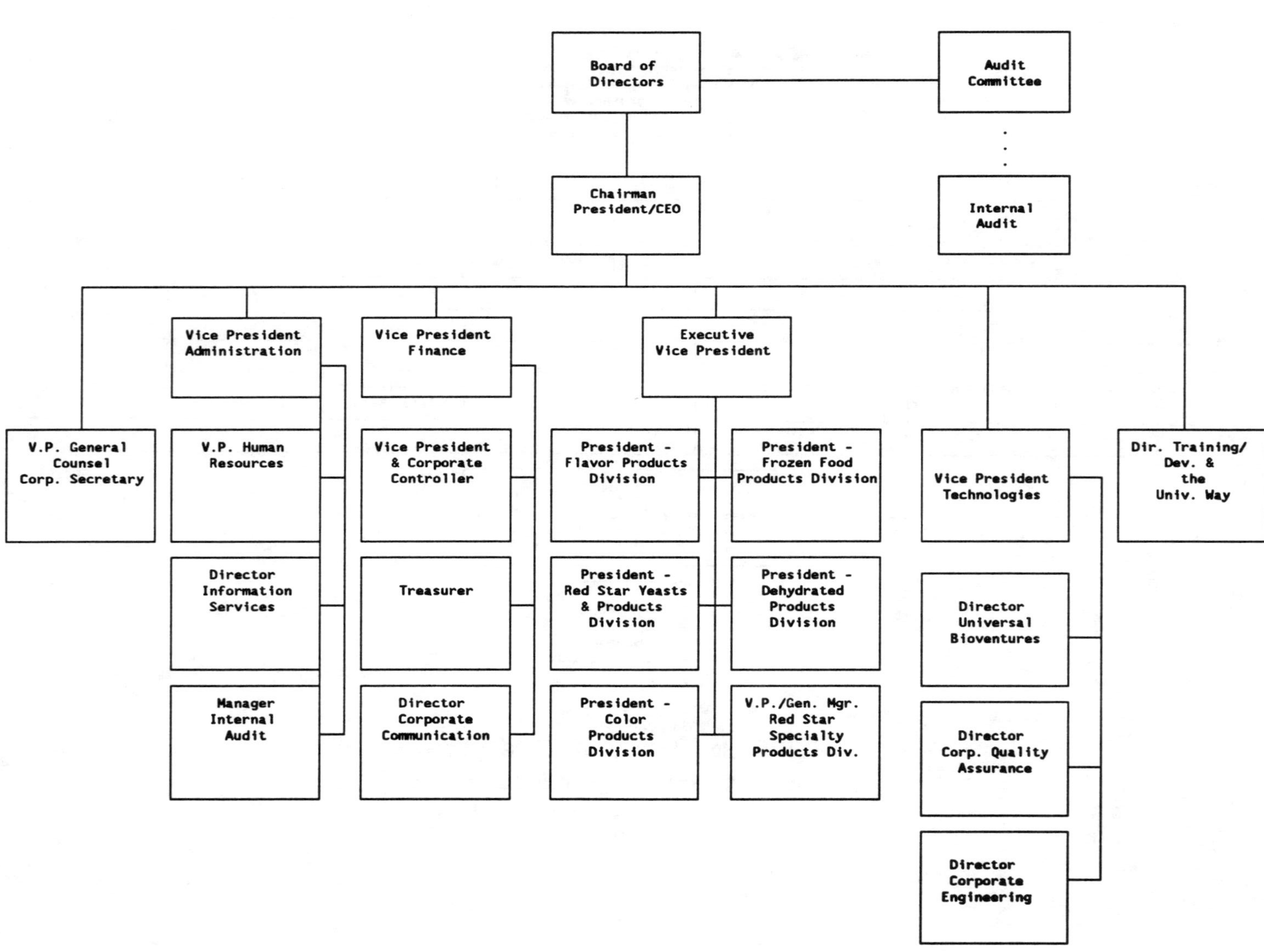

UNIVERSITY OF IDAHO LIBRARY

Source: RQ
29: 525+ (Summer 1990)

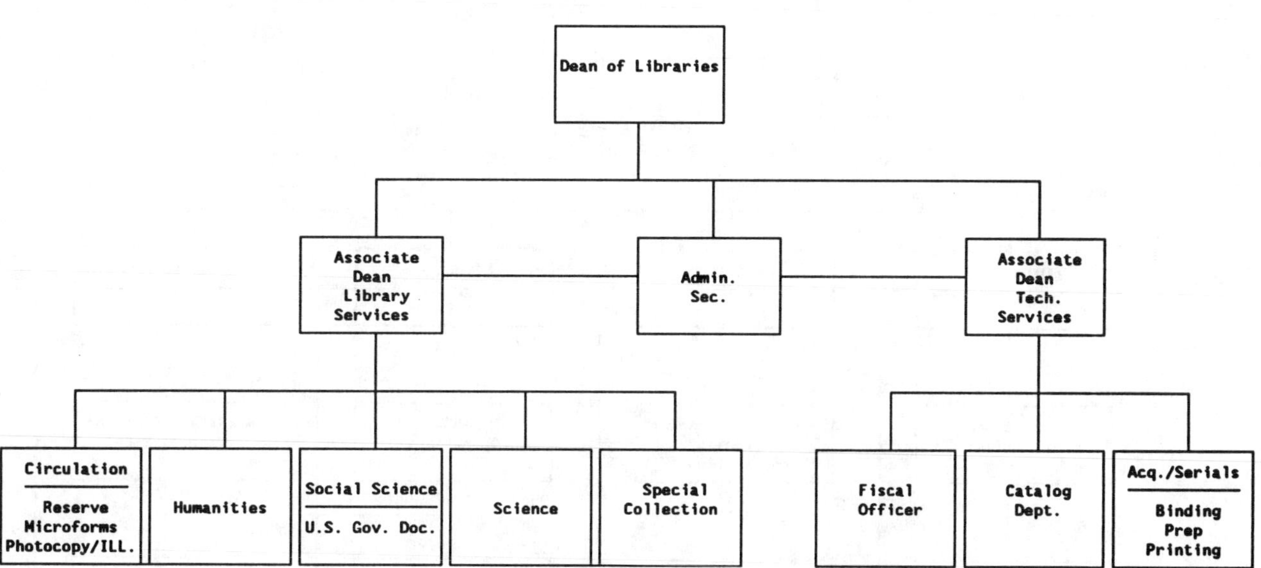

UNIVERSITY OF MARYLAND
PROFESSIONAL SCHOOLS
INFORMATION RESOURCES MANAGEMENT DIV.

Source: LONG RANGE PLANNING
21: 52+ (April 1988)

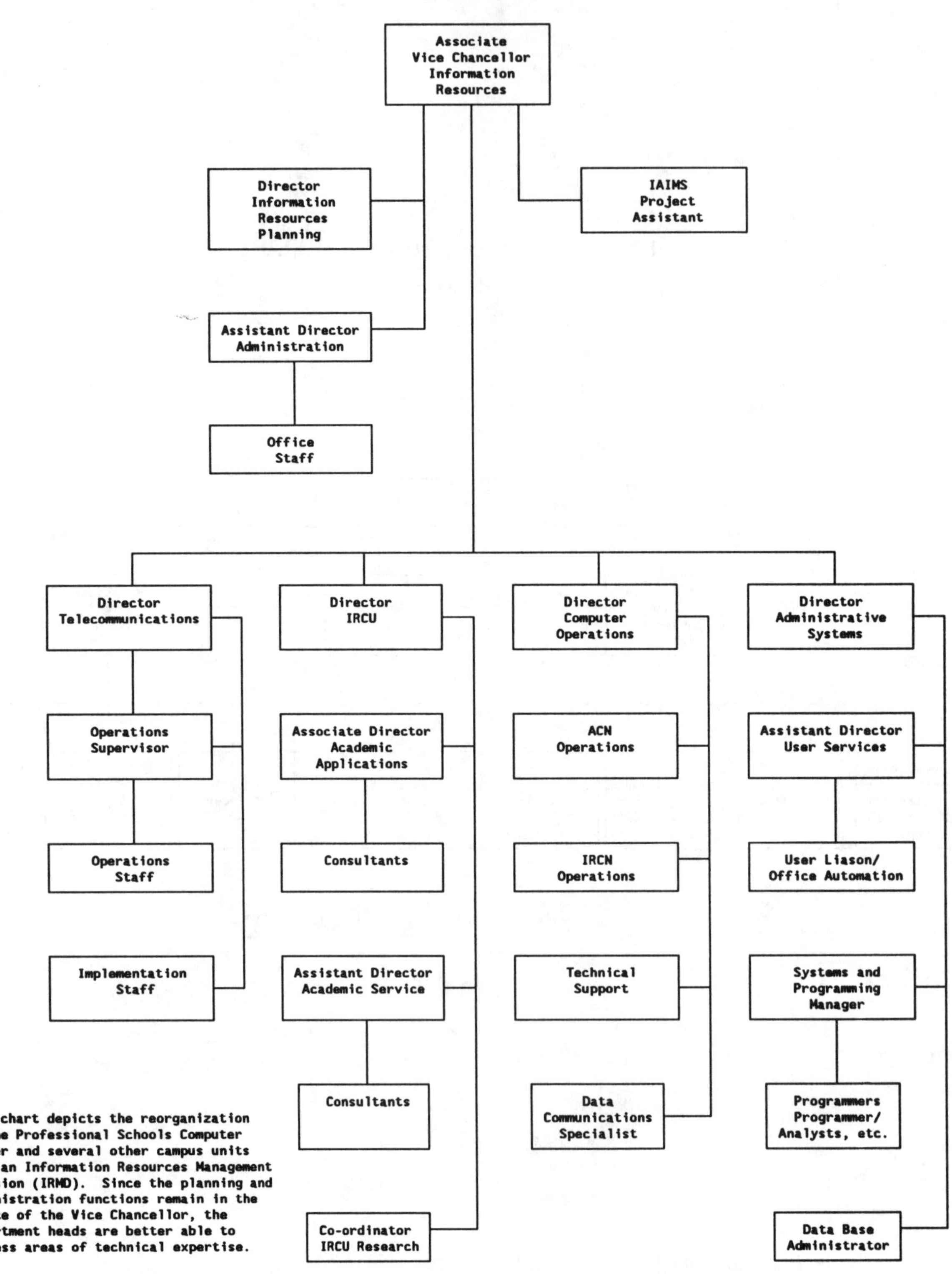

This chart depicts the reorganization of the Professional Schools Computer Center and several other campus units into an Information Resources Management Division (IRMD). Since the planning and administration functions remain in the office of the Vice Chancellor, the department heads are better able to address areas of technical expertise.

VALERO ENERGY CORP.

Source: Company update, 1991

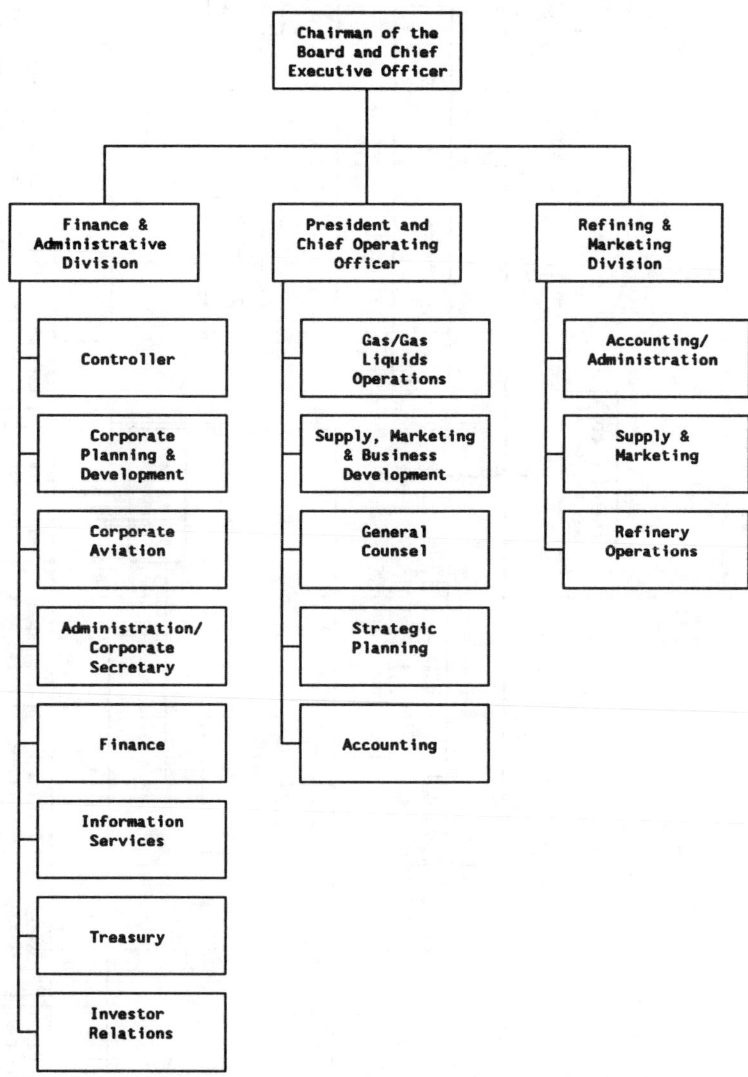

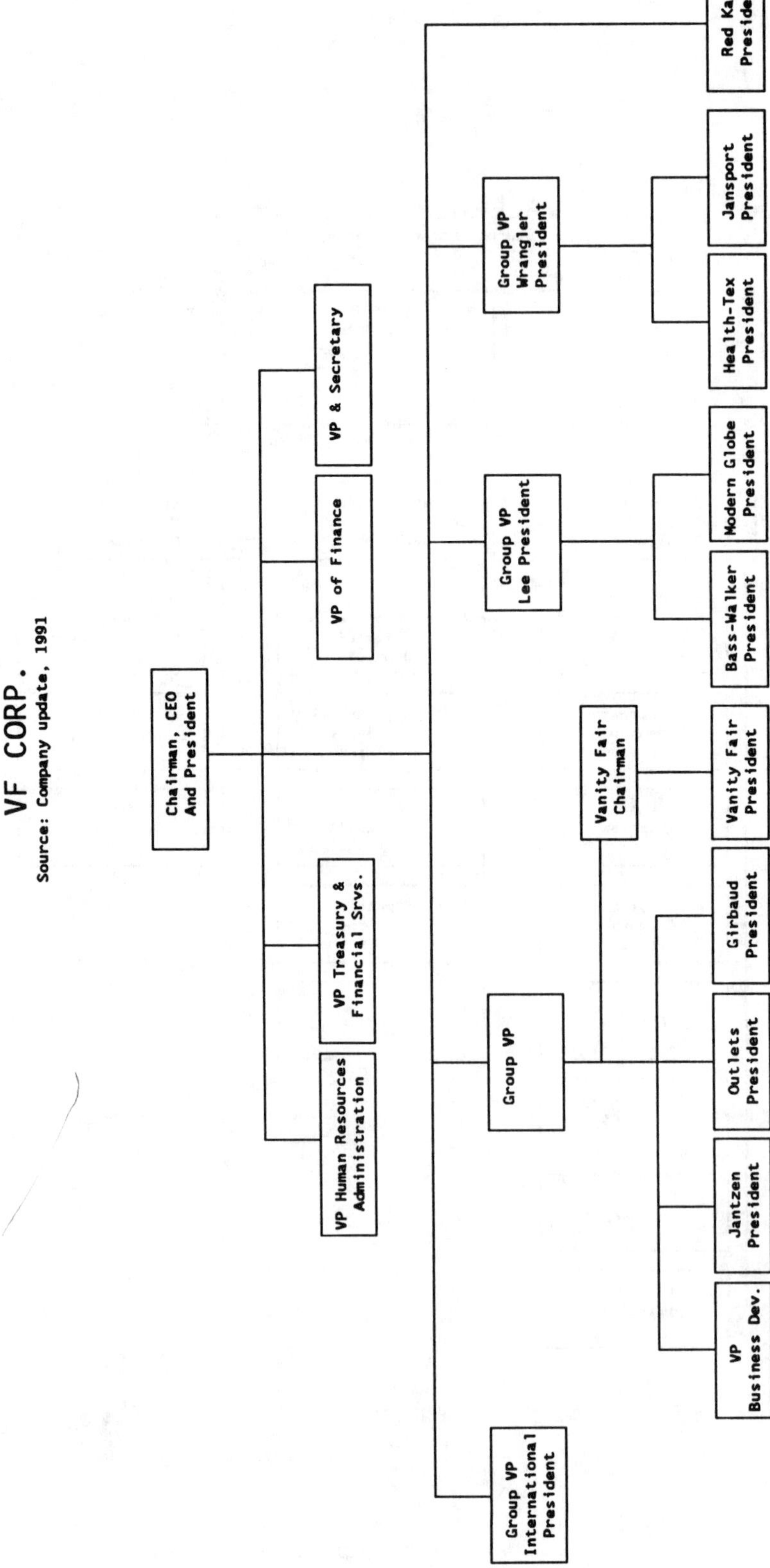
VF CORP.
Source: Company update, 1991
Chairman, CEO And President
VP Human Resources Administration
VP Treasury & Financial Srvs.
VP of Finance
VP & Secretary
Group VP International President
Group VP
Vanity Fair Chairman
Group VP Lee President
Group VP Wrangler President
Red Kap President
VP Business Dev.
Jantzen President
Outlets President
Girbaud President
Vanity Fair President
Bass-Walker President
Modern Globe President
Health-Tex President
Jansport President

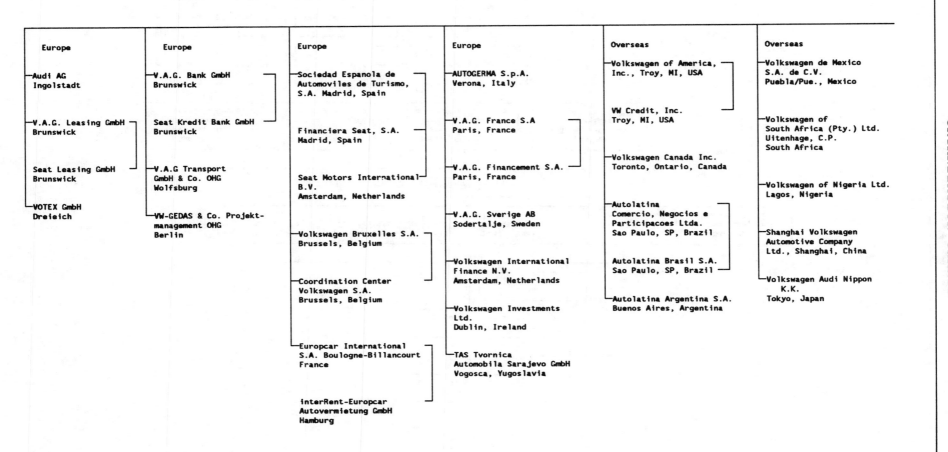

VOLKSWAGEN AG (Germany)

Source: Annual report, 1990

Europe

- Audi AG
  Ingolstadt
- V.A.G. Leasing GmbH
  Brunswick
- Seat Leasing GmbH
  Brunswick
- VOTEX GmbH
  Dreieich

Europe

- V.A.G. Bank GmbH
  Brunswick
- Seat Kredit Bank GmbH
  Brunswick
- V.A.G Transport
  GmbH & Co. OHG
  Wolfsburg
- VW-GEDAS & Co. Projekt-
  management OHG
  Berlin

Europe

- Sociedad Espanola de
  Automoviles de Turismo,
  S.A. Madrid, Spain
- Financiera Seat, S.A.
  Madrid, Spain
- Seat Motors International
  B.V.
  Amsterdam, Netherlands
- Volkswagen Bruxelles S.A.
  Brussels, Belgium
- Coordination Center
  Volkswagen S.A.
  Brussels, Belgium
- Europcar International
  S.A. Boulogne-Billancourt
  France
- interRent-Europcar
  Autovermietung GmbH
  Hamburg

Europe

- AUTOGERMA S.p.A.
  Verona, Italy
- V.A.G. France S.A
  Paris, France
- V.A.G. Financement S.A.
  Paris, France
- V.A.G. Sverige AB
  Sodertalje, Sweden
- Volkswagen International
  Finance N.V.
  Amsterdam, Netherlands
- Volkswagen Investments
  Ltd.
  Dublin, Ireland
- TAS Tvornica
  Automobila Sarajevo GmbH
  Vogosca, Yugoslavia

Overseas

- Volkswagen of America,
  Inc., Troy, MI, USA
- VW Credit, Inc.
  Troy, MI, USA
- Volkswagen Canada Inc.
  Toronto, Ontario, Canada
- Autolatina
  Comercio, Negocios e
  Participacoes Ltda.
  Sao Paulo, SP, Brazil
- Autolatina Brasil S.A.
  Sao Paulo, SP, Brazil
- Autolatina Argentina S.A.
  Buenos Aires, Argentina

Overseas

- Volkswagen de Mexico
  S.A. de C.V.
  Puebla/Pue., Mexico
- Volkswagen of
  South Africa (Pty.) Ltd.
  Uitenhage, C.P.
  South Africa
- Volkswagen of Nigeria Ltd.
  Lagos, Nigeria
- Shanghai Volkswagen
  Automotive Company
  Ltd., Shanghai, China
- Volkswagen Audi Nippon
  K.K.
  Tokyo, Japan

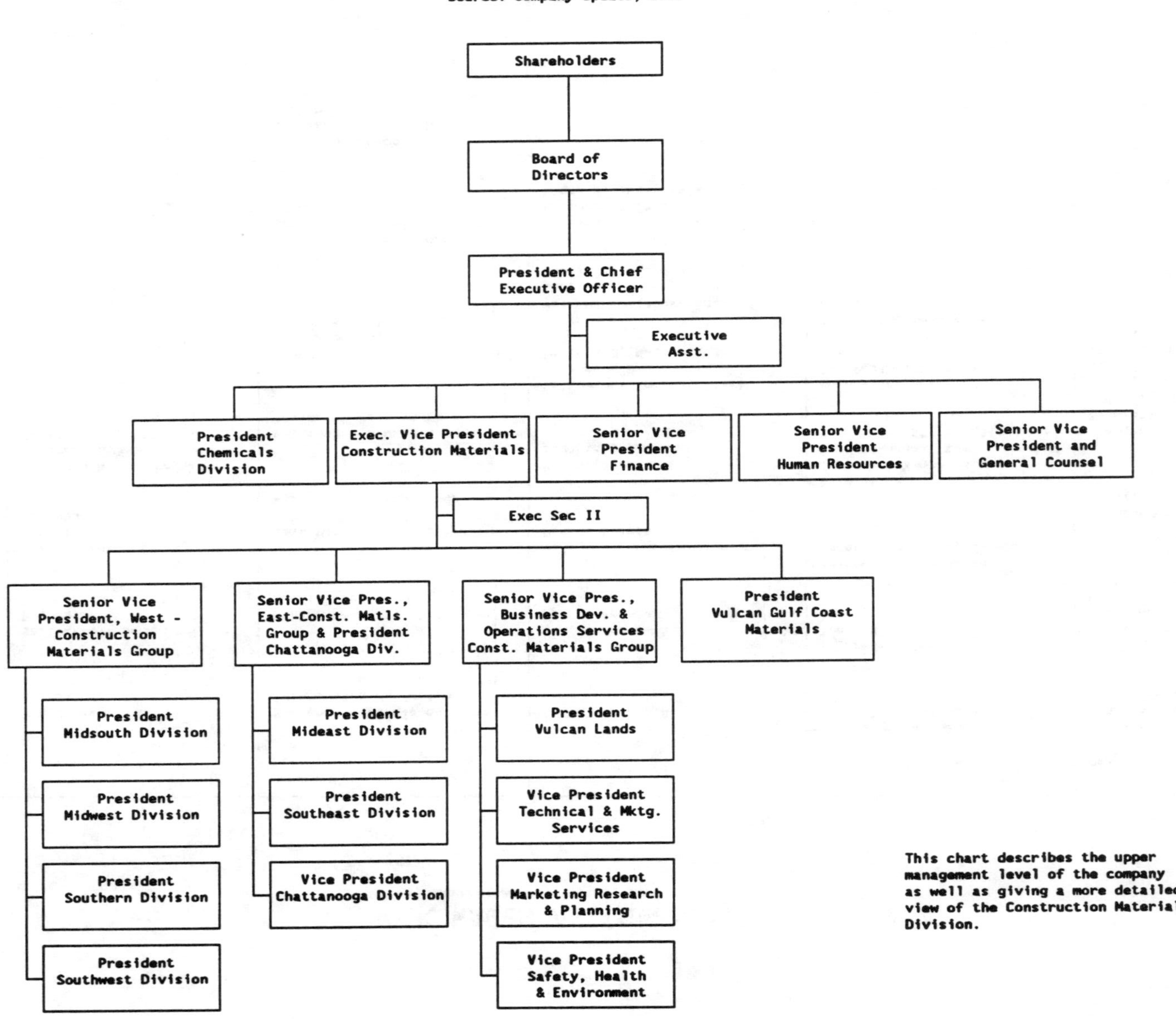

VULCAN MATERIALS CO.
Source: Company update, 1991
Shareholders
Board of Directors
President & Chief Executive Officer
Executive Asst.
President Chemicals Division
Exec. Vice President Construction Materials
Senior Vice President Finance
Senior Vice President Human Resources
Senior Vice President and General Counsel
Exec Sec II
Senior Vice President, West - Construction Materials Group
Senior Vice Pres., East-Const. Matls. Group & President Chattanooga Div.
Senior Vice Pres., Business Dev. & Operations Services Const. Materials Group
President Vulcan Gulf Coast Materials
President Midsouth Division
President Midwest Division
President Southern Division
President Southwest Division
President Mideast Division
President Southeast Division
Vice President Chattanooga Division
President Vulcan Lands
Vice President Technical & Mktg. Services
Vice President Marketing Research & Planning
Vice President Safety, Health & Environment
This chart describes the upper management level of the company as well as giving a more detailed view of the Construction Materials Division.

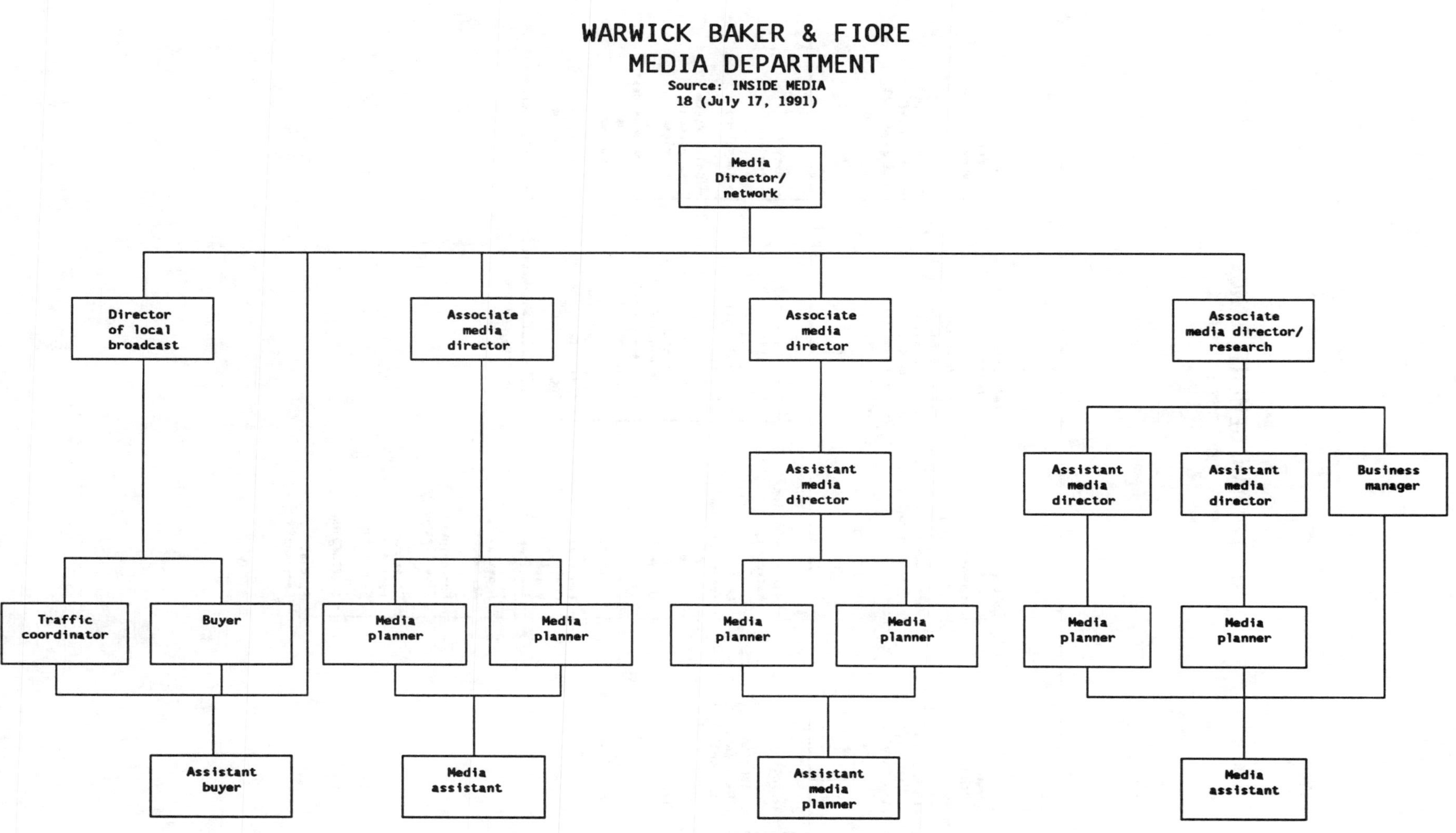
WARWICK BAKER & FIORE
MEDIA DEPARTMENT
Source: INSIDE MEDIA
18 (July 17, 1991)
Media Director/ network
Director of local broadcast
Associate media director
Associate media director
Associate media director/ research
Assistant media director
Assistant media director
Assistant media director
Business manager
Traffic coordinator
Buyer
Media planner
Media planner
Media planner
Media planner
Media planner
Media planner
Assistant buyer
Media assistant
Assistant media planner
Media assistant

WASTE MANAGEMENT, INC.

Source: Annual report, 1990?

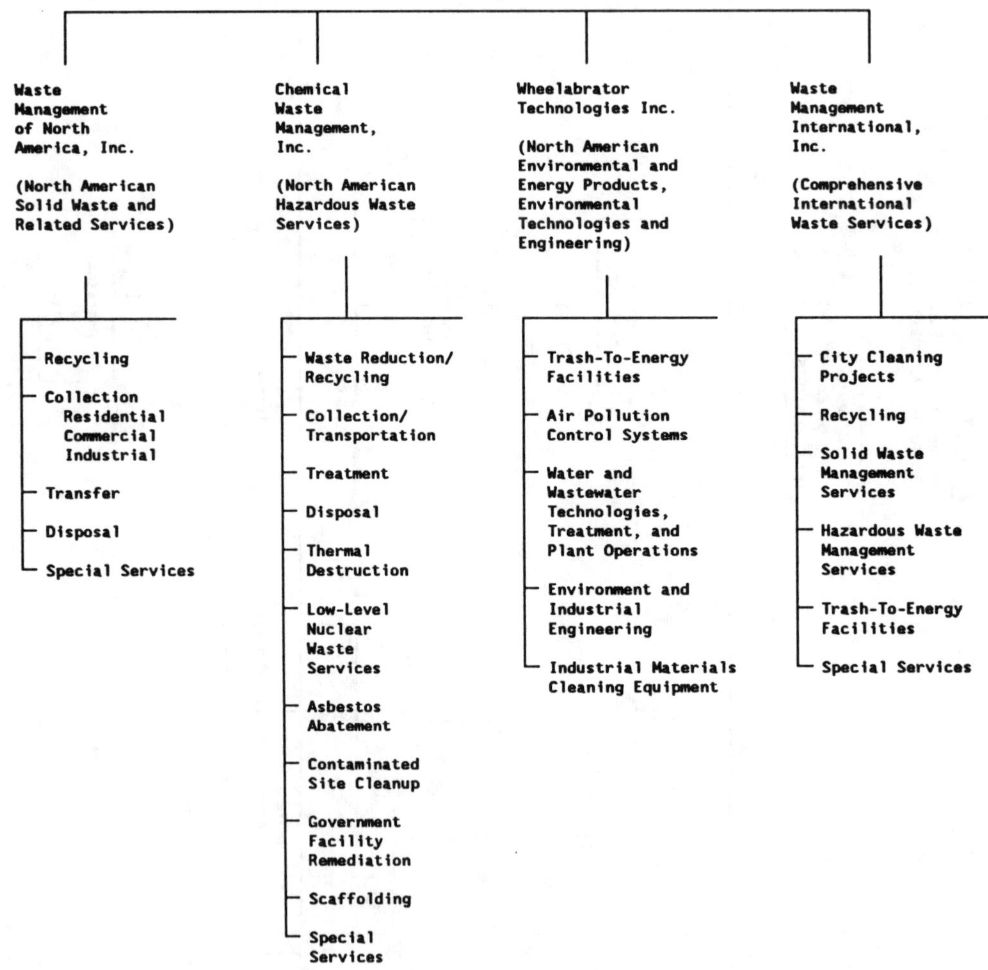
Waste Management of North America, Inc.
(North American Solid Waste and Related Services)
Recycling
Collection
Residential
Commercial
Industrial
Transfer
Disposal
Special Services
Chemical Waste Management, Inc.
(North American Hazardous Waste Services)
Waste Reduction/ Recycling
Collection/ Transportation
Treatment
Disposal
Thermal Destruction
Low-Level Nuclear Waste Services
Asbestos Abatement
Contaminated Site Cleanup
Government Facility Remediation
Scaffolding
Special Services
Wheelabrator Technologies Inc.
(North American Environmental and Energy Products, Environmental Technologies and Engineering)
Trash-To-Energy Facilities
Air Pollution Control Systems
Water and Wastewater Technologies, Treatment, and Plant Operations
Environment and Industrial Engineering
Industrial Materials Cleaning Equipment
Waste Management International, Inc.
(Comprehensive International Waste Services)
City Cleaning Projects
Recycling
Solid Waste Management Services
Hazardous Waste Management Services
Trash-To-Energy Facilities
Special Services

THE WEBB COMPANIES OF WEBB/AMERICA

Source: BUILDING DESIGN & CONSTRUCTION
28: 86+ (March 1987)

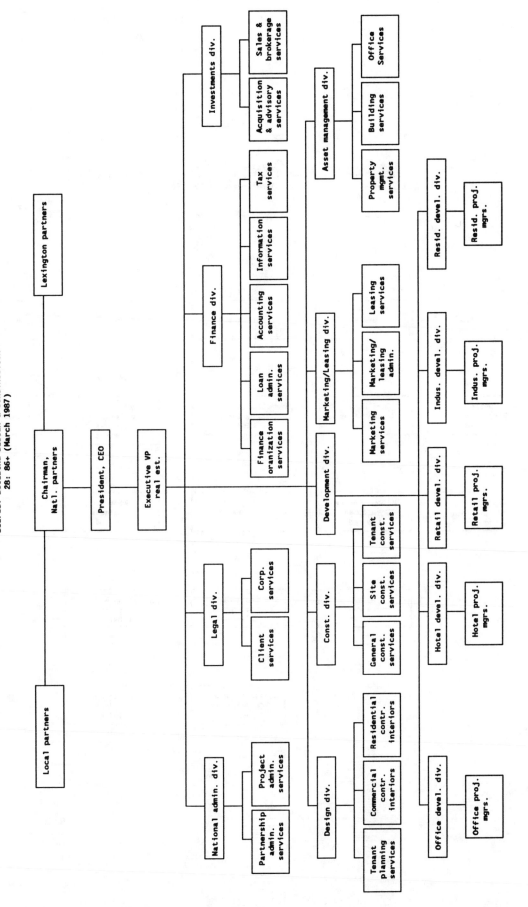

- Local partners
- Chairman, Natl. partners
- Lexington partners

- Chairman, Natl. partners
  - President, CEO
    - Executive VP real est.
      - National admin. div.
        - Partnership admin. services
        - Project admin. services
      - Legal div.
        - Client services
        - Corp. services
      - Finance div.
        - Finance oranization services
        - Loan admin. services
        - Accounting services
        - Information services
        - Tax services
      - Investments div.
        - Acquisition & advisory services
        - Sales & brokerage services
      - Design div.
        - Tenant planning services
        - Commercial contr. interiors
        - Residential contr. interiors
      - Const. div.
        - General const. services
        - Site const. services
        - Tenant const. services
      - Development div.
        - Office devel. div.
          - Office proj. mgrs.
        - Hotel devel. div.
          - Hotel proj. mgrs.
        - Retail devel. div.
          - Retail proj. mgrs.
        - Indus. devel. div.
          - Indus. proj. mgrs.
        - Resid. devel. div.
          - Resid. proj. mgrs.
      - Marketing/Leasing div.
        - Marketing services
        - Marketing/ leasing admin.
        - Leasing services
      - Asset management div.
        - Property mgmt. services
        - Building services
        - Office Services

THE WHARF (HOLDINGS) LTD. (Hong Kong)

Source: Annual report. 1989-90

Property	Hotels	Transport	Terminals	Communications
Wharf Properties Limited	Omni Hotels International Limited	The "Star" Ferry Company Limited	Kowloon Wharf Terminal and Warehouse Limited	Hong Kong Cable Communications Limited
Harbour City Management Limited	Harbour Centre Development Limited	Hongkong Tramways Limited	Modern Terminals Limited	
	Hotel Marco Polo Limited	The Cross-Harbour Tunnel Company Limited	Hong Kong Air Cargo Terminals Limited	
		Allied Investors Corporation Limited	Container Services Limited	

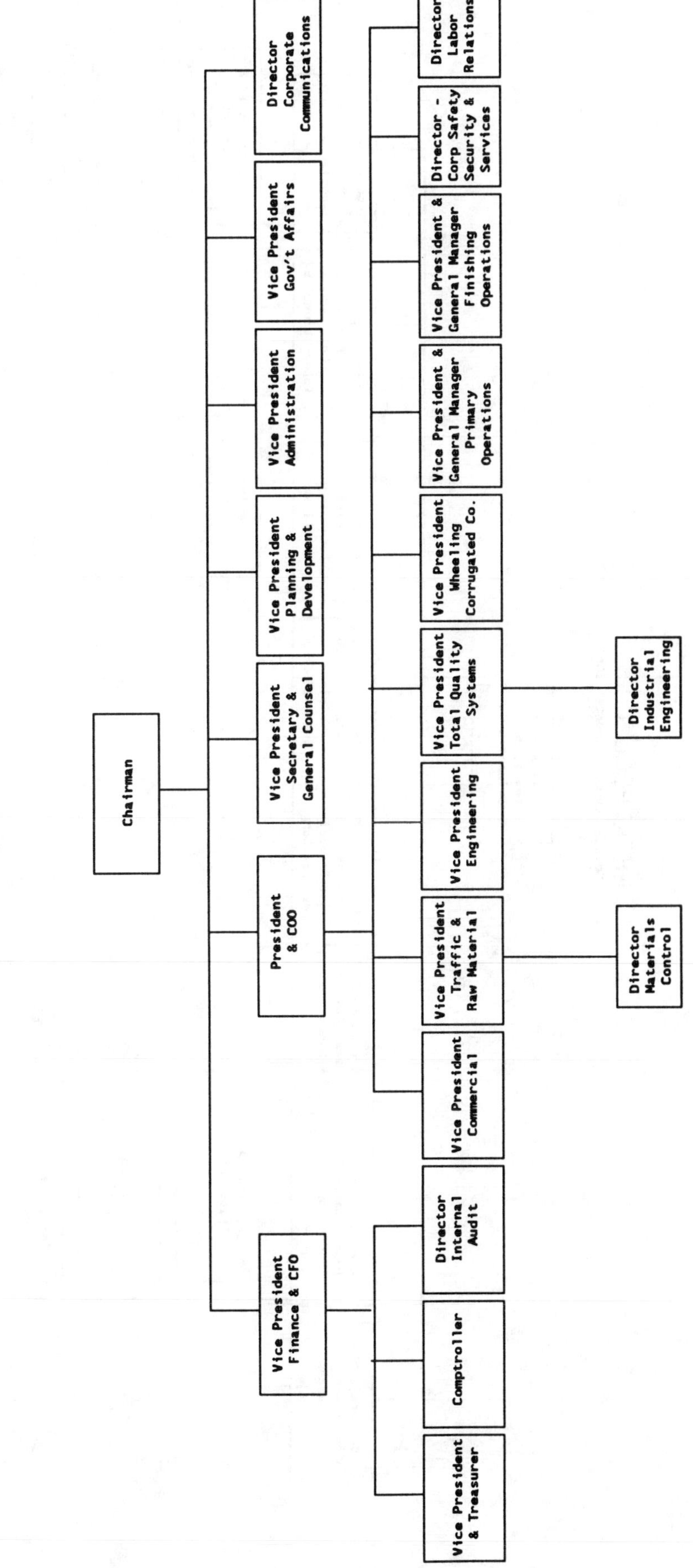
WHEELING-PITTSBURGH STEEL CORP.
Source: Company update, 1991
Chairman
President & COO
Vice President Secretary & General Counsel
Vice President Planning & Development
Vice President Administration
Vice President Gov't Affairs
Director Corporate Communications
Vice President Finance & CFO
Vice President & Treasurer
Comptroller
Director Internal Audit
Vice President Commercial
Vice President Traffic & Raw Material
Director Materials Control
Vice President Engineering
Vice President Total Quality Systems
Director Industrial Engineering
Vice President Wheeling Corrugated Co.
Vice President & General Manager Primary Operations
Vice President & General Manager Finishing Operations
Director - Corp Safety Security & Services
Director Labor Relations

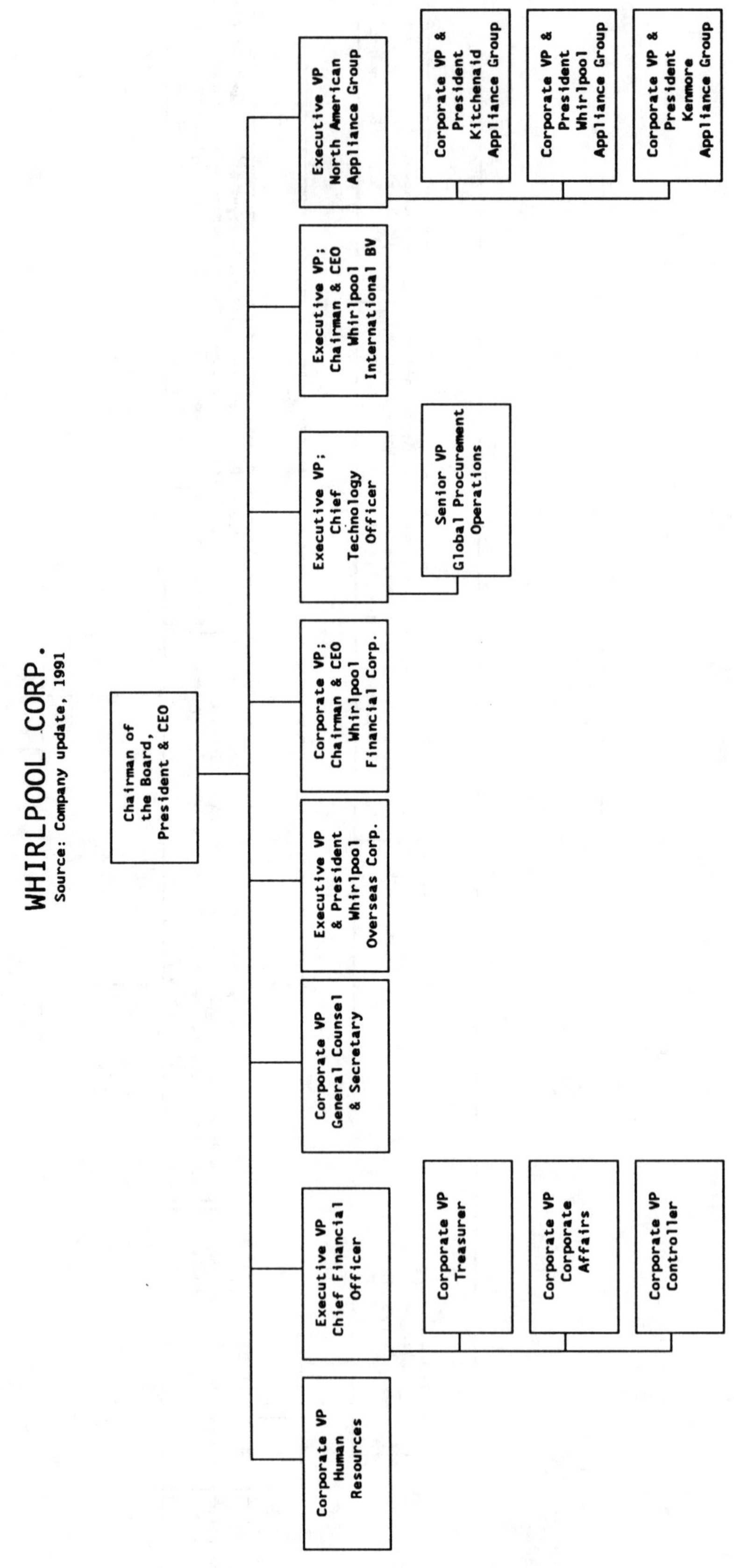
WHIRLPOOL CORP.
Source: Company update, 1991
Chairman of the Board, President & CEO
Corporate VP Human Resources
Executive VP Chief Financial Officer
Corporate VP General Counsel & Secretary
Executive VP & President Whirlpool Overseas Corp.
Corporate VP; Chairman & CEO Whirlpool Financial Corp.
Executive VP; Chief Technology Officer
Executive VP; Chairman & CEO Whirlpool International BV
Executive VP North American Appliance Group
Corporate VP Treasurer
Corporate VP Corporate Affairs
Corporate VP Controller
Senior VP Global Procurement Operations
Corporate VP & President Kitchenaid Appliance Group
Corporate VP & President Whirlpool Appliance Group
Corporate VP & President Kenmore Appliance Group

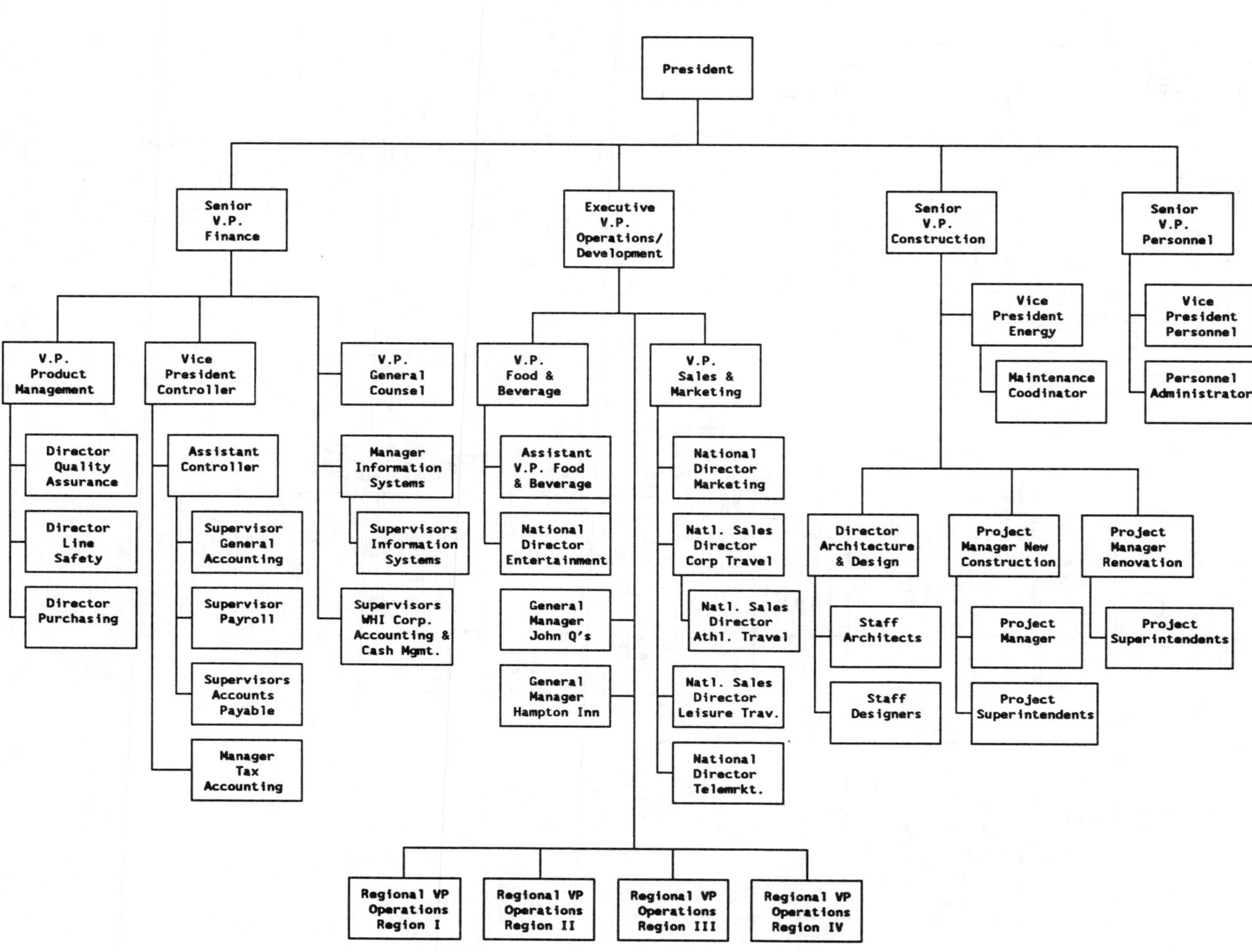
WINEGARDNER & HAMMONS, INC.
Source: Company update, 1991
President
Senior V.P. Finance
Executive V.P. Operations/Development
Senior V.P. Construction
Senior V.P. Personnel
V.P. Product Management
Vice President Controller
V.P. General Counsel
V.P. Food & Beverage
V.P. Sales & Marketing
Vice President Energy
Maintenance Coodinator
Vice President Personnel
Personnel Administrator
Director Quality Assurance
Director Line Safety
Director Purchasing
Assistant Controller
Supervisor General Accounting
Supervisor Payroll
Supervisors Accounts Payable
Manager Tax Accounting
Manager Information Systems
Supervisors Information Systems
Supervisors WHI Corp. Accounting & Cash Mgmt.
Assistant V.P. Food & Beverage
National Director Entertainment
General Manager John Q's
General Manager Hampton Inn
National Director Marketing
Natl. Sales Director Corp Travel
Natl. Sales Director Athl. Travel
Natl. Sales Director Leisure Trav.
National Director Telemrkt.
Director Architecture & Design
Staff Architects
Staff Designers
Project Manager New Construction
Project Manager
Project Superintendents
Project Manager Renovation
Project Superintendents
Regional VP Operations Region I
Regional VP Operations Region II
Regional VP Operations Region III
Regional VP Operations Region IV

WOODWARD GOVERNOR CO.

Source: Annual report, 1990

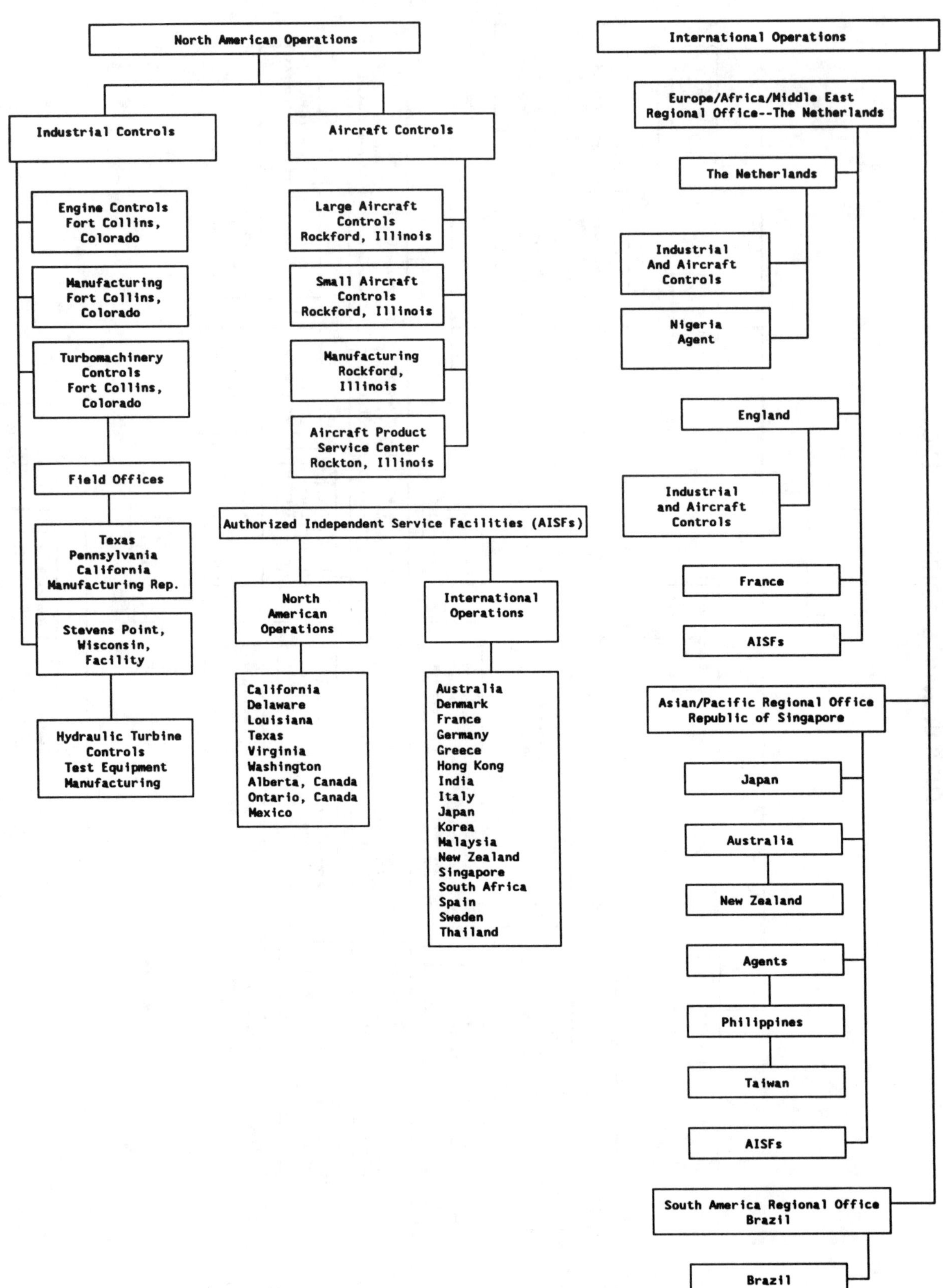

WORLD BANK

Source: FINANCE & DEVELOPMENT 24: 46+ (September 1987)

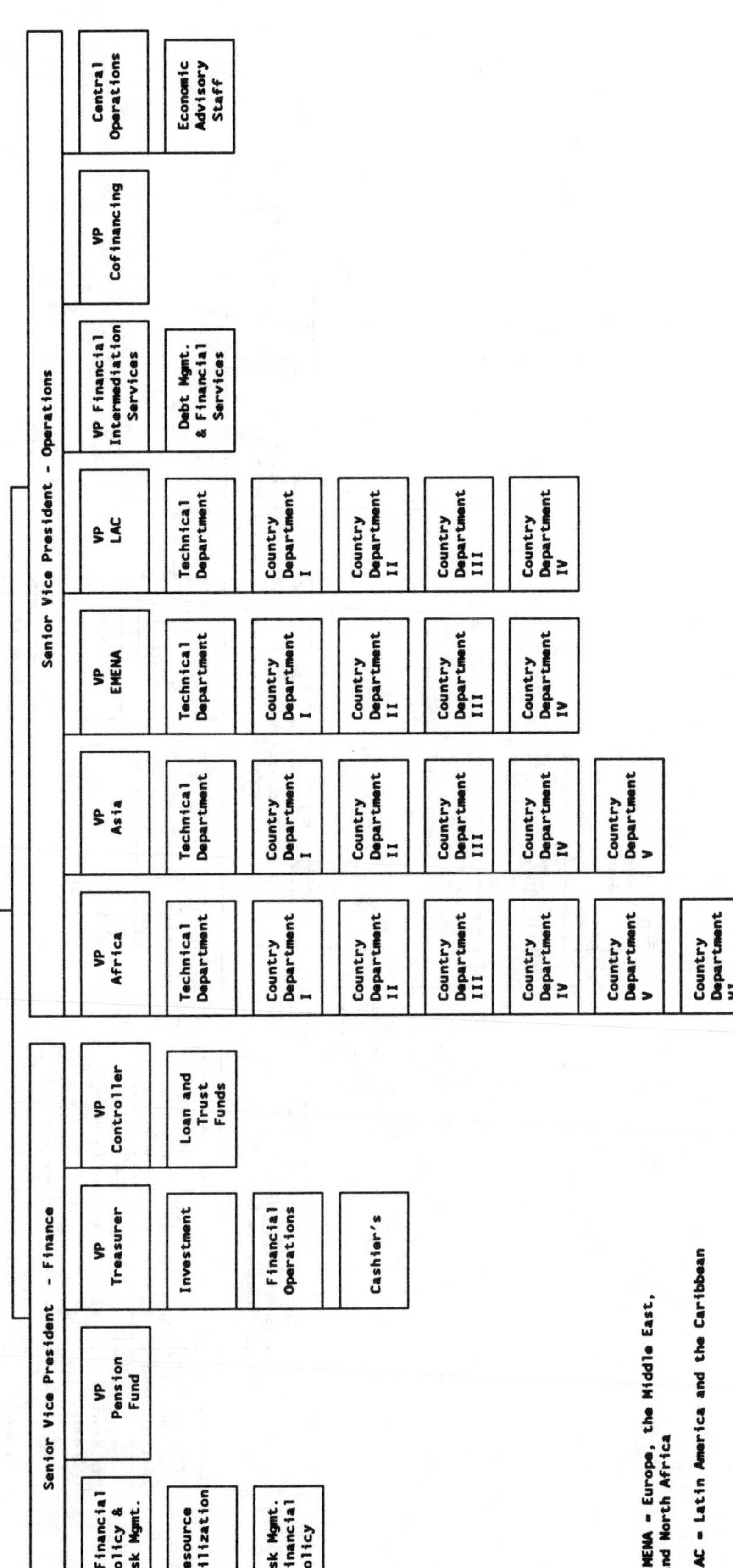
Board of Governors
Executive Directors
President
Senior Vice President - Finance
VP Financial Policy & Risk Mgmt.
Resource Mobilization
Risk Mgmt. & Financial Policy
VP Pension Fund
VP Treasurer
Investment
Financial Operations
Cashier's
VP Controller
Loan and Trust Funds
Senior Vice President - Operations
VP Africa
Technical Department
Country Department I
Country Department II
Country Department III
Country Department IV
Country Department V
Country Department VI
VP Asia
Technical Department
Country Department I
Country Department II
Country Department III
Country Department IV
Country Department V
VP EMENA
Technical Department
Country Department I
Country Department II
Country Department III
Country Department IV
VP LAC
Technical Department
Country Department I
Country Department II
Country Department III
Country Department IV
VP Financial Intermediation Services
Debt Mgmt. & Financial Services
VP Cofinancing
Central Operations
Economic Advisory Staff
EMENA = Europe, the Middle East, and North Africa
LAC = Latin America and the Caribbean

Continued on next page

WORLD BANK
Continued from previous page

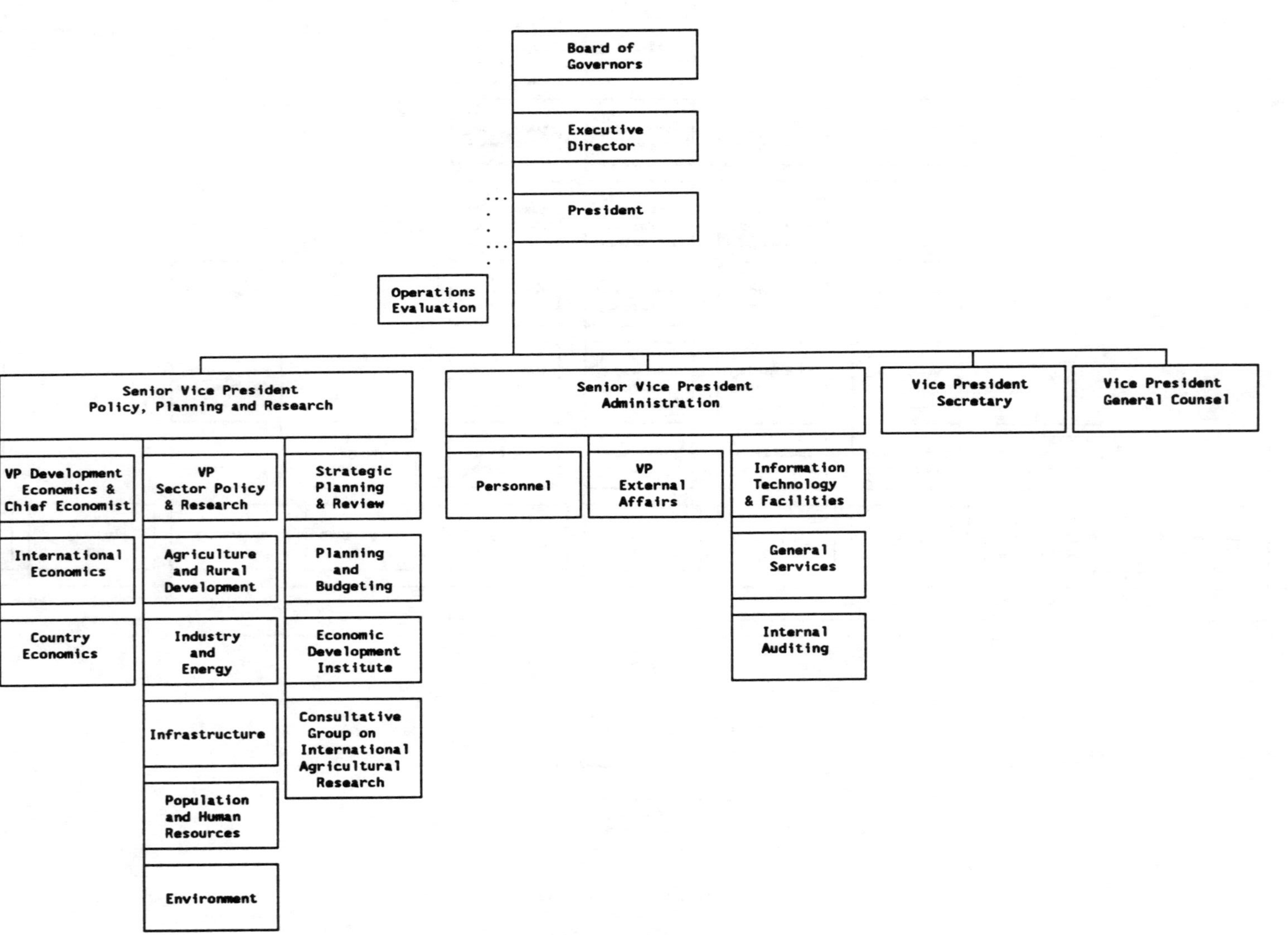

YALE-NEW HAVEN HEALTH SERVICES CORP.

Source: HOSPITAL & HEALTH SERVICES ADMINISTRATION
33:145+ (Summer 1988)

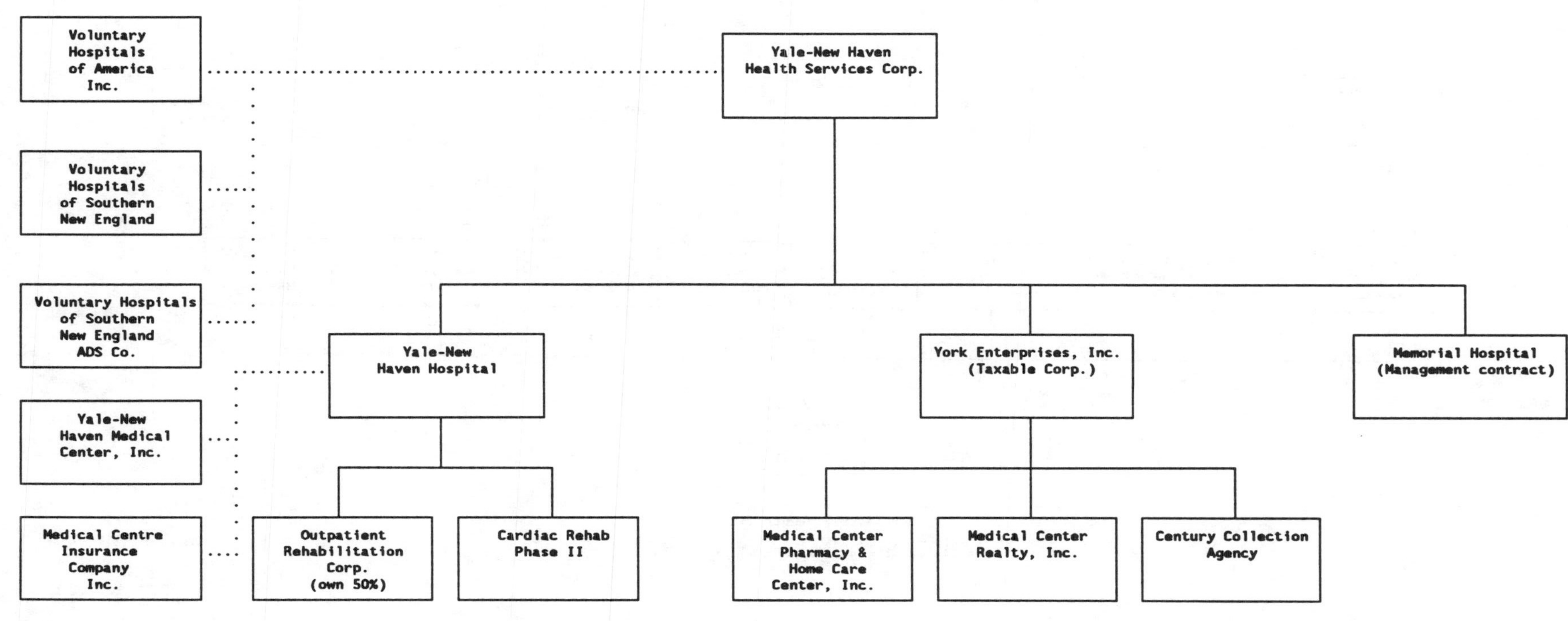

This chart shows the creation of a parent holding company to replace the single hospital corporation concept at this academic medical center. This new structure gives appropriate connections between the holding company and hospital boards.

ZENITH ELECTRONICS CORP.

Source: Company update, 1991

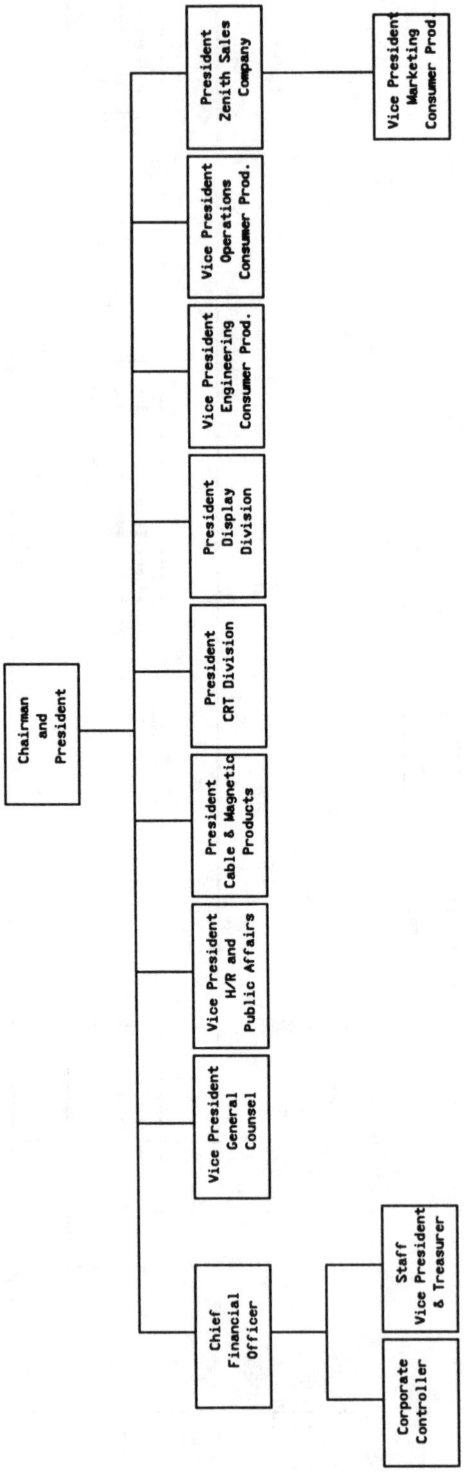

Chairman and President

Chief Financial Officer

Corporate Controller

Staff Vice President & Treasurer

Vice President General Counsel

Vice President H/R and Public Affairs

President Cable & Magnetic Products

President CRT Division

President Display Division

Vice President Engineering Consumer Prod.

Vice President Operations Consumer Prod.

President Zenith Sales Company

Vice President Marketing Consumer Prod.

SAMPLE PRODUCT-LINE MANAGEMENT ORGANIZATION CHART

Source: HOSPITAL & HEALTH SERVICES ADMISTRATION
115 (March/April 1986)

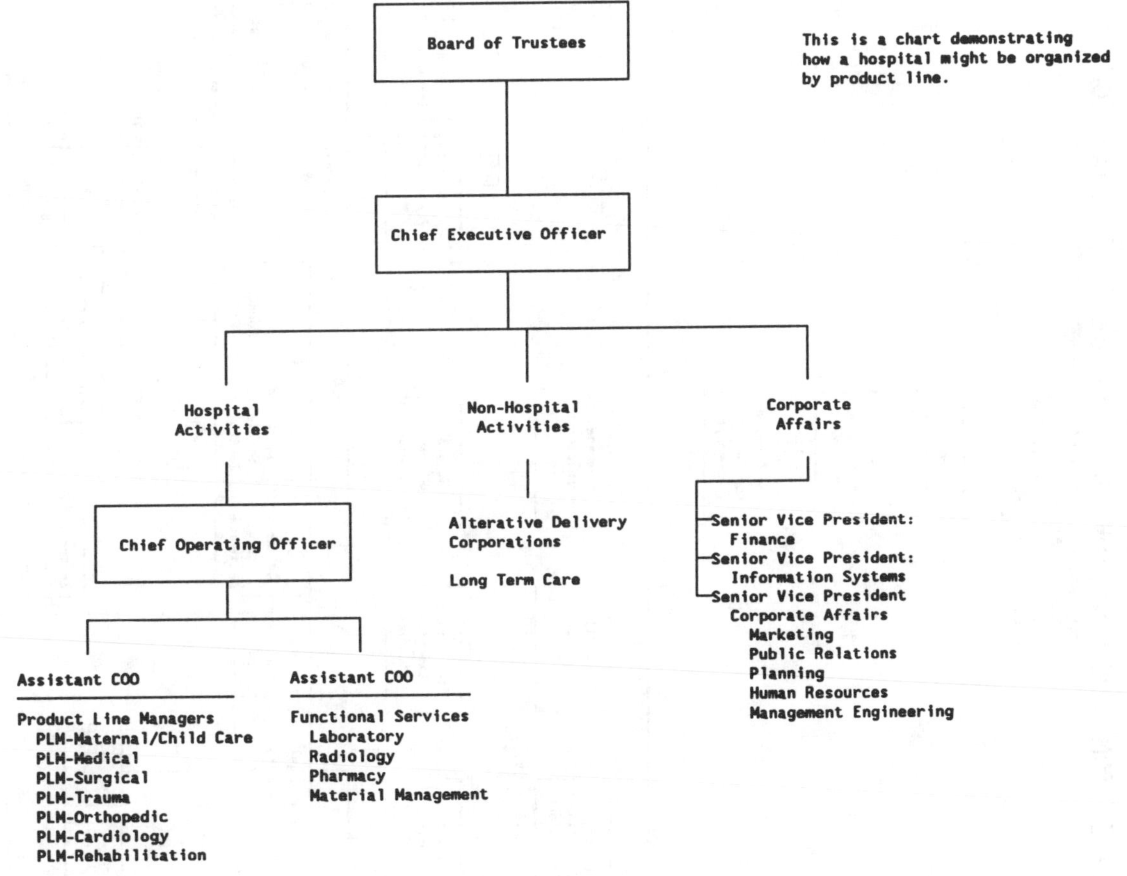

SAMPLE ORGANIZATION CHART OF THE FOOD AND BEVERAGE DIVISION OF A LARGE HOTEL

Source: Lattin, Gerald W. THE LODGING AND FOOD SERVICE INDUSTRY, East Lansing, MI: Educational Institute of the American Hotel & Motel Association, 1989

- Owners
  - President & Managing Director
    - Vice President for Food and Beverage
      - Catering Director
        - Banquet Sales Manager
          - Banquet Sales Representative
        - Banquet Manager
          - Head Houseperson
            - Housepersons
          - Banquet Captain
            - Banquet Servers
          - Banquet Stewards
      - Director Of Culinary Operations
        - Executive Chef
          - Banquet Chef
          - Sous Chef
            - Kitchen Staff
          - Executive Pastry Chef
            - Pastry Chefs
      - Executive Steward
        - Assistant Executive Steward
          - Stewards
      - Beverage Director
        - Assistant Beverage Director
          - Head Bartender Gourmet Restaurant
            - Bartenders
            - Sommelier
          - Head Bartender Specialty Restaurant
            - Bartenders
          - Head Bartender Lounge/ Bars
            - Beverage Servers
            - Bartenders
      - Director of Restaurant Operations
        - Gourmet Restaurant Manager
          - Assistant Manager
            - Captains
            - Servers
            - Bus-persons
        - Specialty Restaurant Manager
          - Assistant Managers
            - Captains
            - Hosts/ Host-esses
            - Servers
            - Bus-persons
        - Coffee Shop Manager
          - Assistant Managers
            - Hosts/ Host-esses
            - Food Servers
            - Bus-persons
        - Room Service Manager
          - Assistant Manager Captains
            - Room Service Attendents
            - Order Takers
            - Room Service Buspersons
          - Cooks
        - Take-out Deli Bar Manager
          - Counter Servers
        - Employee Cafeteria Manager
          - Counter Servers

SAMPLE ORGANIZATION CHART FOR A SMALL RESTAURANT

Source: Lattin, Gerald W. THE LODGING AND FOOD SERVICE INDUSTRY, East Lansing, MI: Educational Institute of the American Hotel & Motel Association, 1989

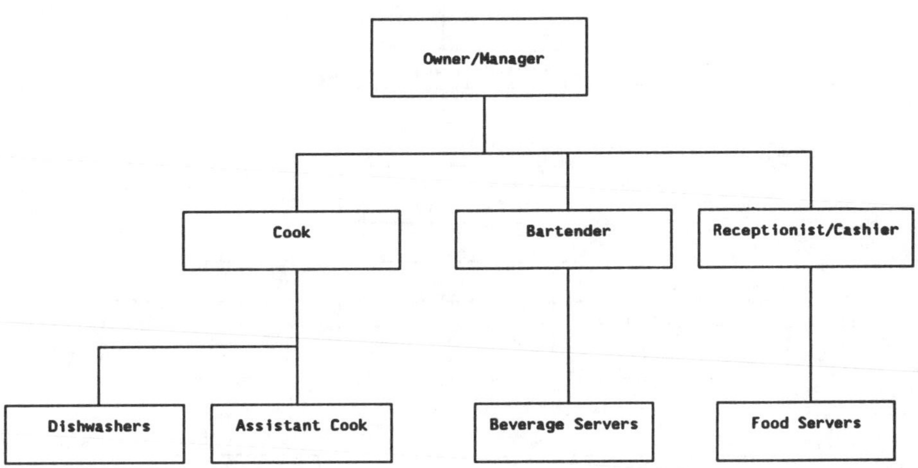

SAMPLE ORGANIZATION CHART OF A MARKETING AND SALES DIVISION IN A LARGE HOTEL

Source: Lattin, Gerald W. THE LODGING AND FOOD SERVICE INDUSTRY, East Lansing, MI: Educational Institute of the American Hotel & Motel Association, 1989

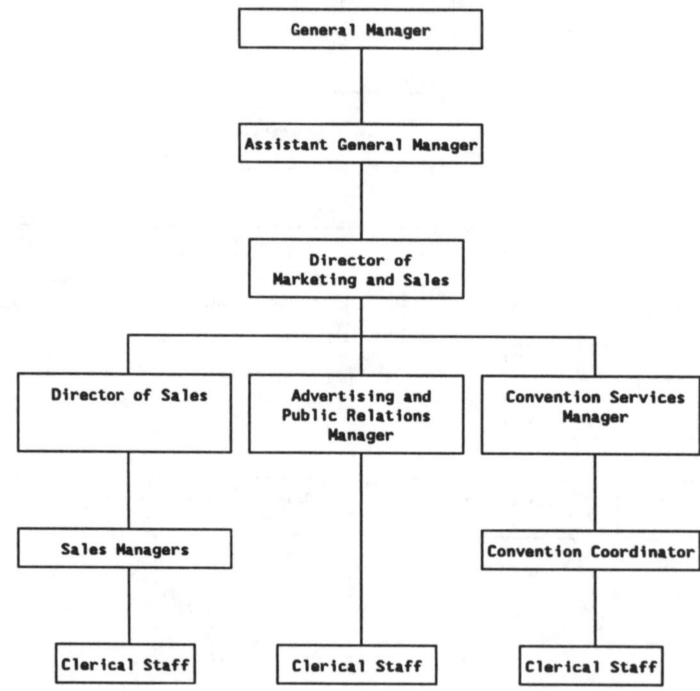

SAMPLE ORGANIZATION CHART OF THE MANAGEMENT OF A LARGE HOTEL

Source: Lattin, Gerald W. THE LODGING AND FOOD SERVICE INDUSTRY, East Lansing, MI: Educational Institute of the American Hotel & Motel Association, 1989

- Board of Directors
  - General Manager
    - Administrative Assistant
    - Resident Manager
      - Human Resources Director
        - Asst. Human Resources Director
      - Director of Property Operations
        - Asst. Director of Property Operations
      - Controller
        - Purchasing Manager
        - Food Beverage Controller
        - Storeroom Manager
        - Assistant Controller
        - Auditor
        - Credit Manager
        - Accounts Receivable Manager
        - Accounts Payable Manager
        - Paymaster
        - Head Cashier
      - Security Director
        - Asst. Security Director
      - Food & Beverage Director
        - Exec. Chef
          - Sous Chef
          - Banquet Chef
          - Pastry Chef
        - Asst. Food & Beverage Director
          - Personnel Manager
          - Restaurant Managers
          - Room Service Manager
        - Exec. Steward
          - Asst. Steward
        - Beverage Director
          - Asst. Beverage Director
        - Catering Director
          - Catering Sales Manager
          - Banquet Manager
            - Asst. Banquet Manager
      - Director of Marketing & Sales
        - Sales Director
        - Public Relations Director
        - Convention Service Manager
      - Rooms Division Manager
        - Exec. House-keeper
          - Asst. Exec. House-keeper
            - Asst. House-keeer
        - Front Office Manager
          - Reservations Manager
          - Chief Operator
          - Night Manager
          - Service Manager
        - Garage Manager
          - Asst. Garage Manager

Index

B

C

D

G

H

I

J

K

L

M

N

O

P

Q

R

T

U

V